PRAISE FOR *VINYL DREAMS*

'A damn good read. The seventies was a crazy, fun era for music where the boys wore the make-up, but I didn't! I was the anti-to the glam. A gender-bending ride, filled with good memories, good times.'

Suzi Quatro, rock legend

'Tony Wellington writes with incredible insight, passion, and intelligence about music and the context in which it was created.'

Stuart Coupe, music journalist

'A thrilling journey that meticulously charts rock music's progress through the chaotic, fertile, high-energy, drug-fuelled innovations that make the seventies possibly its most exciting era.'

David Williamson AO, playwright

'Tackling perhaps the most-maligned of decades, the drug-addled, self-indulgent seventies, in *Vinyl Dreams*, Wellington happily shines a forensic light on the finest musicians of the age, while gleefully exposing the fakes, the frauds and the febrile. What's more, his occasional editorial interjections leave the reader in no doubt about the author's particular musical taste, and challenges readers who lived through the decade to reassess their own fading memories. The only certainty is that seventies continue to confound our certainties, contradict our truths, jumble our facts.

Ten years that began with a bitter, litigious ending (The Beatles) and premature sad loss (Hendrix, Joplin and Morrison) ended with new beginnings (the raw electric rock of The Sex Pistols, the rock/reggae of The Clash and The Police, and the alt-pop of Blondie, Talking Heads and Elvis Costello). In between were Led Zeppelin, Black Sabbath, Deep Purple, Pink Floyd, Simon and Garfunkel, Jethro Tull, ELP, Frank Zappa, The Stooges, Patti Smith, the Ramones, Yes and Genesis, along with Joni Mitchell, Neil Young, Elton John, David Bowie, Billy Joel, Roxy Music, Cat Stevens, Queen, Fleetwood Mac, Dire Straits, ABBA, Bruce Springsteen and the E Street Band, Bob Marley and the Wailers, The Bee Gees, Stevie Wonder and The Eagles. Plus many others, including Australia's own Daddy Cool, Billy Thorpe and the Aztecs, Chain, Skyhooks, AC/DC, Helen Reddy, Renée Geyer and The Saints. Quite a productive, eclectic bunch! The seventies: 'rock's true golden era', as Wellington suggests? Read *Vinyl Dreams* and be the judge.'

Rob Hirst, founding member of Midnight Oil

'One thing I love about this book is how Tony Wellington humanises the rock star. We all know the effect of great rock music on our mental and physical being is beyond magic, but those who create that magic are all too human. Tony takes us into that world and helps us understand how and why the songs we love so much were written by people reacting to the ever-changing world of the seventies.'

Jon Coghill, Powderfinger drummer

Vinyl Dreams

Vinyl Dreams

How the 1970s Changed Music

Tony Wellington

MONASH
UNIVERSITY
PUBLISHING

Published by Monash University Publishing
Matheson Library Annexe
40 Exhibition Walk
Monash University
Clayton, Victoria 3800, Australia
publishing.monash.edu/

Monash University Publishing: the discussion starts here

Vinyl Dreams: How the 1970s Changed Music
ISBN: 9781922979018 (paperback)
ISBN: 9781922979025 (pdf)
ISBN: 9781922979032 (epub)

A catalogue record for this book is available from the National Library of Australia

Cover and text design by Les Thomas
Typesetting by Jo Mullins
Author photograph by Judy Ditter

Printed in Australia by Griffin Press

CONTENTS

PLAYLIST

You may wish to use the QR code below to listen to *Tony Wellington's Vinyl Dreams Official Playlist* on Spotify. Most of the music referred to in the book appears on the playlist. Tunes appear in the same order in which they occur in the text. Please note that some tracks are only available as remixed or remastered versions. At the time of writing, access to the songs of Joni Mitchell and Neil Young is limited because they have removed their albums from Spotify.

Rather than use this playlist, readers may instead search for specific tunes on their preferred music streaming service or else via YouTube. Some will also no doubt hunt through their vinyl and CD collections!

PRELUDE

There are times when I experience pieces of music with such pure joy that I am moved to tears. 'Surrender Rose', from Don Cherry's 1977 album *Hear & Now*, is just one example. It's a sentimental piece, to be sure, but the melody and arrangement – not to mention Cherry's toy-like pocket trumpet juxtaposed with Stan Samole's guitar – make me swoon.

Even The Carpenters' 1970 hit '(They Long to Be) Close to You' can send a shiver down my spine. Of course, there's the angelic perfection of Karen Carpenter's voice, as well as her sublime drumming, but hearing the song also transports me back to my teens and the family television room. The film clip for the song begins with a wide shot of the quintet in a recording studio. The image dissolves to a close shot of brother Richard's hands as he plays the tinkling piano introduction. The camera then tilts up to Karen, sitting behind her drum kit. She begins singing, and between phrases closes her eyes and gently bites her lower lip. Karen Carpenter had that rare capacity to make even the most banal lyric seem deeply personal.

Songs like this remind me of very different times. Ageing is a process of grieving. We have to grieve our lost innocence, our gradual loss of physical capacity, and all the other inevitable consequences of living longer than any previous generation. One of the lost youthful traits that I most often grieve is a sense of wonder – that thrill and visceral excitement that I experienced when discovering something for the first time. Often that something was a piece of music, particularly one that took the art form into new, unimagined realms. In the 1970s, the frontiers of rock music still seemed largely unexplored.

There will inevitably be those who read the ensuing pages and are frustrated that I have given insufficient attention to their favourite performer or album. In my defence, I can assure you that my first draft was more than double the word count agreed to with my publisher. There was so much going on in 1970s music that it could easily fill a very large encyclopedia. I have had to be very selective, focusing on what I consider to be key artists and events. These are not always the most popular or familiar (though oftentimes they are). I am interested in those characters who have been innovative or influential, or whose actions help illustrate the key themes of this book.

I hope this book inspires you to revisit a half-forgotten album, to listen with new appreciation to a familiar performer, or perhaps to discover music you've never heard before. As my wife read one draft, she paused regularly to stream songs as she went. For those who would like to experience the music mentioned in the text, there is a link to a Spotify playlist at the beginning of the book. Alternatively, songs can be located by searching on YouTube or other streaming services.

As Frank Zappa, Elvis Costello, Lester Bangs or someone else once said, 'Writing about music is like dancing about architecture.' So let us dance together in honour of those who laid the architectural foundations on which so much popular music has since been constructed.

1970

The Revolution Will Not Be Televised

The decade began particularly badly for The Who's drummer, Keith Moon.

Four days into the new year, as a neighbourly gesture, Moon, plus his wife and friends, attended the opening of a local pub. Unfortunately, a group of skinheads were also in attendance. When Moon and his entourage attempted to depart in the drummer's Bentley, they found themselves surrounded by the skinheads, who began to pelt the car with stones, and then to rock it back and forth. Moon's chauffeur/bodyguard, Neil Boland, either leapt out of the car or was dragged out by the mob. Panicked, Moon squirmed into the driver's seat and attempted to drive through the melee. A scuffle occurred in front of the car, and Boland was knocked to the ground. As the vehicle lurched forward, the hapless chauffeur was trapped under the car and dragged 100 yards down the road. It was only when bystanders began yelling that Moon stopped the vehicle and discovered the body beneath. Boland's head had been crushed.

Moon was charged with the killing as well as drink driving, plus driving without a licence. Six weeks later, the death was deemed accidental, with the judge noting that Moon had no choice but to act in the way he did. The drummer pleaded guilty to the comparatively minor driving offences. Unfortunately, Boland's family believed there had been a cover-up, and refused subsequent efforts by Moon to look after them. The whole affair had a profound impact on the drummer and, ultimately, the band. As Roger Daltrey put it, 'He didn't get away with it, not by any stretch. He was haunted by it, and his drinking just got worse and worse.'[1]

The year would also prove lethal for a number of rock luminaries, including Jimi Hendrix and Janis Joplin. What's more, the first year of the new decade saw the demise of the world's most influential rock band, The Beatles, as well as superstar duo Simon & Garfunkel. 1970 was a watershed for rock music.

Bob Dylan had become a recluse, no longer 'the voice of a generation'. Even The Rolling Stones were in some disarray following the previous year's dual tragedies of Brian Jones' death and the Altamont Speedway Free Festival murder. Indeed, the Altamont concert was hugely symbolic, peeling away the facade of rock music's supposed unifying power, revealing instead a decidedly ugly underbelly of drugs, alcohol and treachery.

The beginning of the new decade was a clearing house for the detritus of the 1960s, starting with the trial of Charles Manson and his murderous acolytes. The promised revolution had failed to materialise, and the counter-culture was beginning to buckle. As filmmaker and music critic Tony Palmer put it, 'By 1970, popular music had arrived at its worst crisis. The hopes of a generation had come to nothing.'[2]

Authentication

A divide had opened in the late '60s between authentic rock music and commercial pop music; the latter was viewed by many as 'selling out'. Those bands who chased Top 40 chart success released singles (seven-inch discs with one song on each side), while those who considered themselves above commercialism focused entirely on albums or LPs (twelve-inch 'long playing' releases which ran for some twenty-three minutes per side). Singles were often viewed as disposable product for teenyboppers, particularly young girls, while LPs were for serious music enthusiasts.

In the pop versus rock dichotomy, the discerning listener of LPs frowned upon the hysterical fan-worship and pin-up crazes of young women. Of course, this was all a false construct, with males also obsessing over their guitar-wielding, bare-chested heroes. Each cohort could be viewed as blindly loyal. As Robert Wyatt jokingly put it, 'I've always said that the only difference between pop and rock was that pop was for girls and they changed the name to rock for boys. It's like calling perfume "after shave"!'[3]

The distinction between album and single would continue throughout the decade, with the arrival of punk muddying the dichotomy.

Many 1960s music makers were shedding their psychedelia in favour of a more direct, gritty, harder rock sound. To that was added electronic futurism, studio experimentation, and the incorporation of both jazz and classical elements into the rock arsenal. Popular music was evolving at breakneck speed.

In part, this productivity and innovation was because the artists themselves sought greater creative control and less interference. During the 1950s and early '60s, the music industry was hell-bent on regulating product, manufacturing heartthrobs, even dictating which songs would be recorded by which artists. After the 'British Invasion' of 1964, performers increasingly composed their own music. Inevitably, they would eventually insist on greater authority over their art.

Progressive rock drummer Bill Bruford described this musical landscape amusingly:

> There was a brief post-Beatles aberration from the norm, during the late 60s and up to about 1976, that involved so much money flowing into the industry it couldn't be spent fast enough … In the 70s, all manner of stray musicians were turning up in studios. Now we can produce ourselves, let's get an orchestra! (Deep Purple.) Or some jazz guys! (Mahavishnu Orchestra.) Or some jazz guys with an orchestra! (Mahavishnu Orchestra with orchestra.) The crew had mutinied and taken over the ship.[4]

The Rolling Stones were at the coalface, attempting to take greater control of their product while also walking the tightrope between commercialism and authentic, anti-establishment people's music. In 1969, the underground press had hammered the band, labelling them as greedy, capitalist hypocrites thanks to the ticket prices on their US tour. In fact, the whole reason for the band's participation in the Altamont Free Festival was to convince their critics that they hadn't sold out to the capitalist machine.

Perversely, the Altamont murder also played into the phoney persona that Mick Jagger and the Stones had carefully cultivated as a menacing and dangerously subversive bunch of social rebels – domineering sexual marauders, even. Marianne Faithful, Jagger's girlfriend at the time, later noted that Jagger got off on the imagery and undercurrent of their song 'Sympathy for the Devil', dryly noting that Jagger simply wanted 'to have power over people', without thinking 'about whether it's good power, whether it's positive or negative'.[5]

And although they were now dallying with socialites and the 'jet set', as Bill Wyman noted, The Rolling Stones began the new decade broke. Their involvement with rapacious New York manager Allen Klein had left them largely penniless. Apart from his home assets, Wyman reckons he had a bank overdraft of £12,000, and the band was 'technically employed by Klein'.[6] As Keith Richards glumly put it, '[Klein] ended up owning the copyright and master tapes of all our work – anything written or recorded in the time of our contract with Decca.'[7]

The Stones had come to realise that their record label, Decca, was involved in arms manufacture. According to Richards:

> We found out … that all the bread we made for Decca was going into making little black boxes that go into American Air Force bombers to bomb fucking North Vietnam … Goddam, you find out you've helped to kill God knows how many thousands of people without even knowing it. I'd rather the Mafia than Decca.[8]

In response to these revelations, the Stones delivered to Decca tape recordings of such deliberately low fidelity that they couldn't be released. Included was a final contractual single that Decca demanded. 'Schoolboy Blues' (aka 'Cocksucker Blues') contained explicit lyrics about a lonesome schoolboy seeking fellatio and anal sex. As you've no doubt guessed, the song didn't get a release. (Although the track was accidentally included in a four-album box set, *The Rest of the Best*, released in Germany in 1983, before the label recalled the records and the set was reissued without 'Schoolboy

Blues'.) Decca would get their own back on the band by releasing numerous unapproved compilations of Stones' songs from the 1960s.

The legal wrangle between the Stones and Klein would escalate through seven lawsuits. As Keith Richards told *Rolling Stone* magazine, 'The thing [Klein] really wanted was The Beatles and The Stones together, to have them both. He did it. But as he picked one up, he dropped the other.'[9] The Beatles would also find themselves in litigation with Klein.

Country Joe & The Fish released an album simply titled *C.J. Fish*, containing the track 'Hey Bobby', which castigated Bob Dylan for abandoning his role as spokesperson for the counterculture. But Dylan had little interest in politics. In typically mischievous manner, the chameleon of folk rock released *Self Portrait*, a double LP containing covers of well-known pop songs and traditional folk tunes, along with a handful of originals including some from his live set at the 1969 Isle of Wight Festival. An infamous *Rolling Stone* review penned by Greil Marcus began, 'What is this shit?'[10] London's *IT* claimed that Dylan had veered as far to the right as one might get. In his defence, Dylan later stated that the 'scraped together' album was just a joke to hammer a final nail into the coffin of his activist image.

Despite the reaction of the critics, *Self Portrait* sold well, reaching the number four spot in the US charts and the top spot in the UK charts. As a follow-up album, the curmudgeonly songster released *New Morning*, which also went to number one in the UK, but again was no great revelation.

The biggest bust-up

Hope was at times in short supply in 1970. The planet continued to be a restless place full of conflicts and struggle. The post-World War II economic boom was coming to an end for America and its allies. After two decades of strong economic growth, the US dollar was suddenly looking shaky. The term 'stagflation' had been coined by a British politician to refer to a combination of high inflation with economic stagnation, and by mid-1970 the neologism was being sprayed across the Western media.

As well as the economic turnaround, one of the biggest media stories was speculation over the future of The Beatles. Their last effort at recording as a four-piece band had been for the appropriately titled song 'The End' in August 1969. *Let It Be*, released in May 1970, had been recorded a year and a half previously. It was the soundtrack to a documentary on the making of the album, initially titled *Get Back*.

Australia's Molly Meldrum has laid claim to breaking the news of The Beatles' split. In 1969, Meldrum had landed a lowly job at Apple, The Beatles' business conglomerate in London. When John Lennon asked Molly to interview him, the starry-eyed Australian leapt to attention. The taped interview with both John and Yoko Ono was to be printed in Australia's *Go-Set* magazine. When Meldrum sent the tapes back to Melbourne, *Go-Set*'s Phillip Frazer reportedly responded, 'I can't believe The Beatles are breaking up!' A surprised Molly had missed the subtext during his interview: in answer to a query whether he might do something different, other than be a Beatle, Lennon's response was: 'Yes, it could be any minute now.'[11]

In truth, The Beatles had disintegrated well before it became public. At various times during 1969, George Harrison, Ringo Starr and John Lennon had each told their bandmates that they were quitting the group. Manager Allen Klein was in stubborn denial about the disintegration of his gravy train. By 1970, Ringo was recording tracks for his cloying solo effort *Sentimental Journey*, George Harrison was touring with husband-and-wife duo Delaney & Bonnie, while Paul McCartney was secretly recording his first solo album at home. Meanwhile, Lennon was off doing his own thing with Yoko Ono, including their much-ridiculed peace campaign.

The final actual recording of a Beatles song was 'I Me Mine' on 3 January 1970, eight years to the day after The Beatles had failed their audition for Decca Records. Lennon was absent from the recording. Harrison's song has been widely interpreted as referring to the selfishness of Lennon and McCartney.

As the new decade began, Lennon recorded the somewhat acerbic 'Instant Karma!' with his makeshift Plastic Ono Band plus Harrison. In a conscious break from George Martin's producing style, he invited Phil Spector to London to produce the single. The song was completed in one session – just ten takes, with no rehearsal – and released on Apple Records six days later, making it a truly 'instant' record. Spector's approach resulted in lots of reverb on John's voice, a makeshift choir on the chorus, handclaps appearing out of nowhere, and a thudding, incredibly fat drum sound that was as dominant as the vocals.

'Instant Karma!' went to number five in the UK and three in the USA, becoming the first solo disc from a Beatle to sell a million copies. Five days after the single's release, Lennon appeared on BBC TV's *Top of the Pops* miming to it – the first appearance by a Beatle on that show since 1966. Never one to miss an opportunity to promote herself and her performance art, Yoko sat beside John wearing a sanitary pad as a blindfold while knitting.

By March, The Beatles' single 'Let It Be' was released. The McCartney-penned song entered the US charts at number six, the highest position ever for a new single, but was held off the top spot by Simon & Garfunkel's melodramatic 'Bridge Over Troubled Water'. Meanwhile, Klein engaged Phil Spector to remix the documentary soundtrack that would become The Beatles' *Let It Be* album, instructing him to make the record more commercial.

While the other Beatles had been releasing their private projects through Apple Records, Paul arranged to have his solo album released directly by EMI, bypassing Apple. Allen Klein went ballistic when he found out that Paul would be releasing an album at much the same time as Starr's *Sentimental Journey* as well as The Beatles' *Let It Be*. Lennon and Harrison signed a letter instructing EMI to postpone the release of McCartney's solo LP. Ringo was dispatched to take the letter to Paul, which resulted in Paul throwing Ringo out of his house. Among the band members, it was now three against one.

On 9 April, Paul sent out review copies of his new album, simply titled *McCartney*. The media package included a Q&A penned by Paul in which he asked himself if his break from the band was permanent; he answered that he didn't know. He also asked if he could ever see a time when he might again collaborate in songwriting with John Lennon, and provided a curt 'no' in response. The same day, Paul rang John to tell him that he was releasing the covert album, and further that he was leaving the band. A week later, Apple issued a media release explaining that Paul McCartney had left the band due to 'personal, musical and business differences'. Inevitably, the media blamed Paul for breaking up The Beatles.

As McCartney put it, '[T]hese truest friends of mine were now my firmest enemies overnight. Ever since I'd been a child I'd been in this group, I'd grown up in this group, this was my school, my family, my life.'[12] At Paul's insistence, no singles were released from his solo album. Perhaps the key song from the disc is 'Maybe I'm Amazed'. Beginning as a soft paean to his wife Linda, it soon morphs into a screamed verse about being caught in the middle of circumstances that he doesn't fully understand. The album debuted at number two in the UK, held off the top once again by Simon & Garfunkel. After hitting number one in the US, it eventually went double platinum. The critics largely determined the LP to be undercooked, with Robert Christgau saying he found it 'difficult to take seriously as anything more than a million-selling wedding announcement'.[13]

None of The Beatles attended the film premieres of *Let It Be*. Meanwhile, Spector had completely rearranged and remixed the songs on the accompanying LP, even adding an orchestra and female choir to Paul's tune 'The Long and Winding Road'. McCartney was extremely unhappy with the result but was outvoted by the other three. The band's long-time producer George Martin went public, observing that the final album contradicted The Beatles' original intent for a clean, honest rock LP without overdubbing.

By the end of 1970, all four Beatles had released solo albums. Starr's *Sentimental Journey* was widely pilloried. In late November, George Harrison released his triple album *All Things Must Pass*, a critical and commercial success that spawned the hit singles 'My Sweet Lord' – the first by a former Beatle to go number one – and 'What Is Life'. Phil Spector was a co-producer. One of the dissenting voices was again Robert Christgau, who found the album full of 'overblown fatuity' that 'sounds more like Muzak'.[14] But the set went to number one in eleven countries.

From the outset, 'My Sweet Lord' was entangled in provenance issues. Clearly, Harrison had blended a Hare Krishna mantra with the Christian hymn 'Oh Happy Day'. According to some, however, he had also plagiarised The Chiffons' 'He's So Fine', a 1963 hit penned by Ronnie Mack. And so the lawsuits began. Given the degree to which rock and pop music liberally plundered itself – just think about all those identical blues chord progressions with similar melodies – the legal wrangling over 'My Sweet Lord' sent shockwaves through the music business. It also opened the floodgates to more litigation actions.

Lone Lennon

McCartney's personal response to The Beatles' divorce was to spend more time at home with his family. Lennon, however, opted for exorcism.

Both John and Yoko were struggling with heroin addictions. While trying to clean up their act with the help of methadone, the pair were sent a copy of Arthur Janov's book *The Primal Scream*. It outlined his 'Primal Therapy', a treatment that could supposedly cure neuroses by taking adults back to their childhood to re-experience formative pain. The objective was to achieve a peaceful mindset through excruciating catharsis. On meeting Lennon in England, Janov declared him to be 'almost completely non-functional. He couldn't leave the house, he could hardly leave his room … he was just one big ball of pain.'[15] In May, Yoko and John cleared their schedules until September and travelled to Los Angeles, ready for months of daily treatment with Janov. Lennon had to negotiate with the US Embassy to have his visa ban – the product of an earlier drug conviction for possession of hashish – temporarily waived.

At a time when traditional institutions were under challenge and secularism was on the rise, alternative therapies, no matter how outlandish, were being eagerly embraced. Of course, Lennon's new association with Janov was all the publicity the latter's publisher could have wanted.

Even Jann Wenner, editor of *Rolling Stone* magazine, went so far as to declare Primal Therapy to be 'the most important discovery of the 20th century'.[16] Janov himself rashly claimed that his discovery would see the end of all mental disease.

Lennon never completed his course with Janov, having to return to the UK midyear due to his ongoing issues with US immigration. Janov wanted another whole year to work on the ex-Beatle. But instead of more therapy for John, the world got the *John Lennon/Plastic Ono Band* album.

Production credits went to Lennon, Ono and Phil Spector. Recorded at Abbey Road, with trusted friends Ringo Starr on drums and Klaus Voorman on bass, the songs were raw, angry and heartfelt. The album begins ominously, with funeral bells, followed by the brittle, visceral anguish of 'Mother', a song describing how Lennon's parents abandoned him. The track concludes with Lennon pleading for them to stay with him, building in intensity until he screams. Released as a single, it was too excruciating and upsetting to reach single digits in the charts. There was a massive gap between the lilting, wistful 'Julia' from The Beatles' *White Album* and the unbridled screams of 'Mother' on this disc.

'Working Class Hero' is a political folk song, just Lennon with acoustic guitar. It presents a bleak perspective on how working-class people become manipulated: cogs of the middle-class machine and even cannon fodder. Lennon called the song 'revolutionary'. The great irony here is that John Lennon's upbringing was arguably middle-class and comfortable, whereas it was Paul McCartney who came from a more working-class environment.

'Isolation' unpeels Lennon's vulnerability in the face of fame and fortune. 'Well Well Well' sees John and Yoko discussing revolution and women's liberation through a miasma of guilt. 'Look At Me' is about Lennon's search for his true self, while 'God' is a discourse on atheism and identity. Rather like The Fugs' 'Nothing', 'God' contains a litany of the many icons in which Lennon could no longer invest his faith, including Elvis, Dylan and The Beatles. The album closes with a short ditty based on the nursery rhyme 'Three Blind Mice'. Prosaically titled 'My Mummy's Dead', it reprises the theme of the opening track. This time, Lennon is deadpan and emotionless, perhaps implying some degree of resignation.

John Lennon/Plastic Ono Band had a mixed reception. Some considered it far too self-absorbed, with one reviewer suggesting that it wasn't even music but rather a declamation. However, *Village Voice* declared it the best album of 1970. It went to number three in Australia, and one in Canada, but only six and eight in the US and UK, respectively. Today, many view it as Lennon's tour de force. There's no doubting it remains an authentic, harrowing portrait of the man's personal pain; a rock masterpiece, marking a turning point in rock music, away from more universal themes and towards the deeply personal. In the previous decade, Lennon's personal songs disguised their subjective statements beneath a blanket of third-person characters and love song tropes. Now Lennon was laying himself bare. Rock music was hereafter given licence to be disarmingly candid.

Notably, Lennon's focus had shifted from an outward-looking peace campaign to an internal fixation on inner peace. In many ways, this reflected the broader social shift that was going on around him.

Warring songs

If there was one ubiquitous issue that concerned young people in 1970, it was the ongoing Vietnam War. US President Richard Nixon's intentions for the conflict in Vietnam were ambiguous at best. In February, the secret war that America had also been operating in Laos since 1964 finally came to light, much to Nixon's displeasure. National security advisor Henry Kissinger made a public statement that no Americans had been killed during the fighting in Laos. Two days later it emerged that 27 Americans had died in Laos.

In April, Nixon went on national television to explain that he had decided to launch US forces into Cambodia (then Kampuchea). In fact, he and Kissinger had been secretly bombing that unfortunate country for almost a year. In his address, Nixon stated that he had fully consulted with his advisers, however neither Nixon's secretary of state nor his defense secretary knew about the invasion until Nixon's public address.

Internal politics aside, the president failed to appreciate the impact his announcement would have on anti-war sentiment. Protests erupted on campuses across the nation. A rally at Kent State University turned ugly when National Guardsmen fired rifles at students. Although some of the soldiers shot into the air, over the heads of the students, others aimed directly at the crowd. One eyewitness was Chrissie Hynde, who would form The Pretenders at the end of the decade. She wrote, 'I heard the tatatatatatat sound. I thought it was fireworks. An eerie silence fell over the common. Then a young man's voice: "They fucking killed somebody!"'[17]

Over a thirteen-second timeframe, close to seventy shots were fired. Four Kent State students were killed and nine others injured. Three of them were shot in the back. Two of those killed were not even participating in the protests and had simply been walking across the campus. All of those hit by bullets were unarmed. Another student who witnessed the event was Gerard Casale, who would later form the band Devo. He said: 'We saw it happen and we saw the Kent newspaper say, "Students kill guardsmen"! We realised everything we'd been told was a big lie. We were already making music, but when you see something like that it changes you forever.'[18]

The day after the killings, over 900 US colleges and universities shut down, as did many high schools and elementary schools. Five days after the Kent State massacre, more than 250,000 protestors marched on Washington.

Eleven days after the Kent State killings, trouble erupted at Jackson State University. A false rumour had spread that a civil rights leader had been killed. This led to around 100 black students starting fires, throwing rocks and overturning vehicles. Around midnight, after the fire crews had left, the police attempted to disperse a crowd that had gathered in front of a women's dormitory building. Suddenly, the officers opened fire on the building. Forty state highway patrolmen managed to fire off 460 shots in just thirty seconds. Every window in the building was shattered. When the dust settled, two young civilians were dead. But these black deaths didn't generate the same sort of media attention as the white deaths at Kent State.

Various musicians were moved by the shootings. Four days after the Kent State tragedy, the American Symphony Orchestra staged an unrehearsed concert at Carnegie Hall in honour of the students killed. Florida-based garage rock band Third Condition rushed out a single, 'Monday in May (a May Day of Hell)', just seven days after the killings. The song was beginning to garner airplay when Crosby, Stills, Nash & Young (CSNY) put out their own elegy.

On hearing news of Kent State, Neil Young had quickly penned his response, simply titled 'Ohio'. Graham Nash's 'Teach Your Children' was climbing the charts for CSNY at the time of the massacre, but Crosby told Nash that they should record and release 'Ohio' immediately. The song was recorded in just a few takes. The lyrics talk of Nixon's tin soldiers attacking not 'them' but 'us': the band and its listeners pointedly unified with the student victims. As a protest song, it was urgent and unapologetic. During the fadeout, one can hear David Crosby wailing 'How many more?' and 'Why?', with, as he put it, 'the hair standin' up on my arms'.[19]

The single was banned by some radio stations but received considerable airplay on the big-city FM stations. It also delivered political legitimacy to the band members, with CSNY suddenly the new spokespeople for their generation. As Chrissie Hynde wrote, 'I was happy having Young as our spokesman, our voice. It was a big element in easing us out of shock.'[20] Mind you, not everyone was happy about the song's success. Gerald Casale believed it was a case of wealthy hippies making money by exploiting something too political for them to understand. Even Neil Young later admitted, 'I always felt funny about makin' money off that.'[21]

A more universal anti-war anthem was released by Edwin Starr. 'War' had a catchy, brass-heavy hook. Penned by Barrett Strong and Norman Whitfield, the song had already been recorded and released by The Temptations, but Starr's audacious, in-your-face approach delivered more punch. It became a runaway number one hit in the US, and one of the most successful protest songs of the era.

A different Starr, Ringo, wrote and released 'Silent Homecoming' from the perspective of a mother waiting for her son to return from war. At the end of the song we learn that she is actually waiting for a hearse to deliver the body. Released on his second solo album, *Beaucoups of Blues*, it's a simple, pretty song, but suffers from Ringo's vocal limitations. Substantially more interesting – and better sung – was Gordon Lightfoot's 'Sit Down Young Stranger' from his album of the same name. That disc would become his best-selling LP, being renamed *If You Could Read My Mind* when that song smashed the singles charts. 'Sit Down Young Stranger' tells of a young man finally returning to his family home after travelling as a draft dodger. When he gets there, his parents reject him, and he discovers that he no longer belongs in his family home. It's a beautifully poetic and wistful tune.

Other anti-war songs of the year included The Hollies' 'Frightened Lady' and Melanie's massive international hit 'Lay Down (Candles in the Rain)'. A very different feel was evidenced in 'Machine Gun' by Jimi Hendrix, which first appeared on his 1970 *Band of Gypsys* album. Recorded on the first day of the new decade at New York's Fillmore East, it's a semi-improvisatory twelve-minute performance that sees the guitar maestro at his absolute peak. With its rat-a-tat snare drum imitating gunfire, and a confused lyric aligning war with family break-up (perhaps evoking the destruction wrought on Vietnamese households?), the guitar work is considered by many to be among Hendrix's finest: laden with effects pedals, feedback and a bevy of ideas that invoke helicopters, explosions and screams, eventually devolving into tenderness.

Opening side two of David Bowie's *The Man Who Sold the World* album was 'Running Gun Blues', again invoking the atrocities of the Vietnam War (notably the Mỹ Lai Massacre) with lyrics about killing 'gooks' (army slang for Viet Cong). For the US release, the LP cover featured a cartoon of a cowboy holding a gun while standing in front of an asylum. In the UK, the album had a very different cover: a photo of Bowie in a blue dress reclining on a chaise longue. On its first release, the album flopped badly.

It would have to wait for Bowie's *Ziggy Stardust* to surface before the disc would find its audience.

Moratorium marches opposing Australia's involvement in Vietnam were occurring across the nation. These were far and away the largest demonstrations in Australia's history to that point. Senior Liberal Billy Snedden labelled the protest organisers 'political bikies who pack-rape democracy'.[22] But anti-war fervour was no longer dominated by radical long-hairs. There were now Australians from all walks of life campaigning to get Australia out of 'America's war'. At the forefront of the movement was federal Labor MP Dr Jim Cairns. Not long before the May demonstrations, Cairns and his wife, Gwen, had been bashed in their home because of their anti-war stance.

By midyear, polling showed that, for the very first time, a majority of Australians opposed their country's involvement in the war. The tide had finally turned. In response, Prime Minister William McMahon announced that he would start withdrawing Australian troops from the conflict.

By the end of the year, Australia had around 13,000 draft resisters, many of them in hiding. In the US the numbers of draft resisters could be counted in the hundreds of thousands, with many taking up residence in Canada and elsewhere. All manner of trickery was engaged to avoid or fail a draft call-up. The Amboy Dukes' Ted Nugent, later a fiercely vocal conservative and board member of the National Rifle Association, told an underground magazine in 1970 that he had taken crystal meth as well as urinated and defecated in his pants before attending his physical examination. Steppenwolf's song 'Draft Resister' was a rallying cry for those who refused to fight.

Chicago's second album, *Chicago* (generally referred to as *Chicago II*), had been released before the Kent State incident. The album sleeve declared: 'With this album we dedicate ourselves, our futures and our energies to the people of the revolution … And the revolution in all its forms.' The album continued the band's fusion of funk, jazz and rock, tossing up hit singles 'Make Me Smile', 'Colour My World' and '25 or 6 to 4'. It also included an almost side-long suite in four movements titled 'It Better End Soon', with lyrics calling for an end to war.

Chicago's radical rhetoric may have been largely bombast, but they didn't blunder into a political storm like sister jazz-rock outfit Blood, Sweat & Tears, who shot themselves in each of their eighteen feet by accepting US government funding to tour behind the Iron Curtain. The nine band members duly set off on a twenty-six-day tour of Yugoslavia, Romania and Poland. Even though the band waved their fees for the tour, they were ridiculed back home for collaborating with the CIA. It wasn't clear sailing in the Eastern bloc nations either. In Bucharest, authorities were so appalled by the show that they issued a set of instructions for subsequent concerts, which included emphasising the jazz elements and not the rock stylings, lowering the volume and dressing more conservatively. Partway through the subsequent concert, the show was brought to an abrupt halt and the band were ordered to leave the country.

Czech this out

The trials and tribulations of Western rockers were nothing compared to those of the musicians who lived behind the Iron Curtain. The Plastic People of the Universe had formed in 1968, just a month after the Warsaw Pact troops invaded Czechoslovakia to crush the liberalisation process known as the Prague Spring. The band's moniker derived from a Mothers of Invention song, 'Plastic People'.

In Czechoslovakia, the revolutionary power of rock music was tangible. The Plastic People of the Universe unwittingly set in train a movement that would ultimately topple the communist regime two decades later. As reed player Vratislav Brabenec said in 2009: 'Our identity as a band was to do with poetry, not politics … I am one of those whose cultural actions, not political actions, were sufficient to make me a subversive. The politicians made us political by being offended by what we did and the music we played.'[23] As well as their own material, the band performed songs by The Velvet Underground, The Doors, Captain Beefheart, plus those ribald, scandalous American agitators The Fugs. The political regime wasn't impressed.

In 1970, the Czech government revoked the band's music licence, making it extremely difficult for them to perform gigs, let alone rehearse or even purchase equipment. So The Plastic People of the Universe took their music underground. At first, they performed guerrilla gigs under the guise of lectures about Andy Warhol. But the police caught wind of the ruse and began to shut down these events. For a time, they would also play unannounced at weddings and football clubs, but informers frequently reported them to authorities. The band regularly had their equipment confiscated, but they weren't about to give up.

Heavy duties

Polling of college-aged youth in America during 1970–71 revealed that half of those questioned could not name a living countryman whom they held in high regard. Millions of young people across the planet were disenchanted with 'straight' society and its conventions. As Led Zeppelin's Robert Plant put it, 'The 70's were harsher and less innocent times than the preceding decade, and Led Zeppelin were made for them.'[24]

Established in England, Led Zeppelin had been seminal in promulgating a new approach to rock during the late 1960s, at the time dubbed 'hard rock'. It was still blues-based, but it would eventually be seen as the beginnings of heavy metal.

Led Zeppelin's enormous success also helped pioneer the shift from concert halls to stadium venues. But their repeated tours of America were becoming increasingly dangerous. The spring 1970 tour saw Jimmy Page's custom guitar stolen, the band forced off the road by rednecks in Austin, their limo grazed by a bullet in Dallas, and violence erupting outside a venue in Miami. In Memphis, Robert Plant was forced at gunpoint to quell a rowdy audience. The days of playing to relaxed, weed-smoking hippies were over. Sports arenas, coliseums and speedways brought out a very different crowd. Bodyguards packing sidearms became de rigueur.

The Zep's first two albums had been released in 1969 to significant success, and the band was riding high. They were also engaging in immensely debauched offstage behaviour. Taking their lead from members of The Who, they repeatedly trashed hotels, destroyed property and encouraged massively belittling behaviour upon groupies. As Sharon Osbourne put it:

Everyone knew in Hollywood that Zeppelin were in town and those guys were so fucking wild. They'd abuse the chicks. They'd like to push it to see how far they could go: burning them, cutting their hair off, handcuffing them – I mean leaving them handcuffed for a couple of days in the room.[25]

Miss Pamela (Pamela Des Barres) – herself a groupie and regular consort of Led Zeppelin's guitarist Jimmy Page – concurred: 'They were very debauched, and the girls got younger and more willing to do anything. It got to be incredibly sick.'[26] Zep biographer Bob Spitz wrote, 'On early tours with Led Zeppelin, there were many sexual encounters with underage girls.'[27] The band members vied with each other to come up with increasingly depraved ideas.

Of course, Led Zeppelin weren't alone in such antics. Members of The Faces, The Rolling Stones, The Who and others also went on destructive benders while on tour. Rod Stewart happily admits to the incredibly juvenile practice of drawing penises on hotel artworks and 'upon almost anything' he could find.[28] He also helped to flood bathrooms, and drink hotel bars dry. Sometimes Stewart would invite entire audiences back to the band's hotel to assist with the profligate chaos.

These pampered, vainglorious showboats established a benchmark for rock star behaviour, particularly the abuse of women. Inevitably, many had difficulty maintaining functioning relationships and families back home. But their antics as cultural heroes also played into a broader shift towards hedonism and self-indulgence within youth culture.

Jimmy Page had a longstanding obsession with British occultist Aleister Crowley, whom he referred to as 'the great misunderstood genius of the twentieth century'.[29] Crowley promoted the notion that one should do exactly as one pleased all of the time. His teachings and his own behaviour were a masterclass in pure self-indulgence, particularly drug-taking and sexual decadence. Led Zep's next LP would have Crowley's dictum inscribed into the run-out after the last song on each side of the disc: 'So mote be it' and 'Do what thou wilt'. The full version of the latter phrase, from Crowley's *The Book of the Law*, read: 'Do what thou wilt shalt be the whole of the law.' He may have died in 1945, but Crowley was a prototype 'rock god' long before the term was coined.

But Led Zeppelin's live performances were bravura displays of high-energy playing. Their two-and-a-half-hour show at London's Albert Hall prompted Germaine Greer to write:

> Led Zeppelin used discipline and concentration to become the Wagner of rock and roll … For 10 years, rock and roll had been working towards something that would combine the extraordinary capacities of electronic instruments with the anarchic energy of youth, and there, in the Albert Hall on January 9, 1970, I found it.[30]

However, the new global masters of heavy rock were also brazen plagiarists, particularly of American blues artists, with a string of lawsuits the consequence.

Following their fifth US tour, Plant and Page decamped with their families and entourage to a rustic cottage in Wales to write new songs. As Plant put it, 'It created such a dynamic, coming off tour and going up to Wales. It was this thing about trading excess for nothingness, having these great pastoral moments.'[31] They only had acoustic instruments to perform with, but importantly, they were at the time captivated by the likes of Bert Jansch, John Fahey, Joni Mitchell, The Incredible String Band and Fairport Convention. Using one of the first Sony cassette recorders and a stack of Eveready batteries, they set about composing new material with the express intention of demonstrating that the world's greatest rock band could move beyond the explosive eruptions for which they were famous.

The pair then joined bass player John Paul Jones and drummer John Bonham at a sprawling, dank eighteenth-century institutional building known as Headley Grange to record the new material using the Rolling Stones' grandly titled Mobile Studio. In fact, it was simply an eight-track recording console wedged into an RV trailer where the kitchen facilities would otherwise reside.

The general response to the music on *Led Zeppelin III* was bemusement. There was more delicacy to the material than the headbangers were expecting. The album opened with the storming riff and screamed lyrics of 'Immigrant Song', and there were plenty of 'heavy' riffs, such as on 'Out on the Tiles'. But these sat alongside the acoustic guitar, mandolin and banjo featured on the song 'Gallows Pole', a tune lifted from an old Lead Belly recording. 'Tangerine' even employed an uncharacteristic pedal steel guitar, albeit played with a wah-wah pedal. The lilting 'That's the Way', a song about dealing with parental disapproval, was perhaps the first track recorded by a heavy rock band that had no bass or drums.

The album did go number one in the UK, America, Australia and elsewhere, yet *Led Zeppelin III* remains the weakest-selling of the band's first four albums. Speaking to Cameron Crowe in 1975, Plant reflected: 'The third album was the album of albums. If anybody had labelled us a heavy metal group, that destroyed them.'[32] Some critics suggested that Led Zep's foray into contrived folkiness had undermined their reputation as hard rockers. Displaying remarkably thin skin, Jimmy Page lashed out at his detractors, arguing that the band had simply moved too far ahead of the reviewers' capacity to appreciate them. But the critics were put to rest when Led Zeppelin were voted best band in the annual *Melody Maker* poll, finally usurping The Beatles, who had held that spot every year since 1963.

Page's fixation with Aleister Crowley had led him to buy Crowley's former home, known as Boleskin House, on the banks of Loch Ness, in Scotland. But there was another up-and-coming British band that was also inspired by Crowley, and it would incorporate occultism more keenly into its band persona. In 1968, they were playing under the moniker Earth, but found themselves confused with another band that had chosen the same rather obvious name. John Michael 'Ozzy' Osbourne's autobiography suggests that there was a cinema near to the band's rehearsal space which regularly showed popular horror movies, apparently inspiring him and bassist Geezer Butler to write what Osbourne called 'scary music'.[33] Geezer came up with the song title 'Black Sabbath', supposedly lifting it from a Boris Karloff movie of the same name, and it soon became the band's appellation. But this explanation all sounds a bit too cute. Occult and horror themes were not new to rock music in 1970. In the USA, Chicago-based band Coven was also pioneering occult rock. Their debut album, *Witchcraft Destroys Minds & Reaps Souls*, was released in early 1969. Notably, their bass guitarist and co-writer, Michael Osborne, was credited on the album as 'Oz Osborne', and the first track on their album was 'Black Sabbath'. Hmmm.

The British band Black Sabbath, by associating their shtick with Hammer-horror symbolism, and by eschewing the sort of acoustic niceties that still appealed to Led Zeppelin, soon became the foremost progenitors of heavy metal music. As drummer Bill Ward said about writing the track 'Black Sabbath': 'When Oz sang "What is this that stands before me?" it became completely different. Because it hadn't been said quite like that and … this was a different feel. You know, I was playing drums to the words.'[34]

Incredibly, the entire *Black Sabbath* album was recorded in one day. As Ozzy recalled:

> We just set up our gear and played what amounted to a live set without the audience. Once we'd finished, we spent a couple of hours double-tracking some of the guitar and vocals, and that was that. Done. We were in the pub for last orders. It can't have taken any longer than twelve hours in total.[35]

One of the more original aspects to Black Sabbath's sound was Tony Iommi's lead guitar. Iommi had lost the tips of his two middle fingers in a sheet metal factory at age seventeen. After Iommi was told by doctors that he would never play guitar again, his factory manager gave him a copy of a Django Reinhardt LP. The gypsy jazz guitarist had also relearned how to play guitar after losing two fingertips. Inspired, Iommi constructed new fingertips, using molten plastic from detergent bottles and then covering the plastic thimbles with leather. He then detuned his guitar to make it easier to play. There were some chords he couldn't play with his home-grown prosthetics, so he concentrated on a style which paired open strings with fretted strings. His playing helped popularise so-called power chords.

The fuzz-tinged guitar punching out a riff, held in place by powerful bass guitar and busy, corpulent drumming, was the quintessential heavy metal sound that survives to this day. But Geezer wasn't always repeating the riff: often his bass was rushing all over the place. The new metal sound also boasted screamed vocals and buckets of machismo, all delivered with warrior-like ferocity.

The title track was inspired by 'Mars, the Bringer of War' from Gustav Holst's *The Planets*. Geezer Butler was a fan of that classical suite and was mucking around on his bass, trying to play the melody from 'Mars'. When Tommy Iommi heard what he was doing, he turned it into a monster riff.

Whether consciously or not, the riff for the song 'Black Sabbath' uses an inversion of the tritone, which is also known as *diabolus in musica*, as it is supposed to invoke Satanic connotations. The tritone was banned by the church during the Middle Ages. It incorporates a somewhat dissonant 'blue note', with an interval spanning six semitones – or a flattened fifth, in musical parlance. 'Black Sabbath' was certainly one of the first heavy metal tunes to employ the tritone. (The tritone also appears in the opening to Jimi Hendrix's 'Purple Haze'.)

The track 'Behind the Wall of Sleep' takes its inspiration from an H.P. Lovecraft story *Beyond the Wall of Sleep*, and the terribly banal lyrics for 'The Wizard' were inspired by Gandalf from J.R.R. Tolkien's *The Lord of the Rings*. Tolkien's books would inspire a plethora of 1970s music, as well as many band names.

Black Sabbath's collaborative approach to composing was arguably key to their innovative sound. As Iommi explained:

All the songs were written basically the same. We'd go into a rehearsal room with nothing and then just start jamming about … it's peculiar how it all happened … They were just coming out and it was almost like a magical force, pushing these things out that we didn't understand.'[36]

Of course, Iommi was crucial to this process, as was Butler, with the pair bouncing ideas off each other. Having found a riff, they would play it with drummer Bill Ward, while Osbourne picked out a melody, usually singing whatever came into his head. Having established the melody, bassist Butler would then write the lyrics, sometimes inspired by a word or phrase that Osbourne had improvised.

It's instructive to listen to the early Black Sabbath albums and note how the tracks modulate and change so as not to outstay their riff-based welcome – or, as Osbourne put it, 'We like a lot of tempo changes, so that it doesn't get on people's nerves.'[37] Listen to the ominously slow opening track, which speeds up into double time for the last two minutes, or the many changes throughout 'Sleeping Village', which begins with a pastoral feel.

The *Black Sabbath* LP was issued, appropriately, on Friday, 13 February 1970, on the new Vertigo Records label, which had been created to showcase Philips/Phonogram's 'underground' acts. It quickly rose to number eight in the UK, and twenty-three in the US. But the album grew legs and remained in the American charts for more than a year. Critics of the day mostly castigated the record for its dark themes and raw sound, with Lester Bangs describing it as 'Cream clichés'.[38] The band reportedly rushed out to buy all the music papers when the record was released, only to discover they had been roundly savaged. However, few can deny the album's formative influence on the development of rock music.

In mid-1970, just four months later, Black Sabbath went back into the studio to record a follow-up LP, *Paranoid*. It was originally called *War Pigs*, after the opening track, a statement in opposition to the Vietnam War, but the record company, wary of a title that appeared to criticise patriotic veterans, decided to change the album's title. Unfortunately, the cover art had been designed with the *War Pigs* title in mind, and it was too late to alter it. Nevertheless, *Paranoid* would become the blueprint for a genre of music that has survived longer than most, with Sabbath's second outing inspiring countless metal bands over decades. It would also regularly re-enter music charts right up until 2020, when it reappeared (I am tempted to say 'like magic') on the Belgian and Swiss album charts. Chock-a-block with killer hooks and dark, apocalyptic themes, it has been described as a Hieronymus Bosch painting set to music.

Once more, critics mostly hated the heavy rock on *Paranoid*, but audiences knew what they wanted. 'Iron Man' was a fantasy about a superhero ready to wreak revenge on humanity, written, according to Geezer, as a response to global pollution. 'Hand of Doom' was about Vietnam veterans getting hooked on heroin as a means of coping with the horrors of war. 'Jack the Stripper/Fairies Wear Boots' was inspired by an encounter with a group of skinheads. Listen to the structure of this track, with its changes in tempo during the introduction and a brief guitar solo in a different key. Halfway through, when it comes time for Iommi to cut loose, the solo builds superbly, then the whole thing shifts into yet another key and tempo. It's a masterclass in metal shakedown.

Sabbath, like Zeppelin, weren't averse to a dabbling in other genres. Iommi was fascinated with jazz guitarist Joe Pass, and Django Reinhardt's influence is evident on the gentle 'Planet Caravan', a track inspired by Geezer's love of science fiction, closing with an acoustic guitar solo that is well removed from the screaming fuzz distortion of heavy metal. On 'Electric Funeral', by contrast, bass, drums, fuzz guitar and voice are all doing the same riff-based thing, stamping each note with raw primitivism.

With insufficient material for the new album, the track 'Paranoid' was slung together in the studio at the last minute. Tony Iommi came up with the guitar lick, Geezer Butler jotted down some lyrics, Ozzy Osbourne read them as he sang, and twenty minutes later the song was complete. Osbourne later described it as 'a punk song years before punk had been invented'.[39] Turned into a single, 'Paranoid' became the band's only top ten hit. It's a propulsive, urgent song about depression. Butler didn't understand

26

the difference between the terms paranoia and depression when he wrote it, but he certainly knew what the latter was like to experience. As he later explained, 'I used to be a cutter. I'd cut my arms, stick pins in my fingers, that kind of thing. I used to get really depressed and it was the only thing that could bring me out from it.'[40]

Although their albums and songs referenced black magic and the occult, in 1970 Black Sabbath members were publicly distancing themselves from their own marketing ploy. Tony Iommi said, 'Everybody thinks we're a black magic group, but we just picked the name because we like it,'[41] while drummer Bill Ward averred, 'We have never practiced black magic on stage. In fact we're anti-black magic.'[42] Perhaps they were fearful of a media backlash? But they weren't the only ones plundering horror clichés. Other occult rock bands of the era included British six-piece outfit Black Widow. Their theatrical stage act incorporated incantations and a sacrificial ceremony, and their debut 1970 album *Sacrifice* was a mix of Jethro Tull–style progressive rock with heavy rock. In Italy there was also Jacula, a dark progressive rock band with a rare female vocalist.

Absolute shockers

'Shock rock' had precedents going back to the mid-1950s, when Screamin' Jay Hawkins would rise from a coffin and sing into a skull-shaped microphone. In the late 1960s, performing as Dr John the Night Tripper, Mac Rebennack could be found wearing wild costumes and headdresses while enacting mock sacrifices and voodoo ceremonies.

Vincent Furnier also decided he would make a visual impression. The asthmatic kid, whose father was a pastor, established his band, The Spiders, in a Phoenix high school. They changed their name to Alice Cooper after asking a ouija board what they should be called. By 1970, Vincent and his band had relocated to California, where the group were signed by Frank Zappa for his newly hatched Straight Records label. He had already signed the all-female group GTOs (standing for Girls Together Outrageously), which included then groupie and later author Pamela Des Barres. As label stablemates, the GTOs took charge of Alice Cooper's look, helping dress the band in drag and adding purple lipstick to lead singer Furnier.

Alice Cooper's debut album, *Pretties for You*, was mostly in the psychedelic vein, with some free improvisation and lots of effects. It became the first release on Zappa's new label, but it didn't sell. Music critic Lester Bangs called it a waste of plastic. Although it's certainly rough around the edges, I find it more adventurous and interesting than most of Cooper's later efforts. What's more, the music is humorous and decidedly playful, in a similar way to early Soft Machine.

During 1969's Toronto Rock and Roll Revival Concert – which also featured Bo Diddley, Jerry Lee Lewis and Chuck Berry, plus a makeshift band headed by John Lennon and Yoko Ono – Alice Cooper's stage act had included ripping apart some pillows and sending feathers into the air. For some reason, a live chicken was added from backstage. The hapless fowl ended up being tossed into the audience, where it met its demise, with bloodied pieces of chicken being lobbed back onto the stage. The incident made national headlines and soon became embellished, including by a claim that Furnier drank the animal's blood. As he later said, 'All of a sudden we were the most notorious band on the planet.'[43]

But even this hyped publicity couldn't assist Alice Cooper's second album for Straight Records. Titled *Easy Action* and released in mid-1970, it was a lacklustre effort, though again not without a degree of playfulness. At this time, the band enjoyed a reputation for clearing venues: for a period, it became a sort of hip Californian pastime to attend an Alice Cooper show and walk out.

The band relocated to Detroit, Michigan, where they found audiences far more receptive to their idiosyncratic music and increasingly bizarre stage show. The city had already spawned the likes of MC5 and The Stooges, after all. As MC5's Wayne Kramer put it, 'What they were doing was Salvador Dalí with electric guitar, and Detroit was open to that.'[44] Alice Cooper had finally found their niche.

Debuting in 1970 were the Dickensian-titled British band Uriah Heep, with their opening gambit ... *Very 'Eavy ... Very 'Umble*. Critiquing the album on its release (in the US it was retitled simply *Uriah Heep*), *Rolling Stone* reviewer Melissa Mills so loathed the LP that she famously promised to commit suicide should the band become a success. To date, Uriah Heep have released twenty-four studio albums, twenty live albums and forty-one compilation albums. Presumably, Melissa Mills remained alive throughout.

In the face of all this hard rock, pioneering British band Deep Purple were sloughing off their psychedelic and progressive rock pretentions to adopt the new, heavier sound for their fourth album, *Deep Purple in Rock*. Having performed with the Royal Philharmonic Orchestra and released their *Concerto for Group and Orchestra* LP, the band was keen to reassert its rock roots. *In Rock* opens with a blitzkrieg, attention-grabbing assault by Ritchie Blackmore's shrieking, distorted guitar on 'Speed King', before a gentle organ piece with hints of Beethoven's 'Für Elise' by classically trained keyboardist Jon Lord. The song then settles into another of those heavy metal riffs where the guitar and bass play the same thing and the drums thrash about. Ian Gillan's screamed vocals are arrant nonsense, something about a 1950s rocker heading to New Orleans, with many of the lines lifted from 1950s rock 'n' roll songs.

'Flight of the Rat' came about when bassist Roger Glover was toying with a version of Rimsky-Korsakov's 'Flight of the Bumblebee', while 'Into the Fire' was the band's attempt at an anti-drugs song. The ten-minute suite 'Child in Time' is significantly more interesting, with stark lyrics about war. Brazenly, it steals the introduction, riff and melody from the song 'Bombay Calling' which had been released the previous year by American band It's a Beautiful Day. Plagiarism aside, the track allowed the group to stretch out, with a range of feels and tempos, the climax being a definitive high-fretted guitar solo by Richie Blackmore. *Deep Purple in Rock* went to number one on the Australian charts.

Worried that there was no obvious single on the album, the band went back into the studio to try to come up with something more commercial. Scouring for inspiration, they intriguingly found it in Ricky Nelson's up-tempo version of George Gershwin's showtune 'Summertime'. The combined bass and guitar riff on 'Black Night' is a direct purloining of

29

Nelson's recording. 'Black Night' became the band's highest-charting single. Gillan admitted that he had consciously attempted to write banal lyrics, and boy, did he succeed!

Thanks to Led Zeppelin, Black Sabbath and Deep Purple, British music was dominating the hard rock scene in the early 1970s. America's premium hard rock band at the time was Grand Funk Railroad. The name was a punning take on a railway in Michigan, Grand Trunk Western Railroad. Modelled initially on Cream, but without Cream's finesse, and later inspired by Deep Purple, but without Deep Purple's musicality, their first two albums, *On Time* and *Grand Funk* still managed to go gold. This was quite remarkable, given the discs were universally panned by music critics and received next to no radio airplay. But their gung-ho manager, former musician Terry Knight, was brilliant at marketing. Their 1970 album, *Closer to Home*, again failed to impress the critics, but nevertheless went multi-platinum. The LP was backed by a publicity campaign that included a US$100,000 billboard in Times Square. A third 1970 release, the imaginatively titled *Live Album*, also sold in substantial numbers.

Grand Funk was a fascinating case study in popularism. Who was right: the consumers willing to fill arenas and spend on albums, or the music industry and its doyens, who viewed the band as crass, artless or, as the *Rolling Stone Record Guide* put it, 'wretched'?[45] Rod Stewart famously called them the all-time loud white noise. Perhaps the band's appeal was partly their outsider status, with the group's manager capitalising on bad reviews as proof of some sort of elitism within the rock establishment. Having successfully built the band, Knight would end up in protracted litigation with them.

Sliding Doors

America's censorship laws were far less restrictive than those in Britain and Australia. Although there was comparatively less censorship of film and literature in the US, the moral custodians were keenly watching the nation's concert stages. Jefferson Airplane found themselves in hot water following a concert in Oklahoma City during which Grace Slick dropped the f-word. The stage swarmed with police and the band copped a US$1000 fine. Janis Joplin also received a fine for using obscene language in Florida.

Jim Morrison, lead singer of The Doors, was also in a good deal of bother in 1970, up on charges relating to his performance at a Miami concert in late 1969. The extremely drunken singer had teased the audience about taking his clothes off during the song 'Touch Me'. There's little doubt Morrison did ask the audience, 'Do you want to see my cock?', but, as guitarist Robbie Krieger said, 'I personally never saw that happen, nor did [band members] Ray [Manzarek] or John [Densmore], and out of two or three hundred photographs that were taken that night, there's not one shot that shows that happening.'[46] Nevertheless, a clerk in the state attorney's office agreed to serve as complainant, and Jim was charged with a felony of lewd and lascivious behaviour, plus misdemeanours for indecent exposure, profanity and drunkenness.

News of Jim's purported debauchery spread like wildfire, headlining newspapers across the nation. Suddenly Doors concerts were being cancelled. Rallies opposing lewd behaviour popped up across the country, with a 'March for Decency' at the Miami Orange Bowl attracting 30,000 people. The organisers of that event received a special commendatory letter from President Nixon.

Morrison pleaded not guilty to the charges, and bail was posted. After months without performing, some bookings for the band trickled in, but venues were now demanding bonds against lewd behaviour. Similar imposts were being placed on other bands. At a Doors gig in Las Vegas, the local sheriff attended the show with blank warrants made out for each of the band members, ready to be filled out.

In the midst of all this, The Doors released their new album *Morrison Hotel*, named after an actual budget hotel in downtown LA. The record had taken considerable effort to complete over a nine-month period, not helped by Morrison's heavy drinking. Dense with Jim's poetry, the music was a return to the band's blues-rock roots and was warmly received by both critics and fans. The *Creem* magazine editor even went so far as to describe it as the best record he had ever heard. It quickly went gold, reaching number four on the *Billboard* 200, and the group became the first American hard rock act to achieve five gold albums in a row.

Jim's woes were compounding in 1970. The rest of the band wanted their lead singer to give away his distracting filmmaking ambitions and concentrate on music. They also wanted him to shave off his full-face beard and lose weight. His closest female flame was urging him to give away music altogether, and, on top of that, there were a host of unresolved paternity suits.

On an impulse, Morrison suddenly 'married' Patricia Kennely on Midsummer night in a gothic apartment surrounded by candles. Kennely was an editor and critic for *Jazz & Pop* magazine and a practising witch. The 'handfasting' ceremony was conducted by one of Patricia's coven friends and included making small cuts on each of their arms, with drops of their blood mixed with wine, which they then drank. As they were declared married under the Wiccan tradition, Jim reportedly fainted.

Meanwhile, The Doors' *Absolutely Live* was released. It presented the band's extended performance piece 'Celebration of the Lizard', plus several new songs and a couple of blues covers. Cobbled together from various concerts, it only sold half the number that *Morrison Hotel* had managed. This time, the critics were far from kind.

Back in Miami for his trial, Morrison's pending verdict was looking grave. With America's curious blending of politics and the law, the judge appointed to the case was about to face an election and was hungry for publicity. Various witnesses were called, all giving conflicting accounts of the events. At one stage, the trial was paused so The Doors could fly to the UK to perform at the Isle of Wight Festival. Back in court, the judge made an extraordinary determination: the defence would be limited to the same number of witnesses as the prosecution – just seventeen. There had been 100 people lined up to testify, so eighty-three had to be dismissed.

Four weeks after it began, the jury determined that Morrison was not guilty on two of the four charges – lewd behaviour and, curiously, drunkenness (even though Jim had admitted he was drunk) – but guilty of the misdemeanour of profanity and wilful exposure. A month later, Morrison, while still on bail, received the maximum sentence of six months' hard labour. Inevitably, his legal team appealed, but a jail sentence hung over the singer like a sword of Damocles.

Given the relatively poor sales of the live album, the band's label, Elektra, wanted a new LP to meet the Christmas market. A compilation album, titled *13* because it had thirteen tracks, was pushed out in November.

Halfway through a concert in New Orleans on 12 December, Morrison simply gave up performing. He repeatedly bashed the microphone stand into the stage, then threw the stand into the audience and plonked himself down on the drum riser. He remained motionless for the remainder of the gig. The rest of the band realised his touring days were over.

The Doors had been a seminal influence on many other groups, not the least of which was Iggy Pop's outfit The Stooges. Pop (real name James Newell Osterberg Jr) had been captivated by Jim Morrison's stage presence when he saw them perform in 1967. The Stooges' first LP had been produced by John Cale of The Velvet Underground in 1969, though the band could barely play their instruments. The 1970 follow-up, *Fun House*, was recorded with the band playing live in the studio. It was raw, nihilistic and primal. *Fun House* made MC5's *Kick Out the Jams* seem tame by comparison. In other words, it was punk before such a genre existed. Critics were either awed or appalled. Today, *Fun House* is recognised by many as perhaps the most important album in the development of punk and garage rock. However, the band's heroin addictions were already proving problematic.

Despite the legal debacle surrounding the high-profile Doors, The Stooges didn't resile from outrageous stage antics. Singer Iggy Pop smeared himself with meat, cut himself with shards of glass, flashed his genitalia and even dove into the audience (pre-dating crowd surfing). At underground venues, The Stooges were taking confrontational stage performance to a whole new level. But Elektra Records eventually had enough of the band's unpredictable, drug-addled behaviour and dropped them from its roster. At midyear, the band broke up. But Iggy Pop and The Stooges would be back.

Sex machines

There was considerable money to be made from the sexual revolution. X-rated movie theatres were springing up in the US, and New York suddenly had more than 200 adult bookstores. Of course, sex was also a preoccupation of pop and rock music, even slipping into Simon & Garfunkel's mega-hit album *Bridge Over Troubled Water*. Selling around 25 million copies, the LP was in early 1970 the bestselling album of all time, going number one across the globe. In Britain it would remain the bestselling LP for the entire decade.

The track 'Cecilia' is a raunchy, up-tempo song about a highly sexed female lover who takes multiple partners. Even while the first-person singer is in the bathroom washing his face, Cecilia is busy getting off with someone else in the bedroom. Sex also raises its head in 'Baby Driver', about a boy pursuing his sexual initiation, and again in 'The Boxer', in which a runaway boy seeks solace among whores. When recording this track, Simon & Garfunkel became the first musicians to utilise sixteen-track recording, although this was achieved by synchronising two eight-track recorders. Beyond the expected folk rock, the duo dipped their toes into gospel, jazz, reggae and world music, however many critics damned the album for being 'overproduced'.

On *Bridge Over Troubled Water*, Paul Simon finally credited his backing musicians on the LP sleeve, something he had not bothered to do previously. Yet again he appropriated other people's work. The title track had in part been rifled from an old spiritual 'Mary Don't You Weep' that had been recorded by gospel group The Swan Silvertones. Sometime later in his life, Simon reportedly gave Claude Jeter of The Swan Silvertones a cheque to compensate him for the plagiarism. Simon also believed the song 'El Cóndor Pasa (If I Could)' to be a traditional song and thus free of copyright. In fact, it had been penned in 1933 by Peruvian Daniel Alomía Robles, which came to light when Robles' son filed a successful lawsuit against Simon in 1970. The song heralded Paul Simon's increasing forays into world music (and thus, for some, even greater sins of cultural appropriation).

Folk music's clean-cut image took a body blow in 1970 when Peter Yarrow, of Peter, Paul & Mary, pleaded guilty to taking immoral liberties with a fourteen-year-old girl. This was on the back of a previous incomplete case three years earlier involving Yarrow and a fifteen-year-old girl. Yarrow served three months of a one-to-three-year prison sentence. A decade later, in 1981, he was officially pardoned by President Jimmy Carter. It is perhaps the only presidential pardon in US history that has expunged a sexual crime involving a child. Forty years later, in 2021, a new lawsuit was filed by a woman alleging Yarrow had raped her when she was a minor. Of course, Yarrow was the writer of 'Puff, the Magic Dragon'. Of that song, Yarrow once stated: 'It's a sad day when the innocence of childhood departs, and this is what Puff represents to me'.[47]

Various artists were capitalising on the newfound sexual freedoms and shifting moral standards. James Brown's 'Get Up (I Feel Like Being a) Sex Machine' was a rather dull, repetitive slice of funk. The title tells you all you need to know about the stupid lyrics. It nevertheless found plenty of willing ears, hitting the number two spot on the US R&B charts.

But it's The Kinks' 'Lola' that stands out as a watershed song dealing with matters sexual in 1970. Taken from their album *Lola Versus Powerman and the Moneygoround, Part One*, and penned by the increasingly flamboyant Ray Davies, the lyrics detail a romantic encounter between a first-person male protagonist and a trans woman. It became the band's first American hit in four years, the previous being 'Sunny Afternoon' in 1966.

The song's evolution is mired in conflicting stories. Davies claimed the song was inspired by a real-life experience of the band's manager, Robert Wace, however, the band's drummer, Mick Avory, argued that it was simply a product of the band having frequented pubs that featured drag acts. Whatever the case, 'Lola' was truly groundbreaking, being the first big international hit with a non-binary theme. Some stations outright banned the song, including in Australia. Others made terrible edits so they could play a bastardised version. The BBC found a reason to ban the song because the lyrics referred to Coca-Cola, which was in breach of their policy regarding product placement. Ray Davies flew from New York to

London to record new lyrics, changing 'Coca-Cola' to 'cherry cola', and thus rendering it more palatable to the BBC.

Three Dog Night had a hit with 'Mama Told Me (Not to Come)', portraying a naive partygoer who finds himself gobsmacked by a wild, licentious party. The protagonist is offered whisky as well as 'sugar with your tea', a discrete reference to LSD. The song had been written by Randy Newman for Eric Burdon, who recorded it for his *Eric Is Here* album in 1967. P.J. Proby also released a version around the same time, set against a party atmosphere track. But when resurrected by Three Dog Night in 1970, the song's time had finally come, and it shot to number one in the US. Unusually for a hit single, 'Mama Told Me (Not to Come)' features time signature shifts from 3/4 to 2/4.

The Jaggerz' song 'The Rapper' was another big hit. It was not, as the title might suggest, anticipating a new music genre, but rather warning girls about men who seduce women by lying, or 'rapping'. But there were other performers who were pre-empting rap or hip-hop music in 1970.

Proto rap

The roots of hip-hop and rap arguably go back to the African Griot tradition known as toasting, where performers would talk over rhythmic beats. In the 1950s and early '60s, folks like Jamaica's Count Machuki and America's Oscar Brown were adding poetry to reggae and jazz music. Arguably, another watershed occurred in 1965, when Bob Dylan shifted the parameters of popular song lyrics with 'Subterranean Homesick Blues'. Dylan had taken his cue from street performers who were spruiking rhythmic Beat poetry – people like Big Brown (aka William Clifford Brown), whom Dylan witnessed performing in Washington Square Park, and later acknowledged as a seminal influence.

Inevitably, the unparalleled egotist James Brown claimed that he pioneered rap in 1963 with 'Choo-Choo (Locomotion)', which is an odd assertion, because the recorded version was a surf-style twelve-bar blues with no lyrics. To my ear, it owes clear allegiance to Henry Mancini's

'Baby Elephant Walk' from 1961's *Hatari* soundtrack. Brown also claimed that his 1968 release 'America Is My Home' was rap, as well as his 1970 hit 'Get Up, Get Into It, Get Involved'.[48] But Brown has claimed credit for many things.

By the 1970s, the Griot-style toasting tradition was appearing on record in Jamaica. U-Roy (Ewart Beckford) put out two singles there, 'Wake the Town' and 'Wear You to the Ball', which were both local hits. Over reggae music, U-Roy delivered his half-spoken, half-sung toasts.

Meanwhile, in the US, talking blues had fused with jazz and Beat poetry to create a whole new modality. The Last Poets pursued many of the elements that what would later become hip-hop or rap. Their debut album featured three poets, Abiodun Oyewole, Alafia Pudim and Umar Bin Hassan, with themes about ghettoes and revolution set against acoustic and vocalised percussion. Tracks such as 'Wake Up, Niggers', 'Black Wish', and 'When the Revolution Comes' left no doubts about the uncompromising sentiment. Every track was a protest song, with the term 'nigger' being reclaimed from those who would use it as a put-down. *The Last Poets* LP was incendiary, confronting stuff, and yet it became the bestselling American R&B album during May 1970. Such high-profile success put The Last Poets in the sights of the FBI.

Gil Scott-Heron was the most impressive spoken-word exponent of the day. He had witnessed a performance by The Last Poets and suddenly found his calling. His debut LP, *Small Talk at 125th and Lenox*, dealt with a broader selection of topics than the polemical rants of The Last Poets. Scott-Heron's poems courageously considered the hypocrisy exhibited by black revolutionaries, as well as the hollowness of consumerism. Just twenty-one years old, Scott-Heron had already published a volume of poetry, plus his first novel, *The Vulture*. The album's opening track, 'The Revolution Will Not Be Televised', was rerecorded with a full band and released as a single the following year. The album also included the now famous 'Whitey on the Moon', which weighed the cost of the space race against the experience of Americans languishing in poverty. To his credit, Scott-Heron was able to inject dark humour into his subject matter.

Often overlooked in the trajectory of early rap and hip-hop are George Clinton's sister bands with rotating musicians, Funkadelic and Parliament. The opening gambit, *Funkadelic*, blends psychedelia, humour and science fiction into both sung and spoken-word raps laid over funk riffs. Parliament's debut album, *Osmium*, features a huge sound with layered voices sitting on guitar and organ riffing. It's an infectious, underrated masterwork. The track 'Little Ole Country Boy' – a sort of black response to 'Okie from Muskogee' – even incorporates yodelling, pedal steel and jew's harp into its raucous rap-funk. 'Oh Lord, Why Lord/Prayer' steals from Pachelbel's 'Canon in D Major' to produce a rousing gospel song with some truly extraordinary singing.

The disco fad was a few years away, but in New York the groundwork was being prepared. David Mancuso hosted his first Loft Party at his New York home. It was even given a name, 'Love Saves the Day', and it became the template for ongoing weekend dance parties. Mancuso spun the discs and Steve Abramowitz patrolled the door, collecting the $2.50 entrance fee. Blacks, Latinos, straight and gay folks all danced together. The habitués of The Loft were attracted by Mancuso's ability to select dance floor perfection. His home-spun efforts inspired other discothèques, such as The Gallery, Paradise Garage and The Warehouse, as well as a whole swag of deejays. But Mancuso would never be a fan of these more commercial venues, saying, 'I don't like to go in situations that are overcrowded; where you can't dance or where the sound system is so overpowering that your ears are ringing or where beer costs $6 a bottle – this is what I'm rebelling against.'[49]

The hitmakers

Bubblegum music was still receiving plenty of commercial radio airtime, with one-hit wonders such as The Pipkins' 'Gimme Dat Ding', Dawn's 'Knock Three Times', plus longer-flavoured acts like Tommy Roe with 'Jam Up and Jelly Tight'. The genre was often tied into television shows, such as *The Banana Splits* or *The Partridge Family*, and even plundered comic strips such as *The Archies*.

Quality crooning was also holding steady thanks to Barry Manilow, who was recording songs under the moniker Featherbed, Charles Aznavour, France's answer to Frank Sinatra, and Mel Torme, who put out three albums, including one titled *Close to You* that featured his version of the Bacharach/David song '(They Long to Be) Close to You'. That tune had previously been released in 1963 by Richard Chamberlain, followed by Dionne Warwick and Dusty Springfield. But it was the peerless voice of Karen Carpenter, enhanced by her brother's expert arrangement, that commandeered the charts in 1970. Ballads perfectly suited Karen's intimate singing style: she always sounded like she meant every word. The Carpenters' music was all about polish, and both siblings were perfectionists. The single was quickly followed by The Carpenters' bestselling album, also titled *Close to You*.

Irish singer-songwriter Van Morrison was living in Dylan's home turf near Woodstock in upstate New York. Following the commercial failure of his *Astral Weeks* album, 1970's *Moondance* garnered welcome acclaim from critics and helped define his future trajectory. While the LP only rose to twenty-nine in the US and thirty-two in the UK charts, the celebrated disc would continue to sell for the next four decades, going triple platinum by 1996.

Motown was on the nose among critics in 1970, who viewed it as a sausage machine for commercial product. *New Musical Express* called it toytown. Nevertheless, Motown's key act, The Jackson 5, had a stellar year, with four songs reaching the top spot on the US *Billboard* charts. Capitalising on this momentum, Motown issued three Jackson 5 albums in 1970 including a Christmas LP.

But it was America's West Coast, particularly Los Angeles, that operated as a quality hit factory. Queen of LA's Laurel Canyon clique was Joni Mitchell. Although she hadn't attended 1969's Woodstock Festival, she had penned the classic anthem about the event, simply titled 'Woodstock'. The song had been composed in a New York hotel room. As a sort of last hurrah for hippiedom, the lyrics helped sustain the mythic status of the festival, however the song also squeezed in swipes at pollution and war. Ensuring its success, 'Woodstock' was released in three versions in 1970. First out of the blocks was an up-tempo approach by Crosby, Stills, Nash & Young on their LP *Déjà Vu*. This would become the radio-preferred version in the US and Australia. Next was Mitchell's own version, from her *Ladies of the Canyon* LP, released as the B-side to her 'Big Yellow Taxi' single. The final release of 'Woodstock' was a version by a British band (although their name might belie their origin), Matthews Southern Comfort. This now largely forgotten version charted best in the UK, hitting the number one spot.

There was an integrity to Joni Mitchell that endeared her to audiences, as she wore her heart so openly on her sleeve. As she told *Melody Maker*:

> There is a certain amount of my life in my songs. They are honest and personal, and based on truth, but I exercise a writer's license to change details … I like to be straight with people and them with me. But it is not easy to do this all the time, especially in this business where there is so much falsity.[50]

'Big Yellow Taxi', possibly the song for which Mitchell is most famous, only went to number sixty-seven in the US during 1970. It performed far better in Australia, hitting sixth position. The tune had been written during Mitchell's first visit to Hawaii. She had looked out of her hotel window at the verdant green mountains, but found the vista marred by huge parking lots in the foreground. The song became an enduring classic.

Melody Maker readers voted Joni Mitchell the world's top female singer in a 1970 poll, ahead of Grace Slick, Janis Joplin, Aretha Franklin, Joan Baez, Julie Driscoll, Sandy Denny and others. Laurel Canyonites Crosby, Stills, Nash & Young also enjoyed a smash-hit album with *Déjà Vu*. It spawned four singles, including 'Carry On', which Led Zeppelin might be said to have plagiarised for their track 'Friends' on *Led Zeppelin III* (note in particular the imitative down-tuned slack-string guitar intro).

The members of CSNY were in dark places as *Déjà Vu* was being recorded. Stephen Stills' relationship with Judy Collins was on the skids, similarly Graham Nash's liaison with Joni Mitchell, and David Crosby's girlfriend Christine Hinton had been tragically killed in a car crash. On top of that, there was also the matter of four egomaniacs all wanting to be in control. When the outfit was formed, Graham Nash had ominously said, '[W]e don't want to be a group, just individuals, no collective name or anything.'[51] In truth, none of the four could stomach someone else becoming the leader or front person.

Many of the basic tracks for *Déjà Vu* were recorded in solo sessions before being presented to the rest of the members to add their harmony vocals and so on. Engineer Bill Halverson said:

> We spent anywhere from five- to seven-hundred hours of studio time on the second album and a lot of that was rehearsal in the studio and trying to figure out what to do ... there was more and more dissention and there was a lot more distraction ... there was such a negative vibe when they (all) showed up ...[52]

Principal among those 'distractions' was the prodigious quantity of drugs being consumed.

So anticipated was the CSNY disc that Atlantic Records received US$2 million in pre-orders before it hit the shelves. *Déjà Vu*'s success was ultimately a product of those superbly harmonised voices and a couple of standout compositions, but it remains an album that lacks a cohesive soul. The leatherette cover and faux western photo of a sullen band with guns and bandoleers insinuates the group's real nature. But it wasn't just egos and drugs that corrupted CSNY, as their drummer Dallas Taylor opined: 'What started out as our goal to be the world's greatest rock and roll band became trying to be the world's richest rock and roll band. It seemed to happen overnight.'[53]

The subsequent tour was also a disaster, with various band members strung out on drugs and Nash even being stood up by the rest of the band in Chicago. As the Fillmore's lighting director, Joshua White, noted, they 'were stoned and sang flat and the audience went nuts. To me that indicated that times were changing. We were now applauding the presence of the artist. Rather than the performance.'[54]

Enter the troubadour

In the midst of all this US-centric Top 40 product, there was one artist that would commandeer the first half of the decade like no other, and he hailed from the UK. Prior to 1970, Reg Dwight had been working as a support player as well as an impersonator. Cut-price record labels like Avenue or Ace of Clubs put out albums featuring copycat recordings of artists such as Stevie Wonder, The Beach Boys and Creedence Clearwater Revival. Dwight was a dab hand at these caricatures. While also playing keyboards in Long John Baldry's band, young Reg decided to embark on a solo career. He used two of the band members as inspiration for his stage name, saxophonist Elton Dean and band leader John Baldry, and thus dubbed himself Elton John.

Elton's 1969 *Empty Sky* LP was universally overlooked; however, 1970's *Elton John* just couldn't be ignored. With his friend Bernie Taupin providing the lyrics, artful production by Gus Dudgeon and superb orchestral arrangements by Paul Buckmaster, the album bristled with exceptional songs. Carefully planned prior to recording, the whole LP was completed in just four days. At the time, Elton and Bernie were still living in Elton's mother's flat, sleeping in bunk beds in the same room.

Elton John's label, DJM, insisted that the shy, retiring artist go on the road. A trio was thus assembled, with Nigel Olsson on drums and Dee Murray on bass. Booked to support a tour by Latin big-band leader Sérgio Mendes, they found themselves booed off the stage in Paris.

But the album performed well in the UK, so the next step was to see if Elton John might cut through in America. Finding willing venues for an unknown piano-led trio proved almost impossible. Eventually, The Troubadour club in LA was convinced to give Elton a shot on the basis that the record label could guarantee the venue would be packed with notables. The gig almost didn't happen: Elton's nerves were so debilitating that he needed to be coerced into performing. In the audience were the promised stars, with Neil Diamond roped in to act as MC.

Elton decided he would make a visual impression. As he described it amusingly, he wore:

> bright yellow dungarees, a long-sleeved T-shirt covered in stars and a pair of heavy workman's boots, also bright yellow, with a large set of blue wings sprouting from them. This was not the way sensitive singer-songwriters in America in 1970 looked. This was not the way anyone of sound mind in America in 1970 looked.[55]

For the first few songs, the audience chatted among themselves. The presence in the second row of Elton's hero, Leon Russell, threatened to completely paralyse the neophyte. Instead, with determination, he stood up, kicked his piano stool across the stage and commandeered attention by pounding the piano like Jerry Lee Lewis or Little Richard. He even fell to the floor while playing with one hand, then did a handstand on the keyboard. By the end of the set, the audience were cheering and Elton had discovered his performing mojo. Dr Jekyll had become Mr Hyde.

Word travelled fast. Within weeks, much of America knew about the latest rock whiz. In the era of guitar heroes, Elton John helped blaze a new trail for unlikely-looking, piano-playing rock performers, with the likes of Carole King and Billy Joel soon to follow his lead.

His sexual leanings, and particularly his live-in relationship with music manager John Reid, had to be kept secret, because, as he put it, 'Homosexuality had only been decriminalized in Britain for three years: the wider public's knowledge or understanding of the subject was pretty sketchy.'[56]

With *Elton John* a hit on both sides of the Atlantic, Bernie Taupin and Elton John quickly put together a new album, *Tumbleweed Connection*. This time the lyrics celebrated Taupin's fascination with America's wild west. While the LP sold well, not everyone was impressed, with critic Robert Christgau writing, 'Did someone call Grand Funk Railroad a hype? What about this puling phoney?'[57]

In the lead-up to a US tour, his American record distributor decided to release the wistful ballad 'Your Song' as a single. Taupin had tossed off the stream-of-consciousness lyrics over breakfast one morning, and Elton reckoned he composed the tune 'in fifteen minutes flat'.[58] Both Elton and his UK label had already decided the song was not chart material. To everyone's surprise, 'Your Song' went to single digits and became Taupin and John's most enduring success, hatching around fifty cover versions. (It had already appeared on Three Dog Night's *It Ain't Easy* LP.) Elton John was off and running.

Another big success story of 1970 was the release of the double album *Jesus Christ Superstar*, a 'rock opera' by Andrew Lloyd Webber and Tim Rice. At the time the pair were unable to secure backing for a stage production, so they adroitly released the music as a concept album. The recording featured a who's who of British theatre and rock. It was initially banned by the po-faced BBC, whose leaders deemed it sacrilegious, but impresario Robert Stigwood saw an opportunity and snaffled up the performance rights. As well as managing Cream, The Bee Gees and others, he had also produced stage productions of *Hair!* as well as *Oh! Calcutta!*. An expatriate Australian, Stigwood was an early master of 'crossover media', where a product in one medium could help sell product in another. Ultimately, the record helped sell the theatrical performance, which in turn helped sell the movie rights, with the soundtrack from the film completing the circle with even more album sales.

The new British invasion

While the UK was dominating the evolution of hard rock into heavy metal, there was another genre of music that the Brits also presided over: progressive (aka prog) rock.

Groups like Jethro Tull, The Moody Blues, Pink Floyd and Procol Harum had taken tentative steps towards progressive rock, as had Keith Emerson's band The Nice. But when Robert Fripp's King Crimson exploded onto the scene in 1969, it was as a fully realised prog rock act, taking post-psychedelic rock into bold new realms. Their hit debut album *In the Court of the Crimson King* has gone down in history as the most influential progressive rock album of all time.

On these foundations, the early 1970s became progressive rock's golden era, and almost all the successful acts hailed from the UK. The European scene also began generating prog bands; within a couple of years Italy would boast more prog performers than England.

Progressive rock was an attempt by technically skilled rock musicians to enter the pantheon of 'serious music'. The genre was, and still is, characterised by instrumental virtuosity, plus complex compositions, often in suites, with shifting time signatures and a wide dynamic range. In broad brushstrokes, if the 1960s was the era of the electric guitar, then the '70s saw the keyboard become a bona fide leading rock instrument.

Prog acts embraced new technology and were frequently versed in classical music. This was music for concentrating on, not for dancing to, and certainly not as background music. To its detractors it was pretentious, overblown and far removed from the earthy, primal, rebellious spirit of rock 'n' roll. But in the early 1970s, this sort of music was enormously attractive and hugely successful, even though the label 'progressive' had yet to be coined.

So why did Europe, including the UK, embrace prog in ways that American musicians didn't? Rock 'n' roll was born in the US, largely from African-American music, and in the 1960s Britain had picked up that mantle, especially via early Beatles, Animals and Rolling Stones. By 1970, however, some European rock performers were looking closer to home for their inspiration. For many prog rockers, black music was no longer the principal ingredient of rock. The rise of progressive rock was arguably a product of Europe's deep history of classical music.

Of course, England also had centuries of folk music, and that influence would percolate to the surface through idiosyncratic folk rock bands like Fairport Convention, Pentangle, Fotheringay and Steeleye Span, which arguably makes up a third arm of the early 1970s British Invasion.

A few US outfits did eventually dip their toes into prog, but American musicians in 1970 who wanted to expand rock music's vocabulary were more inclined towards jazz rock, because their own culture was the cradle of the jazz tradition. And then, of course, there was America's Frank Zappa, possibly the most individualistic composer working in the rock idiom during the 1960s and '70s. He is variously categorised as prog rock or jazz rock, but arguably deserves a genre all to himself. Zappa released three albums in 1970. *Burnt Weeny Sandwich* is the standout, focused as it is on his instrumental compositions enhanced by some stunning playing, especially from multi-instrumentalist Ian Underwood and violinist Don 'Sugarcane' Harris.

In 1970, King Crimson released *In the Wake of Poseidon*, which followed the stylistic blueprint of *In the Court of the Crimson King*. However, that second LP was soon followed by the far more interesting *Lizard*. This featured four songs on one side and a suite of music on the other. For the first time, every track was written by Robert Fripp. Band leader Fripp was the only remaining member of the original band that had performed *In the Court of the Crimson King* just one year previously. This was a far more jazz-orientated outfit, thanks to keyboard virtuoso Keith Tippett and members of his jazz group. Also providing his skills was Robin Miller, who had been principal oboist with the BBC Symphony Orchestra.

But it wasn't a happy affair making *Lizard*, as some of the rock players found it difficult to connect with Fripp's eclectic compositions. The compositional tour de force taking up the entire second side of *Lizard* covers a remarkable range of territory, from jazz blowing to pastoral chamber music. Despite its tortured genesis, the end result remains exceptional. Critics of the day, however, weren't too sure. Instead of having rock music rub up against jazz and classical elements, for perhaps the first time all three styles were seamlessly integrated into a new whole. What's more, the album lacked the catchy riff-based onslaughts of '21st Century Schizoid Man' or 'Pictures of a City' from Crimson's previous albums. Even though Fripp, in his typically capricious manner, partly disowned the album in later years, *Lizard* was a game-changer in 1970.

Greg Lake, one of the founding members of King Crimson, jumped ship in early 1970 to team up with The Nice keyboardist Keith Emerson plus Carl Palmer, a twenty-year-old drummer who had already worked with Atomic Rooster and The Crazy World of Arthur Brown. Immediately dubbed a 'super group', their debut album revealed a powerful trio hell-bent on exhibiting virtuosity, but also unafraid to appropriate others' compositions. Béla Bartók's piano piece 'Allegro Barbaro' forms the basis for album opener 'The Barbarian', with the track being rudely credited to Emerson, Lake & Palmer on early pressings before Bartók's widow gave them a nudge. 'Knife Edge' is based on an orchestral work by Leoš Janáček, with a bit of J.S. Bach thrown in. The album established a baseplate for the rest of the trio's career.

By 1970, Pink Floyd were up to their fifth album, this one titled *Atom Heart Mother*. As with King Crimson's first couple of albums, Floyd's LP had no writing on the cover, neither band name nor album title. Like a Dadaist conundrum, the cover featured an enigmatic, pastoral image of a cow. When shown to an EMI executive, he reportedly screamed, 'Are you mad? Do you want to destroy this record company?'[59]

The first side, a long, cosmic piece that gave the album its name, was rehearsed in concert before recording, but it remained, as drummer Nick Mason put it, 'unfocused and still unfinished'.[60] So they asked arranger, composer and electronics experimenter Ron Geesin to add some colour. This involved introducing electronic noises as well as orchestral and choir parts. While no critical success, the LP did end up being the band's first number one in the UK. What becomes patently clear when listening to *Atom Heart Mother* is that the Floyd were biting off far more than they could chew, given their limited musical capabilities. Their modus operandi at this time was to come up with brief riffs and extemporise on them until … well, until the cows came home. Nevertheless, they toured *Atom Heart Mother* with a session orchestra.

Genesis, a youthful group comprised of Charterhouse School chums, had recorded their first album, *From Genesis to Revelation*, in 1969, while they were still attending school. In early 1970, their second album, *Trespass*, marked a deep dive into the world of prog. Clearly, they had been listening closely to *In the Court of the Crimson King* and the Moody Blues' *Days of Future Passed*.

Trespass demonstrated all the elements that would become hallmarks of later Genesis work. The emphasis was on changes of mood, aided by mixing acoustic instruments with electronic music. In his memoir, Mike Rutherford is decidedly self-deprecating about *Trespass*, saying, 'Because none of us really knew how to write a song, we'd each write bits. We'd then go and fight the others about which bits we should use ... (we were still just devious schoolboys at heart).'[61] Although *Trespass* failed to chart, its success in Belgium helped keep the band afloat. The subsequent departures of guitarist Anthony Phillips and drummer John Mayhew nearly brought Genesis to a crashing halt, however, the remaining members – Peter Gabriel, Rutherford and Tony Banks – fortuitously co-opted Phil Collins to take over the drum stool and add occasional vocals. Later in their careers, both Gabriel and Collins would ride the crest of the rock roller-coaster as solo performers.

Van der Graaf Generator were dabbling in dark themes on their third album *H to He, Who Am the Only One* – the title referring to the fusion of hydrogen nuclei to form helium, one of the building blocks of the universe. Peter Hammill's vocal delivery matched his philosophical prose, much of which concerned the parlous state of humanity. Thematically, it's much darker than the likes of Alice Cooper and Black Sabbath. Although well received by critics, *H to He* didn't sell well. Nevertheless, some analysts have declared it to be one of the greatest prog albums of all time, and it had an undeniable influence on all manner of later arrivals, including heavy metal bands such as Iron Maiden.

Jazz meets rock

Britain's Soft Machine were an oddity. As drummer Robert Wyatt said, 'It was no longer clear whether Soft Machine were their label's worst-selling rock group or its best-selling jazz act.'[62] Some rock audiences were left nonplussed by the unorthodox time signatures, extended compositions and sheer jazziness of Soft Machine. Jazz audiences were uncomfortable with the loudness of the band, not to mention Wyatt's off-beat vocal contributions. Indeed, early Soft Machine remain difficult to parse. Not exactly prog, eschewing the bombast of ELP and Genesis, they would later be identified as the beginnings of what has become known as the Canterbury scene. Their 1970 album *Third* pushed the boundaries of what could be considered rock music, yet it did so without pretence. Robert Wyatt would only survive one more album, his quirky musical sensibility and wonderful sense of humour then lost to this increasingly dour band.

It was the American jazz trumpeter Miles Davis who can properly take credit for popularizing the jazz-rock hybrid known as fusion. His 1970 album *Bitches Brew* became his highest-charting album, winning him a Grammy Award to boot. In the studio, the players were provided with chord progressions and not much more. Performers sat in a half-circle, with Miles and saxophonist Wayne Shorter in the middle. Semi-conducted by Miles, the players improvised to instructions. The recorded tracks were then edited and assembled for the final LP. In other words, the final arrangements were largely achieved with a razor blade, sometimes with micro-edits of just a second or two. Frank Zappa had taken this approach to extremes with his *Lumpy Gravy* album a few years previously, and here Miles Davis used similar tape editing techniques to generate something new and original.

Where *Lumpy Gravy* remains largely overlooked, *Bitches Brew* is celebrated for its pioneering use of studio technology. Critics mostly fell over each other to praise the album, though some condemned it for its lack of focus. It's interesting to note that, as well as appealing to rock audiences, Miles Davis was also behaving like a rock star, evidencing a voracious appetite for sex and drugs along with an extravagant lifestyle.

Buttons and nobs

One of the novelties of *Bitches Brew* was the channelling of wind and keyboard instruments through guitar effects pedals. Indeed, 1970 was a fruitful year for music technology. Sixteen-track recording was becoming commonplace, with twenty-four-track systems just around the corner.

Audio company Dolby had largely solved the problem of tape hiss by developing its Dolby Noise Reduction System. Eight-track quadraphonic cartridges offered a surround-sound experience for those who wished to be totally immersed in their favourite music. However, records – LPs and singles – remained the dominant music format for consumers. Living rooms were arranged to take best advantage of home stereo systems. Putting together the ideal components became an obsession for the serious music listener, with much debate about the perfect combination of speakers, amplifiers and turntables.

The range of musical instruments was also expanding. It was in 1970 that Robert Moog introduced his Minimoog, a compact version of his earlier Moog Synthesizer. Not much bigger than a typewriter, the Minimoog became a viable touring instrument.

The Fender Rhodes electric piano, with full keyboard range, had been introduced in 1965. But it was still a difficult instrument to lug about, as it incorporated its own large amplifier and speaker. In 1970, inventor Harold Rhodes came up with his Stage Piano model, which featured detachable legs, a sustain pedal and an output jack that could plug into any amplifier. As CBS began mass-marketing the instrument, the sound of the Rhodes quickly became synonymous with '70s music, particularly jazz and soul.

The Mellotron was an early form of sampler, but as this was the era of analogue, it used actual audio tapes. When a keyboard key was pressed, the relevant tape of, say, a violin or flute was pushed against a playback head in the same way as occurs with a tape deck. While this meant that a performer could cart around a virtual orchestra, there were also persistent issues of tape flutter and wow when notes were played and stopped.

Yet these seeming deficiencies were also what gave the instrument its unique quality. British blues-rock musician Graham Bond is credited with being the first rock performer to record with a Mellotron in 1965, and The Beatles used it on their 1966 single 'Strawberry Fields Forever'. Mike Pinder of The Moody Blues was also an early adopter. By 1970, it was a key component of the progressive rock revolution. Spike Milligan famously described the Mellotron thus: 'If you wanted the sound of marching feet in size ten boots accompanied by Chopin and a portrait of Salvador Dalí shaving underwater while whistling "The Blue Bells of Scotland" this was the machine you had to have.'[63]

The original Mellotrons were not intended to be used by touring bands, but rather in studio settings. However, having utilised them in the studio, many performers wanted to replicate the sound on stage. But the Mellotron was a notoriously temperamental beast, highly subject to knocks and bumps as well as variations in temperature which caused the tapes to stretch. What's more, only a limited number of keys could be played at the same time, or else the motor would drag, with the instrument suddenly sounding flat. In 1970, the M400 Mellotron model was released with a thirty-five-note keyboard. It would eventually sell over 1800 units. For bands with classical music sensibilities, it was the cheapest, most convenient way to expand their instrumentation and exercise their orchestral aspirations.

Bigger, louder amplifiers were also being developed by various manufacturers including Marshall, Laney and Randall. But it was a Grateful Dead concert in February 1970 in St Louis that is credited with pioneering the modern concert sound system. A stagehand had put Jerry Garcia in touch with sound engineer Bob Heil. By adding radial horn speakers and ring tweeters, Heil's newly developed rig created a much wider frequency range, meaning that audiences could better understand the lyrics being sung and that the individual instruments had more tonality. He also introduced a unique slightly-out-of-phase two-microphone system. The result was that vocals could be boosted in volume without producing the feedback that had been dogging bands for years.

Boots and all

Bob Heil's revolutionary system was quickly picked up by The Who when they toured the US. But many of The Who's concerts were now being taped by bootleggers. Bootlegs were records made from illegal recordings. Sometimes they were made from unreleased studio tapes, but more often they were live performances recorded by audience members on portable equipment smuggled into concerts. *Melody Maker*'s Richard Williams wrote: 'No money goes to the artist, the songwriters, or the musicians. So it obviously can't be condoned. But the music on some of the bootleg albums which have appeared is so important, and throws so much new light on interesting subjects, that it can't be ignored and suppressed.'[64]

Bootlegs had begun with Bob Dylan outtakes. They were given even greater credibility when a recording of a 1969 concert by The Rolling Stones was released as *Live'r Than You'll Ever Be*, and was positively reviewed in *Rolling Stone* magazine. *Melody Maker*'s Richard Williams claimed it was the best album the band had ever made, and probably the best live rock LP of all time. In response, the Stones released an official live album, *Get Yer Ya-Ya's Out*, which became the first live album to reach number one in the UK.

The Who decided to beat the bootleggers at their own game by bringing out their *Live at Leeds* album, packaging it to look like a bootleg: a blank cover with a rough stamp of the title. With typical braggadocio, Pete Townshend later claimed there was 'little doubt' that the album 'inspired the heavy-metal revolution that soon followed'.[65] Although warmly received by the media and punters alike, with some critics again calling it the best live rock recording of all time, singer Roger Daltrey was less than happy. 'I couldn't hear myself over the band,' he wrote. 'This happened a lot. John played too loud, Moonie was never quiet and Pete amped up to compete. They were all too loud at Leeds. I had to work off the sound reflected back and the only way I could hear myself was to over-sing.'[66]

As concerts in stadiums and arenas became increasingly commonplace, so bootleggers stepped up their output. Artists, of course, loathed bootlegs. As Graham Nash put it, 'For something recorded out of one microphone in front of one of the PA speakers ... for that to have my name on it infuriates me.'[67] An underground magazine soon surfaced titled *Hot Wacks* (aka *Bootleg Bible*), which listed all the available bootlegs and detailed their track listings and sound quality.

The tension between commercial interests and music availability was also playing out in the festival scene. Some counterculture types believed that rock festivals should be free celebrations of 'the people's music'. Phun City was the first attempt at a large-scale free festival in the UK. It didn't start out as a free event, but when financial backing was withdrawn a few days before the festival was due to kick off, the organisers told the scheduled bands that they would have to play for free. There were no fences and no admission fees.

The Bath Festival of Blues & Progressive Music was an attempt to replicate Woodstock near a small town in Somerset, UK. On the bill were top-notch US and UK acts such as Santana, Jefferson Airplane, The Byrds, Frank Zappa, Canned Heat, It's a Beautiful Day, Steppenwolf, Pink Floyd and more. But the narrow country roads leading to the event were quickly choked, which meant that many bands couldn't get to the festival site. In an impromptu free performance, Donovan filled in for two and half hours while the audience waited for the performers and equipment to struggle through the chaos. As with Woodstock, the crowds soon breached the perimeter fencing of the main festival, resulting in it becoming a free festival some 150,000 strong.

Led Zep were the headline act, booked to close the show. To make the biggest spectacle, the band were determined to hit the stage just as the sun was setting. But the previous band, Flock, were too focused on a long-winded jam to relinquish the limelight, so road manager Richard Cole instructed his roadies to kill the power to the stage, stopping Flock mid-flight. Ignoring Flock's complaints, Zep took over as the sky turned orange, doing so at ear-splitting volume, two or three times as loud as any of the preceding acts. Manager and head-kicker Peter Grant missed much of the finale as he had discovered some fellows beneath the stage with recording equipment, presumably aiming to make a bootleg album of the performance. In a scene that would be repeated often, the twenty-seven-stone Grant beat up the would-be pirates and destroyed their equipment.

Australia was also embracing the era of rock festivals. Early off the blocks in January 1970 was the nation's first large-scale, outdoor rock festival, dubbed the Pilgrimage for Pop, held at Ourimbah on the New South Wales Central Coast, north of Sydney. The event was organised by

Emle Stonewall Productions and The Nutwood Rug Band, an American group that had migrated down under in 1967, reputedly to avoid the military draft. The festival was held over a weekend, with an all-Australian bill featuring the best of the Sydney and Melbourne music scenes.

This was something of a test case for Australian music festivals, with everyone on tenterhooks to ensure it didn't turn into Australia's Altamont. There was a uniformed police presence as well as a bevy of plain-clothed detectives. A few arrests were made for minor misdemeanours, and the only serious injury was a chap who nearly drowned in the local swimming hole. The greatest media interest was paid to a young woman in the crowd who took off her top, leading to the headline 'Topless Pop!'. Another paper bemoaned that the 'fascinating spectre of "orgy" with which everybody was so preoccupied never quite materialised'.[68]

Rock festivals were appearing all over the planet, but the biggest and most anticipated was the third Isle of Wight Festival, which featured a number of the acts that had appeared at Woodstock the year before. Attendance figures range between *The Guinness Book of Records*' claim of 600,000 to 700,000 – which would make it the largest rock festival, and one of the largest gatherings of humanity ever – to the organisers' own estimates of around half that number. Acts included Jimi Hendrix, Miles Davis, Jethro Tull, Chicago, Ten Years After, The Doors, The Who, The Moody Blues, Supertramp, Joan Baez, Free, Joni Mitchell, Leonard Cohen, Donovan, Melanie, Kris Kristofferson, Sly and the Family Stone, John Sebastian, Pentangle, plus Emerson, Lake & Palmer in what was only their second live performance.

To ensure cost recovery, the organisers erected security fencing which was patrolled by guards with dogs. A hastily formed British White Panther Party determined they would derail the capitalist promoters and free the people's music from exploitation. The group was led by *IT* editor Mick Farren, who described the event as akin to a prison camp. Along with anarchist comrades, including some Hell's Angels, a gang of around 200 began a series of attacks on the fencing. A nearby hill, dubbed Desolation Row, became the strategic control centre for these blitzes.

Such attitudes frustrated organiser Rikki Farr, who at one point cut loose through the PA system, yelling, 'We put this festival on, you bastards! With a lot of love, we worked for one year for you pigs! And you want to break our walls down and you want to destroy it? Well, you go to hell!'

On the Sunday morning at 10am, when most festival attendees were still asleep, organised raids breached the perimeter fencing in a number of places. Later that day the organisers announced that the festival had become a free event. As with Woodstock, it was a decision borne of necessity.

Oz rock

British and American acts dominated the airwaves in Australia. Owners of Australian commercial radio stations were highly protective of their turf, maintaining pressure on the federal government to ensure no new radio licences were allocated. Indeed, there hadn't been a new radio licence issued for an Australian capital city since the 1930s. The commercial stations also fervently resisted the introduction of FM radio, even though it was long established in America. By 1970, there were close to 700 FM stations in the US, a good proportion of which were rock stations that had shifted to playing LPs rather than singles. Australian listeners were stuck with a handful of low-fidelity AM format stations playing singles, not albums. A dispute between Australian commercial radio stations and six of the largest global record labels further limited what Australian audiences could hear for much of 1970.

But Australia's live music scene was raging. As Billy Thorpe put it, the Melbourne music fans 'didn't give a shit' about the media's perception of the superiority of overseas acts and the inferiority of local acts. As far as the punters were concerned, 'This was their music.'[69] Around forty venues were operating across the southern capital, ranging from clubs and discotheques to suburban town halls. Thursdays to Sundays, many of these venues featured four or five different acts each night. Indeed, Thorpe and The Aztecs were known to play five different venues on a single Saturday, performing a total of around ten hours of music to packed houses.

Australia hatched a handful of progressive bands. Tully were the most experimental and unpredictable. Frequently their presentations became happenings as much as concerts. It was in 1970 that Tully's eponymous album was released, which surprisingly reached eighth position on the charts. I say surprisingly because the album swings between raucous free improvisation, gentle folk rock tunes, solo keyboards and jagged proggish compositions. This was decidedly adventurous stuff.

Tully were chosen to join the Sydney Symphony Orchestra and singer Jeannie Lewis for Peter Sculthorpe's ambitious *Love 200*. The combination of orchestra and rock band had been attempted by the Royal Philharmonic and Deep Purple in the UK, but this was a first for Australia. The premier performance of *Love 200* was such a success that the audience demanded it be performed a second time. Mind you, the sniffy classical critics were unimpressed, with one referring to it as 'a shotgun wedding between serious contemporary music and pop on the very lowest common denominator'.[70] The music ranges from wild folk rock to jazz-inflected free improvisations. At the time, Australian jazz player John Sangster declared that Tully were the best band in the world. Peter Sculthorpe was less enthusiastic, later saying that working with Tully had 'managed to turn me off rock'.[71]

It wasn't in the concert halls but the drinking holes that Australian rock music was developing. Pubs would be proving grounds for many local bands, developing a high-energy, hard rock style with catchy, simple riffs perfectly suited to noisy venues jam-packed with inebriated headbangers. The pub scene was roguishly anti-intellectual, featuring booming music with strong riffs and singalong choruses that would eventually lead to AC/DC, Cold Chisel, Rose Tattoo, Midnight Oil, The Dingoes and The Angels.

Many of the bands in 1970 were multiple personality outfits, with players jumping between groups and styles. For example, while the progressive rock band Sons of the Vegetal Mother was gearing up, a number of its members decided to establish an old-time rock 'n' roll outfit they dubbed Daddy Cool, a tribute to 1950s doo-wop vocal groups. It was initiated as a bit of a joke in late 1970 but would very quickly become a charting success.

Battles of the sexes

By 1970, large numbers of young people were living in full-time relationships without bothering to get married. The availability of contraception – in particular, a decade of access to the contraceptive pill – had turned sexual mores on their head. But as Chrissie Hynde would write, 'So-called women's lib was rather misled by the pill. Women weren't in control of their bodies; the drug was. Taking procreation out of the equation was turning women into sex toys.'[72]

On the upside, having been partially liberated from marriage and child-rearing, increasing numbers of women were gaining a tertiary education. They were also beginning to demand full rights of citizenship in parity with men's. It was early days in the second-wave struggle for women's rights, but Women's Liberation groups were springing up across the Western world, with Australia, England and America all holding their first National Women's Liberation conferences this year. There was also a range of books released on the subject, key among them being Germaine Greer's *The Female Eunuch*, which quickly became an international bestseller.

But the rock industry was spectacularly male-dominated. Apart from singing with bands, or else performing as solo acts with piano or guitar, women were conspicuously absent from rock's stages. Some, however, were appearing on those stages specifically to be demeaned. Rob Tyner from MC5 regularly chose a female audience member to mock rape as part of their act. British outfit Hawkwind had a girl who travelled with the band and danced naked on stage while the all-male band played. Regardless of whether such women were willing participants, their participation served to illustrate their subservience to the male performers. Musically, rock music was an affirmation of male energy.

Some women, however, were courageously bucking the trend. There had been a handful of all-female bands in which the members played instruments – as opposed to purely vocal 'girl groups' – across the planet in the 1960s, but they were largely treated as novelty acts, and none broke through into the mainstream. The Svelts and Wild Honey were two such '60s outfits that transmogrified into Fanny in 1969, being June Millington, her sister Jean Millington, plus Nickey Barclay and Alice de Buhr. There was also the Detroit-based act The Pleasure Seekers, who morphed into Cradle, featuring sisters Suzi and Patti Quatro (Patti would later join Fanny).

The members of Fanny were at pains to ensure their record company didn't exploit them as a novelty act. As immigrants and women of colour, the Millington sisters had enormous hurdles to traverse. June Millington has said, 'We were not supposed to believe in ourselves. It really felt like it was warfare. It was sexism and classism at the same time, and we didn't know whether we were going to make it.'[73]

Fanny worked hard on delivering a powerful stage performance. But an all-female hard rock act was inevitably going to be swimming against the tide in the early 1970s. Their debut album, *Fanny*, was not particularly well received, although their cover of Cream's 'Badge' did garner some airplay. In truth, it was a mediocre album. Even the band were disappointed with how it had been produced. Nevertheless, as pioneers, Fanny would inspire other women musicians.

Naomi Weisstein established a rock group under the title Chicago Women's Liberation Rock Band. Part of their live act included a parody of Mick Jagger singing his deeply misogynistic song 'Under My Thumb'. The band signed with Rounder Records, along with sister band the New Haven Women's Liberation Rock Band. Meanwhile, Annie Nightingale became the first female radio deejay in the UK, and for over a decade was the only one of her kind.

Gay liberation groups were also springing up across Western nations. To commemorate the first anniversary of the Stonewall Riots, a large-scale demonstration in support of gay rights took place in New York. It was called the Christopher Street Gay Liberation Day, with the name an attempt to move attention away from the mafia-controlled Stonewall club and instead focus on the broader street struggle. Despite bomb threats and participants fearful of harassment, a few thousand marchers travelled from Greenwich Village to Central Park, with all local gay and lesbian groups participating. A march was also held the same evening in Los Angeles.

Radical performances

By 1970, most of America's radical activist organisations had been successfully infiltrated by informants, particularly under the FBI's counterintelligence program known as COINTELPRO. Included in their sights were feminist, gay rights, civil rights, anti-war and environmental organisations, plus the American Indian Movement. The activist scene was thus riven with paranoia, often turning on itself.

Bombings had become increasingly common across the US, with each bomb viewed by its perpetrators as an exploding media release. One key far-left militant organisation was initially called The Weathermen, but changed its moniker to the more gender-inclusive Weather Underground. In celebration, they issued a declaration of war against the US government. In the missive, Bernardine Dohrn claimed that the organisation's job was 'to lead white kids into armed revolution', because 'revolutionary violence is the only way' to 'reform the system'.[74] In truth, they were just a hundred or so isolated, deluded zealots.

Concern about air and water pollution was now rife. Smog was choking US cities, the insecticide DDT was poisoning streams, and oil spills were killing marine life. A plan to build a 1300-kilometre pipeline across Alaska was furiously opposed by a range of nascent environmental organisations, including The Wilderness Society, Friends of the Earth and the Environmental Defense Fund. (The project would eventually lead to the catastrophic Exxon Valdez oil spill of 1989.) President Nixon had kicked off the decade with a State of the Union address calling for improved regulations controlling air and water pollution. In truth, he was largely indifferent to environmental concerns. As he reportedly told a meeting with environmentalists at the time, 'All politics is a fad. Your fad is going right now.'[75] The first ever Earth Day in April saw 20 million Americans – 10 per cent of the country's population – taking part in a range of activities.

In Australia, environmental battles were also heating up, including concerns about plans to prospect for oil and to mine for limestone on the

Great Barrier Reef. Tasmanian efforts to save Lake Pedder from a proposed hydroelectric scheme achieved national attention, building with an intensity not seen previously for an environmental concern. Tasmania would become the crucible that would forge the world's first Greens political party.

Cat Stevens' song 'Where Do the Children Play?' demonstrated his concerns about war, ecological disaster and pollution. Three Dog Night's 'Out in the Country' played into the back-to-nature movement, while Spirit's fourth album, *Twelve Dreams of Dr Sardonicus*, featured a couple of tracks that lamented the fate of the planet.

Meanwhile, the civil rights movement had begun to cool in the US. Richard Nixon owed his election to the same forces in the Deep South that had systematically opposed civil rights for black Americans during the 1960s. Although direct action had abated, tensions were still running high, particularly in America's southern states. Neil Young's song 'Southern Man', from his album *After the Gold Rush*, clearly delineated his concerns about the roots of racism in the Deep South, as he asked when the South might make amends for decades of slavery. Curtis Mayfield vented his frustration via a song with the unwieldy title '(Don't Worry) If There's a Hell Below, We're All Going to Go'.

In Australia, a budding land rights movement was rubbing up against an emerging minerals boom. There were three standout Indigenous performers at this time: Auriel Andrew, Lionel Rose and Jimmy Little. Auriel had become a regular on Adelaide television, appearing frequently on Reg Lindsay's *Country and Western Hour*. Indeed, she is thought to be the first Indigenous woman to perform music on Australian television. Lionel Rose, a former boxer who held the bantamweight world title, was enjoying a sideline career as a singer. His 'I Thank You/Pick Me Up on Your Way Down' single sold over 100,000 units and remained in the charts for eight months. He followed up with a debut album, *I Thank You*. Yorta Yorta man Jimmy Little had begun his music career in the 1950s. By 1970 he had released fifteen albums on Festival Records. His 1970 release, *Goodbye Old Rolf*, wasn't a reference to Rolf Harris, but rather a ballad penned by Lorna Bailey about a heroic dog named Rolf.

In the US, the issue of indigenous land rights was also heating up. The Red Power movement had seen Native Americans occupy Alcatraz Island, drawing national attention to civil rights issues, until the government cut off basic resources to the island, including power, water and telephone services. For a time, Johnny Cash erroneously claimed he was part Cherokee. Cash was known to be a champion of the underdog, and none in America were more underdog than their First Nations people. He had penned various songs about Indian rights including an entire album, *Bitter Tears: Ballads of the American Indian*.

In early 1970, Cash released his chart-topping thirty-third album, *Hello, I'm Johnny Cash* – although he hardly needed introducing at this stage of his career. Cash was riding high with his own TV show, on which he had pledged his allegiance to the president. As a public relations stunt, Nixon invited Cash to perform at the White House, providing him with a list of song requests. Among others, the songs included Merle Haggard and Roy Edward Burris' redneck anthem 'Okie from Muskogee', and also 'Welfare Cadillac', Guy Drake's nasty swipe at people on welfare.

But Cash was not a performer who liked to be told what to sing. Indeed, even his own band didn't know what they were going to play from one performance to the next. Cash was not politically aligned, but he viewed the concert at the White House as a means of proving his success to his hideously judgemental father. Dad and the rest of the family were thus invited to attend the White House gig. Inevitably, Cash was widely criticised for accepting the invitation, which many viewed as his personal endorsement of both President Nixon and the Vietnam War.

Cash opened the show with one of the songs that Nixon had requested, 'A Boy Named Sue'. After a few classics such as 'I Walk the Line' and 'Ring of Fire', he performed a newer song, 'What Is Truth'. There can be little doubt that this caused Nixon to squirm in his seat. The lyrics challenge the listener to put themselves in the position of young people, the better to understand them. In one stanza, a long-haired man fails to get a fair trial due to prejudicial attitudes towards his hair and clothes. In another, a child asks why war exists. 'What Is Truth' was not the breast-beating call for God-fearing, conservative values that Nixon was expecting. At the end of the song, Cash respectfully said that he hoped the president might bring the troops home from Vietnam as soon as possible.

Cash wasn't the only performer to associate with Nixon in 1970. Elvis Presley had literally run away from home and travelled like a regular person on a commercial airline. He turned up unannounced and unexpected at the White House wearing a purple velvet suit and gold belt, and packing a Colt .45 pistol in a shoulder holster. Presley had a letter for the president that he wanted to deliver in person. That letter claimed that Presley had done an 'in-depth study of drug abuse and Communist brainwashing techniques'. He was offering his services to the war on drugs.[76]

Highs and lows

Johnny Cash was no stranger to drug and alcohol abuse. He had been in and out of recovery and had frequent brushes with the law. At one point in the 1960s, he had been arrested while smuggling over a thousand amphetamine pills across the Mexican border. Although he would eventually overcome his addictions, in 1970 the monkey was still clinging to his back.

For some people, drugs opened the 'doors of perception', whereas for others those same doors led to nightmare scenarios, incapacity and even death. The hippie routes from Ibiza to Kathmandu and Marrakesh were strewn with listless tragics.

One of the more profound impacts of the '60s counterculture was its tacit acceptance and even encouragement of drug use. Heroin was now rife in the ghettos, and would be the catalyst for gang wars and street violence for decades to come, trapping many poor communities in cycles of poverty and violence. Cocaine became increasingly prevalent. Rod Stewart and his band, rather than stop snorting cocaine to avoid damaging their noses, used capsules to insert the drug anally, where 'they would dissolve effortlessly into the system'.[77] Quaaludes, a barbiturate-like artificial chemical sold under the brand name Mandrax (colloquially known as 'ludes' or 'leg spreaders' and later 'disco biscuits' in the US, and as 'mandies' in Australia), were also becoming popular. Although designed as a sedative, they provided a powerful euphoric high that lasted for some six hours.

Drugs were now a significant part of the rock music scene. As Pete Townshend put it, '[N]arcotics had breached The Who from top to bottom. Everyone in our management team was anaesthetised or high ... and every stratum of our operation was tainted.'[78]

Sly and the Family Stone was one of the most popular acts in the US, but their performances were becoming increasingly erratic, with Sly Stone descending into drug-induced paranoia, hiring gangsters as bodyguards to protect him against imagined enemies, including members of his own band.

James Taylor was in a Massachusetts psychiatric and rehabilitation centre when he finished writing his poignant hit song 'Fire and Rain'. A dour, confessional folk rock tune, it arguably breaks many of the rules about what should comprise hit material. The song opens with his reaction to the suicide of his childhood friend Suzanne. The middle verse, in which his body is aching and he pleads for heavenly guidance, was the product of his return to the US suffering from depression and drug addiction. The third verse bemoans the demise of Taylor's band The Flying Machine. Taylor described the song as 'a postcard from the loony bin before going back out into the world'.[79] His album *Sweet Baby James* went to single digits in the US, the UK and Australia, helping cement a new confessional style among singer-songwriters.

Psychedelic drugs were also having an impact. The 'crazy diamond' Syd Barrett had departed Pink Floyd after becoming unmanageable due to mood swings and hallucinations, likely a product of drug-taking. At the behest of Harvest Records, he nevertheless released a couple of solo albums, *The Madcap Laughs* and *Barrett*. The recording sessions were episodic and difficult, to say the least. Barrett quickly descended into his own living hell.

Chris Kefford of The Move spent decades in mental institutions after taking LSD. Moby Grape's founder Skip Spence eventually ended up in a psychiatric ward after threatening his bandmates with an axe. Folk singer Shelagh McDonald took LSD and then disappeared for thirty-four years. Roky Erickson of The 13th Floor Elevators ended up being subjected to electroshock therapy in a state hospital, while Australia's Stevie Wright, lead singer for The Easybeats, dealt with his addiction problems by admitting himself to the notorious Chelmsford Hospital, where he underwent electroconvulsive therapy and was placed in a drug-induced coma.

Another whose brain was significantly altered by LSD was Peter Green, guitarist and founding member of Fleetwood Mac. As Mick Fleetwood put it, 'LSD fractured his mental stability sooner rather than later.'[80] The band was riding a wave of popularity, having been voted best progressive group in *Melody Maker*'s 1969 year-end polls, with Green third-best composer behind Lennon/McCartney and Jagger/Richards. But Green took to wearing robes and a huge wooden crucifix, jabbering about his search for God and arguing with his bandmates. In Munich, on a sold-out tour, Green attended a local commune where, according to Fleetwood, he 'joined them in getting fried on LSD for a few days'.

The Beach Boys' Brian Wilson was also unravelling in the midst of the band's financial woes. The group had sold the entire catalogue of their music publishing company, Sea of Tunes, for US$700,000 in mid-1969. After signing the consent letter, Wilson went rapidly downhill, even attempting to drive his car off a cliff. He also reportedly dug his own grave in his backyard. Although he did perform with the band at a few gigs in 1970, he was a spent force as far the Beach Boys were concerned, remaining at home most of the time, often in bed.

John Lennon, Keith Richards, Jimmy Page and Eric Clapton were all enduring stretches of heroin addiction. Marianne Faithfull split from Mick Jagger in 1970 and descended into a heroin haze of homelessness, depression and anorexia, for a time surviving on the charity of strangers. Alan 'Blind Owl' Wilson, co-founder, composer and singer with Canned Heat, had attempted suicide on various occasions, and in September was found dead from acute barbiturate intoxication.

On 17 September 1970, Jimi Hendrix made his final live appearance, jamming at Ronnie Scott's Jazz Club in London with his mate Eric Burdon and the band War. In the wee small hours, home from a party where he reportedly took an amphetamine tablet, Jimi asked his girlfriend, Monika Dannemann, for something to help him sleep. She had some very strong German-made sleeping tablets called Vesparax, but it's not known if she witnessed him taking them. Her usual dose was half a tablet. Midmorning, Monika awoke next to Jimi and tiptoed out of the house to buy some cigarettes. When she returned, Jimi had moved his position on the bed but still seemed to be asleep. Monika stepped on a blister pack of her Vesparax, noticing that nine of its ten tablets were missing. One tablet was subsequently found in the bed, but the other eight were presumably consumed. Monika rang Jimi's friend Alvinia, who was spending the night with Eric Burdon, to explain that Jimi wouldn't wake up and might need a doctor. Burdon rang Monika back, telling her to flush any drugs down the toilet and then call an ambulance. By this time, Jimi was vomiting and Monika was hysterical.

Jimi was whisked away by ambulance around 11.30am. He couldn't be resuscitated and was pronounced dead at 12.45pm on 18 September. The coroner concluded that Jimi had likely died from breathing in his own vomit whilst intoxicated with barbiturates. With insufficient evidence about the circumstances surrounding Hendrix's death, the coroner declared an open verdict. Hendrix's legacy, apart from a whole new approach to electric guitar playing, was decades of litigation between family members as they endlessly tussled over his estate.

Just a few weeks later, Janis Joplin concluded an evening of drinking screwdrivers at Barney's Beanery in Los Angeles before returning to her room at the Landmark Motor Hotel. Alone, she skin-popped a dose of heroin. She wandered down to the lobby to buy cigarettes, chatted briefly with the desk clerk, then went back to her room as the heroin kicked in. Collapsing, she hit her head on the nightstand en route to the floor. The heroin Janis had injected turned out to be 'China white', which was half pure rather than the usual 10 per cent strength of street drugs. Janis had overdosed before, but this time there was no one to seek medical help.

Her body was discovered eighteen hours later. The autopsy showed the cause of death to be heroin overdose, likely compounded by alcohol. It could be argued that Joplin died of loneliness. She was at her happiest on stage before adoring fans but had great difficulty being alone. In a bitter irony, a long-awaited letter from her lover, David Niehaus, who was overseas at the time, was waiting for her at the hotel reception desk.

On the last day of 1970, Paul McCartney filed a lawsuit in London's High Court against the other Beatles and Apple Corps Ltd., with the intention of finalising the dissolution of the partnership and divvying up the spoils. Importantly, it was also a means of ensuring that his post-Beatles earnings couldn't be touched by manager Allen Klein.

1971

Gimme Some Truth

Early in 1971, The Rolling Stones announced their departure from Britain. Thanks to serious mismanagement, the band had never paid income tax. With a top British tax rate of 93 per cent, they could not envisage earning enough to make good their debt, so they became tax exiles – a concept that many saw as evidencing an excess of greed and a deficit of patriotism. (The top tax rate in the UK was reduced to 75 per cent during 1971, then raised to 83 per cent in 1974.) The Stones' publicist disingenuously claimed the band were heading to France for the climate. Following a six-week European tour, they held a Goodbye Britain tour, with headlines cunningly asking if this could be the 'last time'.

The fateful Altamont Speedway concert in December 1969 continued to haunt the band. After seventeen days of testimony, Hells Angel Alan Passaro was acquitted on grounds of self-defence over the fatal stabbing of Meredith Hunter. Passaro let out a whoop of joy as the verdict was read, and then headed back to jail, where he was already serving a sentence for marijuana possession. After the trial, he reportedly attempted to sue The Rolling Stones, claiming that their movie *Gimme Shelter* had violated his privacy by showing the stabbing. The victim's mother had attempted to sue the Stones for half a million dollars but settled for just US$10,000.

Years later, an FBI agent revealed that the Hells Angels had plotted to kill Mick Jagger in revenge for his comments about them following the festival debacle. A bunch of bikies attempted to invade Jagger's Long Island holiday home, arriving by boat. As luck would have it, a storm swept them all overboard, foiling the assassination mission.

Battling bugs

The legal action that Paul McCartney had instigated was eventually resolved in his favour. Beatles & Co. was placed into receivership, with the judge noting that Lennon, Starr and Harrison had agreed to increase manager Allen Klein's commission without telling McCartney, something he viewed as a 'grave breach' of their responsibilities to their bandmate. The judge also damned Klein, calling him a 'second-rate salesman'. By this time, Klein had already been convicted on tax charges in the US. But the relationship between the ex-Beatles could never be truly severed, as they all remained directors of Apple Corps, which continued to represent the business and creative interests of The Beatles.

Harrison, Starr and Lennon ended their management contracts with Klein, which set off a new round of litigation. At one stage, Klein claimed commission and expenses of US$42 million, plus damages of over US$10 million. (In early 1977, the whole saga concluded in a deal which saw the three ex-Beatles make Klein a payment of US$4.2 million to get rid of the huckster once and for all. The end of the decade would also see Klein jailed for failing to declare income from the sale of records, including money that was supposed to go to charity from sales of the *Concert for Bangla Desh* album.)

But in 1971, the three non-McCartney Beatles were still at war with Paul. Court documents quoted in *New Musical Express* had Ringo Starr complaining that McCartney was acting like 'a spoilt child' and Harrison whingeing that McCartney had always adopted a 'musically superior' attitude towards him.[1]

John Lennon gave a lengthy, caustic interview with Jann Wenner for *Rolling Stone* that was spread over two issues. The outpouring focused on his litany of gripes, including candid musings about his time with The Beatles. As he summarised it, 'we got fed up being side men for Paul'.[2] During the interview, Lennon opined that he believed himself to be a genius, having known it since he was a child, when he discovered that he was 'cleverer than anybody' at his school. Maliciously, he credited

68

Harrison's post-Beatles success with George having been exposed to 'two fucking brilliant songwriters'.

Such immense egoism sat uneasily alongside Lennon's manifest neuroses. Lennon also called McCartney's debut solo album 'rubbish', arrogantly suggesting that his own album – *John Lennon/Plastic Ono Band* – might 'scare him into doing something decent'. Even the Stones were dismissed as 'a lot of hype', with Mick Jagger singled out as 'a joke, with all that fag dancing'.[3] Lennon also, for no good reason, made public that The Beatles' late manager, Brian Epstein, was a 'fag'. He might've been discovering his inner feminist at this time, but his inner homophobe was off the leash.

Lennon and Ono granted another lengthy interview, this time with Britain's leading left-wing radicals Tariq Ali and Robin Blackburn for their newspaper *Red Mole*. This was a publication which, like *The International Times*, Lennon had assisted with financial support. Inspired by his philosophising with the pair, Lennon went into the recording studio with Phil Spector to tape a contrived anthem, 'Power to the People', the title appropriating a Black Panther catchphrase. Released by The John Lennon/Plastic Ono Band, it achieved single digits on European and American charts. A far cry from the ambivalent stance that he had voiced on his 1968 hit 'Revolution', this time Lennon was urging listeners to get the insurrection happening.

In some ways, 'Power to the People' was a dying gasp of 1960s idealism. Hunter S. Thompson quipped that the song came ten years too late. Paul Simon slammed the record for being condescending, and questioned whether Lennon's motives were primarily about garnering attention. Keith Richards rode in on his high horse, saying that The Beatles should have 'kept it together and realised what they were doing instead of now doing "Power to the People" and disintegrating like that in such a tatty way'.[4]

Lennon's 'Power to the People' was straightforward rock 'n' roll, with a thumping beat from drummer Alan White and a brief sax solo by Bobby Keys. Arguably the real significance of Lennon's tune was not in its broader revolutionary message, but in a very specific one: the third stanza asked male listeners how they were treating their female partners, and urged them to liberate women. This was the first example of a significant male rock star affirming a feminist message in song.

Free women

Like their New York cousins The Last Poets, The Watts Prophets presented fast-paced spoken-word poems set against sparse jazz and funk music. Their 1971 album *Rappin' Black in a White World* featured a rare female voice, Dee Dee McNeil, as well as her piano playing. The album also includes two of her terrifically heartfelt songs, 'What Is a Man' and 'Black in a White World'. This was more proto-rap, and McNeil has been called 'the mother of all rappers'.

The women's movement was inspiring many women to rethink their relationships with men, but also their relationship with their own bodies. Matters previously deemed to be highly personal and thus beyond the purview of politicians and legislators were suddenly political. Pap smears, orgasms, menopause, the clitoris and female masturbation were finally being discussed, much of it thanks to a hugely successful book called *Our Bodies, Ourselves*.

Inevitably, the male-centric nature of rock music became a focus for the new wave of feminists. As an article in *The New York Times* argued, 'Rock music, in fact the entire rock "culture", is tremendously degrading to women'. Author Marion Meade noted that the lyrics of rock songs ranged from 'open contempt to sugar-coated condescension' towards women. Meade rightly singled out The Rolling Stones for their brutish and contemptuous attitude to women displayed in songs such as 'Stupid Girl', 'Under My Thumb', 'Honky Tonk Woman', 'Live With Me' and 'Yesterday's Papers'. Dylan also copped a serve, notably for 'Just Like a Woman'. Meade concluded by decrying the lack of female musicians and calling for women to 'band together and invade the chauvinistic rock scene.'[5]

The Cleves had just one female band member, but they quickly came up against entrenched chauvinism. Formed in New Zealand by siblings

Gaye, Ron and Graham Brown, they relocated to Sydney, releasing an EP and a surprisingly good self-titled album. Gaye Brown performed on bass and then organ, but in the early 1970s this was enough to generate consternation. Heading overseas, they changed the band's name to the more provocative Bitch. In the UK, Gaye found herself being questioned regarding the suitability of a girl appearing as part of a rock band. When Bitch was invited to merge with Spooky Tooth, Gaye was pointedly rejected by both Spooky Tooth's manager and the band's leader, each opposed to having a woman share the stage.

Bonnie Raitt had been signed to Warner Bros for her debut album. Here was a female guitarist who played bottleneck guitar just like that other sex. As Linda Ronstadt put it, 'Bonnie Raitt was the first girl to get up onstage and play guitar and have the guys say, "Hey, she doesn't play like a girl."'[6] While she garnered critical praise, Raitt would struggle to achieve a major hit album until 1989's *Nick of Time*.

Trailblazing all-female rock band Fanny released their second album, *Charity Ball*, offering a broader range of styles than their first LP. The title track, a rocking boogie, became a charting single – the first by an all-female band to reach America's Top 40. Almost inevitably, male critics penned reviews focusing on the band members' appearances rather than their music. The band's name probably wasn't helping them be accepted as serious performers; nor were the bumper stickers calling for fans to 'Get Behind Fanny'.

Lone rangers

Western culture was undergoing another radical shift that would fundamentally alter society forever. It arose, in part, from the 1960s counterculture scene. Psychologist Carl Rogers had inspired the Human Potential Movement, whose adherents believed in the untapped power of the individual. The Esalen Institute, a famous Californian retreat, played a key role in that movement, introducing practices and beliefs that would permeate the yet-to-be-realised New Age scene.

The new emphasis was on self-improvement. That focus was enhanced with the release of Nathaniel Branden's book *The Psychology of Self-Esteem*, which quickly sold over a million copies. Branden argued that one's self-esteem was the most important element in both psychological development and ultimate happiness. He was also working with writer and self-appointed philosopher Ayn Rand (while having a romantic affair with her). In 1964, they had co-written *The Virtue of Selfishness: A New Concept of Egoism*, advocating for a rejection of both altruism and collectivism. Their new way of thinking placed the desires of the individual above the needs of society. According to Rand and Branden, the only social system consistent with this new thinking was laissez-faire capitalism – or, as it would eventually become known, neoliberalism.

This shift from communitarianism, where we view ourselves as part of a collective whole, to individualism, where we view ourselves as a discrete, self-serving unit, had important ramifications for youth culture, not to mention their lingua franca of rock music. Throughout the '70s, rock music would increasingly become about 'me' and less about 'we'. This played into the rapid rise of the singer-songwriter. As Melanie Safka (known professionally simply as Melanie) put it, 'It was an incredibly exciting time to be in the music business, especially if you could play your own guitar or your own piano, and you also wrote your own songs ... We were all scrambling to come up with innovative and deeply personal songs.'[7]

It's tempting to describe this renaissance of confessional songwriting as an escape from the bruising political issues that dominated the 1960s, but perhaps it can also be viewed as symptomatic of the cultural shift towards self-obsession. In the wake of John Lennon's first solo album, autobiographical self-disclosure also played into the notion of authenticity.

Many of these confessional songwriters were cohabiting the Laurel Canyon neighbourhood of LA. Among them was Carole King, who had been penning hit songs since the late 1950s, particularly as part of the famous Brill Building hit factory in New York. In 1970, she had already tested the water as a recording artist with a debut album titled *Writer*, which featured a number of her shop-worn older songs that had already been recorded by others. But 1971's *Tapestry* turned the music industry on its head.

The move from New York to Laurel Canyon found the shy King encouraged by neighbours Joni Mitchell and James Taylor to cut a new album. *Tapestry* showcased ten untested compositions, plus reinterpretations of her songs 'Will You Love Me Tomorrow', which had been a number one hit for The Shirelles in 1960, and '(You Make Me Feel Like) a Natural Woman', which had peaked at number eight for Aretha Franklin in 1967.

Tapestry was recorded at the same time as James Taylor's album *Mud Slide Slim and the Blue Horizon* and shared many of the same musicians. Both LPs featured the song 'You've Got a Friend', which would become another number one hit for Taylor. It had been written by King during the recording sessions, but Taylor begged her to let him record it for his own disc – which was only fair, given her inspiration for the song was a line in Taylor's earlier hit 'Fire and Rain' (on which King had played piano).

King went to the number one spot with 'It's Too Late', while the album itself stayed at number one for fifteen consecutive weeks. It would remain on the charts for an incredible six years, selling in the millions to become the bestselling album of the early 1970s in the US. It scooped the Grammy Awards, with King becoming the first ever female to win the Song of the Year category. *Tapestry*'s time in the charts set a record that lasted four decades, beaten only in 2017 by Adele's album *21*.

King's success was a true watershed for female performers. Produced by Lou Adler for his Ode Records label, *Tapestry* was brim full of memorable songs that have since become pop-rock staples. King had the skill to turn the songs into evocative first-person accounts that bore the ring of truth. The personal pronouns 'I' and 'me' pepper the lyrics. There's only one third-person ballad, 'Smackwater Jack', while all the other tracks come across as confessional tunes. As Robert Christgau wrote, '[I]t established Carole King's individuality as a woman. For Adler's production was so smooth that it slipped a real, potent woman past five million half-suspecting Americans.'[8] Mind you, not all the lyrics were by King. An ex, Gerry Goffin, penned the lyrics for three songs, and Toni Stern supplied lyrics for two others. Even the seemingly female-centric '(You Make Me Feel Like) a Natural Woman' had words by a bloke based on an idea by another bloke: Goffin and Jerry Wexler. Yet the whole album maintained a cohesive feel.

To be honest, I don't find King's voice very appealing. It's nasally and at times harsh (even more so on her concert recordings). But perhaps that played into the album's appeal? King didn't sound too cultivated or professional. Listeners could sing along and not feel outclassed (as they might by, say, Karen Carpenter). What's more, the mix allowed listeners to understand every word that was being sung, again expediting home duetting.

On 'Will You Love Me Tomorrow?', King was supported with harmony vocals by Joni Mitchell and James Taylor. The albums cut by all three of these singer-songwriters demanded close listening, a far cry from the pounding onslaught of 'heavy' music, or the intricacies of prog, where the lyrics were generally bewildering.

James Taylor's awkwardly titled *Mud Slide Slim and the Blue Horizon* showcased his gentle, almost dull, folk rock songs bathed in weary melancholy. The track 'You Can Close Your Eyes', a kind of lullaby written for his one-time girlfriend Joni Mitchell, served as the B-side to his version of King's 'You've Got a Friend'. The follow-up single was 'Long Ago and Far Away', even though those words don't appear in the jumble of cringe-worthy clichés that comprise the lyrics. Joni Mitchell again provided backing vocals and, of course, Carole King tinkled the ivories.

Also hailing from the Laurel Canyon firmament, David Crosby and Graham Nash each released their debut solo albums. But the standout LP, after *Tapestry*, was Joni Mitchell's *Blue*, created when she had split with Nash and was dallying with Taylor (before he moved on to Carly Simon). Almost inevitably, given the claustrophobic nature of the Laurel Canyon imbroglio, the album focuses squarely on interpersonal relationships. Today, *Blue* is viewed as one of popular music's greatest accomplishments, with *The New York Times* declaring it one of twenty-five albums that generated turning points or pinnacles in twentieth-century popular music. *Rolling Stone*'s 500 Greatest Albums of All Time ranks *Blue* at number 3, stating: '*Blue* is the first time any major rock or pop artist had opened up so fully, producing what might be the ultimate breakup album and setting a still-unmatched standard for confessional poetry in pop music.'[9] (Neatly overlooking John Lennon's solo album of 1970.)

Mitchell had not yet discovered her inner jazz buff, so this album is very much in her folk rock phase. She portrays herself as a lonely artist with the courage to take responsibility for her emotional and sexual liberty. Mitchell referred to herself during this period as being like a cellophane wrapper, without any personal defences or guile. 'A Case of You' is emblematic, with its superb lyric about her breakup with either Graham Nash or Leonard Cohen, the words reminding the listener of just how vulnerable love makes us all. The song has since been covered by over 200 different artists, from Prince to Diana Krall.

'Little Green' is probably *Blue*'s most opaque song – unless the listener was aware that Mitchell had given up a child for adoption. 'Carey' is one of her clever observational songs, something she would perfect on later albums. In this case it describes her brief time on the island of Crete, when she lived in a hippie community. This was the album's first single, followed by 'California', written in France while she was pining for her adopted home state. The title track 'Blue' is about a lover caught up in drugs and booze – presumably James Taylor. 'River' is another breakup song, this time set at Christmas, with notable self-recrimination about her own selfishness. The whole album concludes with the decidedly anti-romantic 'The Last Time I Saw Richard', in which she reconnects with a former lover who has become a depressed loner.

Carly Simon was another female singer-songwriter who made an impact in 1971. From her eponymous LP sprang her first Top 40 hit, the wistful social study 'That's the Way I've Always Heard It Should Be'. She quickly followed with another LP, *Anticipation*, containing her smash hit of the same name. The song was reportedly inspired by Simon's experience waiting to go on a date with Cat Stevens. By the end of the year, in this revolving hotbed of performers, Simon would marry James Taylor, instantly magnifying their mutual media cachet.

The Laurel Canyon connection was also present when Stephen Stills contributed guitar to Bill Withers' debut album, *Just as I Am*. Produced and arranged by Booker T. Jones and with a tight rhythm section, it's a fabulous blend of folk, rock, soul and gospel. The LP gave rise to a couple of big singles, including 'Ain't No Sunshine', a superbly idiosyncratic tune that was apparently inspired by the movie *Days of Wine and Roses* about a pair of alcoholics. The strings are superbly arranged, and Withers' scatting, repeated 'I know' gives it a unique edginess. The tune's incredible crossover appeal meant that it made the top ten simultaneously on three *Billboard* charts: Hot 100, Easy Listening and Soul.

Flying solo

Popular music was expanding in every direction, and critics, record stores, radio stations, record labels and even consumers were starting to impose labels on musical styles. As James Brown put it: '[A] funny thing was happening on the radio then. It was starting to get segregated again, not just by black and white but by kinds: country, pop, hard rock, soft rock, every kind you could name. Radio formats became very rigid.'[10]

The Carpenters' third album, cunningly titled *Carpenters*, proved their most successful. Where Karen Carpenter's voice was smooth as silk, Rod Stewart's was like gravel soaked in whisky. Stewart's third solo album, *Every Picture Tells a Story*, was a big seller, particularly on the back of its breakthrough hit, 'Maggie May'. Written by Stewart and guitarist Martin Quittenton, 'Maggie May' describes a young lad jilted after a sexual encounter with an older woman. According to the singer, it was 'a loose recounting of the loss of my virginity in a blink-and-you'll-miss-it encounter with an older woman at the Beaulieu Jazz Festival of 1961'.[11] Stewart was sixteen at the time. Strangely, 'Maggie May' had very nearly been ditched from the album for being 'all verse and no chorus and no hook'.[12] In the end it went to number one in the US, the UK, Australia and Canada. Rod Stewart suddenly had both a number one single and a number one album on both sides of the Atlantic, becoming one of just twelve artists to have achieved that feat.

Harry Nilsson also had a hit with 'Me and My Arrow' from the animated TV show *The Point*, which he had devised. Far more inspiring was his album *Nilsson Schmilsson*. This was Nilsson at the peak of his creativity, before self-indulgence destroyed him. *Nilsson Schmilsson* delivered the hit songs 'Jump into the Fire', 'Coconut' and 'Without You'. The last was a remarkably passionate interpretation of a Badfinger song, showcasing Nilsson's incredible vocal range. 'Without You' enjoyed many weeks at number one in the US, the UK, Australia and elsewhere, along with Grammy nominations and all the rest. It was the sort of orchestrated ballad that few people were attempting at the time.

The decidedly reckless Nilsson generally went into the studio underprepared. The session musicians would turn his music ideas and fragments into full-blown backing tracks, then, at the twelfth hour, as Richard Perry reminisced, 'he lay down on the floor of the studio propping himself up on his elbow with his head resting on his hand, and a sheet of paper on the floor and started to just write lyrics. And so in fifteen minutes he had lyrics.'[13]

Nilsson's 'Jump into the Fire' had to be edited down from a seven-minute studio jam to three and a half minutes for the single. The same approach wasn't attempted for Don McLean's smash hit 'American Pie'. At eight minutes and forty-two seconds, the single was instead spread across two sides of a 45rpm disc. Clunky as that was, the song dominated the airwaves, eventually becoming one the era's classics. For almost half a century, 'American Pie' held the record for the longest song to reach number one in America. And it could have been longer, as McLean had tossed out a whole swag of intended verses when he went to record it.

'American Pie' captured the feeling of regret that was sweeping much of America at the time: a sense that a more simple, reliable and workable society had somehow been left behind. The basic theme, returned to at each chorus, centred around the 1959 plane crash that took out Buddy Holly, Ritchie Valens and the Big Bopper. But 'American Pie' also portrayed the forfeiture of the American dream. It lamented 'the day the music died', meaning music that was easier to assimilate, and that wasn't so loud that it hurt, or so progressive and complex that it couldn't be understood. Simple music was apparently what the world needed, and Don McLean was just the fella to deliver it in 1971. Although *American Pie* is often assumed to be his debut LP, in fact McLean had previously released an album that shared its title with Carole King's *Tapestry*.

The reigning king of singer-songwriters in 1971 was, once again, Elton John. With Bernie Taupin, John wrote music for the British-French teenage romance film *Friends*. The soundtrack LP became his third gold album, following *Elton John* and *Tumbleweed Connection*. There was also a live radio broadcast LP, titled by the date it was recorded, *17-11-70* (released as *11-17-70* in the US). Recordings of the broadcast had already appeared as bootlegs, prompting the release of a properly mastered version. Thirteen original songs were available, but the record company chose to include Elton's version of The Rolling Stones' 'Honky Tonk Women', presumably for marketing reasons. Although it wasn't a huge seller, *17-11-70* still found itself in the Top 100, making Elton John the only performer since The Beatles to have four albums simultaneously in that list. Elton's earnings were generating the expected tax headache. A ten-week, fifty-five-city US tour saw Elton become a millionaire. He was probably the first rock star to take his mother on tour with him.

Later in the year, Elton toured America for the sixth time, which was followed by tours of Japan and Australia. He dubbed the Australian leg a 'nightmare', as he was playing at outdoor football stadiums, tennis centres and a racecourse, often in windy conditions. What's more, there was Commonwealth Police agitation arising from some badges sewn onto his jeans and jacket which were deemed to be indecent. Elastoplast had to be placed over the offending slogans before the police would let the singer rampage across the nation.

A third album release for the year, *Madman Across the Water*, also went gold, although it didn't perform as well in the charts as *Tumbleweed Connection* or *Elton John*. As Elton would put it, 'It's not particularly commercial; there were no huge smash singles, and the songs were much longer and more complex than I'd written before.'[14] Listening to the lush arrangements, it's hard to believe that it was all recorded in just four days –

it was supposed to be five, but they lost a day when Paul Buckmaster spilt a bottle of ink over the scores and had to write them out again.

Taupin's lyrics were becoming more worldly-wise, although the big single 'Tiny Dancer' was a naive panegyric to his wife, with an uncomfortably paternalistic chorus. It's a truly awful bit of lyric, but silly lyrics never stopped Elton John's songs from becoming pop classics. Almost every song on the *Madman* album had lyrics penned in the first person, including 'All the Nasties', which Elton later claimed was about him wondering what might happen if he came out publicly as gay. As he noted, 'Not a single person seemed to notice what I was singing about.'[15]

Gender benders

Gay and lesbian rights organisations were becoming increasingly active across the Western world, but there were, as yet, few pop or rock musicians willing to publicly support the movement. In London, Pink Floyd headed up a benefit concert for gay rights, and David Bowie did likewise. Over in the US, the first ever gay character appeared in the sitcom *All in the Family*. President Richard Nixon hated the episode, and was recorded saying, 'Dammit, I do not think that you glorify on public television homosexuality … By God can I tell you it outraged me.'[16]

T. Rex's Marc Bolan was playing on sexual androgyny, while the band was being hailed as yet another possible 'successor to The Beatles'.[17] Elton John would later praise Bolan as 'the perfect pop star', going on to say, 'He wore make-up during the day, which I'd never seen a man do before.'[18] T. Rex's three singles, 'Get It On', 'Ride a White Swan' and 'Hot Love', were outselling more established artists like The Who in the UK. Police were required to protect band members in their hotels. The comparison with Beatlemania was inevitable. The average T. Rex fan was a girl between the ages of eleven and sixteen. Of course, Marc Bolan's youthful, seraphic beauty played a large part in T. Rex's appeal. An appearance on the BBC's *Top of the Pops* in March, with Bolan sporting glitter and satin clothing, saw the British launch of what would come to be known as glam rock or glitter rock.

Fellow Brit David Bowie was also toying with sexual ambiguity, but a more dominant theme was flamboyant self-absorption. His album *The Man Who Sold the World* had slumped in the UK but garnered some interest in the US. Without a work permit, he couldn't perform any gigs in the States, so Mercury Records sent Bowie on a radio promo tour. Bowie wore a stylish dress to interviews in the US and even on the street, at one stage inspiring an offended Texan to threaten him with a gun.

But he returned home none the worse for the experience, and immediately began writing new songs as well as developing a new stage character for himself. Using a piano rather than guitar, he penned over three dozen songs, many of which appeared on his next two albums. Peter Noone of Herman's Hermits heard a demo of the first song written, 'Oh! You Pretty Things', and released it as his debut solo single, with Bowie on piano. When Noone's version went to number twelve on the UK singles chart, it became Bowie's biggest success since 1969's 'Space Oddity'.

Bowie's *Hunky Dory* album includes tribute songs to Bob Dylan, Andy Warhol and The Velvet Underground. It opens with the lead single 'Changes', a somewhat autobiographical song about the need to reinvent oneself as well as disappoint one's parents. With its shifting time signatures and unconventional chord progressions, it's a curiously episodic slice of art rock. On its release in early 1972, the song flopped, as did the album. Both would have to wait to find an audience. Indeed, *Hunky Dory* would eventually be reissued many times. 'Changes' was rereleased with 'Space Oddity' as a single in 1975, and Bowie finally achieved his first UK number one hit. 'Changes' became the quintessential Bowie tune; it would also be the last song he performed on stage before his death in 2016.

Making labels with sticky fingers

The story of 1970s music is also the story of record labels, and it's worth taking a moment to consider their role.

Early independent labels in America included Chicago's Chess Records, which released Ike Turner's 'Rocket 88' in 1951, a song many point to as marking the beginning of rock 'n' roll. Sun Records, Mercury, Vee-Jay, Motown, Stax and others followed. As the late '60s and early '70s music scene expanded and diversified, more independent labels emerged. Many of the top-selling albums in 1971 were made with little or no input from the big record companies. As the decade progressed, some of these new labels established their own styles. Buying an album on a given label would thus guarantee a certain quality and approach. Record buyers like me would frequently take a stab on an unheard artist simply because they were on a boutique label alongside better-known acts. What's more, having a top-selling artist on an independent label could help subsidise non-commercial artists on that same label.

The major labels fought back by creating their own niche sub-labels. These weren't independent as such, but they were designed to give that impression. Decca, for example, introduced Deram, EMI created the Harvest label, and Philips came up with the Vertigo label. Some of the genuinely independent labels at this time were RAK Records, established by producer Mickie Most, Chrysalis Records, Charisma Records and radio deejay John Peel's short-lived Dandelion Records. Although they could control their product, most independent labels still had to cut deals with the majors to get their records distributed.

Successful bands were also creating their own labels, the most obvious being The Beatles' Apple Records. The Moody Blues established Threshold Records, The Rolling Stones launched Rolling Stones Records, Jefferson Airplane formed Grunt Records, The Beach Boys had Brother Records, Frank Zappa created Straight Records and the Bizarre label, and Deep purple established Purple Records.

Meanwhile, the big record companies were busy gobbling up smaller companies to create enormous conglomerates. For example, the Kinney Corporation, which was founded on cleaning and carparking empires, bought Warner-Seven Arts and all of its labels, then added Elektra, which amalgamated with David Geffen's Asylum Records, and the whole lot morphed into Warner Communications, with further holdings in film, television and print. Music was big business. By the mid-1970s, the top four record corporations controlled more than half of all records and tapes sold. What's more, conglomerates like CBS were also buying up record stores, as well as Fender guitars, Leslie speakers, Rhodes pianos, Rogers drums and so on. While much of the creative side of making music was contracted out to independent labels and producers, the real power remained in the hands of industry behemoths.

Despite the legal shenanigans swirling around the former moptops, the Apple label continued to release records. *Ram*, released in 1971, was the only album credited to Linda and Paul McCartney before the pair created the band Wings. As with McCartney's 1970 solo effort, the new LP topped the charts in the UK and performed very well elsewhere, and again it was savaged by the critics. *Rolling Stone*'s John Landau was particularly fierce, calling *Ram* 'inept', 'inconsequential' and 'emotionally vacuous'.[19] McCartney was stung by the criticisms.

Perhaps it was the playfulness and humour across the disc that took everyone by surprise? Have a listen to the sweeping shifts of mood on 'The Back Seat of My Car' and be amazed at the very evident influence of Brian Wilson circa *Pet Sounds*. The track is a *coup de maître*. Another song rejected by The Beatles, the charmingly silly 'Uncle Albert/Admiral Halsey', has echoes of 'Yellow Submarine' and other mid-career Beatles tunes that have since become children's favourites. What many viewed as twee and self-indulgent could also have been considered endearing and witty. Released as a single in the US, 'Uncle Albert' was Paul's first post-Beatles number one in America.

The *Ram* sessions also produced 'Another Day', a non-album single credited to 'Mr. and Mrs. McCartney'. It's a sort of 'Eleanor Rigby' theme, about the drudgery of life for a depressed, unattached woman. There's even a hint that she may commit suicide. Hardly the breezy stuff of Top 40 radio, yet 'Another Day' went to number one in Australia, two in the UK and five in the US.

While The Rolling Stones were investing in their new, bespoke label, their old label, Decca, released a compilation of Stones' songs, clumsily titled *Stone Age*. The band were so incensed that they took out full-page ads in the music press denouncing the LP, despite which the record reached number four in the UK charts.

The first LP to appear on the Rolling Stones Records label was *Brian Jones Presents the Pipes of Pan at Joujouka*, a recording of a Moroccan Sufi group. The Stones were now exiled in France, dallying with the Riviera jet set, while their business adviser, Prince Rupert Loewenstein, was investing their moolah in various offshore tax shelters. Jagger's lavish wedding to Nicaraguan-born model Bianca Pérez-Mora de Macías in St Tropez was attended by rock stars, socialites, actors and British royals. Of the Stones, only Keith Richards was invited to the ceremony, though the others got to attend the reception. It was a shotgun wedding, with Bianca already four months pregnant. The guests had just 24-hours notice to attend. Photos of the bride invoke the proverbial rabbit in the headlights.

As Richard Neville wrote in *Ink* magazine: 'That day in St Tropez marked the end of any further pretence of Jagger as the figurehead of a radical lifestyle.'[20] Indeed, the wedding was proof to many that rock music had 'sold out' to celebrity status, tax avoidance and gaudy self-indulgence. Filmmaker Donald Cammell, who had co-directed Jagger in the movie *Performance*, pinned the basis of the marriage on Jagger's narcissism, saying, 'Mick looked into Bianca's face and saw – Mick. It was as close as he could get to making love with himself.'[21]

The Stones' *Sticky Fingers* album appeared, with its infamously risqué LP cover. Designed by Andy Warhol, it featured the crotch of a pair of jeans, replete with bulge from an unrestrained and sizeable penis. Jagger and Co.'s braggadocio was yet again on full display, with most people assuming the image was of Jagger's front package. (There are various stories about who modelled for the image, with Joe Dallesandro being one obvious contender.)

The elaborate design initially included a real zipper that opened to reveal white material underneath. Those associated with the design had failed to consider that the zippers would damage the vinyl records when they were stacked for shipment. The actual zippers were quickly replaced by a photograph of a zipper. The album also featured the first airing of the now iconic tongue and lips logo that would become synonymous with the band. It was also the first of the Stones' many albums to feature the vulgar COC catalogue number. *Sticky Fingers* was the band's first LP to hit the number one position in both the UK and US charts. This return to their blues-rock roots would become one of the most celebrated rock albums of all time.

The opener and single 'Brown Sugar' was partially composed while Jagger was in Australia performing in the disastrous *Ned Kelly* movie. Initially titled 'Black Pussy', Jagger's lyrics were a lewd story of white slave owners who both beat and sexually exploit their black slaves. As a result, the upbeat feel comes across like a celebration of rape, female denigration and underage sex. Presumably listeners were captivated by the musical feel rather than the thematic intent. It was just more evidence of the band's collective tin ear when it came to matters of race and sexual politics.

And it wasn't like this was going unnoticed in 1971, with *Rolling Stone* magazine asking Keith Richards about the 'down-on-chicks' attitude evidenced in their songs. Richards' response proved the point, saying it was a 'spinoff from our environment ... hotels, and too many dumb chicks'.[22] Jagger had enjoyed an affair with African-American Marsha Hunt, a back-up singer, model and actress, with whom he also had his first child. For some strange reason, Hunt later asserted that 'Brown Sugar' was based on her – though why anyone would want to associate themselves with this brutal song escapes me.

The B-side to 'Brown Sugar' was a song titled 'Bitch', with yet another lyric, like 'Honky Tonk Women', about how Jagger is able to have sex under any circumstance or in any condition. The 'bitch' in this case refers to desire itself, not womanhood. 'You Gotta Move' is the only track not written by band members, instead based on a traditional African-American spiritual, and performed by Jagger in a faux-Southern black voice supported by jangling slide guitar from Mick Taylor. It has the rough-and-ready, tinny feel of early blues recordings – a homage to the 1950s records that inspired the band's formation.

'Sister Morphine' was initially credited to both Jagger and Richards, yet it was Marianne Faithfull who had penned the lyrics. The song had previously been released by Faithfull as a B-side to her 'Something Better' single in early 1969. Sadly, it took a legal battle for Faithfull to secure her rights as co-author.

Sticky Fingers closes with the lengthy, otherworldly 'Moonlight Mile', full of shifting dynamics and wistful instrumentals. Thematically, it's yet another song about the loneliness of being on the road as a touring musician, but musically it stands apart, with a sumptuous string arrangement by Paul Buckmaster. It's a strangely prog-like ending to an otherwise dour blues-rock album.

At the end of the year, another Rolling Stones compilation album was released on London Records, a Decca offshoot. Titled *Hot Rocks 1964–1971*, it would ironically become the bestselling release by the band, even though they had nothing to do with putting it together. *Hot Rocks 1964–1971* spent an incredible 378 weeks on the *Billboard* chart, eventually going twelve times platinum.

Ambitious projects

Following the incredible success of Deep Purple's *In Rock* album, the subsequent *Fireball* LP further cemented the band as a substantial international act. The up-tempo, frenetic title track, released as a single, begins with the sound of an air conditioner being turned on, although the band tried to convince everyone it was a 'special' synthesiser noise. Throughout the LP, the elementary riffs are alleviated by extended instrumental solos, often traded between Ritchie Blackmore's fine guitar playing and Jon Lord's dynamic organ. 'The Mule' stands out with its borrowings from '60s psychedelia alongside frenetic drumming by Ian Paice, while the lyrically clunky 'Anyone's Daughter' delves into country rock, with Blackmore on acoustic guitar and Lord playing honky-tonk piano. It was all a long way from Lord's classical-rock-fusion ambitions, which he would continue to pursue as a solo artist.

Speaking of ambitions, The Who's Pete Townshend was struggling to devise a follow-up to the band's hit rock opera *Tommy*. Fuelled by idealism and drugs, he conceived of a project called *Lifehouse*. The plot, such as it was, involved a future in which pollution had become so unbearable that humans were forced to live indoors wearing experience suits, via which their senses were stimulated (perhaps partly inspired by Frank Herbert's *Dune*). A character called Bobby hacks into the grid that feeds stimuli to individual suits. He somehow converts everyone's data into musical notes, and those notes combine into one single note that sets them all free. Just to make things even more abstruse, Townshend conceived of a combined stage musical and film that would respond to an audience's desires – a transcendent experience whereby performers and audience could become a single entity of creativity and understanding. Uh-huh ...

It was, to say the least, wildly idealistic. Struggling to marry his celebrity status with his reticence, Townshend wrote to *Melody Maker*: 'The idea is to make the first real superstar. The first real star who can really stand and say he deserves the name. The star would be us all.'[23] At the time Townshend was experiencing depressive episodes, while continuing as a disciple of Sufi guru Meher Baba. (Baba had died in January 1969, his last words reportedly being, 'Do not forget that I am God.')

The band spent hours trying to knock Townshend's idea into some sort of workable shape. As Roger Daltrey described the *Lifehouse* project, 'It was a mess ... Keith and John would start drinking, just to make the time pass faster. On one particularly long evening, Keith just started taking his clothes off. Then he stood on his head and rested his bollocks on the table.'[24] Workshopping the concept at the Young Vic Theatre brought Townshend crashing back to terra firma. He'd had far too much faith in the capacity, let alone the willingness, of an audience to participate in the creative process. At the workshops, nothing was achieved, with everyone – audience and performers – departing frustrated and confused. At the same time, Townshend was suffering panic attacks and drinking heavily. The Who's manager, Kit Lambert, was spaced out on hard drugs, and the band were yet again on the brink of busting apart.

From the detritus of the *Lifehouse* project arose the album *Who's Next*. Most of the LP tracks were songs penned for *Lifehouse*. The only non-Townshend number was 'My Wife', by John Entwistle, originally intended for his solo album. The LP cover featured the four members of the band doing up their trousers after urinating on a concrete obelisk. The reference to *2001: A Space Odyssey* was obvious, but there was also a rather distasteful suggestion that the band held everything – audience included – in contempt. But *Who's Next* was an immediate success, and many still consider it among rock's greatest albums. The reason, according to Daltrey, is that, for once, the band had the compositions well ahead of the recording sessions. Even though the *Lifehouse* project had fizzled, the band had road-tested many of the songs in a live setting, and even begun to record them at an aborted studio session in New York. By the time they put down the final tracks in their homeland, all four performers were comfortable with the material.

The opening track, 'Baba O'Riley', got its moniker from Townshend's guru conjoined with minimalist composer Terry Riley, though the song is often referred to as 'Teenage Wasteland' – words which appear in the chorus. Apparently, those words were inspired by the rubbish left behind at the end of outdoor concerts such as Woodstock and the Isle of Wight Festival. But the lyrics are largely opaque: something about rejecting the madness of teenage rebellion for a quiet, simpler life with loved ones. It certainly wasn't revelling in any nihilistic teenage wasteland. The original version was reportedly half an hour long, but it was edited down to five minutes for the LP with a breathless violin climax courtesy of guest artist Dave Arbus. (In 2012, The Who would perform it for the closing ceremony of the London Olympics.)

Entwistle's 'My Wife' was no ode to his missus, but rather a driving rocker about a man avoiding his spouse so he doesn't have to explain his bad behaviour. 'Behind Blue Eyes' was also about being tempted by evil ways, with a plaintive cry that no one understands how difficult life is for rock stars. Such constant bleating by rock stars about the difficulty of life on the road inevitably fell on deaf ears. Compared to the lives of their fans, the touring life of the professional rocker seemed pretty much ideal, particularly as they appeared to get away with doing whatever they wanted.

'Won't Get Fooled Again' became the hit single from the album, charting around the world. The closing number for the LP, it was a belligerent statement about the futility of revolution, and how hankering for social change simply leads down endless dark alleys. In many ways, it was the perfect anthem for the new decade, with Townshend averring, as Jagger did in 'Street Fighting Man', that he's simply going to get on with playing his music – the revolution be damned. Some radicals felt compelled to write to Townshend, complaining about his overarching pessimism towards the possibility of social or political change. Such barbs only infuriated the misanthrope even further.

The hypersensitive Townshend maintained a dialogue with his critics throughout 1971 via the pages of the music press. As with The Rolling Stones, The Who were now being labelled as sellout capitalists. By the end of the year, Townshend had lost patience with his critics, penning a rant in which he told them all to 'fuck off'.

An altogether different multimedia project, but no less radical than *Lifehouse*, was Frank Zappa's *200 Motels*. Indeed, there is one degree of separation, with The Who's Keith Moon working on the Zappa project immediately before workshopping *Lifehouse* at the Young Vic.

200 Motels was a movie and double album built around the concept of life on the road for rock musicians. The band get stuck in the fictional town of Centreville and proceed to demonstrate how touring can make one crazy. Two hundred was the number of lodgings in which Zappa estimated he had stayed during his rock career. The movie was directed by Zappa along with British director and critic Tony Palmer, who had already made films and TV shows about Cream, Colosseum, Fairport Convention, Juicy Lucy and others.

The budget, stumped up by United Artists, was a tight US$679,000, and the whole thing was shot in one week at London's Pinewood Studios. Zappa and his band, The Mothers of Invention, perform the music along with the Royal Philharmonic Orchestra (in a stalag set). This was the Zappa band fronted by Mark Volman and Howard Kaylan from The Turtles, along with the great British drummer Aynsley Dunbar and jazz keyboardist George Duke. The 'acting' cast included Ringo Starr performing as Larry the Dwarf but dressed up to look like Frank Zappa; Keith Moon as a harpist dressed as a nun; actor and folk singer Theodore Bikel as the group's manager; and notorious groupie and GTO member Pamela Des Barres as an interviewer. Even Ringo's driver, Martin Lickert, was awarded a role after actor Wilfred Bramble stormed out in disgust. There were also plenty of groupies, including the infamous Cynthia Plaster-Caster, renowned for making plaster casts of erect rock star penises.

Inevitably, Zappa and Palmer clashed on set. The producer, Jerry Goode, had to step in and resolve the situation by instructing Zappa to direct the actors and Palmer to direct the cameras. Much of the dialogue was improvised. By the end of their allotted studio days, Zappa had only managed to complete one-third of his shooting script.

The outcome was an eye-watering pastiche of surreal vignettes, shot on videotape with masses of video effects, and finally transferred from tape to 35mm film – the first feature film to attempt this process. Like all of Zappa's screen experiments, *200 Motels* was an assault on the senses. Where Zappa's music was at times challenging, his use of visual media went even further, with frenzied editing and montages mixing animation, live music performances and real conversations all jumbled together in a chaotic mess. Famed movie critic Roger Ebert gave *200 Motels* three out of four stars, but many others were far less kind. I suggest ignoring the film and instead going straight to the double album soundtrack, which has some sublime moments. Here you will find Zappa's avant-garde classical work, solid rock songs, touches of jazz and his trademark comedy tunes about sexual matters.

Zappa's insistence on devolving to schoolyard smuttiness has always challenged critics, and even many fans of his music. This second incarnation of The Mothers of Invention, with Volman and Kaylan (aka Flo & Eddie) taking lead vocals, represents a period when Zappa was at great pains to test the squeamishness of his audience. On one hand, the composer obviously found such frolics amusing. On another, he knew that pushing the boundaries of sexual mores would appeal to teenagers who might otherwise ignore his challenging music. And indeed, albums like *The Mothers, Fillmore East – June 1971* were bought by many young people for their titillation content: it hit *Billboard* at number thirty-eight, and ranked twenty-fourth on the album charts for the year in Australia.

But 1971 was not Zappa's best year. After filming *200 Motels*, a planned concert at the Royal Albert Hall featuring both his band and the Royal Philharmonic Orchestra was suddenly cancelled when hall management got a whiff of Zappa's libretto. A subsequent lawsuit in which Zappa's manager attempted to sue the Royal Albert Hall for breach of contract was eventually lost. Having 'Penis Dimension' played in court no doubt sealed the verdict.

Back in New York, John Lennon asked to meet Zappa. At a planned Zappa concert that evening, both Lennon and Ono, bolstered by cocaine, appeared on stage towards the end of the show. As usual, Ono's caterwauling ruined what could have been a wonderful jam session. Part of the concert was released on *The Mothers, Fillmore East – June 1971* just two months later. But Lennon and Ono's contributions were left off the album, as Zappa refused to deal with Lennon's manager Allen Klein. Lennon and Ono used the tapes on their own *Some Time in New York City* album, claiming copyright for the entire improvisatory jam, including segments featuring Zappa's composition 'King Kong' retitled as 'Jam Rag' (British slang for a sanitary napkin). Inevitably, Zappa wasn't happy.

But things were about to get much, much worse for FZ. The Mothers toured Europe in November and December. Whilst performing at the ballroom in the Montreux Casino, an audience member fired a flare gun, which set alight the rattan-covered ceiling. As the audience panicked, Zappa tried to calm them down, but the stage was overrun by terrified punters. Incredibly, the building managers had chained the exit doors to prevent a crowd outside from sneaking into the concert. The only exits were the front door and a small window beside the stage. The road crew smashed the window and helped people to climb out. Thankfully, there were no fatalities and just a few minor injuries. The band retreated to their hotel and watched as the building, along with all their musical equipment, lit up the Swiss sky.

The upside to this disaster was that the band Deep Purple were also in the audience. Watching the fire from the safety of their hotel across Lake Geneva, bass player Roger Glover grabbed a napkin and jotted down the words 'smoke on the water' – and thus a rock classic arose like a phoenix from Zappa's calamity.

But Zappa's *annus horribilis* hadn't ended. The band voted to continue the tour in England with new and borrowed gear. A week after Montreux, they were playing a concert at the Rainbow Theatre in London. As the Mothers launched into a typically twisted cover of The Beatles' 'I Want to Hold Your Hand', a member of the audience, Trevor Howell, leapt to the stage and punched Zappa, who fell fifteen feet into the orchestra pit in front of the stage. It appeared at first that he was dead, with one leg bent beneath his body and blood pouring from wounds in his head. Howell was grabbed by the road crew and held until police arrived.

Zappa suffered a broken rib, paralysed wrist, fractured leg, gashes in his head and a crushed larynx. Initially, Zappa's team were told that he might never be able to perform again. Visiting him in hospital the following day, the band found Frank wrapped up like a mummy, with holes for his eyes and mouth. His first utterance was to call a tune, as if they were all on stage: '"Peaches En Regalia",' he croaked. 'One, two, three.' Everyone fell about laughing.[25]

Howell was sentenced to twelve months' jail. Zappa was in plaster up to his hip for four months, then in a wheelchair for a long time afterward. He ended up with one leg permanently bent and somewhat shorter than the other, and would suffer chronic back pain for the rest of his life. The only positive was that his voice dropped by a third, which he claimed was an improvement. While recuperating in a wheelchair, the workaholic managed to put together three very different albums, *Just Another Band From L.A.*, *Waka/Jawaka* and *The Grand Wazoo*.

Fused

Many viewed Zappa as a crossover rock and jazz artist, but the predominant melding of those styles came from the jazz side of the equation. Some in the jazz field decided the incorporation of electronic instruments and rock rhythms was a bridge too far. Others, like Joachim-Ernst Berendt, believed that rock had gone as far as it could, and thus the incorporation of jazz elements and sensibilities made rock more sophisticated.

The Mahavishnu Orchestra was headed by English guitar whiz John McLaughlin. The rest of the original line-up was Panamanian-born drummer Billy Cobham, Czechoslovakian keyboardist Jan Hammer, American violinist Jerry Goodman and Irish bass player Rick Laird. McLaughlin had already been a member of Miles Davis' band, as well as Tony Williams' Lifetime, and he had three solo LPs under his belt.

The music on Mahavishnu Orchestra's debut album, *The Inner Mounting Flame*, is electric jazz-rock with tight, rapid-fire compositions, complex time signatures and precision playing. Peaking at number eleven on the *Billboard* jazz albums chart, it helped bolster the new fusion genre. McLaughlin's jet-propelled, super-fast electric guitar soloing became a focus of the outfit, wowing many guitar-heads who had previously been turned on by the likes of Clapton, Hendrix and Page. (Meanwhile, Gary Boyle, Terje Rypdal, Derek Bailey, Ralph Towner, Volker Kriegel, Philip Catherine, Ray Russell, Jukka Tolonen and others were also creating waves by combining post-Hendrix guitar shredding with modern jazz.) Of note on Mahavishnu's initial outing was the muscular, technically astounding drummer Billy Cobham, who propelled the entire unit with enormous ferocity. As Cobham put it, 'I want my playing to be simple enough for the audience to understand but intricate enough for them to be awed by what I'm doing.'[26]

In Britain, the jazz-rock fusion thing was being driven by Ian Carr's outfit Nucleus, plus Keith Tippett, Mike Gibbs and a whole swag of expatriate South Africans who were members of The Blue Notes and Chris McGregor's Brotherhood of Breath. These expats formed a jazz-rock band called Assagai. In 1971, their only two albums, *Assagai* and *Zimbabwe*, were both released. They're cracking examples of African-flavoured big-band jazz-rock. There's even a version of The Beatles' 'Hey Jude' on the first album, performed with a Caribbean feel.

On a similar journey but even more successful was Osibisa. They were the first all-black band to appear on Britain's *Top of the Pops* TV show. Comprised of four expatriate West Africans and three Caribbeans, their influence was considerable, helping to establish African rock as a marketable commodity as well as pioneering what would become known as world music. In the studio, the band captured their live feel by recording everything in just one take. The debut disc, *Osibisa*, was quickly followed by another album, *Woyaya*, both of which rated well. LP covers featured artwork by Roger Dean, who would soon be creating covers for Yes, Uriah Heep, Gentle Giant and others. However, it wasn't smooth sailing for black bands in Britain. The members of the white supremacist National Front – 17,000 in number and growing – were making their presence felt, and black Britons also had to contend with considerable police harassment.

In Australia, jazz was also making occasional bedfellows with rock and even folk and classical music. The very versatile Jeannie Lewis, a familiar sight at many activist demonstrations, recorded with the Ray Price Jazz Quintet, and also headed up her own band, Gypsy Train. She helped stage the Mood and Mode Variations concert at Sydney Town Hall, which saw folk, pop and classical musicians sharing the stage. The Daly-Wilson Big Band were also busy touring their blend of jazz and rock, while in Perth a so-called rock mass was staged at St George's Cathedral with rock band Bakery and a jazz ensemble. This resulted in a popular LP titled *Rock Mass for Love*, a curious blend of jazz, rock and religious proselytising.

Aussies on the march

With *Jesus Christ Superstar* making waves, a Capitol Records executive, the superbly named Artie Mogull, reckoned that the song 'I Don't Know How to Love Him' had the makings of a hit single. He first approached Linda Ronstadt to record it, but she disliked the tune. At around the same time, Mogull was being harangued by Helen Reddy's husband and manager, Jeff Wald. Mogull happened to catch Helen Reddy's performance on *The Tonight Show*, and finally offered her a contract to record a single. He suggested she try 'I Don't Know How to Love Him'. Reddy wasn't keen, later writing, 'Why would I waste this opportunity on a whiny song structured around a vocally awkward major sixth musical interval?'[27] But Mogull was insistent.

While recording what she hoped would be the A-side, 'I Believe in Music', Reddy found herself extremely nervous and disheartened. But those emotions served her well when they moved on to record 'I Don't Know How to Love Him'. On release, a small radio station in Connecticut began playing the tune. Reddy's friends and relatives all phoned in requests to hear the song over and over. The assertive Jeff Wald was also working the phones, as well as wining and dining deejays. That was the way the game was played. Eventually, Reddy's single made its way into the charts.

In Australia, the song went to number two, becoming Reddy's first hit in her native land. It eventually charted in Europe, Canada and America. Capitol had a burgeoning success on their hands, and so they rushed out a Helen Reddy LP, using her hit single as the title track. Notably, the *I Don't Know How to Love Him* long-player included an early version of her feminist anthem, 'I Am Woman'. Reddy suggests in her autobiography that she was motivated to write an empowering song for women after experiencing the way men treated women in the entertainment business.[28] Her expatriate friend Lillian Roxon, a pioneering rock journalist, was also a major influence. While Reddy may have penned the lyric, it was fellow Australian Ray Burton who wrote the music for 'I Am Woman'. He also takes credit for the inchoation of the song, claiming it was he who suggested Reddy should write a song about women's issues. But the timing wasn't yet right for that piece of pop polemic.

Olivia Newton-John, another expat Aussie, also debuted with her LP *If Not for You*, with the title track, a Bob Dylan song, becoming her first international hit. Another track from the album, the nineteenth-century murder ballad 'Banks of the Ohio', also performed well.

Back at the bottom of the world, Scottish-born, Adelaide-dwelling Eric Bogle wrote a simple song about a catastrophic event that was deeply embedded in his adopted land's national psyche: the Gallipoli campaign during the First World War. Not long after arriving in the country, Bogle had witnessed a Remembrance Day parade in Canberra, inspiring the tune that he will forever be remembered for. 'And the Band Played Waltzing Matilda' was a ballad about the terrible cost of war, and its gloomy tone was all the more poignant in the shadow of the Vietnam conflict. Although penned and performed in 1971, the song didn't gain broad attention until it won a prize at a National Folk Festival in Brisbane in 1974. Bogle recalled, '[T]here was a second's silence after I finished. I thought, "I've fucked it here." I hadn't sung it very well. Then this storm of applause broke out ...'[29] Eventually the song was picked up by English folk singer June Tabor, and then it was covered by everyone from Joan Baez and Christy Moore to The Dubliners and Midnight Oil.

Despite the parlous state of Australian radio, the land down under wasn't entirely a cultural wasteland when it came to rock music. Discerning Australian music consumers were keeping abreast of overseas trends and buying plenty of non-commercial rock albums, especially prog rock, with some prog LPs charting better in Australia than in the UK. But those hankering after broader, more adventurous radio programming were defeated by the stranglehold that commercial radio stations had on the politicians and thus radio licensing.

In 1971, Australian radio finally came of age thanks to music guru Chris Winter and visionary producer Ted Robinson. We still didn't have FM radio, nor pirate radio, to expand the repertoire, but Winter saw an opportunity and somehow convinced the Australian Broadcasting Corporation to grant him a two-hour night-time slot in which he could play non-mainstream rock music on the national broadcaster's AM station. *Room to Move* was, as Marius Webb succinctly put it, 'an independent beacon in a sea of musical commercialisation and the idea that led to the eventual establishment of Double/Triple J in 1975'.[30] Winter was the epitome of cool, spinning album tracks by Zappa, Weather Report or Genesis, and

Room to Move was an education for all who listened. Chris Winter was a true musicologist, immersed in global music and passionate about all of it, and he became a seminal figure in Australia's musical trajectory.

Australia's commercial radio stations finally twigged that local acts had selling power, and 1971 became something of a watershed year for Aussie pop music. Various Australian artists became top-selling chartbusters, with Spectrum, Chain and Daddy Cool all enjoying number one hits and each releasing an album.

Daddy Cool was the joke that quickly stopped being a joke. At the Odyssey Pop Festival in Wallacia, it became abundantly clear that there was an audience for throwback music. Their hit song 'Eagle Rock' was promoted with an early film clip by Chris Löfvén. As he recalled, 'There were a few music TV shows that occasionally played film clips if artists weren't available to appear live in the studio.' Nascent music videos of the day were 'inspired by Dick Lester's innovative, fresh approach with The Beatles' *A Hard Day's Night* movie'.[31] 'Eagle Rock' stayed at number one in Australia for an incredible seventeen weeks straight. Two months later, the band's debut album, *Daddy Who? Daddy Cool!*, topped the album charts, setting a benchmark for Australian sales. As producer Robie Porter noted, the album was recorded over two nights and every song was either a first or second take, with the whole shebang mixed in just nine hours.

Those eagles had a reptile offspring. It has been suggested that Elton John's 1972 hit 'Crocodile Rock' was inspired by Daddy Cool's 'Eagle Rock'. Certainly, both Elton and lyricist Bernie Taupin were aware of Daddy Cool. Indeed, there wasn't much going on in pop and rock that Elton John failed to notice. What's more, Taupin had been photographed wearing Daddy Cool promotional paraphernalia.

On the back of their unexpected Australian success, Daddy Cool headed for the West Coast of the US, including a week-long stint at the Whisky a Go Go. A follow-up US tour occurred a few months later, but this quirky band from the antipodes only managed to generate a cult following overseas. In September, new single 'Come Back Again', paired with 'Just as Long as We're Together', hit the number two spot on the

Australian charts. The integration of 1950s doo-wop with contemporary styling proved irresistible. What's more, covers of songs like 'Baby Let Me Bang Your Box' suited the cheeky irreverence of Australian youth culture. But Daddy Cool would be a short-lived band.

Ted Mulry had arrived in Australia from Britain and teamed up with Harry Vanda and George Young at Alberts to release the revoltingly cheesy 'Falling in Love Again'. (If you ever need a good laugh, have a look at the film clip for this song.) Former Easybeats members Vanda and Young were flitting back and forth between London and Sydney, releasing singles under a wide range of pseudonyms. Meanwhile, George's younger brothers, Malcolm and Angus, were hanging around Ted Mulry's gigs, with Malcolm sometimes joining them on stage while underage Angus watched from the front row. Both dreamed of having their own rock band. They couldn't have guessed in 1971 that one day they would enjoy the second-highest album sales of all time.

Australians may have been listening to a lot of British prog, but there weren't many local prog bands on the scene. There was MacKenzie Theory, led by guitarist Rob MacKenzie and augmented by viola player Cleis Pearce, both of whom had enjoyed classical training. Also leaning towards prog was Company Caine, with their debut album *A Product of a Broken Reality*. The music melds guitar-based hard rock jamming with keyboard and saxophone amid jazz-psychedelia and silly pop songs. Many view this LP as an influential milestone in Australian music. Don Walker, who would establish Cold Chisel, noted: 'The Australian music scene in the early 70s was not as you say artistically encouraging ... I remember me and my mates getting very excited over the Company Caine record for example – that an Australian band could put out a serious musical record like that.'[32]

Without any sizeable venues in Australia, visiting acts were forced to stage outdoor shows at tennis centres, and absurd venues such as Sydney's Randwick Racecourse. Pink Floyd played there on a blustery day that threatened to blow the band off the makeshift stage. Deep Purple played at Perth's Beatty Park Aquatic Centre, with a swimming pool between band and audience. But a Bee Gees concert at Subiaco Oval in the same city devolved into a riot. When some young girls attempted to climb onto the stage, a roadie grabbed one of the girls and roughly tossed her back, injuring the poor lass. The crowd yelled their disapproval. Maurice Gibb was perhaps less than diplomatic in response, telling the crowd to shut up. During the encore, the mob's fury peaked, with audience members leaping on to the stage to smash the band's equipment. Intervention by the police inspired chants of 'Kill the pigs!'

A few weeks later, in Greensborough, North Carolina, Robin Gibb collapsed from ingesting too many amphetamines and had to be hospitalised. Brother Maurice, meanwhile, was grappling with alcohol addiction. As he noted, it was John Lennon who had introduced him to drinking alcohol – when Maurice was seventeen. 'I was drinking every day. I started to drink in the mornings. I was starting to be sick in the mornings. I was hugging the toilet every morning, and things like that.'[33] As brother Barry put it, 'There were instances when Maurice would actually have to feel his way along the wall to the stage.'[34] Things escalated until, as Maurice admitted, 'I was verbally abusive, very arrogant, obnoxious, belligerent, you know … It was all me, me, me. Whatever I had to do … I was a loving dad, and I still am. But I was very selfish. Very selfish about everything. I would always put myself before my wife and my children, which is what the disease does to you.'[35] For Maurice, his indulgences would peak in 1991, when, after a month-long binge, he found himself waving a loaded gun at his wife and children.

Bowing out

Another artist struggling with alcohol dependency was The Doors' Jim Morrison. His band's final studio recording, *L.A. Woman*, was released in April. The stripped-down accompaniment was a big departure from the embellished *Soft Parade* and much closer to *Morrison Hotel*. Elvis Presley's bass player, Jerry Scheff, and rhythm guitarist Marc Benno were co-opted to help out. The single 'Love Her Madly' became one of their highest-charting hits. Their swan song LP included some of The Doors' best material, such as 'Riders on the Storm', inspired by an old cowboy song called 'Ghost Riders in the Sky'. It would be the last tune ever recorded with the mercurial Morrison.

Morrison knew he needed to escape the LA environment. He headed to Paris, where one of his more regular flames, Pamela Courson, was ensconced. At around 6am on 3 July, Courson found Morrison dead in her bathtub. He had joined Hendrix, Joplin and Brian Jones in the 27 Club. The official cause of death was listed as heart failure, though there can be little doubt that self-abuse through drugs and alcohol played its part. Three years later, Courson would join the 27 Club herself.

The Allman Brothers Band were also grappling with addictions in their ranks. They released their live *At Fillmore East* double album to great success, hailed in *Rolling Stone* as 'the best damn rock and roll band this country has produced in the past five years'.[36] Because they tended to use their songs as vehicles for long, improvised soloing, two sides of the set contained just one song each. The Allmans were pioneers of Southern white rock, helping shift entrenched attitudes towards America's south-east, which was generally viewed as being backward and racist. What's more, they had two drummers, one of them black and one white.

The Allman Brothers didn't go for the machismo and bombast of Britain's heavy rock acts, instead favouring musicality over theatre. The band's leader was guitar maestro Duane Allman, whom many considered to be as good as Eric Clapton. He had been invited by Clapton to play on Eric and the Dominos' album *Layla and Other Assorted Love Songs*. 'Layla' is famous for its intense blending of the two great guitarists. Indeed, the singing plays a distant second fiddle to the guitars in the original mix, but the extended outro always struck me as overwrought (and with one guitar slightly out of tune).

As well as guitar chops, the other thing that Clapton and Allman had in common was their fixation with heroin. In October, four members of the Allman Brothers Band and crew – Duane, Berry Oakley and two roadies – checked into a rehab centre to deal with their heroin dependences. A few weeks later, Duane Allman was riding his Harley-Davidson when he swerved to miss a truck that had stopped in an intersection. He was thrown from his bike, which landed on top of him. Duane Allman was three years short of joining the 27 Club.

High on cocaine, the rest of the band played at Duane's funeral. Immediately afterwards they shared some pot and decided that the band should carry on. The Allman Brothers' next LP, *Eat a Peach*, featured both live and studio recordings that included Duane. Duane Allman's posthumous album would also be the band's first to break into the Top 10 on the US charts.

Another posthumous release, Janis Joplin's *Pearl*, also charted well, hitting the top spot in the US, Australia and elsewhere. Recorded between July and October 1970, all the tracks featured Janis except 'Buried Alive in the Blues', which was an unfinished backing track. The last song she recorded before her death was the a cappella 'Mercedes Benz'. Janis was the classic tortured artist. Haunted by the cruel taunting of her high-school peers, and forever hungry for validation, she made even the most banal lyrics seem like passionate purging. Almost single-handedly, Janis blazed a trail for assertive, uncompromising women in the music business. That path would lead directly to the likes of Patti Smith, Madonna, Pink and many more.

Singles lifted from *Pearl* included Joplin's version of Kris Kristofferson's 'Me and Bobby McGee', with the gender of the protagonists swapped without needing to alter the lyrics. It went to number one in Australia and America and was the late artist's biggest hit. This was only the second time in American chart history that a song by a dead performer had reached the top of the charts, the previous being Otis Redding's '(Sittin' on) The Dock of the Bay', in 1968.

Metal mayhem

The coining of the term 'heavy metal' is often credited to *Creem* magazine, which used those words to describe the debut album *Kingdom Come* by New York power trio Sir Lord Baltimore. Certainly, that album contains all the hallmarks of the genre. However, the two words had also appeared together in 1968, buried in the lyrics of Steppenwolf's ode to freedom, 'Born to Be Wild'. Even further back, there was a character, Uranian Willy, the Heavy Metal Kid, in William Burroughs' novel *The Soft Machine*. Given that many declare Black Sabbath to be the beginnings of the heavy metal genre, it seems neatly coincidental that Sir Lord Baltimore was their opening act in New York during Sabbath's Paranoid tour.

Black Sabbath's third album, *Master of Reality*, once again went gold in the UK and platinum in the US. Historically, *Master of Reality* has been viewed as an important precursor of doom metal and stoner rock, and is today considered one of the all-time great albums in the metal canon. But critics in 1971 were still inclined to stick the boot into heavy metal, with *Village Voice*'s Robert Christgau writing, 'I don't care how many rebels and incipient groovers are buying. I don't even care if the band members believe in their own Christian/satanist/liberal muck. This is dim-witted, amoral exploitation.'[37] *Los Angeles Times* critic John Mendelsohn wrote, 'Black Sabbath's ... new songs are as indistinguishable from its old songs as its old songs are from one another.'[38] But critics aren't punters, and the punters loved it.

The sound on *Master of Reality* went deeper into the black void, with brutal force and plenty of distortion. The track 'Sweet Leaf' opens the album with coughing. It was penned by Geezer Butler in praise of the marijuana the band members were consuming. As Ozzy Osbourne wrote about this era: 'Every day I'd be smoking dope, boozing, having a few toots of coke, fucking around with speed or barbiturates or cough syrup, doing acid, you name it. I didn't know what day it was most of the time.'[39] Perhaps to atone for their depravities, the track 'After Forever' urges listeners to put their faith in God, as that's the only way to be saved from sin: hardly what one might call satanist or demonic.

Led Zeppelin were anticipating touring their new album. As for their previous disc, they began recording at Hedley Grange, getting a monster drum sound by recording the kit in the entrance hall, which had a high cathedral ceiling. Further recording continued at Island studios. As engineer Andy Johns noted, they were highly disciplined in their approach, which he compared with a band like the Stones, who could spend 'days and days trying to get a basic track'.[40] But the album's release hit delays, not least of which was wrangling with their record company over the artwork for the sleeve. The band wanted no mention of their collective or individual names on the cover. Of course, there had been precedents to this approach, such as Pink Floyd and King Crimson, but this time there would be no writing anywhere on the jacket, with the band instead identifying themselves via runic symbols. There wouldn't even be any record company information. The record executives were aghast at the idea, calling countless meetings to try to dissuade the band, but Zep understood the power of hype and intrigue.

Robert Plant had been reading a book on the Scottish border wars when he penned the lyrics for 'The Battle of Evermore'. As he put it, 'I realised that I needed another completely different voice, as well as my own, to give that song its full impact. So I asked Sandy Denny along ...'[41] Denny had by this time left Fairport Convention and was focusing on a solo career. She got her own symbol on the album cover.

Plant and Page had been listening incessantly to Joni Mitchell's *Blue*. Thus arose 'Going to California', with Plant's lyrics channelling his desire to meet the songstress. The shifting rhythms of 'Four Sticks' had drummer Bonzo Bonham flummoxed. However, he witnessed a performance by Ginger Baker's Airforce, inspiring him to not only concentrate properly in the studio, but also to play with four drumsticks instead of two.

The standout track on *Led Zeppelin IV* is 'Stairway to Heaven'. As it gained popularity, Atlantic Records begged the band to release a single version, but Jimmy Page was adamant that would never happen. By way of argument, Atlantic referred to the success of million-selling singles from The Rolling Stones' *Sticky Fingers* LP, but *Zep IV* was already selling twice the number of units as the Stones' album. In the ideological battle between singles and LPs, Led Zeppelin were determined not to become known as a singles band. In 1975, Page told Cameron Crowe, 'To me, I thought "Stairway" crystallised the essence of the band. It had everything there and showed the band at its best ... We were careful never to release it as a single. It was a milestone for us.'[42]

Led Zeppelin had a solid history of plagiarism, and in the case of 'Stairway' they appear to have purloined the guitar introduction from American band Spirit's 1968 instrumental 'Taurus'. Led Zep had toured with Spirit in their early days and had recorded an unreleased version of Spirit's song 'Fresh Garbage' for their first album. The tussle over copyright of 'Stairway' would lead to a protracted series of court battles decades later.

Plagiarism or not, 'Stairway to Heaven' makes many lists of greatest ever rock songs and became the most requested song on American FM stations for many years. As well as metal, the tune also contains elements of prog and folk rock. The convoluted lyrics have confounded millions of listeners. Plant has attempted to explain them as being about a woman getting everything she wanted without consequences – which sounds a lot like an Aleister Crowley–influenced approach to life. John Paul Jones more honestly stated, 'Nobody's quite sure what "stairway to heaven" means.'[43] Of course, there are many cover versions, but, for the awesome fun of it, have a listen to the live interpretation by Frank Zappa's band, recorded during his final tour, which appears on the album *The Best Band You Never Heard in Your Life*.

Led Zeppelin IV was, like Carole King's *Tapestry*, another watershed in record sales. In the US alone it has sold over 24 million copies. The band were thus able to dictate their own terms with tour promoters. They demanded and achieved a ninety/ten split on their sold-out arena concerts. To avoid tax scrutiny, management stuffed mountains of cash into travel bags, with band members taking whatever they needed whenever they desired. Meanwhile, the performances also swelled, often running to three hours of aural assault.

Jimmy was now playing on a custom twin-necked guitar featuring both six and twelve strings, inspired by one played by Earl Hooker, Sonny Boy Williamson's guitarist. Being able to swap between six and twelve strings was the only way he could perform 'Stairway to Heaven' without changing instruments mid-song. Meanwhile, perpetual schoolboys Plant and Bonham were busy winding each other up. At one concert, Robert proffered a banana during Bonzo's extended drum solo. A row between

Bonzo and Plant resulted in the drummer punching the singer and then picking a fight with a hotel chef. The fracas was resolved when tour manager Richard Cole decked the drummer, breaking his nose.

In Japan, tension again spilled over between band members mid-show, with Bonham giving Plant a split lip and then refusing to return to the stage. Their continuing alcohol-and-drug-fuelled hijinks also played a major part in the mayhem that swirled around the band. In Japan, as an indicative snapshot, one of the team ran naked across rooftops after his clothes were thrown out of the hotel window. Another was forced to return to his motel from a restaurant sans clothing. At a members-only disco, Bonham urinated from a balcony onto the deejay. On a train ride from Hiroshima, he defecated into the handbag of Jimmy Page's Japanese groupie. Bonham and Richard Cole bought samurai swords, which they used to destroy a hotel suite. As Jimmy Page put it, 'Night after night after night, we had all this stuff going on, and we got away with murder.'[44]

Disturbances also became increasingly routine at Led Zep concerts, particularly as concert tickets sold so quickly that many disgruntled fans were left trying to gain access by any means. One frightening episode occurred at a government-sponsored festival in Milan. The event turned chaotic when a crowd clashed with 2000 riot police outside the stadium, with the fracas migrating into the venue. The band decided that they might be able to reduce the tension by performing, but their music had the opposite effect. First the drum roadie copped a beer bottle in the head. Then a tear gas cannister exploded in front of the stage. As the band called it quits, the battle escalated, with 'thirty or forty cannisters of tear gas all going at once'.[45] The band and crew barricaded themselves in the dressing room and wrapped wet towels around their heads, but the windows were broken and more tear gas cannisters were dropped into the room from the street. In the end, everyone survived, but Led Zep never played Italy again, and thereafter doubled their security team.

Alice Cooper put out *Love It to Death*, their third and final album for Zappa's Straight Records label, from which erupted a hit single, 'I'm Eighteen', reaching number twenty-one on the *Billboard* chart. Mind you, band members and their extended families worked the phones, ringing hundreds of radio stations across the country to request the song. 'I'm Eighteen' spoke to the awkward confusion of being simultaneously boy and man. *Village Voice* critic Robert Christgau called it 'one of the great singles of all time'.[46] The band's music, now produced by Bob Ezrin, had lost much of the impishness that defined their previous albums and was entering into a more polished, less adventurous, hard rock sound. Weirdly, *Love It to Death* closed with a cover of Harry Butler and Rolf Harris's quasi-Aboriginal 1960s hit 'Sun Arise'. There was no digeridoo or wobble-board in Alice Cooper's version.

On the strength of 'I'm Eighteen', Warner Bros. Records sniffed an opportunity and picked up the contract from Zappa's Straight label, rereleasing *Love It to Death* with some genuine promotion. Touring to support the album, the increasingly theatrical stage act included props such as gothic torture devices, and the show climaxed with Vincent Furnier being fried in an electric chair.

The progable sons

The list of prog albums released in 1971 is very, very long, so I'll just focus on a few of them. Gentle Giant had been formed in 1970. *Acquiring the Taste*, their second LP, established a wholly new sound in the prog realm (as the title might suggest). It was rock combined with folk, jazz, medieval madrigals, baroque, chamber and even musical rounds, and band members played on a staggering array of instruments. This was the most idiosyncratic of all the progressive rock developments, and one that had zero peers. As a result, Gentle Giant also had fewer fans than bands like Yes, Genesis and their ilk.

Caravan's *In the Land of Grey and Pink* was their third outing, injecting a good deal of surreal, quirky humour into what was becoming a rather po-faced and self-reverential genre. (The few other prog bands that employed humour and whimsy included Gong, Hatfield & the North, plus Dutch outfit Supersister.) Many musicologists place this Caravan album high in their lists of best all-time prog releases. It combines catchy melodies with extremely witty lyrics – particularly on the title track and on 'Golf Girl'.

Emerson, Lake & Palmer had a big year, releasing two albums, *Tarkus*, followed by *Pictures at an Exhibition*. As was becoming de rigueur in prog circles, side one of *Tarkus* was a suite of interconnected tunes. Greg Lake described the whole album as being 'songs united by themes of science fiction, violence and the futility of war'.[47] It was certainly a far more aggressive set than their debut disc. This is yet another of the era's records that garnered poor reviews but enjoyed enthusiastic listener response. *Rolling Stone*'s critic complained that the band had failed to become 'creators' and instead churned out 'mediocrity', while *NME*'s Richard Green said it was 'cacophonous ostentation' containing 'a mixture of sounds completely incomprehensible to my ear'.[48] Nevertheless, *Tarkus* reached the top spot on the UK charts, and single digits in Australia and the US.

Perhaps *Rolling Stone* was unimpressed with ELP's magpie-like pilfering from classical music? If so, they would've been even less pleased with *Pictures at an Exhibition*, a rock adaptation of Mussorgsky's piano suite, recorded live. The enthusiastic roar of the Newcastle City Hall audience demonstrates that prog was meeting demand and was not out of touch, as some like to suggest. The band's label, Atlantic, couldn't decide how to promote the album, and even considered putting it out on their classical label, Nonesuch. For a time, it was placed in the too-hard basket and shelved. However, when a New York radio station played the recording in its entirety, the listener reaction was such that Atlantic agreed to release it.

Contrary to the label's fears, it sold very well. Lake suggests that the album helped 'tear down the walls of prejudice and bigotry', going on to assert, 'It was perhaps the first time that a young rock audience had ever been offered up an honest, serious attempt at performing a piece of classical music with a rock sentiment and a rock feeling, but not in a corny, piss-taking way.'[49] Lake's analysis, like the music itself, is somewhat overblown. There had been various earlier efforts to marry classical music with rock.

Yes managed to put out two excellent albums in 1971, *The Yes Album*, followed by *Fragile*. *The Yes Album* was a breakthrough for the band, catapulting them into the pantheons of prog elite. Like Led Zeppelin, Yes had taken time out to reside at a country retreat while honing their composing skills. In keeping with the film frame concept of the cover, the album had a very cinematic quality. Tracks like 'Yours Is No Disgrace' and 'I've Seen All Good People' were the quintessential, crowd-pleasing Yes formula.

While Yes were going from strength to strength, they had membership difficulties. Keyboardist Tony Kaye was resistant to playing the newfangled keyboards that prog now demanded, so he was ditched in favour of Rick Wakeman, at the time a member of Strawbs. Wakeman enjoyed playing as many different keyboards as could be wedged around him. In order to pay for that array of keyboards, the group rushed out the album *Fragile*. The opening tune, 'Roundabout', begins with elegant acoustic guitar featuring harmonics, followed by a superbly busy bass line, then a suite of riffs and shifting feels. It even ends with a CSNY-styled vocal harmony. Released as a single, cut back to three and a half minutes (and thus missing some of the tastier aspects of the album version), it charted well in the US. *Fragile* was the first of many Yes albums to enjoy cover art by Roger Dean.

Genesis added guitarist Steve Hackett in January and by midyear were recording the album *Nursery Cryme*. The LP failed to appeal to critics and buyers in England, but found more enthusiastic reception on the Continent. Genesis would play to crowds of 20,000 in Italian arenas, and then go home to perform for a few dozen punters in British clubs.

With no fixed ideas about what to include on their sixth disc, Pink Floyd attempted to compose new material in the studio. Days and days of effort came to nought. At one stage the band considered calling the new album *Return of the Son of Nothings*. The end result, *Meddle*, was as unfocused as the approach. 'San Tropez' stands out because it was the only song brought into the studio pre-composed and ready to put to tape. But it's far from inspired, being a crooning jazz shuffle with a flaccid piano solo. The whole LP was closer to German electronic band Tangerine Dream in its atmospherics than a foot-tapping rock album. Inexplicably, it peaked at number three on the UK charts but failed to sell in the US.

In Italy prog rock was positively booming, with the genre now labelled Rock Progressivo Italiano (RPI). Many Italian bands were creating music that was truly original and often experimental. Chief among them was the sublime Premiata Forneria Marconi (generally shortened to PFM). They signed with RCA Records' Italian label, Numero Uno. The New Trolls were another Italian progressive outfit that fused classical with rock music. Their 1971 album *Concerto Grosso per i New Trolls*, a baroque-rock suite produced in collaboration with Luis Bacalov from Argentina, was a wonderful example of symphonic rock and a milestone album for the band, selling close to a million copies in Italy alone.

British outfit Hawkwind helped pioneer space rock, with music and lyrics invoking science fiction (they collaborated for a period with sci-fi author Michael Moorcock). *In Search of Space*, Hawkwind's 1971 album, met with a degree of commercial success. The album originally came with an interlocking die-cut sleeve that unfolded into a hawk-like shape, plus a twenty-four-page booklet about the discovery of a spacecraft titled *The Hawkwind Log*. This was 'head music', probably best experienced under the influence of something.

The Netherlands was also spawning progressive groups including Focus, Earth & Fire, Kayak, Alquin, and – my personal favourite – the witty Supersister. *Present from Nancy* was a truly amazing 1971 debut from this fabulous quartet.

Germany had its own eclectic prog bands, such as Parzival. Their 1971 album *Legend* is full of blind corners and dynamic shifts. Just when you think you've got a hold on a tune, it darts off somewhere altogether new. Many other German acts were leaning towards the avant-garde. In part, the Krautrock music scene was an extension of the classical avant-garde, with the obvious father figure being Karlheinz Stockhausen. This was music generally being developed in homes and recording studios, not on concert stages. Much Krautrock was anarchic and decidedly punk long before punk reared its spiky head, and 1970 to 1975 was its golden era.

Big gigs

In August 1971, some rock superstars gave their time to a cause greater than themselves: the cyclone-ravaged, starving people of blighted, war-torn Bangla Desh (formerly East Pakistan, and today known as Bangladesh). The initiative began with sitar master Ravi Shankar, who had been befriended by ex-Beatle George Harrison. George spent three months on the phone, twisting rock arms and doing deals for a fundraising stage and movie spectacular.

Two performances were mounted and filmed at Madison Square Garden. At the end of the concerts a cheque for US$243,000 was handed to UNICEF from the ticket sales. However, the millions of dollars raised from the film and the album sales were held up in an IRS tax escrow account. The Concert for Bangla Desh was an artistic and humanitarian success, but the actual 'aid' turned into a debacle. It took over a decade for around US$12 million to finally be sent to Bangladesh.

The three-album box set was a huge seller. Performers included Bob Dylan, Leon Russell, Billy Preston, Jim Keltner, Eric Clapton, Klaus Voormann, Ravi Shankar, Ringo Starr and others. This was the first time that Ringo and Harrison had shared a stage since 1966 (not counting the Apple rooftop). Harrison had attempted to get Paul McCartney and John Lennon to join in, but McCartney didn't want to participate in anything that Allen Klein was involved in. The invitation to Lennon was for him alone, not Yoko. This resulted in a ding-dong battle between Lennon and Ono, with John departing New York in a rage two days before the concerts. Dylan's participation was also in flux right up until the day of the concerts. When he finally relented, it marked his first appearance at a major US concert in five years.

While preparing for the big event, Harrison recorded a single, 'Bangla Desh', and rushed it out just four days before the concerts. The disc is viewed as rock's first charity single, becoming a Top 10 hit in the UK and Europe. The B-side for the single was 'Deep Blue', a song about grief and helplessness – a product of Harrison watching his mother succumb to cancer. Ravi Shankar also released a benefit EP of his own, 'Joi Bangla', produced by Harrison.

The original concept for the recording of the Madison Square Garden concerts was to have the live album released within days of the event, ideally to beat the bootleggers, but it didn't hit the shelves until almost five months later. Phil Spector was involved in the recording and mixing, which didn't help, particularly as he was in and out of hospital at the time. Even more problematic was a disagreement between Apple Records' distributor, Capitol Records, and Dylan's label, Columbia Records, about who held the rights to the material. The quibbling over money for a charity fundraiser was ignominious for the music industry and their obscenely wealthy executives. As many critics noted, the record companies were profiteering at the expense of famine victims. The British government also insisted on a purchase tax on the box set, pushing the price sky-high; one politician reportedly told Harrison that England needed the money as much as Bangladesh.

But the concert itself did more for rock music's public image than almost any other event. It demonstrated that some of the biggest names in the business could work together harmoniously as good global citizens. Valuable lessons were learnt that would influence later charity events, such as 1985's Live Aid. Of course, Harrison rightly enjoyed the reflected glory, though Ravi Shankar's seminal and practical roles were rudely overlooked. UNICEF also benefited from the publicity, receiving considerable donations as well as seeing increased numbers of volunteers.

Although Harrison declined an offer to repeat the New York concerts in London, an English version did take place under the banner 'Goodbye to Summer – A Rock Concert in Aid of Famine Relief of Bangla Desh'. Performers included The Who, The Faces, Mott the Hoople, America, Lindisfarne and Quintessence.

Other big rock festivals continued to roll out. The Weeley Festival in Essex was a complete shamble. Poorly organised, it was also marred by heavy-handed bullying by the Hells Angels. As *NME*'s correspondent wrote, 'Brandishing scaffolding poles and any other handy weapons, they set about enforcing their version of order amongst a peaceable majority and took over the press pen, the stage area and the backstage area. One girl was savagely beaten, and her clothes ripped when she rejected their amorous advances.'[50] In the end, a group of angry stallholders and festival staff, plus what organiser Colin King referred to as SAS paratroopers, set upon the Angels, including their motorbikes, ultimately driving them off. The battle left a trail of casualties.

Other countries faced bigger challenges. An enormous festival occurred on the shores of Mexico's Lake Avándaro. In a repressive political climate, during the Mexican Dirty War, rock music was considered subversive and dangerous. Courageous Mexican hippies created La Onda (The Wave), a group of like-minded artists and intellectuals seeking social change. Oddly, the concert was also aiming to promote a car-racing event at the same location, but the race was cancelled when ticket sales exceeded expectations. Organisers had planned for 25,000 attendees but 300,000 turned up. The event was broadcast live on radio, but the band Peace & Love upset authorities by playing their song 'Marihuana' and also imitating Country Joe's 'fuck cheer' from Woodstock. After the festival, President Luis Echeverría cracked down on La Onda and banned any songs commemorating the event. Festival organiser Justino Compean was forced to flee Mexico.

The state of things

1971 would prove a significant turning point in US history. The US dollar was cut loose from gold reserves and allowed to float free: basically, America no longer held enough gold to back its own currency. The year was also the last hurrah of large-scale 1960s activism. At the end of April, the biggest ever demonstration against the Vietnam War occurred in Washington, with an estimated 500,000 citizens rallying. The sheer scale of the event took the nation's breath away.

Activists then attempted to shut down Washington DC by blockading streets. They were met with 12,000 federal troops, 5000 police and 1500 national guardsmen, plus tanks and helicopters. The nation's capital resembled a battle zone. So many people were arrested that emergency detention centres had to be established, including a fenced football stadium. The incarcerated protestors entertained themselves by singing songs – including, inevitably, Lennon's 'Power to the People'. The *Ann Arbor Sun* described the whole event as '5 days of tear gas and music'.[51] In the end, 12,614 people were arrested, making it the largest mass arrest in US history. Of that incredible number of arrests, only seventy-nine people were ultimately convicted, with charges dismissed for twelve and a half thousand people. A subsequent class-action suit ordered the federal government to pay settlement to the many thousands wrongfully arrested.

Johnny Cash and his wife, June Carter Cash, travelled to Vietnam to perform for the soldiers, and the trip had a catalytic impact on Cash's attitude. In the division between 'doves' and 'hawks', Cash subsequently described himself as a 'dove with claws'. Two songs penned by Cash referenced his Vietnam experiences. The first was 'Man in Black', a protest song against the way poor people are treated by wealthy politicians which also referenced the Vietnam War. The more pointed song was 'Singin' in Viet Nam Talkin' Blues', which neatly described Cash's experience in the warzone. Both songs appeared on his 1971 album, *Man in Black*.

When soul singer Freda Payne released her single 'Bring the Boys Home', it spent thirteen weeks on the *Billboard* Hot 100, becoming her second gold record. That said much about how far ordinary Americans had come in their thinking about the Vietnam conflict. Some of that shifting opinion could be sheeted home to the exposure of the Mỹ Lai Massacre, in which more than 500 innocent civilians – women, children and the elderly – were raped, tortured and slaughtered by US troops in a sickening killing spree. Of twenty-six officers and soldiers charged over the massacre, only one, Second Lieutenant William Calley, was found guilty. He was sentenced to life imprisonment, but after he spent just three days in jail, President Nixon ordered him released to house arrest. He ended up paroled in 1974. The Vietnam War Song Project has identified 118 songs that reference Calley and/or the Mỹ Lai Massacre.

In June, *The New York Times* began to publish the Pentagon Papers, revealing the top-secret history of America's involvement in Vietnam.

The revelations laid bare much of the duplicity around the government's role in the conflict.

Some remnant counterculture activists still hoped that disruption itself would lead to some sort of political upheaval and a change for the better. In Britain, a group calling itself The Angry Brigade were bombing embassies, shops and corporate buildings. Bombings were a daily issue for Americans, particularly in big cities such as New York and San Francisco. Over an eighteen-month period between 1971 and 1972, an astounding 2500 bombings occurred on American soil. That amounts to almost five blasts per day.[52] Some historians have argued that this incredibly violent period of US history has been purposefully brushed over.

The FBI were also more than willing to participate in illegitimate activities. They were busy arranging the bombing of offices of the free press and counterculture groups, as well as carrying out mass intimidation of targeted citizens. They also illegally used hundreds of postal workers and switchboard operators to spy on their behalf. So-called 'black-bag jobs', which included illegal break-ins, were becoming rampant. The FBI also financed, armed and directed a civilian vigilante group known as the Secret Army Organisation. This cohort of extreme right-wing citizens fire-bombed cars, burglarised homes and ransacked the workplaces of those who participated in the anti-war movement.

In response to such tactics, a group calling itself the Citizen's Commission to Investigate the FBI invaded a small FBI office, stealing over 1000 classified documents. They mailed these to members of Congress and several newspapers, thus exposing the many ways that FBI operations infringed on the laws of the land as well as the First Amendment rights of civilians. Included in the documents were references to COINTELPRO (Counterintelligence Program), the covert system of illegal wiretaps, and harassment and smear campaigns that had been running for two decades. With the cat out of the proverbial bag, the FBI were seen to be little better than their prey, and the massive COINTELPRO program had to be dissolved by Bureau boss J. Edgar Hoover.

Britain versus Oz

The British economy was faltering. In the second half of 1970, economic growth had been a reasonable 3.3 per cent, but in the first half of 1971 it slumped to 0.3 per cent. By the end of the year, close to a million Britons were unemployed, figures not seen since 1940.[53] Battles raged between unionists and the government. On 28 October, the House of Commons voted in favour of joining the European Common Market, with a decisive 356–244 majority. Entry to the European Union was driven by Tory prime minister Edward Heath, his final words in the debate being that 'many millions of people right across the world will rejoice that we have taken our rightful place in a truly united Europe'. A half-century later, the same political party championed Brexit.

Oz magazine had its start in Australia, where it attracted obscenity charges. In the late 1960s it was transplanted to London, where it quickly became a leading mouthpiece of political dissent and rock music information. The Schoolkids' Issue saw editors Richard Neville, Jim Anderson and Felix Dennis on charges including 'conspiracy to corrupt public morals'. Absurdly, this charge carried an unlimited custodial sentence, making the trial deadly serious. The *Oz* hearings would become Britain's longest-running obscenity trial.

A benefit concert was staged, while artists like David Hockney donated paintings to help pay for legal costs. John Lennon sold his white piano, and also penned a new tune, 'God Save Oz', which soon became a sort of all-purpose protest song, with the words readily changed to 'God save us'. Session singer Bill Elliott performed lead vocals, and the single was released as Bill Elliott and the Elastic Oz Band. On the flip side was a repetitive, raucous dirge of a track titled 'Do the Oz', with Lennon on vocals. It featuring imbecilic lyrics based on the children's ditty 'Hokey Pokey', embellished with Yoko's wailing. The single failed to chart.

In the end, the *Oz* three were found not guilty on the conspiracy charge but guilty of two lesser offences, and were thus sentenced to prison terms.

They were taken from the court to prison, where their hair was forcibly lopped, at the time a hugely symbolic act. For three weeks, the trio were kept incarcerated while they awaited the outcome of a bail application. Fifteen Labour MPs were so appalled at the severity of the sentences that they tabled a motion in the House of Commons, claiming that the English system of justice had been discredited. Many in the media also viewed the whole affair as a national disgrace. John Lennon came out swinging, telling *The Evening Standard* that the authorities should now arrest all of Soho (the city's red-light district). Mick Jagger said, 'If there has been a moral crime committed it is by police and the judge.'[54]

Eventually, the convicts were released on condition that they not commit any more similar offences while on bail. A protest march through London's streets found Lennon and Ono at the front of the column, with Lennon singing 'Power to the People' through a loudhailer. At the appeal trial, the three defendants wore long wigs. Barrister John Mortimer carefully explained how Justice Argyle had misdirected the jury on no less than seventy-eight occasions. The convictions were overturned.

Black writes

Race messaging continued to occupy many musical minds. Arguably, the key song to bubble up from the black rights firmament at this time was Marvin Gaye's 'What's Going On'. Recorded not long after the Kent and Jackson State killings, it wasn't released until early 1971, in part thanks to a squabble between Gaye and Motown's Berry Gordy. As Gordy told *The Wall Street Journal* in 2011:

At first I didn't want Marvin to do it … Up until then, Marvin's career had been based on a positive image, and his fans loved him for it … Motown was about music for all people – white, black, blue and green, cops and robbers. I was reluctant to have our music alienate anyone. This was a big risk for Gaye's image.[55]

In particular, Gordy wanted a line referring to police brutality removed, but Gaye refused to tone the song down. Juxtaposed with a party atmosphere, 'What's Going On' deals with war, picket lines, discrimination against longhairs and the unnecessary deaths of black people. Gaye's partner, Tammi Terrell, had recently died of a brain tumour, and his brother Frankie had just returned from Vietnam, so he was certainly primed to delve into issues somewhat weightier than romance.

'What's Going On' was an instant smash hit, selling over 200,000 copies in a week, and staying at number one for five weeks on the *Billboard* R&B charts, while reaching number two on *Billboard*'s Hot 100. There's no denying the song's power. On the strength of the hit song, Gordy gave Gaye just one month to put together an album. The LP, named for the hit song, stayed on the *Billboard* chart for over a year. At the time of writing this book, Gaye's *What's Going On* LP is ranked by *Rolling Stone* as the greatest album of all time, calling it 'soul music's first concept album, and one of the most important and influential LPs ever made'.[56] Praise doesn't come any higher than that. Whilst speaking on behalf of black America, the various songs on the LP tackle racial injustice, environmental degradation, religion and drug addiction.

Blackness was also being celebrated on the silver screen. *Shaft* was both a hit movie and a key song of 1971. The film starred Richard Roundtree as a black private detective, but largely stereotyped other African-American characters as gangsters and whores. Nevertheless, its box-office success proved there was money to be made in movies for and about black folk, and it thus inspired a whole genre of 'blaxploitation' movies. Isaac Hayes' award-winning score for *Shaft* became Stax Records' fastest and biggest-selling album, raking in over US$3 million in just three weeks. The 'Theme from Shaft' single, released two months later, was also a massive hit. Over scratchy, strummed wah-wah guitar and stabbing brass, the spoken lyrics describe the movie character's sex appeal and coolness. The song won an Academy Award for Best Original Song, with Hayes the first African-American to receive that honour.

Hayes had penned hits for Stax Records artists including Sam & Dave. He had also released big-selling soul albums on which he embellished popular songs into studio extravaganzas. His version of Jimmy Webb's 'By the Time I Get to Phoenix', for example, ran for eighteen minutes, opening with an improvised rap about the power of love, followed by much extemporising on the tune, all of which built to a massive climax. Hayes dragged Webb's decidedly white song 'over to the black market', as he put it.[57] Similarly, his twelve-minute version of George Harrison's 'Something' became a corpulent concoction of funky jazz soloing over lush orchestral arrangements. These lavish reworkings succeeded on both the R&B and jazz charts.

Surprisingly, Hayes couldn't read or write music. He'd hum the parts, or play them on the piano, and arranger Dale Warren would then score them. Pat Lewis was allowed free rein to imagine how the backing voices should sound. The albums were thus genuinely collaborative affairs. What nobody realised at the time was that Isaac Hayes' work would find its way onto discotheque turntables, becoming part of the formula that would ultimately define disco music.

Racial issues also found their way onto an Australian single in 1971. 'Gurindji Blues' was based on a poem written by Ted Egan and sung by Galarrwuy Yunupingu. To a backing of didgeridoo and clap sticks, Yunupingu gave an account of the dispossession of Aboriginal land and the Wave Hill workers' strike, which had begun in 1966. Because the tune included the words 'poor bugger me' it didn't garner radio airplay, but the single sold in the thousands, helping kick-start Ted Egan's long career. This was also the year that the Aboriginal flag, designed by Luritja artist Harold Thomas, was flown for the first time at a land rights rally in Adelaide. It would become an enduring symbol for Australia's First Nations people.

Protesting too much

The protest movement that had galvanised so many in the 1960s was dissipating. Leading light Phil Ochs was now strung out on pills and alcohol, battling depression and suffering from writer's block. Joan Baez attempted to keep the flame alight. Her double album *Blessed Are . . .* was her last on the Vanguard label, selling well and generating a hit single with a version of The Band's 'The Night They Drove Old Dixie Down'. Her first album for A&M Records, *Come From the Shadows*, included her song 'To Bobby', in which Baez castigated her old friend and lover Bob Dylan for having abandoned the protest movement. Then, out of the blue, Dylan released 'George Jackson', about a Black Panther leader who had been killed by guards at San Quentin prison. Although some radio stations refused to spin the single, many Dylan fans welcomed the reclusive artist's apparent rediscovery of his social conscience.

While songs about civil rights were waning, environmental messaging was on the rise. Marvin Gaye's 'Mercy Mercy Me (The Ecology)' rose to number four on the *Billboard* pop chart and number one on the R&B chart. It would become an iconic song not only for Gaye but also for the environmental movement, its litany of woes including bomb testing, oil spills, overpopulation and air pollution. John Prine's 'Paradise', about the impacts of strip mining, was personal for the singer-songwriter: his parents hailed from a town in Kentucky which was destroyed by a coal company.

The Beach Boys' album *Surf's Up* presented a harder edge to their music, opening track 'Don't Go Near the Water' being a case in point: the surf might've been up, but the water was filthy. The album also contained the unusually jagged and bleak 'A Day in the Life of a Tree', a song about environmental pollution written in the first person from the perspective of a tree. Even the cover of *Surf's Up* was a miserable, dark image. Based on the James Earl Fraser sculpture known as 'End of the Trail', it depicted a Native American on a horse, the warrior slumped in despair. In a rare interview, Brian Wilson noted that the band's clean-cut image was doing them more harm than good. John Wetton, bass player with many seminal British prog bands, called *Surf's Up* his favourite 'prog' album of all-time, explaining that the LP 'shifted my parameters, blurring all the boundaries of my musical vocabulary'.[58]

Beatle blues

Lennon invited his old bandmate George Harrison to participate on his new album, including the now notorious track 'How Do You Sleep?' – a vicious attack on Paul McCartney. The lyrics were co-written by John and Yoko, although some reports suggest that Allen Klein also added his two bits.

Oz magazine's Felix Dennis was at the Lennon abode to witness the recording of the track. Ringo Starr happened to be present also, and Dennis watched Ringo get more and more upset: '[A]t one point I have a clear memory of his saying "That's enough, John" … but as usual, Lennon ploughed his furrow and he just didn't give a shit whether people liked it or not.'[59] The line in the song suggesting Paul's sole achievement was the song 'Yesterday' exposed the massive chip on Lennon's shoulder. He was always resentful that The Beatles' most successful tune was created without his involvement, either as composer or performer. McCartney responded to the vicious rebuke with a far more conciliatory song, 'Dear Friend', released on Wings' *Wild Life* album.

Vitriol notwithstanding, the new Lennon album, *Imagine*, provided much easier listening than the *Plastic Ono Band* LP. Indeed, Lennon described it as 'Plastic Ono Band with sugar coating'.[60] There were a couple of protest songs: 'Gimme Some Truth', about hypocrisy and chauvinism in politics, plus 'I Don't Wanna Be a Soldier, Mama', with minimalist lyrics offering little more than the song's title.

As well as some rock 'n' roll numbers, the album featured a couple of songs that would become classics. 'Jealous Guy' had been rejected during The Beatles' *White Album* sessions. Reworked for *Imagine*, the song is a remarkably self-effacing account of Lennon's feelings of inadequacy as a husband and partner, almost cringeworthy in its unmasking. Similarly, 'How?' acknowledges the swathe of uncertainties plaguing the man, most notably his difficulty comprehending love.

But it was the album's title track that became one of the greatest, most enduring songs in popular music. Its utopian idealism has since been co-opted to all manner of causes and purposes, from human rights to anti-globalisation. It remains Amnesty International's official song. Partly a response to Harrison's earlier song 'My Sweet Lord', it was also a clear statement of Lennon's belief, unfiltered and reportedly written in a rush. If ever there was to be a secular hymn, 'Imagine' fits the bill. The song resonates because almost every human at some stage has wished for a less fractious and more humane world, without battles over theology, land and wealth.

John and Paul continued to slug it out in the pages of *Melody Maker*. While Lennon was leaning on drugs, Paul had spent a dark period swigging alcohol. McCartney's next album eschewed use of his famous name and came out simply under his new band, Wings. *Wild Life* was recorded in just eight days at Abbey Road studios, and featured his wife Linda, as well as guitarist Denny Laine, formerly of The Moody Blues, plus drummer Denny Seiwell. Five of the eight tracks were recorded in a single take. In fact, the opening track, 'Mumbo', was simply the band jamming in the studio with McCartney adlibbing nonsense vocals, its inclusion the result of engineer Tony Clark deciding to hit the record button. Critics once again found the album second-rate, and much of it certainly was, particularly the tedious blues 'Bip Bop'. Many also ridiculed McCartney for including his wife in the band, an attitude that was both chauvinistic and unfair.

John Lennon and Yoko Ono were now ensconced in New York. Unlike in London, the couple could wander the streets without being pestered by fans. As Lennon put it, 'I'm just known enough to keep my ego floating, but unknown enough to get around, which is nice.'[61] They were both keen to escape the British media, which had been vitriolic, if not racist, towards Yoko, even calling her ugly.

But their real reason for being in the US was to try to reclaim Yoko's daughter, Kyoko, from former husband Tony Cox. Cox had joined a religious cult, Church of the Living World, and vanished along with Kyoko. Towards the end of the year, Cox surfaced in Houston, where he began legal action to garner equal access rights to their daughter. Eight-year-old Kyoko was still hidden away, and Cox ignored repeated court orders to produce her.

Eventually he was declared in contempt of court and imprisoned for five days. The judge finally ordered that Kyoko be handed over to her mother, but Cox, his new wife and Kyoko simply disappeared again. Yoko Ono would not hear from her daughter until after Lennon's death in 1980.

Briefly filled with revolutionary fervour, Lennon became obsessed with the struggles in Northern Ireland. He wrote a folk song with the ironic title 'The Luck of the Irish'. Unfortunately, the song's lyrics were offensively simplistic. Lennon also aired his new bluesy, stomping song for jailed activist John Sinclair. The poet, leader of the White Panther Party, and former manager of Detroit band MC5, had been jailed for ten years simply for offering an undercover police officer two marijuana joints.

The John Sinclair Freedom Rally, also known as the Ten for Two Rally, was held at the University of Michigan, and Lennon's starring role turned the show into a significant event. As well as John and Yoko, the performers included Phil Ochs, The Up, Bob Seger, Stevie Wonder and Archie Shepp. A telephone call to the Jackson State Prison allowed the audience to hear John Sinclair speaking with his wife. As Lennon told the crowd, 'We came here to say that apathy isn't it, and that we can still do something. So flower power didn't work. So what? We start again.'[62] Three days after the event, the Michigan Supreme Court determined that the state's marijuana statutes were unconstitutional, and Sinclair was released from prison. To many it seemed as though Lennon's rally had precipitated Sinclair's release. Sinclair and his wife travelled to New York to personally thank John and Yoko for their support.

December also saw the release of a new single by John, Yoko, The Plastic Ono Band and The Harlem Community Choir. His seventh post-Beatles release, 'Happy Xmas (War Is Over)', was a continuation of the peace campaign that had included bed-ins and billboards. The single appeared too late to capitalise on the American yuletide, receiving limited airplay and promotion. In England, its release was delayed for a whole year as Lennon's British publishers, Northern Songs, were none too happy about crediting the single as a Lennon and Ono collaboration. Historically, the song has enjoyed staying power, reappearing in the charts many times over, most notably after Lennon's death in 1980, when it reached number two, just behind the reissue of 'Imagine'. And, of course, it would be covered by everyone from The Incredible Penguins to Neil Diamond, Diana Ross, Céline Dion and Miley Cyrus.

1972

All the Young Dudes

Topping the album sales in the UK in 1972 were two K-Tel compilations packaged specifically for telemarketing: *20 Dynamic Hits* and *20 All Time Hits of the 50s*. The *Dynamic* disc featured tracks by Deep Purple, Santana, Sly and the Family Stone plus Blood, Sweat & Tears. The Canadian-based company had pioneered compilation albums in the late 1960s, licensing songs to appear on budget-priced LPs. On one hand, they were treating music as cheap, consumer product, sold not in record shops but in department or even hardware stores. On the other hand, the compilations successfully introduced listeners to artists they may not otherwise have bothered with.

A very different compilation album of 1972 deserves a special mention. Lenny Kaye, who would later become lead guitarist for Patti Smith, was working at the Village Oldies record shop in New York. Kaye wanted to put together a collection of psychedelic and garage rock singles from the '60s, with eight LPs focusing on different regions of the US. Elektra Records was on board but convinced Kaye that one double album would be a more marketable proposition. Thus appeared *Nuggets: Original Artyfacts from the First Psychedelic Era, 1965–1968*. The liner notes on the sleeve included one of the first uses of the term 'punk rock'. The twenty-seven bands represented included The Electric Prunes, The Leaves and The Strangeloves (who pretended to hail from Australia). This somewhat obscure release would become formative for the punk movement.

Bellicose Beatles

Paul McCartney made a flying visit to John Lennon's New York apartment and the pair finally agreed to bury hatchets, at least publicly. However, their relationship was far from amicable. Paul regularly telephoned John, but was usually met with a gruff response; one of them would generally hang up on the other.

The presence of John and Yoko in New York may have breathed some momentary life into the radical activist movement there, but it would prove a temporary fillip. Over four days in January, the pair became co-hosts of the popular *Mike Douglas Show*, which aired on daytime TV. They used the opportunity to introduce their radical friends Jerry Rubin, Bobby Seale and Ralph Nader, as well as a New York bar band named Elephant's Memory, which would become the new Plastic Ono Band. A show highlight occurred when Lennon invited one of his childhood heroes, Chuck Berry, onto the program. With Elephant's Memory plus John and Yoko, Berry went through rough versions of his songs 'Johnny B. Goode' and 'Memphis, Tennessee'.

John and Yoko had arrived in New York on visitor visas, but Republican senator Strom Thurmond recommended deportation proceedings as a 'strategic countermeasure', particularly as 1972 was a presidential election year. The visa case dragged on through the courts, with each hearing affording another temporary postponement of the deportation order. Ono was granted permanent residency, but Lennon's problems ostensibly dated back to his 1968 London conviction for possession of hashish. Despite the tenuous nature of his American residency, Lennon continued to participate in anti-war efforts, including a National Peace Rally in New York, where he led the crowd in a sing-along of 'Give Peace a Chance'. Meanwhile, the FBI were bugging the phones of both Lennon and his legal team. Even John's personal photographer, Bob Gruen, found himself being tailed by FBI heavies. Lennon's outspoken views on Northern Ireland had also resulted in Britain's MI5 sending information to the FBI to bolster its case against the rock star.

Northern Ireland's Bloody Sunday massacre became a significant flashpoint in that conflict, with British soldiers shooting dead thirteen unarmed people in Londonderry. Lennon had already written the ironic 'The Luck of the Irish', but now he and Yoko were moved to compose a new protest song, 'Sunday Bloody Sunday', this time an angry polemic over a very basic rock riff. Both songs would appear on the *Some Time in New York City* album, released midyear. Eventually, John and Yoko would be forced to abandon their support for the IRA following indiscriminate bomb attacks on British civilians.

The release of 'Sunday Bloody Sunday' was held up in publishing wrangles again because of Ono's co-writing credit, so the first songwriter to release a single inspired by the Bloody Sunday events turned out to be Paul McCartney. 'Give Ireland Back to the Irish' was written by Paul and Linda two days after the 30 January massacre and released as a Wings single a few weeks later. It was McCartney's first foray into protest songwriting, but the clunky lyric was hardly uncompromising: while questioning Britain's role in Northern Ireland, the song also praised the UK as 'tremendous'. Inevitably, 'Give Ireland Back to the Irish' was banned by the BBC and other stations, yet it charted reasonably well.

Wings were busy touring Britain in a small van, just like the early days of The Beatles. They performed unannounced concerts at universities and the like – in keeping with Paul's idealised vision for The Beatles' *Get Back/Let It Be* project.

The cover for Lennon's *Some Time in New York City* album was a parody of *The New York Times*. The front included images of Nixon's and Mao's heads pasted onto the bodies of nude dancers. This was widely censored across the US. A postcard was included with the original release showing the Statue of Liberty wearing a Black Power glove. There was also a mailable petition requesting that 'the Lennons' not be expelled from the US. As for the music, the double LP was a collection of Lennon's most obdurate sermons on topics that included jailed activists John Sinclair and Angela Davis (both of whom had been exonerated and freed from jail by the time of the album's release), the Attica Correctional Facility, male chauvinism and colonialism. These were augmented by live performances from a 1969 UNICEF charity concert with George Harrison in London, and the 1971 Fillmore East jam with Frank Zappa and the Mothers of Invention. For the studio material, Lennon and Ono were supported by Elephant's Memory, held in place by Jim Keltner's drums.

The album release was preceded by a single, 'Woman Is the Nigger of the World'. The disc became Lennon's lowest-charting single of all time. It was damned for its use of the pejorative term 'nigger', and for conflating women's issues with black rights, yet it did win plaudits from the National Organization for Women. The song was performed live on *The Dick Cavett Show*, with Cavett instructed by his network to apologise in advance for the song's content. Cavett did so begrudgingly, later explaining that the only objections received were 600 in response to the scripted introduction. There were no complaints regarding the song itself.

Lennon would argue that 'Woman Is the Nigger of the World' was the world's first women's liberation song – but, of course, Helen Reddy's 'I Am Woman' had already been recorded and released; it just hadn't become a hit. Musically, the propulsive 'Woman Is the Nigger of the World' is one of the better tracks on *Some Time in New York City*. Lennon's voice is in top form and there's a nice, lyrical sax solo by Stan Bronstein. At this time, Lennon and Ono were busy filming their every activity, with plans for movies and documentaries tumbling over one another. This massive self-absorption also produced another diary song in the style of 'The Ballad of John and Yoko'. Titled 'New York City', it played as an old-fashioned rock 'n' roll number bursting with descriptions of their new life in the Big Apple.

Some Time in New York City was not well received on its release. Stephen Holden in *Rolling Stone* described the album as 'artistic suicide', adding: 'The tunes are shallow and derivative and the words little more than sloppy nursery-rhymes that patronise the issues and individuals they seek to exalt. Only monumental smugness could allow the Lennons to think that this witless doggerel wouldn't insult the intelligence and feelings of any audience.'[1] Robert Christgau said the songs 'attack issues so simplistically that you wonder whether the artists believe themselves ... Agitprop is one thing. Wrong-headed agitprop is another ... While striving to enlighten, they condescend.'[2]

With an eye on the immigration department, Lennon began to curtail his activist pursuits, but he and Yoko continued to provide covert financial support for various causes. Midyear, the pair instigated a concert in New York for a non-controversial cause: intellectually challenged kids. Called the One to One Festival, organiser Geraldo Rivera wanted to bring handicapped kids out of institutions and into a public space where people could relate to them on a one-to-one basis. Lennon and Allen Klein – the latter participating under sufferance – purchased US$50,000 of tickets and gave them away to intellectually challenged kids and volunteers. Leading up to the event, John went into a panic about performing live. According to Rivera, he and Yoko rang Paul and Linda McCartney asking them to join the concert, but the McCartneys declined. In the end, John and Yoko performed with the backing of Elephant's Memory. Lennon had promised the band that it would be the start of a national tour, but the tour never eventuated.

Just before the charity event, Allen Klein had told Lennon that he was the one audiences wanted to see, not his wife. This home truth didn't go down well, particularly with Yoko. In the end, however, the performance was largely John with band. Yoko did get to perform her song 'Sister O Sister', and she appeared to be playing keyboards on other songs. John performed 'Instant Karma', 'It's So Hard', 'Cold Turkey', 'Imagine', 'Come Together', 'Hound Dog' and even 'Mother', which he introduced by quipping that it was 'from one of those albums I made since I left The Rolling Stones'.[3] Lennon was preceded on stage by Sha Na Na, Stevie Wonder and Roberta Flack, who all reassembled for the finale of 'Give Peace a Chance'. Just a week later, John and Yoko were back on stage for a charity telethon to raise money for the disabled. It would be the last time John and Yoko would appear on stage together.

Lennon had been stung by the responses of critics to his live performances, as well as by their reactions to *Some Time in New York City*, and he slid into depression. His marriage was increasingly rocky, and he was tussling with his drug habits. Yoko's shift from conceptual artist, filmmaker and avant-garde screamer to thoughtful songwriter and straight-ahead musical performer was also putting strain on the relationship. Inspired by her newfound capabilities, Yoko was churning out songs at breakneck speed, while John was sinking into writer's block.

Towards the end of the year, John produced Yoko's double album, *Approximately Infinite Universe*, but he had no new material of his own. He was moving away from politics and from Yoko, and even inching away from music. Another problem was his growing dissatisfaction with the man he had once championed to Paul McCartney: Allen Klein. A *New York* magazine article exposed that The Beatles' manager had been secretly diverting money from the sale of *Concert for Bangla Desh* albums into his own ABKCO business, rather than providing it to the Bangladesh relief effort. Lennon's opinion of Klein was now little better than McCartney's.

Festivals in the line of fire

The British government introduced its proposed Night Assemblies Bill, which aimed to control outdoor rock festivals. Interviewed in Hollywood, Mick Jagger referred to the bill as 'disgusting', before offering his naive approach to politics in general: 'My slogan is: "Good Government Is No Government". England doesn't need a government because it can govern itself.'[4]

A British free festival was attempted at Windsor Great Park, just below Windsor Castle. Promoting it as 'Rent Strike: The People's Free Festival', the organisers hadn't bothered to seek permission to use the Crown land, so a banning order attempted to stymie the event. In the end, just 700 people turned up to discover they were outnumbered by police. The coppers were unnecessarily brutal in shutting down the festival, leading to a public outcry.

Over in the US, the wonderfully titled Erie Canal Soda Pop Festival anticipated attendees around the 55,000 mark but, in a now familiar story, ended up with some 300,000 and roads blocked for thirty kilometres.

Many advertised acts – including Black Sabbath, The Allman Brothers, Joe Cocker, Fleetwood Mac, The Doors, Slade and John Mayall – failed to reach the festival site. Those who did make it onto the stage included Black Oak Arkansas, Albert King, Santana, Canned Heat, Ravi Shankar, The Eagles and that most eccentric of British prog bands, Gentle Giant. Over three days, the festival devolved into chaos, with insufficient food and water, not to mention torrential rainfall. Angry at the prices charged by food vendors, festival-goers took revenge by upturning their vans and robbing them. Some hungry punters killed a local cow but had no means of butchering the hapless animal. Three revellers drowned in the local river, and the concert closed when the remaining punters set fire to the stage. The promoters found themselves facing a bevy of legal actions.

But it remained far more dangerous to attempt to stage rock festivals in other countries. The Festivali i Këngës 11 in Albania, organised by Albanian Public Radio and Television, found itself on the wrong side of Albanian dictator Enver Hoxha. He declared the organisers to be enemies of the state, accused them of plotting against the government and had most of them murdered.

The Mar Y Sol Pop Festival in Puerto Rico boasted a diverse line-up including The Allman Brothers Band, The Dave Brubeck Quartet, Alice Cooper, Mahavishnu Orchestra, Herbie Mann, Osibisa, Dr John, B.B. King, Faces with Rod Stewart, and Emerson, Lake & Palmer. But it was newcomer Billy Joel who won the audience over, at the same time garnering the attention of Columbia Records' Clive Davis. Several accidental deaths occurred at the festival, as well as one murder. An arrest warrant was issued for the promoter, who fled before the festival had concluded.

Thickening

Australia's second-bestselling album of 1972 was Jethro Tull's *Thick as a Brick*. There were no individual songs on the LP, just one track that spanned both sides of the disc. *Thick as a Brick* spent eleven weeks at number one in Australia, as well as going to the top spot in America, Canada and Holland.

The original gatefold cover opened into a twelve-page tabloid – parodying a small-town English newspaper. Tull's music had morphed into a no-holds-barred prog rock extravaganza, although front man and songwriter Ian Anderson claimed the LP was actually a satire on both prog rock and concept albums. Record buyers may not have picked up on the humour, but attendees at Tull concerts were often witness to the band's cynicism, such as when drum solos devolved into all band members belting tiny cymbals. The show frequently began with men in coats sweeping the stage and inspecting the building, until some of them picked up instruments to reveal themselves as band members. Sometimes the whole band would stop mid-performance to read news reports or answer a telephone. At other times, a man in scuba gear would wander onto the stage for no apparent purpose. This was Theatre of the Absurd meets rock.

The album's conceptual story, such as it was, concerned a young boy named Gerald Bostock. Anderson claimed he was inspired by his own 1950s' childhood 'in that era of post-war Biggles hero mentality': 'Not the passage of a boy to man, it was the passage of child to adolescent. The album was about all the misconceptions that came out of the way we, as children, get brainwashed.'[5] I doubt many listeners were able to glean any of that.

Much of *Thick as a Brick* was composed in the recording studio. The addition of harpsichord, classical percussion instruments, saxophone and strings were a big leap from Tull's previous albums. Critics struggled with it. Some, like *New Musical Express*, doubted that the album had any chance of success. Running with the popular tide for a change, *Rolling Stone* heaped praise, calling it 'one of rock's most sophisticated and ground-breaking products'.[6] It says much about this golden era of rock and its adventurous listeners that an album as polymorphic and challenging as *Thick as a Brick* could be so successful.

As well as Tull, Australia was also knee-deep in Cat Stevens, with *Teaser and the Firecat* the number one album for the year, *Tea for the Tillerman* at eight and *Catch Bull at Four* at twelve. Born Steven Demetre Georgiou, he chose the name Cat because a girlfriend suggested he had feline eyes. In just two more years, Cat Stevens would receive a plaque representing forty gold records sold in Australia. American critic Robert Christgau found Cat Stevens decidedly offensive, writing that 'he is without doubt the most mindless of the major singer-songwriters, even running slightly ahead of John Denver, and all the time he's spouting his romantic and generational clichés he's also playing the guru'.[7]

Stevens' one-time girlfriend, Carly Simon, also released an album that went number one in Australia as well as in her homeland. *No Secrets* included her top-charting single 'You're So Vain'. An acerbic attack on a self-absorbed male, it has kept tongues wagging for decades. In 2003, the president of NBC Sports won an auction, paying $50,000 for the privilege of having Simon tell him who the song was about, on the condition that he keep the answer to himself. Simon has hinted that there may have been three arrogant males on her mind, one of which she confirmed to be Warren Beatty. Other frontrunners include Mick Jagger, David Geffen, Jack Nicholson, Cat Stevens, Kris Kristofferson and David Bowie. The intrigue has certainly helped the song to live well beyond its shelf-life, but some bemoaned its overblown pretentiousness, such as the rhyming of yacht, apricot and gavotte (an archaic French dance). Pompous or not, it was an important statement of female assertiveness. 'You're So Vain' was also a necessary exposé of the increasingly unbridled self-adoration of many male celebrities.

Other singer-songwriters were also making good internationally. Loudon Wainwright III enjoyed a surprise hit with his flippant 'Dead Skunk (in the Middle of the Road)'. Written in fifteen minutes after an actual experience with the subject matter, it appeared on his *Album III*, which curiously charted best in Australia. Dylan was the yardstick by which many male singer-songwriters were still being judged, with Wainwright, David Bromberg, John Prine, Bruce Springsteen, Steve Goodman, Steve Forbert and even Leonard Cohen variously being hailed as 'the new Bob Dylan'.

Absurdly, Dylan complained that Neil Young's hit 'Heart of Gold' was too imitative of his own style. Young's album *Harvest* topped the charts across the globe, as well as generating a second hit single, 'Old Man'. Eventually, it was bumped from the charts by the band America's irritatingly inane 'Horse With No Name' – which Neil Young viewed as plagiarising his style! (Young's father did congratulate his boy after hearing 'Horse With No Name' on the radio, assuming it was his son's doing.) For my money, 'Horse With No Name' takes the cake for imbecilic song lyrics.

Neil Young's *Harvest* also included a live version of his cautionary tale 'The Needle and the Damage Done', about heroin addiction. His friend Danny Whitten would be booted off Young's tour, only to die the very next day of drug and alcohol poisoning. For years afterwards, Young blamed himself for Whitton's death.

Jackson Browne was also enjoying some success writing songs for others, notably 'Take It Easy', which he had co-written with Glenn Frey, and which became a hit for Frey's new band The Eagles. The Eagles' eponymous debut LP also offered up a couple more charting singles, 'Witchy Woman' and 'Peaceful Easy Feeling'. Robert Christgau complained that the album was evidence of the new trend in America towards hedonistic individualism, full of songs about the 'new alternative man who goes it alone'.[8]

Since breaking up his famous duo in 1970, Paul Simon had done some teaching of songwriting craft at New York University, but there had been no recordings since 1970's runaway hit *Bridge Over Troubled Water*, which remained the bestselling album of all time. Simon finally released his solo LP, simply titled *Paul Simon*. He was never a prolific songwriter, but as he told *Rolling Stone*: 'Having a track record to live up to and the history of successes had become a hindrance. It becomes harder to break out of what people expect you to do.'[9] The title of the opening track, 'Mother and Child Reunion', came from a chicken and egg dish on a restaurant menu. With its ska beat, it immediately reinforced Simon's interest in world music. The song was recorded in Jamaica with Jimmy Cliff's backing group. Released as a single, it went to single digits. Although superficially upbeat, it's actually a song about bereavement and grief.

The world music influence was also evident on the narrative ballad 'Duncan', performed by Simon with Paris-based Andean folk group Los Incas. Elsewhere, the album incorporated elements of blues and jazz, with the likes of Stéphane Grappelli, Airto Moreira and Ron Carter included in the stellar list of accompanists. Indeed, 'Hobo's Blues' is a simple duet between Simon on strummed guitar and Grappelli doing his thing, almost a homage to the violin virtuoso's dalliances with Django Reinhardt. A second single, 'Me and Julio Down by the Schoolyard', was not very successful at the time but has proven to have staying power. The confusing narrative this time concerns a couple of young people who have broken the law for some unspecified crime, what Simon imagined as being 'something sexual'.[10] Many years later, Simon called the lyrics 'inscrutable doggerel'.[11]

Critics were generally kind to Paul Simon, but many demanded some new form of magic. His live performing was largely limited to support concerts for presidential hopeful George McGovern, including a reunion with Art Garfunkel. Columbia Records, capitalising on the brief get-together, issued *Simon & Garfunkel's Greatest Hits*, which again sold a bucketload.

According to Paul Simon at the time, the most 'flagrant' bootlegging wasn't of unreleased material or live concerts, but rather people copying legitimate LPs onto tape.[12] The sound quality of tape had improved markedly, and the Advent Corporation introduced their tape deck, which incorporated Dolby type B noise reduction and chromium dioxide tape performance. Stereo cassette tape decks could be added to home sound systems everywhere. The music industry had yet to get its collective head around the financial impacts.

Out of exile

The Rolling Stones' double album *Exile on Main Street* had mostly been recorded in the hot, cramped basement of Keith Richards' villa in southern France, before final touches were added at LA's Sunset Sound Studios. The album is dominated by Richards, the reason being, as he said, 'It was just a matter of who was available to record … I was there all the time and I just kept on blowing.'[13]

True to form, the new Stones LP was obsessed with sex and hedonism. The opening track, bearing the unsubtle title 'Rocks Off', was about the frustrations of not being able to achieve orgasm. Singles lifted from the disc included 'Happy', with Richards taking the lead vocal task, 'Sweet Virginia', a country music ballad, and 'Tumbling Dice', which was yet another of Jagger's braggadocio songs sung in the first person, this time about a gambler who must have sex with anything that moves.

Mind you, the lyrics were barely audible. The whole affair suffered from poor recording and muddy mixing. (More recent remastered versions of the album enjoyed much brighter, cleaner mixes.) The prosaically titled 'Turd on the Run' perpetuates the Jagger/Richards misogynistic trajectory, about a jilted man who fantasises about trussing up the female protagonist and making her scream until she wishes she wasn't alive. As Robert Christgau put it in *Newsday*, 'almost as soon as Jagger and Richards began to compose, they created a persona whose hostility to women rose above and beyond the call of realism'.[14]

'Sweet Black Angel' was, like Lennon & Ono's 'Angela', Jagger's nod to jailed activist Angela Davis. Her name is never mentioned in the awful lyrics, and the casual listener may not have realised who the song was about. An acoustic ballad with a Caribbean rhythm, written while the band were in Jamaica, the outcome is so bad that some Stones fans have attempted to excuse it as a parody. The reference to 'ten little niggers' again shows how tin-eared Jagger was to race sensitivities.

Mick Jagger has said that '*Exile on Main Street* is not one of my favourite albums ... when I listen to *Exile* it has some of the worst mixes I've ever heard ... *Exile* is really a mixture of bits and pieces left over from the previous album ... everyone loves it, but I don't really know why.'[15] Proving his point, *Rolling Stone* magazine currently ranks it at fourteen in its 500 Greatest Albums of All Time, calling it a 'dirty whirl of basement blues and punk boogie'.[16]

Allen Klein sued the band because he believed that five of the songs on *Exile* were composed while Jagger and Richards were still under contract to his company ABKCO. Klein ended up getting a share of the record royalties, and by the end of the year he had released another Rolling Stones compilation album. It was lumbered with the appalling title *More Hot*

Rocks (Big Hits & Fazed Cookies), and was a sequel to the previous year's compilation *Hot Rocks 1964–1971*. Earlier in 1972, Decca had also put out yet another compilation Stones LP, *Milestones*, and towards the end of the year released the *Rock 'n' Rolling Stones* compilation. That's three compilations in one year, all assembled and released without the band's consent.

With *Exile* finally in the shops, the band embarked on their first American tour since 1969's Altamont debacle, playing fifty-one shows to more than 750,000 people. Jagger banned VIPs from the first twenty rows, thus ensuring those seats were filled with fans. He strutted the stage in a sequined white jumpsuit split open to his groin, where a rolled-up sock exaggerated the size of his appendage. Truman Capote travelled with the band, intending to write an article for *Rolling Stone* magazine, but the final product never eventuated. Capote alleged that the tour doctor raped a high school student on the band's jet. A movie of the tour by filmmaker Robert Frank was never formally released, as the band were horrified at what was revealed in the footage. Excerpts and bootleg copies did, inevitably, leak out, which reportedly show Mick and Keith off their faces, Keith injecting heroin, Jagger snorting cocaine through a $100 bill, and orgies on the tour aircraft.

In Vancouver, more than thirty fans had to be hospitalised after clashing with the Royal Canadian Mounted Police. In Montreal, a bomb blew up in the Stones' equipment van, after which it was discovered that thousands of counterfeit tickets had been sold, resulting in another riot. In San Diego, police barricades were set alight ahead of a battle that saw sixty punters thrown in jail and fifteen injured. In Houston, eighty-one were arrested; in Washington DC, sixty-five were arrested. Both were eclipsed by Tucson, where police managed to arrest more than 300. In Rhode Island, the only people arrested were Jagger and Richards, for attacking a photographer. The mayor arranged for them to be released in time for their evening concert, to avoid yet another riot by fans. The injured photographer later sued.

While they were in Chicago for three appearances, the band stayed as a guest of Hugh Hefner in his Playboy Mansion, with 'bunnies' on tap.

Of course, Jagger was married to Bianca, with whom he had a child, but he had also just had an affair with another doppelganger, Carly Simon, and he wasn't above dallying with groupies and others on tour. Former squeeze Marianne Faithfull would later characterise Jagger as 'a woman-hater and very bisexual'.[17] He was also paranoid, reportedly packing a pistol in his jacket pocket as well as having two bodyguards.

Stevie Wonder was the support act for the Stones' tour. He had just released his pioneering album *Music of My Mind*, his fourteenth studio disc, but the first on which he had full artistic control. After turning twenty-one, Wonder had demanded the royalties that had been held in trust by Motown's Berry Gordy, and spent some $250,000 making *Music of My Mind*. On the disc he was supported by electronic music pioneers Malcolm Cecil and Robert Margouleff, of Tonto's Expanding Head Band. *Music of My Mind* reintroduced Wonder to a white audience, as did the tour supporting the Stones. The year also saw Wonder's massive hit 'Superstition' released, from his other 1972 album, *Talking Book*. This was his first American number one since 1963. With a theme very relevant to the credulous 1970s (and, perhaps, today), 'Superstition' warns of falling prey to superstitious beliefs.

Like Stevie Wonder, Elton John was able to compose new songs at a cracking pace. Elton described the process in his autobiography:

> Bernie would bash out his lyrics and leave them for me on the piano. I'd wake up early, go to the dining room, see what he'd come up with and write songs while I was having breakfast. The first morning … I had three done by the time the band drifted downstairs looking for something to eat.[18]

Honky Chateaux became the first of his LPs to go to number one in America, performing almost as well across the world, supported by hit singles 'Rocket Man' and 'Honky Cat'.

Dressed to thrill

Elton John was still performing in outrageous costumes, and rock music was becoming increasingly fixated on theatrical presentation. Of course, this didn't sit well with everyone. In *The New York Times*, Grace Lichtenstein wrote that 'freakishness is too often a substitute for strong musical ideas. Give the boys and girls a circus, the thinking seems to be, and they'll forget you're laying down the same tired old chords.'[19]

Peter Gabriel of Genesis went even further than Elton John with his get-ups. The somewhat naive, surrealist painting on the cover of the band's *Foxtrot* album featured a female figure in a red dress with a fox's head. It was the third Genesis cover by artist Paul Whitehead, although none of the band members was happy with the result. Nevertheless, Gabriel picked up on the motif and began wearing a red dress and fox headpiece on their subsequent tour, generating significant media attention, including a *Melody Maker* front cover.

The rest of the band had no idea about the stunt until Gabriel walked onstage for the first show. For the rest of the tour, he worked his way through an array of outlandish costumes, and by the end had affected a quasi-ancient-Egyptian look, with theatrical eye make-up and an inverted Mohican hairstyle. Where David Bowie adopted singular character creations, Gabriel would go through multiple outlandish outfits in a single show. As bassist Mike Rutherford noted, 'We had no idea of what Pete was going to do in advance – he knew if he'd run it by us we would have stopped him. After that, it was almost as though we all agreed to ignore Pete's stage look.'[20] Drummer Phil Collins would later say, 'I always felt a bit frustrated that the music wasn't, I felt, being listened to. It was being watched.'[21]

Without a trace of irony, David Bowie criticised Alice Cooper, opining: 'I think he's trying to be outrageous … I find him very demeaning. It's very premeditated, but quite fitting with our era.'[22] Meanwhile, a music writer described a 1972 Bowie performance as follows: 'Dedicated to bringing theatrics back to rock music, David Bowie swirled and captivated … queening his way through old and new songs.'[23]

Speaking of 'queening', Bowie famously told *Melody Maker* in 1972 that he had always been gay. Such assertions appear to have been part of a calculated aim to maximise attention, much like his dress-wearing in 1971. At the time he was married to, and had a child with, Angela Barnett. Not that that meant he couldn't be gay or bisexual, except that he later recanted the assertion, telling *Rolling Stone*: 'The biggest mistake I ever made was telling that *Melody Maker* writer that I was bisexual.'[24]. As *Melody Maker*'s Michael Watts put it, 'he likes to put us on a little'.[25] Indeed, putting people on was exactly what David Bowie was best at. While he may have helped make non-heterosexuality acceptable in 1972, it could also be argued that Bowie was exploiting gay culture for the sole purpose of self-promotion.

Bowie's album *The Rise and Fall of Ziggy Stardust and the Spiders from Mars* was a continuation of the material written for *Hunky Dory*. This time it was collated into a rough concept album built around a tale of an androgynous, bisexual rock artist who arrives on Earth. Reviews were generally favourable, and Bowie set off on his iconic Ziggy Stardust tour. Now, I must confess that I was never enamoured of Bowie's music, nor of his manufactured personas – sorry, Bowie fans. In researching this book, I even read Will Brooker's nauseatingly sycophantic *Why Bowie Matters*, but I remain largely unmoved.

The lead single from the *Ziggy* album was 'Starman'. With a chorus melody that somewhat echoes that old chestnut 'Over the Rainbow', it became Bowie's first big hit since 1969's 'Space Oddity'. But it was a performance on *Top of the Pops* that caused ripples through British culture, with the singer dressed in a rainbow jumpsuit, sporting red hair and white fingernail polish. The rest of the band were also dressed outlandishly, but it was Bowie draping his arm over guitarist Mick Ronson that really stiffened the upper lips of many British parents. That seminal moment of British TV supposedly influenced many wannabe musicians who would later become household names, including Boy George, Adam Ant, Morrissey, Siouxsie Sioux and even Noel Gallagher. As then fifteen-year-old Gary Numan put it, 'I think it stands as one of the pivotal moments of modern music, or, if not music, certainly a pivotal moment in show business ... To say it stood out is an epic understatement.'[26]

At this time, there was a curiously reverential alliance between Bowie, Iggy Pop and Lou Reed. Reed's album *Transformer*, produced by Bowie and Mick Ronson, included an early paean to gay liberation titled 'Make Up'. Mind you, Reed had long been attracted to subcultures, and the drag element of the gay scene excited him just as prostitutes titillated his imagination. The single 'Walk on the Wild Side' quickly became an international scandal as well as a hit. The lyrics described a series of characters, some transgender, all heading to New York to become part of Warhol's coterie of instant superstars. This was as risqué in 1972 as had been The Kinks' 'Lola' two years previously. RCA even released a less raunchy version of 'Walk on the Wild Side', removing the references to 'coloured' girls and oral sex. Where Bowie could sing in tune, the same can't be said of Lou Reed.

At the same time, Bowie was nurturing Mott the Hoople, writing and producing their breakthrough hit single 'All the Young Dudes'. This glam anthem peaked at number three in the UK, and became the title of their 1972 LP, again produced by Bowie. The lyric described the disaffected youth of the era: the next iteration after the 1960s generation. Like The Who's 1964 hit 'My Generation', the young dudes in Mott the Hoople's song also wanted to die before they turned twenty-five years old.

While Bowie was camping it up in Britain, the New York Dolls were confounding US audiences with sexual ambiguity draped over garage music. For a time, they had a residency at New York's Mercer Arts Centre. As Roy Hollingworth gushed, 'They might just be the best rock 'n' roll band in the world'. He went on to describe them as a band with no manager, no record company, no publicity unit and precious little equipment, and decided they embodied 'the rebellion needed to crush the languid cloud of nothingness that rolls out from the rock establishment and falls like drizzle on the ears'.[27] Before it had been named, Hollingworth was being wooed by the essence of punk.

The New York Dolls (all males) dressed both offstage and onstage in all manner of gender-bending outfits that incorporated fishnet stockings, gold lamé, leopard-print tights, polka-dot dresses, feather boas, spandex, teased bouffant wigs, plus lurid and badly applied make-up. Academic Van M. Cagle perhaps described their music most accurately: 'The band's inspired rush of musical energy, its technical amateurism, and its lacklustre attitude toward contrived rock formats operated in a coherent manner to demarcate the band as one that was reconstructing rock primitivism for a new decade of listeners.'[28]

The Dolls flew to London to open for the Faces. After the gig, Dolls drummer Billy Murcia passed out from a drug overdose. He was put in a bath and force-fed coffee, which resulted in asphyxiation. Adhering to the aforementioned demands of 'All the Young Dudes', he was dead at twenty-one. The incident only enhancing the band's notoriety, aiding their edgy image. Back in New York with a new drummer, the Dolls signed to Mercury Records and took on a manager while they continued to challenge cultural and musical sensibilities.

In the previous decade, appearances mattered, but they didn't dominate the music. Janis Joplin was no beauty queen. Bands like The Turtles and Canned Heat were far from handsome. Hendrix may have enjoyed dressing up in military jackets and feather boas, and Jagger may have worn a dress at 1969's Stones in the Park concert, but they were still predominantly focused on the music. The accoutrements were an addendum (and Jagger shed the dress once the initial impact had been achieved). By 1972, however, there was a distinct shift in musical journalism, with a greater focus on appearances: '[C]an anything dim the splendour of this ravishing creature?' asked Michael Watts while discussing Bowie.[29]

In part, glam's appeal paralleled a growing acceptance not only of theatrics in rock, but of gay camp. In this era before the AIDS epidemic, when sexual liberation was integral to youth culture, the exploration of diverse sexual practices was genuinely liberating. Glitter/glam was moving queerness from subtext to text, celebrating sexual diversity and making that diversity palatable.

But glam wasn't just about putting on a good show while appropriating gay fashion – it was also a hyped-up form of narcissism. As Bowie admitted,

'I'm not a musician. I'm not into music, you see, on that level. I don't profess to have music as my big wheel and there are a number of other things as important to me apart from music. Theatre and mime for instance.'[30] Glam was all 'notice me, notice me, notice me'. What the artists were wearing and doing mattered just as much as the music they were creating. This new emphasis on style over substance was symptomatic of a broader cultural shift towards self-centredness.

Prognosticating

Roxy Music was also unafraid to camp it up. They borrowed from 1950s, '60s and '70s music, as well as from each era's couture, sporting a mishmash of suits, sequins, ties, leather, leopardskin and eye make-up. The band introduced art school student Brian Peter George St John le Baptiste de la Salle Eno to the world. Eno's influence on the development of 1970s rock would be very significant. At this stage, as a self-declared non-musician (in fact he could play basic guitar), he was already signalling that the manipulation of sound and texture could have equivalent value to traditional musicianship.

Initially, Eno wasn't on stage at all, but stationed at the mixing desk, where he treated the sounds from the instruments. But he soon migrated to the stage, wearing outrageous costumes à la Elton John, and, like a mad professor, twiddling nobs. He also made great copy for journalists, ever happy to expound on musical theories and his approach to life. Inevitably, Eno was also somewhat threatening for those rock musicians whose self-concept was very much rooted in their technical mastery of instruments. During the apogee of prog and fusion, when technique was the pinnacle of rock accomplishment, Eno was a sort of Prince of Darkness.

Being glam-ish, Roxy Music's appeal included many younger listeners, especially females. The band's appearance on *Top of the Pops* performing 'Virginia Plain' – dull as that song was – nevertheless became a lightning rod for the glam movement, and, thanks to Eno, an important introduction of electronic music to mainstream audiences. But not everyone was impressed with these latest rock heroes, with critic and filmmaker Tony Palmer writing, 'Like all glam bands, Roxy Music are more interested in getting their names in the social register and trying on different kinds of clothes than doing anything about real rock and roll. In Roxy Music, you see the triumph of artifice.'[31]

Eno may have been challenging technical virtuosity, but prog was still championing the cause. In Italy, the country's most successful prog band, PFM, released their first album *Storia di un Minuto*. Full of scintillating compositions, it became the first ever Italian rock album to top the country's charts in the first week of release. Later in the year, they released their second LP, *Per un Amico*, which was even better than the first, in part because they had access to sixteen-track production. But the music on both of these discs is exhilarating, and the second LP brought them attention right across Europe.

The first discussions around what would become Pink Floyd's *Dark Side of the Moon* occurred around drummer Nick Mason's kitchen table. Roger Waters had an idea for an album as well as having some songs in development, including one with an unusual 7/8 time signature. As the band talked, the issue of stress became a thematic thread. Within just a few weeks, 'Dark Side of the Moon, a Piece for Assorted Lunatics' was performed at London's Rainbow Theatre over four sellout nights. Studio recording of the work happened sporadically over the rest of the year, but the album wouldn't surface until March 1973.

Yes followed up their hugely successful *Fragile* album with *Close to the Edge*. It would be the band's biggest commercial success, going to single digits in the UK and US and garnering extremely favourable reviews. There were just three tracks, each dense with ideas. Once recording was complete, however, drummer Bill Bruford said no to Yes and went off to join the more challenging King Crimson. For the Yes world tour, Alan White took over the drum stool. Working from tapes to learn the material, he had just one full day's rehearsal with the band before hitting the stage. The massive tour lasted from July 1972 to April 1973.

Speaking of excellent drummers, Soft Machine's Robert Wyatt had been booted out of the very band he had established, resulting in a good deal of personal trauma for the sensitive musician. At one low point he even attempted suicide, slashing his wrists in a bath. Despite his personal difficulties, and thanks to his unique drumming style, offers of work did appear, finding him playing with pianist Paul Bley, and at the Berlin Jazz Festival. But Wyatt's inclinations were towards quirky songs and tonal experimentation rather than jazz improvisation, so he established a very different group and named them Matching Mole – a play on the French for Soft Machine, *machine molle*.

The eponymous debut LP by Matching Mole is a disarming blend of prog rock, twisted pop and avant-garde improvising. The opening track, 'O Caroline', sung in Wyatt's highly distinctive, quavering voice, is a corker. It allowed him to delve deeper into the idiosyncratic and deeply personal songwriting that he had pioneered while in Soft Machine. As co-composer Dave Sinclair said, '[I]t was so honest as well, because it was coming from inside him. It was pouring out.'[32] Humble sincerity would be a hallmark of Wyatt's body of work. Elsewhere on the *Matching Mole* album, Wyatt uses his idiosyncratic voice as an additional instrument, as on 'Instant Pussy', while 'Signed Curtain' is a witty deconstruction of a pop song, with lyrics about the business of songwriting. The rest of the album is jazz-inflected avant-garde rock, with plenty of improvising. Crimson's Robert Fripp was in the producer's chair.

Later in the year, an even better Matching Mole album appeared, this time titled *Little Red Record*, the title a reference to Mao's *Little Red Book*. It features an amusing cover image of band members painted in the style of a Cultural Revolution propaganda poster. Brian Eno guests, and actress Julie Christie (listed as Ruby Crystal) helps out with vocals. Of particular note are the Wyatt vocal tracks. 'Gloria Gloom' begins as a sombre Tangerine Dream–ish soundscape, evolving into a mass of voice snippets and then becoming another of Wyatt's wonderful self-effacing songs in which he ponders whether he wouldn't be better off fighting for socialism than playing in a rock band. It all devolves into a description of a nightmare. Next is the exceptional 'God Song', with Wyatt speaking directly to God about his many frustrations apropos organised religion.

These songs may sound portentous or even indulgent, but in Wyatt's expert hands they come across as quirky and charming. Again, much of the rest of the album is improvised avant-garde rock, with Wyatt's exceptional drumming a feature.

Two albums emanated from the fertile minds of Gentle Giant this year. *Three Friends* is a concept album, about three schoolfriends who take different life paths. Their first self-produced LP, it was also their first to chart in America. Having got their somewhat operatic inclinations out of their system, the next album, *Octopus*, marks a high-water mark for this extraordinary band. The title is a pun, based on '*octo opus*', meaning eight musical works. No two tracks on *Octopus* are alike, as the band toy with musical rounds, madrigals and rock motifs, not to mention nifty time signatures. The songs often have a literary edge, being inspired by Rabelais, Camus and the poetry of psychiatrist R.D. Laing. As usual, band members play a panoply of instruments, while new drummer John Weathers is the perfect fit, his exuberant personality colouring the disc. 'Knots' is a highlight, with its melange of overlapping voices expanding on Laing's brainteasing verse. For its sheer inventiveness and originality, taking rock music in a direction inhabited by no one else, *Octopus* is the perfect introduction to Gentle Giant.

Emerson, Lake & Palmer's third, *Trilogy*, was another huge success, going to number two in their homeland and five in the US. Unfortunately, the Hipgnosis-designed cover is a shocker, showing profiles of the three band members seemingly naked and staring blankly. Apparently, Salvador Dalí was invited to produce cover art for the disc, but he wanted too much money. The album includes ELP's version of Aaron Copland's 'Hoedown', from the 1942 ballet *Rodeo*. Americana also inspired 'The Sheriff', while George Gershwin gets a nod in 'Trilogy'. Various critics panned the album for being highbrow and pretentious. As Greg Lake put it, 'ELP seemed to have a special knack when it came to infuriating music critics to a point where they lost self-control.'[33]

From Greece sprang Aphrodite's Child, with their double album titled *666*, based on the Book of Revelation. The band had been established in

1967 and achieved considerable European success with hit singles and two previous albums. Aphrodite's Child featured two performers who would become giants on the global music scene: singer Demis Roussos and composer/performer Vangelis Papathanassiou (better known simply as Vangelis). The *666* album took the band into prog rock territory, mostly under Vangelis' influence, which did not sit well with those band members who wanted to further their pop-hit status. Roussos was also moving towards a solo career, having already released a solo LP, *On the Greek Side of My Mind*. By the time *666* hit the market, Aphrodite's Child had dissolved, but the LP remains a unique, scattergun illustration of these disparate talents.

Many European bands were beginning to take a more idiosyncratic approach to their music-making. Experimental music, an important tranche of modern classical music, was now firmly ensconced in the rock field. Can and Amon Düül were two of the bigger names in contemporary German avant rock. As Can's keyboardist Irmin Schmidt put it, '[P]eople on the Continent no longer think making music means imitating British or American groups.'[34] Schmidt and bandmate Holger Czukay had both studied under avant-garde composer Karlheinz Stockhausen. The band's double album of 1971, *Tago Mago*, was a groundbreaking melange of free improvisation, electronica, *musique concrète* and buried, tuneless vocalising. Once again, British occultist Aleister Crowley was a seminal inspiration. *Tago Mago* has been cited as an influence on many British and American performers, including John Lydon of The Sex Pistols and various 1980s outfits such as Jesus and Mary Chain, Radiohead and The Flaming Lips.

Can's 1972 offering was slightly more accessible, but still challenging. *Ege Bamyasi* even spawned a single, 'Spoon', which managed to chart in Germany. Listen to the frantically edgy opening track, 'Pinch', and you'll discover that Can was really a punk band before punk had arrived.

Rock music was busting out all over.

Heavy times

In order to reduce our massive urban conurbations into manageable tribes, we humans adopt clothing that delineates our chosen subculture. As Frank Zappa once quipped to his audience, 'Everyone in this room is wearing a uniform.' In the late 1960s and the 1970s, skinheads adopted a confronting anti-hippie visage of closely cropped hair, heavy Doc Martens boots and jeans with braces – a sort of aggressively proletarian, chauvinistic version of working-class attire.

British rock band Slade had at one stage attempted to delineate themselves by adopting the short-haired guise of skinheads. As bass player Jim Lea explained, 'The only reason we had our hair cut was we were just fed up with looking the same as every other group.'[35] But promoters and venues fretted about the sort of crowd they might attract, so they grew their hair and were adopted by former Animals bassist and Hendrix manager Chas Chandler. Under Chandler's instruction, they became a glam rock act. Slade revamped an old Little Richard hit, 'Get Down and Get With It', after which came the foot-stamping 'Coz I Luv You', which reached number one in the British Isles and seven in Australia. Another single with phonetic spelling, 'Look Wot You Dun', also charted well, followed by a big-selling album, *Slade Alive!*, then another hit, 'Take Me Bak 'Ome'. On a roll, by the end of the year, a further album with silly spelling, *Slayed?*, peaked at number one in the UK and Australia.

Was it all a case of style over substance? As music scribe Nick Logan admitted, 'Personally, I find Slade, apart from anything else, too crude a musical band for my tastes, but to dismiss them out of hand would be to ignore the demands and opinions of a considerable body of people.'[36] And here we have a dilemma that permeated music in the 1970s. Many rock audiences were not exactly discerning aesthetes. Millions of young people didn't discriminate between genuine creative talent and hyped-up, visceral showmanship. Indeed, Chandler urged his new band to keep it simple (the KIS principle – soon to be emulated by Kiss). As vocalist and guitarist Noddy Holder put it, 'We were trying to make the arrangement of the songs too complicated. Chas was always drumming it into us that we were trying to be too complicated.'[37] In an era where prog rock, fusion and avant-garde rock were becoming increasingly complex, there was inevitably going to be an audience for repetitive, riff-based blues rock.

Which inevitably brings us to Status Quo. The band had a long evolution, starting life as The Scorpions in 1962. Their big breakthrough didn't happen until they signed with Vertigo in 1972 and released the not-so-subtly titled *Piledriver*. It was actually their fifth LP. The opening track is a derivative twelve-bar blues performed as a raucous boogie shuffle – sort of Canned Heat without finesse. From there, it's all graceless, derivative, head-banging stuff. In their time, Status Quo released close to 100 singles, spent more than 400 weeks in the UK singles charts and 500 weeks in the UK albums charts.

Deep Purple's *Machine Head* was the first release on their Purple Records label. The album went to number one in the UK within a week of its release, becoming the band's bestselling disc. With banal lyrics and chunky riff-based songs, it turned into another classic of the heavy metal genre. Blackmore's guitar playing established a standard of virtuosity that set a real benchmark. There's little suggestion of Jon Lord's classical pretentions – although the 'Smoke on the Water' riff has been compared with the opening of Beethoven's 'Fifth Symphony', and Blackmore described the chord pattern for 'Highway Star' as a Bach progression. At the time, the band didn't see the commercial potential of 'Smoke on the Water'. Finally released as a single in May 1973, it became a global hit.

Black Sabbath's fourth album, cleverly titled *Vol. 4*, was the first produced by their guitarist Tommy Iommi. During the making, they were staying in a Bel Air mansion. As Ozzy described it, 'We never left the house. Booze, drugs, food, groupies – everything was delivered.' Indeed, they were going through so much 'blow' that it had to be delivered twice a day. It's no wonder Osbourne refers to the LP by the name of one of the songs, 'Snowblind', which Vertigo refused to allow as an album title. As he later lamented regarding cocaine, '[I]t took over our lives. It got to the point where we couldn't do anything without it. Then it got to the point where we couldn't do anything with it, either.'[38] Much of the time during recording sessions, the players simply couldn't function. At a Hollywood Bowl gig to promote the album, Iommi had taken so many drugs that he walked off stage and collapsed.

Vol. 4 didn't impress the critics, but it was the band's fourth album in a row to sell a million copies in America. Curiously, in an interview at the time, Ozzy Osbourne paid tribute to Yes, claiming that Rick Wakeman was the world's best keyboard player and that the Yes band on stage was 'perfect'.[39]

The tragic singer-songwriter Judee Sill was in London on a tour midyear when *Melody Maker* roped her into one of their blind listening tests. They played her Alice Cooper's 'Be My Lover' from the band's album *Killer*. Sills' response was classic: 'Oh God, disgusting. Dog puke. It's so unoriginal ... Agggh, I can't listen anymore. Maybe that's the worst record I have heard in my life.' While not everyone's cup of cha, Alice Cooper nevertheless found their mark with their 1972 album, *School's Out*. The LP, with its cover of a vandalised school desk, reached number two in the US. The title track also charted well across the world, living on as the signature song for which the band is best remembered. Some radio stations banned 'School's Out' because it supposedly encouraged rebelliousness among schoolkids. Teachers, parent groups and even some psychologists voiced their antagonism as well. Nothing guaranteed rock success like moral outrage.

The Alice Cooper roadshow was getting bigger with each album. The School's Out tour included ten dancers, a small orchestra, lavish backdrops and hints of *West Side Story*. For a performance at the Hollywood Bowl, Wolfman Jack rode onto the stage on a camel, and helicopters dropped hundreds of girls' panties onto the audience. In that crowd was young Elton John, who would later say, 'It was a show I'll never forget. I remember the helicopter coming over, and me fighting people in the crowd I so desperately wanted a pair of these panties. For me, it was the perfect rock and roll show of that time.'[40] But Vincent Furnier was also losing his real self in the constant demand to be Alice Cooper, bolstered by vast quantities of alcohol.

Where Alice Cooper was all shock theatrics, Iggy Pop was the real deal and the blood wasn't faked. For a taste of Iggy Pop's stage act, try this description from *Melody Maker*'s Michael Watts:

A feature of his act has been to jump from the stage into the arms of his fans and invite them to beat him up a little bit ... And Jesus, is that really hot wax he's pouring over his torso? Ladies and gentlemen, is Iggy Stooge your kind of meat?[41]

Self-mutilation became Iggy Pop's incomparable affectation.

Another idiosyncratic, volatile iconoclast was Captain Beefheart. At least Beefheart's 1972 *Clear Spot* disc was more accessible than his previous albums *Trout Mask Replica* or *Lick My Decals Off Baby*. Beefheart told *New Musical Express* that he had written all the material for *Clear Spot* in just two and a half hours, while driving between Harvard and Yale, but you could never swallow the Captain's word without adding a big grain of salt. Nevertheless, Beefheart, like Iggy Pop, was an important bridge between 1960s rock and 1970s anarchic punk. There was simply no category for what Don Van Vliet was doing with his band.

Jazzing things up

Jazz continued to interface with rock. Keyboardist Chick Corea founded the appallingly titled but highly influential outfit Return to Forever, who released their debut eponymous LP. The album was recorded for Manfred Eicher's independent ECM label, which was already beginning to command a hallowed place in the presentation of superbly recorded music. Fellow jazz pianist Herbie Hancock released his tenth album, *Crossings*, an early example of free jazz blended with electronica.

Of some interest here is Frank Zappa's foray into the big band jazz-fusion field with both *Waka/Jawaka* and *The Grand Wazoo*. In his downtime from touring, still confined to a wheelchair, Zappa decided to focus on musicianship and composition, rather than his more crowd-pleasing excursions into silly songs and sex vamps. The albums employ both jazz and rock musicians and the horns are bulked out, with the emphasis very much on the musical arrangements.

Of a very different ilk was another 1972 Zappa release, this one recorded live the previous year before his hard landing in an orchestra pit. Featuring The Mothers of Invention, at the time incorporating ex-Turtles members Howard Kaylan and Mark Volman, on the first side of *Just Another Band From L.A.* was one of Zappa's humorous, surreal rock operas, 'Billy the Mountain'. As with the previous year's live *Fillmore East – June 1971* disc, the racy sexual inuendo and wacky humour resulted in *Just Another Band* charting in both the US and Australia.

Women up front

Another landmark fusion of styles was Annette Peacock's debut solo album *I'm the One*. Sexiness oozes from the album via her breathy voice and the sensual nature of her lyrics. The album was a unique blend of soul, jazz, rock and avant-garde electronic music all performed by some stalwart musicians. Criminally ignored at the time, both Peacock and her debut LP nevertheless had an influence on many artists. Retrospective reviews have finally begun to acknowledge just how groundbreaking and fresh Peacock's music was in 1972. As John Fordham wrote in 2011, '[T]he uncompromising, sound-manipulating focus still sounds contemporary.'[42]

Annette Peacock's life story is remarkable in itself. A self-taught musician who found herself at the Julliard School, she married jazzers Gary Peacock and then Paul Bley, and became an associate of LSD guru Timothy Leary. She was one of the first Westerners to study Zen Macrobiotics, and she was a pioneer of the Moog synthesiser (perhaps even the first female Moog player). What's more, Peacock toured with Albert Ayler, collaborated with Salvador Dalí, and worked with Karlheinz Stockhausen, Brian Eno, Bill Bruford, Mick Ronson and various others. Having got *I'm the One* off her chest, it would be another six years before her second, equally sensuous LP *X-Dreams*, would appear.

If you're interested, just give the opening title track of *I'm the One* a try. Don't be put off by the free-form jazz opening, just go with the flow; about two minutes in, the track settles into a groove, and thereafter the shifting textures and that remarkable voice can't help but carry you to new horizons. The only cover song on the album is the quirkiest version of Elvis Presley's 'Love Me Tender' that you are ever likely to hear.

Women were still a comparative rarity in rock music, but the women's movement was going from strength to strength. In Australia, the Women's Electoral Lobby was formed with the aim of influencing elections in favour of women's issues. Thousands of women and supporters hit the streets in Sydney and Melbourne demanding equal pay, equal opportunities, free childcare, free contraception and safe, legal abortions. In the UK, Rose Heilbron became the first female judge at the Old Bailey. In America, women were allowed to compete in the Boston Marathon for the first time, the FBI hired its first female agents, and Sally Priesand became the first female rabbi. Feminism was also beginning to penetrate the rock industry, with Paul Simon telling *Rolling Stone*, 'I believe that the sex roles that we culturally assume are restricting to both males and females. They're more than restricting, they're damaging ...'[43]

Neil Young's stupid response to the rise of feminism was 'A Man Needs a Maid', in which the singer requires a woman to cook and clean and then to go away. Country Joe McDonald went hard in the opposite direction, swapping roles with his partner and taking over house and childcare duties. What's more, he practised positive discrimination in his support band, hiring women in non-traditional female roles.

Argent enjoyed their biggest international hit with 'Hold Your Head Up', from the album *All Together Now*, its decidedly simplistic lyrics calling on women to do just what the title suggested. The riff, written by Chris White, sounded as though it had been borrowed from The Rolling Stones, but Rod Argent's organ solo on the album version is a cracker. Indeed, Rick Wakeman declared it to be the greatest organ solo ever.

Of greater significance, this was the year that finally saw the ascendency of the world's first popular feminist anthem: 'I Am Woman' by Helen

Reddy. Reddy's image was mainstream, not radical chic, and arguably her song was even more palatable for that. At first, many radio stations refused to play 'I Am Woman', but Reddy began performing the song on TV variety shows, and when women started phoning radio stations to request the song be played, the game was up. By December, after nine months in the charts, it finally hit number one, becoming Capitol Record's first number one song in five years.

A new gender-ation

The 1970s were a curious confluence of ardent feminism and opposition to censorship, with the two issues becoming entangled in strange ways. It was also a watershed for the Gay Liberation Front and the Campaign Against Moral Persecution (CAMP). In the antipodes, South Australia became Australia's first state or territory to decriminalise some homosexual acts. While the gay scene wasn't as overt in Australia or Britain as it was in New York, there was a definite increase in the number of gay venues in places like Sydney's Darlinghurst and London's Soho. Same-sex attracted men were no longer hiding: they were coming out across the Western world, creating precincts where they could both feel safe and build a sense of community. Venues catering specifically to lesbians were in much shorter supply.

Lavender Country was a gay-themed country music band out of Seattle, Washington. Patrick Haggarty and his bandmates recorded their debut eponymous album, featuring tracks such as 'Cryin' These Cocksucking Tears', 'Come Out Singing' and 'Back in the Closet Again'. It is considered the first queer country music album.

Transgender and intersex folk were hardly on the radar, yet there was one trailblazer worth mentioning. Born Wayne Rogers, soon to become Jayne Rogers, Wayne County or Jayne County, she was gender non-conforming even at school, and brave enough to wear make-up in the southern state of Georgia. Rogers left the south at age nineteen to arrive in New York in time for the historic Stonewall Riots. After liaising with Warhol and treading the theatre boards alongside Patti Smith, in 1972 she formed Queen Elizabeth, a pioneering proto-punk band. The stage act was decidedly raunchy, catching the attention of David Bowie, with Rogers being signed to his management firm.

Another transgender artist yet to come out was Moog pioneer Wendy Carlos. The commercial success of her album (released under her original name, Walter Carlos) *Switched-On Bach* in the late 1960s afforded her the courage and funds to undergo gender reassignment surgery in early 1972, making her a pioneer in a very different field. Wendy was terrified about appearing in public, and, for marketing purposes, continued to release albums as Walter. Carlos contributed to the soundtrack for Stanley Kubrick's movie *A Clockwork Orange*. She also released her own album of music not included in the official soundtrack disc, titled *Walter Carlos' Clockwork Orange*. What's more, before Eno had begun to popularise ambient music, Carlos was already venturing down that path with her double album *Sonic Seasonings*, which would have a long-lasting influence on later creators of ambient and New Age music. Each side of the disc represented a season, and the synthesised music was interwoven with field recordings of nature. But Wendy lived a tortured double life until she finally came out publicly in 1979.

Rolling diggers

Despite the sexual revolution, sex could still raise hackles. Various Australian church leaders and politicians were offended by the title of Daddy Cool's album *Sex, Dope, Rock'n'Roll: Teenage Heaven*. It wasn't all retro teen-themed music this time. 'Please, Please America' was a tongue-in-cheek plea for the band to find success in the land of the free, while 'Make Your Stash' was a shamelessly Zappa-influenced melody and arrangement. On this track, one can sense how the band were struggling with the musical strictures of their retro concept, wanting instead to stretch out musically. By midyear, Daddy Cool decided the joke had gone on long enough.

The first Sunbury Rock Festival was billed as 'the Rock Happening of 1972', and 35,000 punters descended on a private farm in country Victoria. The promoters had decided to only feature home-grown acts, booking all of the usual suspects. As well as a film, a number of LPs resulted from Sunbury event, including the big-selling Billy Thorpe & the Aztecs double disc, *Aztecs Live! At Sunbury*, which peaked at number three on the albums chart.

Billy and his Aztecs were the quintessential Aussie rock band, playing hard, blues-based rock. Their single 'Most People I Know (Think that I'm Crazy)' was a massive hit in 1972, becoming one of Australia's most iconic rock anthems. The single was also released in the UK, and by the end of the year the band would head off to the motherland, where – following the oft-repeated pattern of so many Australian acts – they were to discover that their larrikin sensibility and primitive power was not such a good match with British ears.

Buffalo, however, were another story. The American-sounding moniker gives a clue to the band's ambitions. Buffalo were one of the few successful Australian rock exports at this time, and the first Australian band to appear on Phonogram's progressive Vertigo label. Their single 'Dead Forever' sold well, as did their debut LP of the same name, despite a ridiculous cover image. But the music was hardly original: simply more derivative, riff-based heavy rock. Even the title track sounded like Black Sabbath with even clunkier lyrics. Thanks to their label, the band found a bigger audience in Europe than in Australia.

Creeps and global ructions

Down under the land down under, a group of advocates formed the United Tasmania Group to challenge the Tasmanian state elections – the first environmental party to contest elections anywhere in the world. The UTG would eventually morph into the Tasmanian Greens, which in turn inspired the national Australian Greens party and the global Greens political movement. Meanwhile, in the US, the Don't Make a Wave Committee resolved to change its name to the Greenpeace Foundation.

The environment was on many people's minds thanks to France's decision to start testing nuclear weapons in the Pacific. There were protests all over, and Greenpeace set off from Auckland in a yacht to the test site at Mururoa Atoll. After all manner of high-seas shenanigans, a French naval minesweeper rammed the yacht in a flagrant breach of maritime law.

Matters environmental were now part of mainstream music-making. Paul Simon's eponymous solo album included 'Papa Hobo', about vehicle emissions – dubbed 'Detroit perfume'. Air pollution was also referenced in Stevie Wonder's 'Superstition' and The Stylistics' 'People Make the World Go Round'. Even The Osmonds, with their song 'Crazy Horses', used the horses of the apocalypse as a metaphor for atmospheric pollution.

Randy Newman saw a news story about a river in Ohio that was so polluted it caught on fire, and immediately wrote the elegiac 'Burn On', which appeared on his *Sail Away* album. Albert Hammond released 'Down by the River', which told of a swim in a country river that ended up causing a trip to the doctor. Country Joe McDonald's *Incredible! Live!* album took such concerns even further, with a track imagining a future where the world is so polluted that everyone has to live inside giant plastic domes. And John Denver released his version of John Prine's song 'Paradise', about the environmental impact of strip mining.

While the West was irritated by smog, large swathes of South-East Asia had been rendered uninhabitable by munitions and defoliants. President Nixon announced the withdrawal of an additional 70,000 soldiers from Vietnam and revealed that Henry Kissinger had been in secret negotiations with the North Vietnamese. Protestors and activists continued to march and campaign, while draft dodgers were still being hunted down and arrested. The month of March saw the North Vietnamese launch a major offensive, the scale and ferocity of which caught America off-guard. In response, Nixon ordered the resumption of bombing in the North.

When peace talks yet again broke down, Nixon engaged his 'Madman Theory' – wanting the North Vietnamese to believe that he would do anything to end the war. Over eleven days of almost constant bombardment, US aircraft released 28,000 tons of bombs, more than all the bombs dropped on North Vietnam over the previous three years. The 'madman' was certainly on the loose. Around the globe, national leaders accused Nixon of mass murder, and the Swedish prime minister compared the bombings to the Nazis' execution of Jews during World War II.

The bombings and their impacts were witnessed firsthand by folk singer Joan Baez, who was in North Vietnam with a human rights mission. In Hanoi, she experienced 'the heaviest bombing in the history of the world'[44] by her own countrymen. She also taped the sound of the bombs exploding, which were included on the title track of her 1973 album *Where Are You Now, My Son?*. She later described the album as 'my gift to the Vietnamese people, and my prayer of thanks for being alive'.[45]

By the end of 1972, Vietnamese-American photographer Nick Ut had taken his Pulitzer-winning photograph of children fleeing a napalm attack. At the centre of the image was a naked nine-year-old girl, Phan Thi Kim Phùc, screaming in fear and pain after napalm had been dropped on her village. The image had an enormous impact on public sentiment. Nixon claimed the image was faked.

A group of active-duty GIs from Idaho, calling themselves the Covered Wagon Musicians, recorded their song 'Napalm Sticks to Kids'. Buffy Sainte-Marie released 'Moratorium', highlighting the diversity of people now supporting the protest movement. Neil Young penned 'War Song' and released it with Graham Nash, while Country Joe McDonald recorded songs such as 'Kiss My Arse' and 'Tricky Dicky'.

The Pentagon Papers, which had been leaked by Daniel Ellsberg, inspired Texan band Bloodrock to release their song 'Thank You Daniel Ellsberg'. Attempts to hit Ellsberg with conspiracy and espionage charges would eventually founder when it was revealed that the Nixon White House had ordered unlawful activities intended to discredit Ellsberg.

The men who undertook those activities were known as 'the plumbers', because they were supposed to stop further leaks of the type perpetrated by Ellsberg. The operatives had been engaged by the Committee to Re-Elect the President – referred to in the media by the wonderful acronym CREEP – which included Attorney General John Mitchell, Nixon's counsel John Dean, and a right-wing loose cannon named G. Gordon Liddy. CREEP embarked on illegal surveillance of Democrat presidential contenders, infiltration of opposing campaigns, violence or threats of violence to intimidate political opponents, the use of call girls for political blackmailing, and agents provocateurs to disrupt rallies and political meetings.

But everything started to unravel on 17 June, when five of CREEP's bumbling 'plumbers' broke into the Democratic National Committee's offices in the Watergate building in Washington, with the whole gang arrested before they could escape. Soon, Liddy and White House aide E. Howard Hunt were also arrested. Nixon pleaded total ignorance. Incredible as it now seems, a majority of Americans preferred to believe that the president and the White House were not involved in the Watergate break-in. However, *The Washington Post* was determined to keep the story alive.

In the lead-up to the November 1972 election, soul singer James Brown once again publicly supported Nixon. He later argued that he had secured commitments from Nixon to declare Martin Luther King Jr's birthday a public holiday, as well as to provide more drug clinics. But his overt support for Nixon resulted in pickets and boycotts, plus heckling at his concerts. In the end, Nixon failed to make good on any of his promises to Brown. Brown's overt support for the government also didn't rescue him from a stoush over US$4.5 million in unpaid taxes.

Stevie Wonder released his album *Talking Back*, which included the song 'Big Brother', about surveillance and intimidation of anti-government folk living in the ghettos. The O'Jays' number one hit 'Back Stabbers' reflected the paranoia that was sweeping across black America. Sly and the Family Stone's album *There's a Riot Going On* also captured the zeitgeist, brimming with pessimism and cynicism. As *Rolling Stone*'s critic wrote:

At first I hated it for its weakness and lack of energy ... But then I began to respect the album's honesty ... Sly was laying himself out in all his fuck-ups. And at the same time holding a mirror up to all of us ... It's hard to take, but *There's a Riot Going On* is one of the most important fucking albums this year.[46]

The LP's title track, which, according to the liner notes, closed side one of the disc, was actually non-existent: there was no riot going on.

Just twelve days before the US presidential election, federal national security advisor Dr Henry Kissinger gave a media conference to speak about his ceasefire negotiations with the North Vietnamese, claiming that 'peace is within reach in a matter of weeks or less'.[47] It was a lie, but it took the wind out of the opposition's sails.

On election day, voter turnout was the lowest it had been since 1948, with only 55 per cent of the electorate taking part. Nixon won by a landslide, capturing 61 per cent of the popular vote. He received almost 18 million more votes than the Democrats' George McGovern, and still holds the record for the widest popular vote margin in any post–World War II presidential election. But Watergate was set to expose the dark underbelly of the US government.

John Lennon responded to the news of Nixon's re-election by imbibing large amounts of alcohol. He and Yoko then attended a party at Jerry Rubin's apartment. John unleashed his fury on almost everyone, complaining that their political failure had robbed him of creative energy. When a female attendee tried to console him, he reportedly ranted in her face, threatening her and saying he was going to join The Weathermen. As guests took their leave of the scene, John took a shine to Rubin's female flatmate and went off to a bedroom with her. One of the guests put on a Bob Dylan record to try to drown out their very vocal lovemaking.

John's sexual appetite was never matched by Yoko, and in this instance she did her stoic best to be understanding. As she put it, 'I felt very sad for myself. I didn't like it. But at the same time, I understood what he was going through.'[48] Sated, John emerged and motioned to Yoko for them both to leave. The next day, John was contrite, and they were back in the studio working on Ono's feminist album.

The world was a fractious place in 1972. Italy saw the founding of the Red Brigade, one of the most 'successful' terrorist groups. During their campaign of political assassinations and kidnappings – a period known as 'the years of lead' – they managed to kill some 350 businesspeople and judges. They would also capture and kill the Italian prime minister, Aldo Moro. The Japanese Red Army had also executed many people, including their own defectors.

Perhaps the most significant terrorist incident of the year was the attack on the Israeli Olympic team at the 1972 Summer Games in Munich, by affiliates of the Palestinian Black September group. Disguised as athletes, eight terrorists forced their way into the living quarters of the Israelis, killing athletes and taking hostages.

A time it was

Australia was one of the safer places on the globe. The conservative prime minister, Billy McMahon, had become a laughing-stock, while the Labor leader, Gough Whitlam, was offering to end to military conscription and retreat from the Vietnam War – and even to drag Australia into the future. The political scene was electric.

Whitlam was a rare party leader with a genuine interest in the arts, and his party's election campaign became defined by a pop song. The 'It's Time' Australian Labor campaign plagiarised ideas from the New Zealand Labour Party's successful 1972 campaign, while the emphasis on personality rather than policy was lifted from the American campaigning playbook. A whole swag of screen and stage celebrities gathered to belt out the tune 'It's Time' for a TV commercial, with Alison MacCallum taking lead vocals. She had enjoyed chart success earlier in the year with a debut solo single, 'Superman' (another Vanda and Young composition), plus an album, *Fresh Water*. But her real fame came as the principal singer on the 'It's Time' advertisement. There were consequences: MacCallum's home was strewn with garbage, and she, along with other celebrities who appeared in the ad, was blacklisted from performing in certain clubs.

On 2 December 1972, Gough Whitlam's Labor Party was elected with a comfortable majority, and Gough became the first elected Labor prime minister since 1949. The lurch to the left was seismic, with Whitlam wasting no time in reforming the political and social landscape. Straightaway, conscription was abolished, draft resisters were freed from prison and Australia's remaining personnel in Vietnam were recalled. There was a stop placed on the granting of new mining leases on Aboriginal reserves, and a Ministry of Aboriginal Affairs was created. The National Wage and Equal Pay cases were reopened before the Commonwealth Conciliation and Arbitration Commission, and within a fortnight they had brought down a judgement that women performing the same work as men should be paid the same wage. This led to an estimated overall rise in women's wages of around 30 per cent.

The changes continued at breakneck speed. In its first year, the Whitlam government established more than 100 expert commissions to report back on a wide range of issues. The year before Whitlam's reign, the parliament had passed 700 pages of legislation. In the first year of the Whitlam regime, that figure would be 2200 pages.

The end of the year also saw the release of Neil Diamond's double live album *Hot August Night*. While it went to number five in the US, the album rocketed to the top spot in Australasia. It has gone down in history as one of the biggest-selling albums in Australia, spending twenty-nine weeks at number one. What's more, it charted from 1972 to 1976, again in 1982, yet again in 1991–92, and then once more in 2014. Australia was the Diamond express.

1973

What a Bastard the World Is

While the planet seemed to be spinning out of control thanks to terrorism and economic meltdowns, rock music also appeared to be on the edge of chaos. All manner of rock stars began to spit the dummy. Both Leonard Cohen and The Kinks' Ray Davies announced they were throwing in the towel, while David Bowie gave his supposed farewell concert at London's Hammersmith Odeon, claiming he was also leaving it all behind.

Neil Young was concerned with the very scale of the music business. Horrified at the sight of an enthusiastic fan being beaten by a policeman at the Oakland Coliseum in California, he said:

> Filling a 20,000-seat hall is not rock 'n' roll, but rock 'n' roll business … Who needs to be a dot in the distance for 20,000 people and give the cops another excuse to get uptight and stop kids being happy? The circus might be all right for some acts, but it's not for me anymore.[1]

Even The Who's Pete Townshend, no stranger to on-stage theatrics or grandiose rock musicals, found it all too much in 1973, saying, 'People like Alice Cooper, good as they are, are inventions of a hungry industry. They might think they're real. I know better.'[2] Captain Beefheart weighed in too: '[I]t's getting to where groups aren't really playing. The theatre is more important than the music.'[3]

Going to water

Two weeks into the year, an Elvis concert in Hawaii became the first global telecast by an entertainer to be viewed by more people than had watched the moon landing back in 1969. Broadcast live via satellite, the show was viewed by 1.5 billion people in forty countries. Presley wore a white jumpsuit; the King wanted it to 'say America'. The jewel-encrusted outfit featured a bald eagle on the back, plus an enormous belt sporting a repeated motif of the Great Seal of the United States. The whole ludicrous ensemble incorporated 6500 gemstones.

In part, Elvis appealed because he was a sort of clean slate onto which people could project their own fantasy Elvis. He didn't get involved in public scandals, wasn't arrested, didn't trash hotel rooms or get into fights. He never did anything publicly that might undermine a fan's opinion about the sort of character he was.

On the evening of 23 January, three days after being sworn in for his second term, President Nixon appeared on television screens across America to announce that 'we today have concluded an agreement to end the war and bring peace with honour in Vietnam and Southeast Asia'. Neil Young was in the middle of a concert when he was handed a piece of paper. When he announced that peace had finally been declared, a mighty roar rose from the audience.

But the war in Vietnam did not end. The North Vietnamese, now free from US air raids, continued their land grab in the south. Meanwhile, America's bombing of Cambodia and Laos continued, and wouldn't end until a congressional determination in August. The total tonnage of bombs dropped on Cambodia over four years was 540,000 tons. But it was Laos that went down in the record books as the most bombed nation, on a per-capita basis. From 1964 to 1973, the number of secret CIA and US Air Force bombing missions over Laos amounted to an incredible 580,000 sorties – equivalent to a planeload of bombs every eight minutes, twenty-four hours a day, for nine years. By 1973, one-tenth of the Laotian population had been killed, most of them civilians. The secret war left 37 per cent of all agricultural land in Laos hazardous. Almost a third of the bombs, including cluster bombs, had failed to detonate. Even today, many Laotians, including children, are maimed or killed by old bombs.

To celebrate the end of the Vietnam War, Funkadelic came up with 'March to the Witch's Castle'. The spoken lyrics pointedly note that the nightmare had just begun for soldiers attempting to readjust to civilian life, not least because so many were returning with drug addictions.

With the war supposedly over, Vietnam quickly disappeared from both news reports and rock songs. The Watergate saga instead occupied America's consciousness. The Senate Watergate Committee began nationally televised hearings in May, and America's naivety was dealt a swift uppercut. FBI director L. Patrick Gray admitted that he had destroyed evidence and was forced to resign. Testifying before a Senate committee, former White House aide John Dean revealed that the president had authorised payment of 'hush money' to the men arrested over the Watergate break-in, and admitted that he had discussed the Watergate cover-up with President Nixon on at least thirty-five occasions.

When a White House staffer told the committee that President Nixon had secretly recorded all conversations that occurred in the Oval Office, it set off a constitutional crisis over the president's right to keep those tapes secret. American democracy and its president were dragged deeper into a quagmire from which they would never fully emerge. During a scheduled appearance before the media, Nixon uttered the words with which he would forever be tarnished: 'People have got to know whether or not their president is a crook. Well, I am not a crook.' The rats, however, were abandoning the sinking ship, with various Nixon aides asking for preferred treatment in return for inside information about the president's actions.

Virgins wearing bells

Despite – or perhaps because of – the world's woes, the music industry was making record profits. Large companies previously unrelated to the sector were now making significant investments in the record business. Back in

1955, the American music industry was worth a quarter of a million US dollars, but by 1973 it was raking in US$2 billion annually.[4]

Similar increases occurred in Britain, and young Richard Branson wanted a bigger slice. After securing loans, Branson bought an old manor house just north of Oxford. Converted into a recording studio, The Manor would play a central role in the development of British and European rock music. After a minor hiccup – being nabbed for illegally rorting excise duty – Branson and his team also expanded their Virgin Record stores, with fourteen open by the beginning of 1973. With Simon Draper, Branson then established the Virgin Music label. The first act signed to the new label would prove to be most propitious: Mike Oldfield.

Perhaps not surprisingly, Branson was more interested in making money than music. As his business partner Simon Draper later said, '[H]e wasn't really interested in music – he had the long hair but that was about it. But everyone else who worked at Virgin was passionate about it.'[5] Peter Blegvad, whose band Slapp Happy were also signed to Virgin, agreed, saying, 'He had the trappings of a hippie, but I think he was always a hard-nosed business-man with his eye on the main chance of making money. That's what drove him.'[6] It was Draper, a fan of Soft Machine, Kevin Ayers and the like, plus assistant Donald 'Jumbo' Vanrenen, who championed the signing of Oldfield.

Mike Oldfield was a wunderkind. By the time he was twelve, the self-taught guitarist was playing at local clubs and dances. At fifteen he refused a directive from his headmaster to cut his hair, and left school to play music full-time. After a stint with his sister performing as The Sallyangie, he found himself a member of Kevin Ayers' The Whole World band. Performing on two of Ayers' solo albums plus one by The Edgar Broughton Band provided the young prodigy with exposure to recording techniques. Classical composer David Bedford had given Oldfield a copy of Frederick Delius' orchestral tone poem based on the traditional English folk song 'Brigg Fair'. These variations on a simple tune became a sort of template for Oldfield's expansive compositions.

While working as a session player at Virgin's Manor studio, Oldfield began using studio down time to record his multi-instrumental piece, initially titled 'Opus One'. On becoming the first artist signed to the new Virgin label, he was invited to record 'Opus One' properly. According to Branson, Oldfield generated over 2300 separate recordings to make up what would become a sort of one-man symphony, 'Tubular Bells', playing most of the instruments himself.

On 25 May 1973, Virgin Music released its first four albums: Mike Oldfield's *Tubular Bells*, Gong's *Flying Teapot*, Steve York's *Camelo Pardalis*, and *The Faust Tapes* by German eccentrics Faust. It was mostly left-field stuff, although both Faust and Gong already had niche followings. At the same time, a subsidiary label was established by Virgin, called Caroline Records, to showcase less commercial artists on budget-priced discs.

Luckily for Virgin Records, *Tubular Bells* became an international hit. Its British sales were advanced when John Peel not only gushed over the LP but also played the work in its entirety on his influential radio show *Top Gear*.

Branson planned a live performance with a multi-star cast including Kevin Ayers, Viv Stanshall, both of Oldfield's siblings, plus members of Gong, Henry Cow, and even Rolling Stones' guitarist Mick Taylor. Oldfield, however, had developed a fear of appearing live. Branson managed to bribe the protégé into performing by offering him his Bentley. The show was a huge success. After the standing ovation, according to Branson, the hyper-sensitive Oldfield was 'too shattered' to speak with the press; seeing people queueing to buy his album, he muttered, 'I feel as if I've been raped,' before rushing away.[7]

At an international music fair in Cannes, Branson struggled to elicit interest from American distributors, being told that *Tubular Bells* couldn't possibly sell in the US market. By the end of the year, however, its opening theme had been used for the soundtrack of the smash horror film *The Exorcist* – a movie that Oldfield was too afraid to watch. The movie soundtrack became a hit album, and America's Atlantic Records also released a short excerpt from *Tubular Bells* as a single. Incredibly, the LP stayed in the charts for the next five years. As Branson biographer Tom Bower put it, 'The album's phenomenal success made Branson a millionaire at twenty-three. Skilfully, he had retained all the rights, leaving Oldfield with a comparative pittance.'[8]

There's much to thank – or blame – *Tubular Bells* for. The album helped bankroll the behemoth that Branson's businesses would become. With *Tubular Bells* raining dough, Virgin Records took risks with some of the greatest and least heard progressive and avant-garde acts of the era, including the unparalleled Henry Cow, their mates Slapp Happy, Canterbury-styled proggers Hatfield and the North, guitarist Steve Hillage, Can, Lol Coxhill, The Flying Lizards and the world's most iconoclastic wit, Ivor Cutler. For this array of eccentric talent, the label was dubbed an 'audio arts council'.[9]

Gong's *Flying Teapot* may have been thoroughly overshadowed by *Tubular Bells*, but it remains one of the most endearingly silly and infectious albums in all of prog rock. It's the first of a trio of discs presenting Daevid Allen's madcap Gong mythology, the other two parts being *Angel's Egg* and *You*.

With its Op Art cover, *The Faust Tapes* was the third album by the German musical adventurers. The deal cut with Virgin was that the tapes would be provided nil charge, so the album sold for just 49p – the price of a single. As a result, *The Faust Tapes* secured sales of 60,000 copies. The disc is really a knitting-together of song fragments, ranging from electric folk to prog to electronic and industrial noise plus treated vocals, the whole thing careening from the melodic to borderline unlistenable. Their subsequent album, *Faust IV*, recorded at The Manor and also released this year, became a Krautrock classic.

Faust toured with Henry Cow, whose debut album, punningly titled *Legend* ('leg end', with the cover artwork showing a sock), was also recorded at The Manor. (Their next two albums also featured plastic woven socks.) Primarily an instrumental album, the intricate pieces are largely uncategorisable, veering from free jazz improvisation to tightly controlled ensemble playing. Some of Fred Frith's composing utilised John Cage's chance methodology. With Chris Cutler laying down his busy drumming bed and John Greaves weaving superbly intricate base lines (just listen to 'Teenbeat Reprise'), the soloing is taken by Geoff Leigh and Tim Hodgkinson on wind instruments, plus the incredible guitar chops of Fred Frith.

Members of Henry Cow also pioneered Rock in Opposition, a collective of experimental European rock groups that included Italy's Stormy Six, France's Etron Fou Leloublan, Belgium's rather dour and gothic Univers Zero, and my personal favourite, the virtuosic Swedish outfit Samla Mammas Manna. The 'opposition' in their collective moniker was in relation to the established rock business and their determination to pursue personal ideals regardless of the commercial music industry.

Virgin's mail order service had been selling a lot of Krautrock, especially Tangerine Dream, so Draper and Branson offered band members Edgar Froese, Peter Baumann and Christopher Franke a five-year contract. A modular Moog synthesiser was acquired for The Manor, and the trio spent six weeks recording what would become the surprise hit album *Phaedra*. As there were no presets for the Moog in 1973, the band had to spend hours each day just tuning the beast. Soon, German electronic music pioneer Klaus Schulze would also join the Virgin stable.

In 1973, Virgin began to stage its own concert series, using the same marketing approach it had taken with *The Faust Tapes*: bargain-priced admission. At a Rainbow Theatre gig, Faust's performance was augmented by thirty TV sets stacked on top of one another, plus a guy jackhammering a lump of concrete on the stage.

Under the Rainbow

The Rainbow Theatre was also the scene of Eric Clapton's return to the stage. Clapton hadn't been seen in public since 1971's Concert for Bangla Desh. He remained holed up with his girlfriend, Alice Ormsby-Gore, both of them strung out on heroin. His musical mates were worried about him, so Pete Townshend organised Ronnie Woods, Steve Winwood, Jim Capaldi, Jim Karstein and Rick Grech to gather with Clapton for ten days of rehearsals in London. As Clapton put it, '[T]his was something that I would never have managed to do on my own, but because it was Pete, I went along with it.'[10]

On 13 January, they performed before a packed house at the Rainbow Theatre. Clapton and Alice arrived late and stoned. In the audience were Ahmet Ertegun, Elton John, Jimmy Page, Joe Cocker and Ringo Starr, plus George Harrison and his wife Pattie Boyd. The band opened with 'Layla', the song Clapton had written to try and seduce Boyd away from Harrison. But Townshend's efforts didn't resolve his friend's drug issues, as Clapton wrote: 'After the Rainbow concert, I went back into hiding, and though I understood that Pete cared for me and wanted to help by getting me back in the music scene, I just wasn't ready.'[11] He continued to burn through £1000 worth of heroin each week. Alice Ormsby-Gore would eventually die of an overdose in 1995.

The unfortunate truth is that many of the era's rock luminaries were vile people (we'll come back to Clapton on that score). As Led Zeppelin began their twenty-four-date British tour, young music journalist Nick Kent was assigned by *New Musical Express* to cover the action. His article laid bare the infantile self-indulgence of the band members. It began by describing the departure of a roadie after John Paul Jones petulantly destroyed a Mellotron that wasn't functioning to his liking. He also described the 'barely pubescent' girls hanging around the dressing rooms, and a fight that involved throwing beer cans, bottles and food.[12] Years later, Kent explained that he had never witnessed worse behaviour than that exhibited by drummer John 'Bonzo' Bonham and tour manager Richard Cole: 'I once saw them beat a guy senseless and then drop money on his face. It makes me feel sick when I hear Plant talking about what a great geezer Bonzo was, because the guy was a schizophrenic animal.'[13] Groupie-turned-author Pamela Des Barres concurs, writing, 'Bonzo was a big, overgrown baby. I witnessed him beat up so many people.'[14]

Zep's fifth studio album – the first with a proper title, *Houses of the Holy* – copped a mixed response. It largely avoided their expected heavy blues-rock in favour of a brighter, cleaner sound. It was, inevitably, a hit, going to single digits across the planet, including the top spot in the UK, US and Australia. As with The Rolling Stones, anything Led Zeppelin released at this time turned to gold. Jimmy Page told an interviewer that the tracks 'The Crunge' and 'D'yer Mak'er' were 'just a giggle. They're just two send-ups.'[15] The latter was a Caribbean-styled number, while 'The Crunge' was a tasteless slice of American black funk. It almost seemed as though the band were treating their fans with contempt. 'The Rain Song' was an epic ballad with acoustic guitar, piano and orchestral (Mellotron) pretensions, which would've sounded more appropriate on a Moody Blues LP. Plainly, Led Zep were keen to demonstrate they could produce more than riff-based rock and ferocious solos. No doubt they also wanted to distance themselves from the likes of Black Sabbath and Status Quo. But success also lent them a massive dollop of arrogance.

Still smarting from having been outdone by The Rolling Stones in America during 1972, Led Zep realised they needed to spruce up their public image. So they met with heavy-hitting PR firm Solters/Sabinson/Roskin in Paris. To keep the musos occupied, their management brought in high-class prostitutes to stage a private sex show while the meetings with the PR agency were going on. Appropriately enough, the PR firm made no bones about the fact that Led Zep were viewed as barbarians. Yet the band didn't seem to understand why they couldn't garner the magazine covers that their rivals enjoyed.

To trump the Stones, they set about generating a new benchmark for rock spectaculars when on their ninth American tour. They added laser lights, smoke bombs, an exploding cannon and giant video screens. They also beefed up the sound wattage and donned sparkly clothing. What's more, they began to provide journalists with concert tickets, plane journeys, hotel suites and, of course, prostitutes. After eighty-seven days on the road, they had broken the US$4 million gross takings record set by the Stones. Playing three-hour sets to massive crowds, they set a new attendance record in Tampa, Florida of 56,800 people. The New York shows were filmed for the troubled documentary *The Song Remains the Same*. Like the Stones, Led Zep now had their own jet, a Boeing 720, emblazoned with their name.

Meanwhile, the offstage debauchery continued. Women were selected and corralled by Richard Cole, Beep Fallon and others, and, like disposable product, they were used, abused and tossed aside. When Jimmy was shown a photograph of fourteen-year-old Lori Mattix, he knew he had to have her. Richard Cole and Peter Grant pulled the terrified girl into a limo and delivered her to the rock star. As Lori later said, 'I know he fell in love with me because of my innocence. He was twenty-nine; I was fourteen. It was no secret he liked young girls.'[16] Sadly, Lori's mother conceded to the liaison.

Meanwhile, Bonzo was busy breaking artworks over people's heads, dangling hapless people by their feet from balconies, and trashing hotel rooms and vehicles. On his birthday he punched his drum tech, drove a motorcycle through hotel corridors and threw TVs and furniture from windows. At his party, George Harrison started a massive food fight, and Peter Grant attempted to drive a rented Cadillac into a swimming pool, but instead got it wedged between two palm trees. In Seattle, more shenanigans occurred, with Cole and Bonzo catching numerous mud sharks, which they rubbed on a bevy of girls (reprising the antics immortalised on Zappa's 'The Mud Shark' from *Fillmore East – June 1971*). John Paul Jones dismantled Bonzo's room and sent every item that could be unbolted into the sea. The hotel manager reportedly thanked them for only trashing the one room this time, whereas Rod Stewart's crowd had recently destroyed five. A *New York Post* photographer had his camera broken and his face injured when attacked by Peter Grant, resulting in Grant's arrest. At the end of the tour, $200,000 went missing from the band's safe deposit box at their New York hotel, with the FBI investigating. The perpetrator was never found, though it may well have been an inside job.

Back at home in England, the excesses of the tour had left Jimmy Page in a bad way. He turned from cocaine to heroin and became increasingly infatuated with the occult, collecting masses of Aleister Crowley memorabilia. John Paul Jones was disheartened and threatening to quit. Efforts to reconvene the band to begin a new album were repeatedly foiled, as Jones never showed up. It would be another eighteen months before the band again set foot on a stage.

Stress fractures were also evident in The Who. While rehearsing for their Quadrophenia tour, Roger Daltrey and Pete Townshend came to blows. Townshend had downed the best part of a bottle of brandy before swinging his guitar at the singer, saying, 'Oh shut up, you cunt.'[17] As Daltrey described it, 'I replied with an uppercut to the jaw. Pete went up and backwards like he'd been poleaxed. And then he fell down hard, cracking his head on the stage. I thought I'd killed him.'[18] Two weeks later, during a gig in Newcastle, Townshend attacked the band's sound engineer, tossing a tape machine at him before storming off the stage. The local newspaper aptly called him childish.

In San Francisco, drummer Keith Moon downed a bottle of brandy, plus what Daltrey described as 'a handful of horse tranquillisers and something else we never quite discovered'. Partway through the show, in front of 15,000 people, Moon lost consciousness. Dragged offstage by roadies, he was showered, injected with something by a doctor, and plonked back at the drum kit. But he only lasted one tune before passing out again. As their drummer was being carted away, the remaining trio attempted to keep performing. Pete Townshend then asked if there was anyone in the audience who could play drums. Nineteen-year-old Scot Halpin volunteered, was given a shot of brandy for his nerves, and managed to percuss The Who through the rest of the set.

As darkness fell

Pink Floyd was yet to melt down. Drummer Nick Mason remembers the recording sessions for *Dark Side of the Moon* as being conscientious, with the band acting as its own producer. Unusually for the Floyd, the music had been honed during numerous live performances, rather than contrived in the studio. The Abbey Road studios now offered sixteen-track recording, and the Floyd used every one of them, sometimes going to second-generation copies for more than sixteen tracks. Sound effects, tape loops and plenty of synthesisers were employed. Vocals were treated in various ways, including double-tracking, flanging (the same track played ever-so-slightly out-of-sync with itself) and other trickery. Clare Torry was brought in to sing on what would become 'The Great Gig in the Sky', producing a wordless improvisation for which she immediately apologised, worried it was too exuberant. But the band loved it. Torry was only paid a standard session fee, however, in 2004 she sued for 50 per cent of the royalties, claiming her improvising had amounted to co-authorship. The case was settled out of court, and all subsequent releases credited the track to Richard Wright and Torry.

Roger Waters took the finished mix home for his wife to hear. As it concluded, she burst into tears. Plainly this album was something quite special.

Dark Side completed the band's commitment to Capitol Records. The lads were toying with jumping ship, so their label put in extra effort to promote the disc. Pink Floyd set about touring the music, starting at Earls Court, where various film clips accompanied songs – including footage from the Australian surf film *Crystal Voyager* – and a fifteen-foot plane shot to the stage over the audience's heads to burst into a ball of fire.

Dark Side of the Moon remains one of the bestselling albums of all time. Even though it only sat at number one in the US for a week, it had such long legs that it remained in the *Billboard* charts for 741 non-consecutive weeks until mid-1988. It would reappear in the charts on further reissues. Oddly, the album never reached number one in the UK, only making it to number two, but is still in the top ten bestselling albums there. Indeed, statistics suggest that one in four households in Britain owned a copy of *Dark Side* by the turn of the century. In global terms, the album has sold something in the order of 50 million copies.

Cogitating on the phenomenal success, Nick Mason suggested: 'The overall idea that linked those songs together – the pressure of modern life – found a universal response and continues to capture people's imagination … And the musical quality spearheaded by David's guitar and voice and Rick's keyboards established a fundamental Pink Floyd sound.' Mason also noted that the additional voices and saxophone, plus the overall sonic quality achieved by engineer Alan Parsons and mixer Chris Thomas, was 'state of the art'. In particular, *Dark Side* made full use of stereophonic hi-fi, becoming the go-to album when people wanted to demonstrate the quality of their home music systems.

Dark Side of the Moon takes the band away from the noodling psyche-delia for which they were famous. The album also deals with themes generally considered taboo in popular music, notably mental illness and depression. As a high-water mark for the rock idiom, it remains as fresh and interesting as it was in 1973.

Of course, the worst aspect of having a smash hit album was the expectation to equal or better it. Pink Floyd came up with the idea for an entire album produced without the use of any musical instruments – pure *musique concrète*. For two months, band members laboured over field recordings for a project to be called *Household Objects*. While it provided a terrific distraction, nothing substantial ever came of it.

Pink Floyd had long enjoyed a strong communal relationship with Soft Machine, dating back to the underground era of the short-lived but hugely influential UFO Club in 1967. In May 1973, Nick Mason received a postcard from former Softs drummer Robert Wyatt. It asked him if he would care to produce Wyatt's next album with a reformed Matching Mole. Mason received the request on the same day that he heard Wyatt had fallen from a window.

Wyatt and his girlfriend, Alfreda Benge, had attended a party at the fourth-floor apartment of June Campbell Cramer, aka 'Lady June'. As was his want at the time, Wyatt drank too much and somehow ended up leaving the party by the quickest route. As he humorously described it, 'I didn't fall on my head, I fell on my left heel – although the rest of me obviously followed quite quickly, not having become detached en route.'[19] The alcohol kept his body relaxed, possibly saving his life, but he broke his twelfth vertebra and was paralysed from the waist down.

Pink Floyd teamed up with Soft Machine to play a benefit concert for Wyatt at the Rainbow Theatre. Compered by John Peel, the event raised £10,000. In a *Melody Maker* article, Steve Lake explained Wyatt's significance thus: 'It's not generally acknowledged yet, but Robert was a true innovator as far as drumming's concerned in the mid-60s, single-handedly responsible, I think, for a lot of the cross fertilisation that has occurred between rock and jazz.'[20]

Stoned again

The Rolling Stones performed a benefit concert for the victims of a Nicaraguan earthquake, with support acts Santana plus comedians Cheech & Chong. The Stones were aiming to tour the Pacific next, but the Australian immigration department initially refused them entry. Jagger's 1969 drug conviction meant that a Japanese visa request was also refused. Eventually, Australia relented, and the band set off on their tour of Hawaii, New Zealand and Australia. The last time the band had toured Australasia was in 1966.

The Stones still revelled in their reputation as a 'dangerous' band. In Adelaide, some 5000 fans clashed with police and twenty-one punters ended up arrested. However, immigration minister Al Grassby came out swinging on behalf of the band, claiming he had gone out on a limb to allow the Stones into the country, and they were an excellent example to Australian youth. On returning to London, Keith Richards was busted for possession of cannabis, heroin, Mandrax and firearms.

In an interview with *Melody Maker*, Jagger's contempt for women was on full display. When asked about his wife's filmmaking ambitions, he said, 'When girls get together, there's always talk but they never get anything done.' One of the reporters was so shocked with this comment that he asked Jagger to repeat it. On why his wife didn't go on tour with him, Jagger explained: 'You wouldn't take your wife to the office with you, would you? I've never taken any old lady on tour.' (Other bands happily toured with wives and girlfriends.) To top it all off, in reference to Linda McCartney, Jagger gracelessly opined, 'I wouldn't let my old lady play the piano.'[21]

The Stones released *Goats Head Soup*, which had been recorded in piecemeal fashion in Jamaica, the US and the UK. Many critics consider the record substandard, but, of course, it went to number one in many countries. The cover image of Jagger's lipsticked head masked in chiffon was shot by David Bailey, who apparently had in mind Katharine Hepburn from the movie *The African Queen*. The back cover showed Richards looking the epitome of a wasted drug addict.

The first hit from the album was 'Angie'. Driven by an acoustic guitar and piano, the slow ballad went somewhat against the band's hard-rocking reputation. *New Musical Express* called the single 'atrocious', but 'Angie' became an iconic tune, floating to the top of the charts and becoming a live staple for the band. Credited to Jagger and Richards, it was rumoured to be about Jagger's relationship with Bowie's wife, but was more likely written about an imaginary person. The song avoided the sort of mean-spirited misogyny that tainted many of the band's songs and was uncharacteristically tender.

'Coming Down Again' was an ode to infidelity, while 'Doo Doo Doo Doo Doo (Heartbreaker)' offered a confused lyric that began with a New York policeman shooting an innocent boy, then moved on to a description of a young girl shooting up heroin. Even the band's eulogy to rock music, 'Can You Hear the Music', was slow and turgid.

The closing track, 'Star Star', was originally called 'Starfucker' before Warner-Elektra-Atlantic Records objected. This dull rock 'n' roller gained notoriety because of its obscene lyrics, which are all about a groupie and her willingness to engage in sexual antics involving fruit. Its repeated massed chorus yelling 'starfucker' is presumably intended to maintain the band's edgy, liberated image, but 'Star Star' tries so hard to shock, and is so musically clichéd, that it instead stands as a grotesque finale for The Rolling Stones' golden era.

Oh no

Yoko Ono's *Approximately Infinite Universe* double album continued her shift towards more conventional rock forms, while espousing her feminist leanings. On that score, she had her limits. The track 'What a Bastard the World Is' was described as a satire about the militancy of some feminists, with Ono saying, 'So they would scream and shout and kick out all men.

Then what are they going to do?'²² The album sleeve included Ono's essay 'The Feminization of Society'.

Rather than illuminating their relationship, 'Song for John' was pure doggerel. Once again, the backing was provided by Elephant's Memory, with Mick Jagger guesting on guitar on one track, but it couldn't rise above 193 on *Billboard*.

On April Fool's Day, Lennon and Ono staged a press conference in New York announcing themselves ambassadors for the state of Nutopia, its flag being all white. They moved into the architecturally eclectic Dakota building, joining various actors, film directors and sundry bohemians. The apartments had been a principal location for the horror film *Rosemary's Baby*. The pair did surface to attend a couple of New York demonstrations, but Yoko was busy churning out songs for her next album. Once again, she planned a double album, but EMI/Apple insisted it be a single disc. After a composing hiatus, John was finally tinkering with a couple of tunes himself, hoping also to put out an LP.

When it came time to record Yoko's new disc, John's involvement was now limited. He didn't even get a producing credit and his guitar playing on two tracks was billed as John O'Cean. The entire *Feeling the Space* album furthered Ono's feminist messaging, as one might guess from song titles such as 'Angry Young Woman', 'She Hits Back', 'Men, Men, Men' and the single from the album, 'Woman Power'. The latter anticipates rap music, with Ono riffing the spoken words over a repetitive rhythm track. John found Ono's backing band to his liking, so he used the same musos on his own material, recorded in July and August, which would eventually become *Mind Games*.

In a strange attempt to deal with their growing marital strife, Yoko encouraged the couple's twenty-three-year-old assistant, May Pang, to have an affair with John, and told them to decamp to LA. And so began what would come to be known as the 'lost weekend'. As Lennon's friend Elliot Mintz put it, 'The lost weekend was a combination of a remarkable party, an exercise into the depths of foolishness, and I think John's last effort to assert his manhood.'²³

LA also happened to be the centre of the American recording industry, and Lennon was determined to record an album of classic old rock 'n' roll tunes. A few weeks after landing in the city of fallen angels, Lennon met up with Elton John. The two bonded immediately. Between intense bouts of work, Elton managed to squeeze in some serious imbibing with Lennon.

Yoko visited Paul McCartney in London, as a result of which Paul was dispatched to LA with a message of conciliation from Yoko. McCartney found his old bandmate embroiled with 'three beautiful total alcohol nutters': Harry Nilsson, Keith Moon and Jesse Ed Davis. He said John was being 'a teenager again … being his old Liverpool self, just a wild, wild boy'.[24] He dutifully delivered Yoko's message.

Mind Games hit the shelves at the end of October. It was Lennon's first self-produced solo work without help from Phil Spector. Once again, the disc was brimming with personal outpourings, from gloomy odes to Yoko to more light-hearted songs, such as the jaunty 'Intuition', plus the rockabilly 'Tight A\$'. The title track harks back to the Beatles era in both musical style and its love-is-all-you-need subject matter, but the verses remind us that love can be a battle of wits. Overall, the album feels half-baked, no doubt because Lennon's life direction at this point was one long stumble – away from politics and revolution and further from his wife.

Paul McCartney's Wings released their second album, *Red Rose Speedway*, along with its single 'My Love'. The album went to number one in the US and Australia, and number five in the UK. Critics, however, mostly found the album uneven and mediocre. History has it that McCartney wanted to put out a double album, but EMI thought the material wasn't strong enough. The band also recorded the non-album singles 'Mary Had a Little Lamb' and 'Hi, Hi, Hi'. The BBC banned the latter, believing the title was a drug reference and that the lyrics contained sexually explicit content, but as McCartney told *Rolling Stone*:

> The daft thing about all that was our publishing company, Northern Songs, owned by Lew Grade, got the lyrics wrong and sent them round to the radio station and it said, 'Get ready for my body gun,'

which is far more suggestive than anything I put. 'Get ready for my polygon' … I mean, it was suggestive, but abstract suggestive.[25]

Wings also enjoyed a hit with the theme song for the James Bond film *Live and Let Die*. Recording the tune had reunited Paul with George Martin, who arranged the orchestra. The song was a smash hit across the world, as well as being nominated for an Oscar. McCartney also found himself in court, pleading guilty to growing marijuana and receiving a fine.

When Wings began to rehearse songs for their next album, band members Henry McCullough and Denny Seiwell were unhappy. Depending on which version one reads, they were either disgruntled about the inclusion of Linda McCartney in the band, upset at Paul McCartney's tendency towards autocracy, dissatisfied with the style of music they were being asked to perform or simply unwilling to travel to Nigeria to record. That's right, Paul McCartney got it into his head that he'd like to record the new album somewhere exotic, and he chose Nigeria.

Nigeria was an impoverished nation run by a military government. What's more, the EMI studios in Lagos had just one eight-track recording machine. Having lost his lead guitarist and drummer, it fell to McCartney to play drums, guitar and bass, with Denny Laine also playing guitar. However, life in Africa was far from smooth sailing. At one point Paul and Linda were robbed at knifepoint, with the thieves stealing not only money but also Paul's notebook, in which he had written songs and lyrics, plus cassettes of demos that had yet to be recorded. It took six weeks for Paul, Linda and Denny to lay down the basic tracks for the new disc, after which they returned to the safety of England. Further overdubs, plus some string arrangements by Tony Visconti, were added. Sax player Howie Casey also contributed and would eventually join Wings.

The album spawned two hit singles, 'Jet' and 'Band on the Run'. The latter was a deeply personal song – well, a medley of three tunes, really – illustrating where McCartney's head was at. In the opening, he muses about feeling trapped in his rock star role. The second section sees him toying with the idea of giving away his riches to charity and taking up a simple life. It then moves into the song proper, a somewhat repetitive hook with lyrics plainly about the departure of McCullough and Sewell.

'Jet' was inspired by either a puppy the McCartneys had bred or else a pony that Paul once owned – depending on which of his explanations you choose. McCartney has also said the words were inspired by meeting Linda's intimidating father, but rhyming 'jet' with 'suffragette' made for pure nonsense. It's basically a dippy, pointless song with a big, fat sound. Overall, *Band on the Run* was viewed as a belated return to form for McCartney, going to number one in the UK, US, Australia and elsewhere and becoming the biggest-selling album in both the UK and Australia during 1974. It would also be McCartney's last record on the Apple label.

While the McCartneys were in Nigeria, Lennon, Starr, Harrison, Ono and Apple began action against Allen Klein and ABKCO, citing excessive commissions, fraud and mismanagement. ABKCO countersued them all, claiming a cool US$63.5 million plus future earnings. ABKCO also claimed that Paul had conspired with the other ex-Beatles to damage or injure Klein, and sought a further US$34 million in damages for that.[26]

George and Ringo weren't musically idle either. George Harrison's *Living in the Material World* became his second number one album in America. It's loaded with Harrison's ongoing philosophical tug-of-war between spirituality and earth-bound reality (a conflict from which material-ism would emerge the winner, with Harrison taking up residence in a 120-room mansion augmented with a massive collection of expensive automobiles). *Rolling Stone* lauded Harrison's album as a pop classic, whereas Tony Tyler in *New Musical Express* called it 'turgid, repetitive and so damn holy I could scream'.[27]

Ringo Starr's third album, *Ringo*, was notable for its inclusion of all the ex-Beatles, plus a wide range of support stars including Marc Bolan, Harry Nilsson, Tom Scott, James Booker and Robbie Robertson, to name but a few. Such assemblages of big names would become Starr's signature approach to recording. The individual tracks were composed by Starr himself, his fellow ex-Beatles and Randy Newman, and he included the old chestnut 'You're Sixteen' by Bob and Dick Sherman. The opening track, Lennon's 'I'm the Greatest', is significant for being the only time that Starr, Harrison and Lennon recorded together post-Beatles. Plainly inspired by Muhammad Ali's famous slogan, it was Lennon's tongue-in-cheek take on fame.

Box of tricks

Starr's natural voice was limited, but some rock singers were looking for ways to enhance their vocal abilities. Musicians had been toying with devices that made instruments sound like voices since 1939, when Alvino Rey attached a microphone to his wife, who was concealed behind a curtain. Her voice was then magically channelled through his pedal steel. (There's film of this floating around – just hunt for Alvino Rey plays 'St Louis Blues' with Stringy the talking steel guitar.) In the early 1960s, Pete Drake also used a talk box device on his album *Forever*. It was designed by Bill West, husband of country singer Dottie West. Bill gifted his home-made device to Joe Walsh, who used it on 'Rocky Mountain Way', from his 1973 release *The Smoker You Drink, the Player You Get*.

Walsh also showed the device to Bob Heil, the sound engineer who was famous for developing the unique sound systems used by The Grateful Dead and The Who. Together Walsh and Heil developed a better version, dubbed the Heil Talk Box, that could work in a live setting. Peter Frampton's girlfriend bought one of these newfangled talk boxes as a birthday present for her beau. When Frampton began using it live, the crowd went wild: have a listen to 'Show Me the Way' and 'Do You Feel Like We Do' from his 1976 release, *Frampton Comes Alive!*.

Another way to achieve voice-like instrumental effects was via a vocoder. Emerson, Lake & Palmer used the device for the track 'Karn Evil 9: 3rd Impression' on *Brain Salad Surgery*. Today, in the era of samplers, this all sounds a bit ho-hum, but it held great novelty in the early '70s. The vocoder was a good fit with the sci-fi pretensions of prog, finding its way onto albums by The Alan Parsons Project, Pink Floyd, Space Art, Electric Light Orchestra, Mike Oldfield, and Jean-Michel Jarre. But it has also had application to other genres, being utilised by artists as diverse as Herbie Hancock, Stevie Wonder, Neil Young and Michael Jackson.

While touring in Italy, Emerson, Lake & Palmer were introduced to PFM: one three-letter band meets another! ELP arranged for PFM to join them on their own label, Manticore Records. The result was the album *Photos of Ghosts*. Most of the tracks were reworkings of songs from PFM's first two Italian LPs, but now with English lyrics penned by former King Crimson lyricist Pete Sinfield. For the first time, an Italian rock band achieved mass appeal across the globe. *Photos of Ghosts* also helped awaken young American music consumers to Europe as a source of progressive music.

Moving well away from complex compositions, King Crimson's eccentric leader Robert Fripp was joined by self-proclaimed non-musician Brian Eno for some quirky, minimalist space music. Eno had departed Roxy Music with a £15,000 debt and no firm direction. But he had been listening to pioneering avant-garde composers such as Steve Reich and Terry Riley, in particular Reich's work using tape recorders as instruments. In his home studio, Eno demonstrated to Fripp the tape delay system that had been developed by the likes of Karlheinz Stockhausen and Pauline Oliveros. Fripp was so intrigued that he and Eno recorded the first side of what would become *No Pussyfooting* there and then, in just two takes.

Fripp laid down some guitar sounds that Eno transformed through echo and tape delay, providing a bed for the guitarist to then improvise over. With pure Fripp arrogance, he dubbed it Frippertronics. The second side was recorded much later, with a VCS3 synthesiser providing the drone bed, but again with Fripp weaving hypnotically over the top. As one music scribe put it, 'The result is somewhere between Terry Riley's *Rainbow in Curved Air* and John Martyn's longer guitar pieces.'[28]

No Pussyfooting delivered minimalism to a new audience. It was a far cry from both Eno's debut solo effort, *Here Come the Warm Jets*, and King Crimson's 1973 release *Larks' Tongues in Aspic*. Island Records only released *No Pussyfooting* begrudgingly, and then at a discount price. Although it didn't sell in huge numbers, *No Pussyfooting* performed remarkably well for a decidedly avant-garde offering.

Larks' Tongues in Aspic featured the third incarnation of King Crimson. For Fripp, it was now time to put the 'progressive' back into prog rock. With drummer Bill Bruford poached from Yes, and bassist John Wetton from Family, he added violinist David Cross and avant-garde percussionist Jamie Muir. The album saw Crimson moving even further away from rock, towards a more European, free improvisatory approach. Indeed, listening to *Lark's Tongues*, it is often impossible to tell what is improvised and what is composed. Gone are the hippie-surreal Pete Sinfield lyrics, with the few words penned by Richard Palmer-James, a founding member of Supertramp. The LP takes dynamics to new extremes, particularly on the two title tracks, which veer from gentle, tinkling subtlety to full-blown fury. At a time when many music aficionados were lying in the dark umbilically connected to their hi-fi, this was the ultimate headphone experience.

Fripp's unique electric guitar sound was admired by many. Guitar treatments were also the gambit of aforementioned British singer-songwriter John Martyn. His album *Solid Air*, recorded the previous year but released on Island Records in early 1973, was a mighty declaration of intent. Although not a runaway success in its day, *Solid Air* remains a hugely pivotal and influential album in the history of British music. With support from the cream of the folk rock scene, especially members of Fairport Convention, Martyn created a stirring blend of folk, blues and space rock with traces of jazz. Even his drawled vocals seem a world apart from what everyone else was doing at the time. Pivotal to the sound of the LP was Danny Thompson's majestic, super-mellow double bass. To get an idea of how wonderful that instrument can be, just listen to the title track, a tribute to Nick Drake. 'Solid Air' even has Tristan Fry chiming in on a vibraphone and Tony Coe on breathy, lilting saxophone. It is absolutely, breathtakingly gorgeous. As drummer Dave Mattacks declared of those recording sessions, 'Blimey, if this is the kind of stuff these folkies are up to, I'll have some more of it!'[29]

Also recorded and released in 1973 was John Martyn's album *Inside Out*, which was even more experimental than *Solid Air*. Although pigeonholed as folk, Martyn professed his love for jazz saxophonist Pharoah Sanders and the keyboard textures of Joe Zawinul. The track 'Make No Mistake', for example, references John Coltrane's 'A Love Supreme'. For *Inside Out*, Martyn was joined by members of Traffic, including Steve Winwood, Chris Wood and Remi Kabaka, as well as the saxophone of Bobby Keys, who was touring at the time with The Rolling Stones. Thankfully, Danny Thompson was again in the mix. So these are mostly rock musicians being asked to stretch out like jazz players.

Genesis completed their year-long Foxtrot tour, which covered the UK, Europe and North America. During touring, drummer Phil Collins would record each performance and obsessively replay the tapes in his motel room, making notes for improvement and slipping suggestions under the doors of his bandmates. While composing new material for *Selling England by the Pound*, Collins had been listening to Mahavishnu Orchestra, leading to some complicated time signatures on the new album. The opening track is a classic prog tour de force, with eight minutes of shifting moods, inscrutable lyrics and bravura ensemble playing. From *Selling England*, Genesis managed to garner their only Top 40 hit from these early years: 'I Know What I Like (In Your Wardrobe)'. It's probably the least interesting track on the LP, but it also doesn't shift and change too much, no doubt rendering it more radio-friendly. Genesis declined an offer to appear on *Top of the Pops* because, as Rutherford put it, 'we were an albums band, not a singles band'.[30]

The staging for the Selling England tour included large, curved screens and explosive flashboxes, as well as Gabriel suddenly flying above the stage on wires. It didn't work so well during their Rainbow Theatre concert, as Mike Rutherford related:

[H]is wires began slowly, slowly crossing. Very gradually he was being spun around to face the wrong way, leaving the audience to stare at his back. Pete spent the rest of the song trying to sing and twist round at the same time – I know because from where I was standing all I could see were his feet paddling in mid-air.[31]

More portentous prog appeared in the guise of Rick Wakeman's *The Six Wives of Henry VIII*. Having read a book on the subject while on tour with Yes, Wakeman began to assemble his concept album, recording it in breaks from touring and utilising members of both Yes and his old band Strawbs.

Wakeman had a solo record deal with A&M Records at the time. At first the boffins at A&M were reluctant to release an instrumental rock album, but they finally relented, pressing an initial batch of just 12,500 copies. It would go on to reach single digits in the UK and Australian charts, eventually selling in the millions. Today, many of the synthesiser sounds appear dated, although the album's success did help cement the synth as a legitimate lead instrument. About one and three-quarter minutes into 'Anne of Cleves', for some reason the melody from The Hollies' song 'Bus Stop' comes through loud and clear.

Perhaps this was the album that broke prog's back, dividing critics between those who found it offensively pretentious and those who loved its excesses. Mind you, it's nowhere near as flamboyant as much of Wakeman's later work. On *Six Wives*, Wakeman's mastery of all manner of keyboards is clearly evident, but musically the album is wildly fragmented, more like a showpiece of technique than a musical vision.

This was the pinnacle year for Dutch band Focus, starring keyboard and flute player Thijs van Leer and guitar whiz Jan Akkerman. The double album *Focus 3* charted well, and they also had hits with 'Hocus Pocus' and 'Sylvia', marking the first time in a decade that a band had two singles without lyrics in the UK Top 40. To support the new album, Focus enjoyed a sellout tour in the UK, as well as North American tours supporting Yes, Gentle Giant and Frank Zappa. A live disc, *At the Rainbow*, was also a big seller. So popular were Focus that Jan Akkerman bumped Eric Clapton off the top spot in *Melody Maker*'s annual best guitarist poll.

John Lennon and Yoko Ono at the John Sinclair Freedom Rally 1971

Linda and Paul McCartney with Bhaskar Menon

Mick Jagger

The Kent State Massacre 1970

Robert Plant and Jimmy Page of Led Zeppelin perform acoustic segment 1973

Sunbury Pop Festival 1973

Black Sabbath   Vietnamese refugees 1975

Pink Floyd perform *Dark Side of the Moon* 1973

David Bowie   Joni Mitchell   Alice Cooper

The Who

Karen and Richard Carpenter

Elton John

Peter Gabriel in Genesis

Brian Eno

Johnny Cash meets Richard Nixon at The White House 1972

Helen Reddy

The Bee Gees

Suzi Quatro

The 1973 version of King Crimson

T. Rex's Marc Bolan

Slade

New York Dolls

AC/DC

Gentle Giant

10cc

Johnny Rotten performing with The Sex Pistols

Blondie

The Ramones

Patti Smith

The Runaways

ABBA

Stevie Wonder

Carole King

Gloria Gaynor

Donna Summer

Dazzle dealers

One of the more interesting bands to have a hit album in 1973 was 10cc. Here was intelligent pop music crafted with style and wit. The line-up consisted initially of Graham Gouldman, Eric Stewart, Kevin Godley and Lol Creme. Their breakthrough hit single, 'Donna', was an ironic take on banal Top 40 music, in some ways reminiscent of Zappa's toying with the doowop idiom. 'Rubber Bullets', a catchy, shape-shifting song about a jailhouse riot, rocketed to number one in the UK and three in Australia. The success of the song wasn't impeded by the BBC wrongly assuming it was about Northern Ireland and thus banning it.

Many of 10cc's songs were little feasts, unafraid to employ key changes, shifting feels and character-filled vocals with hook-based rock 'n' roll clichés. The debut album is jam-packed with ideas and recording studio mastery, plus humour. Have a listen to the anthemic, stadium-like build on 'Fresh Air for Mama', or the wicked wit of 'Sand in My Face', about the then ubiquitous magazine advertisements for muscle-building con-traptions. 'Speed Kills' might have been a frantic twelve-bar blues, but it was layered with fourteen guitar parts, a sort of experiment in electric guitar potential, with psychedelic lyrics à la 'Eight Miles High' sung at a different tempo to the instruments. 10cc were fortunate to also have four excellent vocalists.

Roxy Music released *For Your Pleasure*, their last LP to include Brian Eno. It went to number four in the UK charts but wasn't so well received elsewhere. Lead singer Bryan Ferry's castration complex – a barely contained fear of losing his masculinity to sexually predatory females – pervades the disc, from 'Beauty Queen' to the seductive sirens of 'Editions of You', reaching its apotheosis with 'In Every Dream Home a Heartache', wherein a wealthy male playboy becomes subjugated by a blow-up doll. Revenge against the evils of womanhood emerges with 'The Bogus Man', a song about a male stalker. In this case, the music leans towards Krautrock, with discordant sax playing, treated vocals and a monotonous keyboard and drum bed. This pitiable obsession with women's power over men was also brandished on the cover, with Ferry's girlfriend and model Amanda Lear dressed as a dominatrix holding a panther on a leash.

Musically, it was all well removed from the Top 40, so no singles were released. Instead, a separate song, 'Pyjamarama', was put out as a single. While they were in Paris, Amanda Lear introduced the band to Salvador Dalí. Afterwards, Ferry referred to Dalí as 'a master self-publicist.'[32] Takes one to know one.

Roxy Music was very much Ferry's band, and he was leaning towards traditional music styles, whereas Eno was pushing the band towards the avant-garde while also becoming increasingly flamboyant on stage. Friction was inevitable. With Eno gone, Roxy Music recorded and released their second LP for the year, *Stranded*. The band were now much more mainstream, and for the first time Ferry was not the sole songwriter. The album went to number one in the UK but struggled in other territories. The whole LP has a metallic, dispassionate feel. Again, the cover featured a sexy female model, this time in a wet dress looking submissive.

But the real master of self-publicity, David Bowie, was shedding one identity to slip into a new one. Trouble was, Bowie's carefully honed stage personas were undermined whenever he was interviewed. In a TV interview with Russell Harty, he acknowledged that he had 'a hotchpotch philosophy which really is very minimal'. Questioned as to whether he indulged in any sort of religious worship, Bowie said, 'Um, I love. I love life very much indeed.' Asked who the real David Bowie was, he told Harty, 'I find that I am a person who can take on the guises of different people that I meet.'[33] The bling-bedecked starship trooper turned out to be a dull, decidedly shallow disappointment. A long, rambling interview with Roy Hollingworth for *Melody Maker* further demonstrated just how inarticulate and unfocused Bowie could be. As he intoned, '[W]e are easy people. And maybe in a lot of ways ... very simple. If only they could see. Oh God, this intellectual confusion that surrounds us all. Why, why ... why?' With unbelievable conceit, Bowie concluded the interview by saying, 'I never thought Ziggy would become the most talked about man in the world.'[34]

Aladdin Sane was the punning follow-up album to *The Rise and Fall of Ziggy Stardust*. The LP cover featured his new post-Ziggy look, with a red and blue lightning bolt painted across his face. The album release was preceded by hit singles 'The Jean Genie', and 'Drive-In Saturday'. Most of the songs on the album were maudlin, focused on the trials of being a celebrity or else portraying images of urban decay. The most interesting track was the title one, with some superb bass playing by Trevor Bolder and fabulous Keith Tippett–like piano playing by Mike Garson, although the melody is insignificant. It's worth hearing for the piano solo alone.

The Bo Diddley–inspired 'Jean Genie' began life as a jam session on a tour bus. The song may have been a hit, but it's an ordinary composition with lyrics that are just plain dreadful in almost every way, clumsily linking Iggy Pop with playwright Jean Genet. Other tracks on *Aladdin Sane* are musically and thematically superior. Reviewing the album, one critic noted, 'There is much to dazzle the eye and ear, but little to move the mind or heart. It is clever, but icy cold.'[35] Nevertheless, sales-wise, it surpassed Bowie's previous albums, going to the top spot in the UK and performing well elsewhere.

Queen had begun life as Smile, before Zanzibar-born Farrokh Bulsara changed his name to Freddy Mercury and joined the band, at the same time convincing the rest of the team to adopt a more regal moniker. After a few poorly attended gigs in 1972, the band decided to go to ground and record an album, even though they had no record deal. They were given access to Trident Studios on downtime when other artists were not using the facility. Months spent trying to find a record company willing to release the resulting album came to nought. In February 1973, they managed to get the unreleased album played on BBC Radio 1. A few weeks later the band struck a release deal with EMI Records, which put out the single 'Keep Yourself Alive', followed by the eponymous album.

While generally well received by critics, neither LP nor single set the world on fire. Mind you, *NME*'s Nick Kent found the band far too derivative, and even referred to their 'stupid name' as being 'like a bucket of stale urine'.[36] But Queen were hugely ambitious, keen to distinguish their act from the plethora of other bands seeking attention. They set about recording their next LP while touring with Mott the Hoople and building a fan base. For a time, all members of Queen wore only black and white, with Mercury's outfits becoming increasingly outrageous.

It was steadily more difficult for hard rock bands to distinguish themselves. The crowded field also included Thin Lizzy, Budgie, Nazareth, Wishbone Ash, Golden Earring, Aerosmith, Blue Öyster Cult (the first to utilise a nonsensical umlaut), The Amboy Dukes, Lynyrd Skynyrd (the name was a phonetical spelling of a high-school gym teacher's name), Montrose, Mountain, Bachman–Turner Overdrive and a whole host of others. Finding a point of difference for those churning out similar riff-based songs became the holy grail. The members of Kiss solved the problem by donning ridiculous comic-book costumes, apparently with individual personas: Starchild, Demon, Spaceman and Catman. With garish make-up that disguised their real faces, and shows that incorporated fire-breathing, shooting rockets and spitting blood, this daft silliness somehow found a massive audience.

Slade's awful haircuts and even more ridiculous outfits were also no impediment to success, with number one singles and a sellout concert at Earls Court. Three days after that concert, drummer Don Powell was critically injured in a car accident that took the life of his twenty-year-old girlfriend and put the drummer in a coma for a week. In order to meet a commitment to play a gig on the Isle of Man, eighteen-year-old plumber Frank Lea filled the vacancy with minimal rehearsal. Mind you, Slade's music wasn't too demanding and, as one critic quipped, 'I doubt whether anyone noticed the difference.'[37] Just ten weeks after surgery, Powell was able to join his bandmates in New York to record 'Merry Xmas Everybody', their sixth and final number-one UK single. Manager Chas Chandler had pressed the band to record a Xmas tune, which bore fruit when half a million copies were on advance order before it had even been released. The lyric suggested that everybody was having fun, but few people in Britain could have believed that, given the state of the economy. In 2009, it was determined that 42 per cent of the world's population was likely to have heard this very ordinary Slade tune. In 2015, the song reportedly continued to rake in £500,000 annually in royalties.

Status Quo were making a big impression on very young girls across the UK. As founder/guitarist Francis Rossi unkindly put it following one show, 'They were so bleedin' young. I mean, we went on stage and they were nibblin' at yer feet.'[38] Critics attending such events noted that every song sounded the same, but they did get progressively louder and more frantic as the show headed towards its climax. The band's new album, *Hello!*, became the first of four to top the UK albums charts. Status Quo were the McDonald's of rock music: formulaic grunge-boogie with yelled catchphrase choruses. On their Australian tour they were supported by local glam band Hush, who were equally contrived and derivative but also managed to get teenyboppers screaming.

Alice Cooper commandeered the shock rock end of the market with his macabre tomfoolery. The *Billion Dollar Babies* album hit number one in the UK and US, as well as spawning a string of rather dreadful hit singles. The album's title reflected the band's surprise at their own good fortune. The subject matter of the new material included necrophilia, visits to the dentist and sexual abuse. In some sort of domination fantasy, 'Raped and Freezin'' inverted expectations, with the male hitchhiker protagonist being used and abused by a woman driver. 'Generation Landslide' portrayed a generation disowned by their fathers and feminist mothers while they indulged in alcohol, razor blades and needles. It's all decidedly silly.

Capitalising on their respective notoriety, and like Brian Ferry before him, Cooper met with Salvador Dalí in a blaze of media, with the visual artist proffering a sculpture of the singer's brain, replete with ants and a chocolate eclair. Dalí's theatricality and fantastical persona had been a big influence on young Vincent Furnier.

America's biggest rock act in 1973 was arguably The Allman Brothers Band. The LP *Brothers and Sisters* was a huge American success, peaking at number one. The band were also touring again, playing stadiums and arenas. The LP features some nice solos among a lot of dog-eared twelve-bar blues patterns, but on 'Jelly Jelly' the lead guitar is so out of tune it grates. Mind you, the singing is often off-pitch also. As one of them told a reporter in 1973, 'I don't get interested in new ideas, and I don't think anybody else in the band does. We're more interested in the old things.' And then, without a trace of irony: 'If we studied new music as such, we'd wind up copying someone else.'[39]

After having a song rejected by the rest of the band during rehearsals for *Brothers and Sisters*, Gregg Allman decided to start cutting an album of his own, *Laid Back*. As Allman described his situation, he was 'like the guy who has a girlfriend across town so as to keep his marriage together' – as if that made sense.[40] The rest of the band tried to ignore Allman's other album affair.

The Allman Brothers were one of just three bands to play the largest rock festival of all time, The Summer Jam, which attracted 600,000 punters to the Watkins Glen Grand Prix raceway in New York state. The other two acts were The Grateful Dead and The Band. As was the case with Woodstock and many other massive festivals, the numbers of people overwhelmed the organisers, who were forced to turn it into a free event. Given the population of America at the time, it has been calculated that one in every 350 Americans attended the festival, including one in every three people aged seventeen to twenty-four who lived in either Boston or New York at the time.

One of the technical breakthroughs was a 50,000-watt sound system that incorporated digital delay lines to compensate for the speed of sound through the air. These devices were capable of milliseconds of delay. Thus, four speaker towers placed a distance from the stage were fed with 350 and 525 milliseconds of delay so their output matched the sound arriving from the stage speakers. There were no reports of violence, however a skydiver died when one of his flares engulfed him in flames. His body was found some time later in a nearby forest.

But tragedies were aplenty across the music scene. American singer-songwriter Gram Parsons had recorded as a solo artist and as a member of The Byrds and The Flying Burrito Brothers, but years of drug abuse had taken its toll, and the influential country-rock performer checked out on a toxic mix of morphine and alcohol. That set off a train of events that included his assistant Michael Martin and friend Phil Kaufman stealing Parsons' body from LA airport, then driving it to Joshua Tree National Park, where they failed in a bungled attempt at cremation. They were arrested and fined. The charred remains of the musician were finally buried in a cemetery in Louisiana.

The Stooges' former bassist Zeke Zettner also took his leave this year with help from heroin, and Ron 'Pigpen' McKernan, organist with The Grateful Dead, joined the 27 Club after years of alcohol abuse.

Happenstance also took its toll. Jim Croce had recorded a fistful of albums and enjoyed a number of charting singles. A week after recording his latest album, Croce and five others were killed when their chartered plane hit a tree during take-off in Louisiana.

Acting alone

Van Morrison was building a reputation for ignoring his audience at live gigs. As one critic wrote, 'I bore witness to what I can only describe as a most incredible non-performance ... He stood in the shadow of a battery of dark-blue spotlights and, except for some finger-poppin' with his right hand, remained immobile.'[41]

The polar opposite was Gary Glitter (Paul Francis Gadd), with his bouffant hair, Liberace bling and overt narcissism. He began as Paul Raven but the glam movement inspired his new moniker and look. Glitter had a number of egotistical UK pop hits in 1973, notably 'I'm the Leader of the Gang (I Am)' and 'I Love You Love Me Love'. His bestselling album, with the tacky title *Touch Me*, peaked at number two on the UK charts, spawning more hits: 'Do You Wanna Touch Me' (later covered raucously by Joan Jett) and 'Hello, Hello, I'm Back Again'. Although the contrived Glitter phenomenon failed to enthuse Americans, I'm sorry to say the album reached number eleven in Australia – and one in Finland! When his star began to wane, Glitter moved to France and Australia, and was at one stage declared bankrupt. His ignominy was compounded when he was convicted of possessing child pornography in England and then jailed in Vietnam on child sex charges, followed by further sex charges back in the UK.

In 1973, the glam phenomenon was so contrived that a manufactured pop star could be substituted without anyone realising. Peter Shelley of Magnet Records created a character called Alvin Stardust, no doubt drawing on Bowie's Ziggy Stardust. When Alvin Stardust's debut single, 'My Coo Ca Choo', began rising in the charts, Shelley wasn't interested in performing, so he cast Bernard Jewry as himself. Jewry lip-synced to 'My Coo Ca Choo' on *Top of the Pops*, and thereafter took on the camp role of Alvin with a series of chart successes on which he did actually sing.

A more enduring talent, Paul Simon, released his third solo studio album, *There Goes Rhymin' Simon*. Both album and lead single 'Kodachrome' were huge hits, although 'Kodachrome' couldn't be played on the radio in Britain because it utilised a trademarked business name. Further singles included 'Loves Me Like a Rock', 'Take Me to the Mardi Gras' and 'American Tune'. The latter had a melody plagiarised from a hymn, 'O Sacred Head, Now Wounded', and was, Simon admitted, as close as he had ever come to penning a political tune – which is an odd thing to say from someone who conceived '7 O'Clock News/Silent Night' for the 1966 LP *Parsley, Sage, Rosemary and Thyme*, and who had made the decidedly polemic 1969 TV special *Simon & Garfunkel: Songs of America*. Like 'America' from *Bookends*, 'American Tune' used personal ennui as an analogy for the nation's broader failings. Notably, Simon wrote the song just after Richard Nixon was elected president. Critics fell over each other to praise the album.

Billy Joel also experienced a crescendo with his second LP, *Piano Man*. At age twenty-two, he had been signed to Paramount Records' Family Productions, naively signing away almost all of his publishing rights. At the time he was broke, and, as he said, 'I didn't know what I was signing.'[42] As the album went gold, he only received US$8000 in royalties. What's more, his first album had been mastered at the wrong speed by the record company, so he ended up sounding somewhat chipmunk-like.

It was yet another huge year for Elton John with the release of *Don't Shoot Me I'm Only the Piano Player*, followed by *Goodbye Yellow Brick Road*.

The former went number one in the UK, US, Australia and elsewhere, yielding the hits 'Crocodile Rock' and 'Daniel'. The latter was also huge, staying at number one for two months and generating more hit singles: 'Bennie and the Jets', 'Goodbye Yellow Brick Road', 'Candle in the Wind', 'Saturday Night's Alright for Fighting' and 'Funeral for a Friend/Love Lies Bleeding'. His stage shows were increasingly flamboyant, and he was now employing professional costume designers, who were urged to create the most outrageous garb they could imagine.

Elton's entrances were also reaching beyond the absurd. At a Hollywood Bowl performance, the stage was dominated by a huge image of him in top hat and tails. Porn star Linda Lovelace was introduced, followed by impersonators of the Queen, Batman and Robin, Frankenstein's Monster and the Pope, each making their way down an illuminated staircase. Eventually Elton appeared to the strains of the 20th Century Fox theme, dressed in an outfit completely covered in feathers. As he descended, the lids on five pianos sprang open to spell out his name. Hundreds of doves were supposed to appear from within the pianos, but they either didn't survive the ordeal or else suffered stage fright. In fact, neither his band nor his songwriting partner, Bernie Taupin, were happy with this over-the-top showbiz pizzazz, believing it distracted from the quality of the music.

The success of *Goodbye Yellow Brick Road* caught Elton John by surprise. He described it as 'quite a dark record in a lot of ways. Songs about sadness and disillusion, songs about alcoholics and prostitutes and murders, a song about a sixteen-year-old lesbian who ends up dead in a subway. But it just kept selling and selling and selling ...'[43] Taupin said his lyrics for the song 'Benny and the Jets' were intended as a satire on the music industry of the time.

Elton John was now so big that he could commandeer the Boeing 720 that had been used by Led Zeppelin, having it repainted to his specification. He tells an amusing tale of taking his mother on tour, and her watching the famous porn movie *Deep Throat* on the plane while attempting to eat her lunch. But the man himself was rapidly transmogrifying into a spoilt, sulky, tantrum-throwing, juvenile pop star. It would only get worse as drugs entered the fray.

It was a make-or-break year for Bruce Springsteen. His debut album, *Greetings from Asbury Park, N.J.*, was released to generally good reviews but modest sales. With his E Street Band, Springsteen opened for numerous touring artists and headlined in smaller venues. By September, when the second album, *The Wild, the Innocent & the E Street Shuffle*, appeared, his work had become more intrinsic, and was again well received by critics, but also failed to set the cash registers ringing. The song 'Rosalita (Come Out Tonight)' was described by Springsteen as 'my musical autobiography'.[44] As a teenager, he'd had a girlfriend whose mother had threatened to take out a court injunction to keep him away from her daughter. He said he wrote 'Rosalita' 'as a kiss-off to everybody who counted you out, put you down or decided you weren't good enough'.[45]

The irrepressible Stevie Wonder released *Innervisions*, which quickly became a smash hit, making a huge impact on soul and black music. Wonder performed all the instruments, including drums, on seven of the nine tracks. Brimming with influences, the songs speak to drug abuse, racism and, of course, love.

Three days after the album's release, Wonder was sleeping in the passenger seat of a car driven by a friend when they collided with a logging truck. One of the logs broke through the windshield, hitting Wonder in the forehead. The musical genius was taken to hospital, where he lay in a coma for a week and a half. When he finally awoke, he had lost his sense of smell. Tour director Ira Tucker brought a keyboard to the sickbed, and to everyone's relief Wonder found he could still play. But his recuperation would take a long time, and Wonder would be moved to take a more spiritual journey because of it.

The key track on *Innervisions* is arguably 'Living for the City', a portrait of black oppression which also managed to squeeze in a comment about air pollution. The closing track, 'He's Misstra Know-It-All', is seemingly about a confidence trickster, but many took it to be a pointed attack on President Nixon. Both became hits, along with 'Higher Ground', a song about reincarnation.

More MOR

MOR (middle-of-the-road) rock – aka soft rock – was also big in 1973. Bread were still on the ... er, rise, but the band was crumbling. Nevertheless, the release of their *Best of Bread* album became one of the biggest-selling LPs for the year.

The group named after a dildo from a William Burroughs novel, Steely Dan, was also riding the crest, as were The Eagles. The latter's second album, *Desperado*, was named after a song that is so recognisable it is often assumed to have been a hit single, which it wasn't. Don Henley had composed the basics of the piece at his Laurel Canyon home in the late 1960s, but it was finally completed in collaboration with Eagles bandmate Glenn Frey. Linda Ronstadt recorded it for her *Don't Cry Now* album, and The Carpenters would also record the tune. The Eagles' album also produced another signature song for the band, 'Tequila Sunrise', cementing the successful songwriting partnership of Henley and Frey.

And, while we're in the middle of the road, over in Sweden, a group called Björn & Benny, Agnetha & Frida released their debut album, *Ring Ring*, with the title track becoming a successful single in Europe and South Africa. Their manager began calling them by the palindromic acronym ABBA, which was also the name of a fish canning company in Sweden. Failing to qualify for the Eurovision Song Contest in 1973, they set their sights on the 1974 competition.

Emerging subcultures

Ska had appeared in Jamaica in the early 1960s, using fast tempos, bouncing bass lines and stabbing horns. Rocksteady used fewer horns, and the bass played notes in clusters rather than continuously. Rocksteady also slowed the music down to make it more sensuous. Out of all this came reggae, which put further emphasis on rhythm and pushed the bass to the foreground. But reggae also had a moral conscience, much of it derived from Rastafarianism. Ras Tafari was the original name of Ethiopian emperor Haile Selassie, who was revered as the second coming of Christ in Rastafarianism theology. Ganja, or marijuana, was considered a sacred herb by Rastafarians.

Chris Blackwell, a white Englishman, had established Island Records in Jamaica during the late 1950s, but relocated to London in 1962 – the year in which Jamaica achieved independence from Britain. When Bob Marley & The Wailers finished a tour of the UK in 1973, they didn't have enough money to return home to Jamaica, so Blackwell advanced them the plane tickets and funded the recording of a new album in Jamaica. Blackwell reworked the resulting tapes and added some guitar by Wayne Perkins. Although not a huge seller, it was a breakthrough album for the reggae form, and today *Catch a Fire* is recognised as one of the best reggae albums of all time.

Marley's next album for Island, also released in 1973, was *Burnin'*, featuring two songs that would become reggae classics, 'I Shot the Sheriff' and 'Get Up, Stand Up'. While the former outstays its welcome with far too much tedious repetition of the chorus, the latter is a cracking call to activism.

Just as reggae had evolved in the ghettoes of Jamaica, so New York's ghettoes were developing their own musical culture. The Bronx, in particular, was an urban catastrophe, with high rates of both unemployment and crime. Many disreputable landlords set their buildings ablaze to collect insurance money. At one stage, fires were lit in twenty-two buildings in just one fortnight. On the upside, some residents enjoyed an intrinsic sense of community. Block parties were all the go, particularly among African-American, Caribbean and Latino folk. These were street events that often involved closing off a road to traffic so the locals could have barbecues and dance to music pumped out from a sound system controlled by a deejay. Power for these events was often achieved by hacking into the street lighting.

Since late 1971, dances had been held at the old Concourse Plaza Hotel, which was now housing families who had lost their homes in fires. In the hotel was a popular discotheque called the Tunnel Plaza; however, in 1973, the police shut it down for operating without a licence.

Jamaican-born DJ Kool Herc (Clive Campbell) was so named because, like Hercules, he was big and imposing. Just eighteen, he commanded respect and was able to keep control of dance party events. What's more, his events were alcohol- and drug-free. Most historians view 11 August 1973 as the beginnings of hip-hop, thanks to a 'Back to School Jam' party held for Herc's sister. The aim was to raise enough money for young Cindy to buy new clothes for the school year. Hand-drawn fliers advertised admission prices of twenty-five cents for girls and fifty cents for boys, with the party running from 9pm to 4am. Using two turntables, Herc experimented with moving the record back and forth to create a rhythm, which would become known as 'scratching'. He also used a mixer to switch between two discs. By focusing on the instrumental breaks in the songs, he allowed the young dancers – then called b-boys and later break dancers – to demonstrate their moves. Soon he learned to isolate the instrumental and percussion breaks on various songs and string them together as the party peaked. He referred to this as the merry-go-round.

Herc quickly became famous, thanks to his massive sound system (the speakers became known as Herculoids), and the fact that he played the sort of music that wasn't being played on the radio, including tracks by Baby Huey, Booker T & the M.G.'s, Mandrill and Cymande. A whole new subculture was underway.

America's commercial discotheques also became hungry for music that would keep people on the dance floor. The party drugs of choice among disco dancers were cocaine and 'poppers' (amyl nitrate – a heart stimulant that generates a sudden surge of blood to the brain). Nascent disco music included Harold Melvin and the Blue Notes' 'The Love I Lost', with its thumping bass and incessant four-four beat, and 'Dancing Machine' by The Jackson 5, which was recorded in early 1973 but not released until February 1974.

During a performance of 'Dancing Machine' on the TV show *Soul Train*, Michael Jackson did the robot dance. That style of dancing had been created in the late 1960s by Charles Washington, but Jackson did it faster and with more precision than anyone before.

At the time it was just called party music, but other artists favoured by discotheque deejays included Diana Ross, Isaac Hayes, Kool & the Gang and MFSB. Earth, Wind & Fire's fourth album, *Head to the Sky*, also capitalised on the hunger for dance music. Almost all these party/dance releases were by black artists.

Down with the echidnas

Australian entrepreneur Robert Stigwood brought Frank Zappa and the Mothers of Invention down under for the first time. They played Sydney's Hordern Pavilion during a series of unionised power stoppages that blacked out the city; fortunately, the Hordern had its own generator. This was Zappa's hot band, featuring Jean-Luc Ponty on violin. While in Sydney, Zappa managed to witness Barry Leef perform with Bakery at Chequers nightclub. Presumably because they knew Zappa was in the audience, Bakery rocked out a version of Zappa's blues tune 'Road Ladies'. Zappa was so impressed with Leef's singing that he invited the Aussie to perform 'Road Ladies' with The Mothers at their concerts in Sydney and Melbourne. Zappa also asked Leef to join his band on a more permanent basis, but Leef's contract with Bakery prevented him becoming a new Mother. The concert tour by Zappa and his band is considered by many – including me – as one of the best Australian tours of the era.

While in Melbourne, Zappa and some of his band visited a wildlife sanctuary, where they were seemingly taken with the echidnas. Soon after, Zappa would compose his breathless, difficult tune 'Echidna's Arf (Of You)', one of the most extraordinary compositions in his oeuvre (in particular, have a listen to the live version recorded in Helsinki on *You Can't Do That on Stage Anymore Vol 2*). Three years later, on a return visit, he would come face-to-face with an even stranger antipodean creature, the satirical little Aussie bleeder Norman Gunston.

Michael Gudinski and Ray Evans' new Mushroom Records label released the nation's first three-disc set, *The Great Australian Rock Festival: Sunbury 1973*. The neophyte label had already released its first single, a catchy tune by Madder Lake with the terrible title 'Goodbye Lollipop'. This was an art rock band with an arty name – madder lake being a painting pigment. Their debut album, *Stillpoint*, performed extremely well also.

Prog band MacKenzie Theory's debut album, *Out of the Blue*, was Mushroom Records' second LP. Recorded live in the studio in front of a small audience, the album disappointed its makers, failing to reach the energetic highs of their uninhibited concert performances. Nevertheless, the album marked another high point in progressive rock for Australian acts.

And Jeannie Lewis released her debut folk-jazz album, *Free Fall through Featherless Flight*, with a cover designed by Martin Sharp and music arranged and directed by Michael Carlos.

Of the twenty-five top-selling albums in Australia for the year, only two were home-grown, and they both appeared well down the list – and both were by Brian Cadd. The focus for Australian record buyers remained Britain and America. It's not surprising that many Australian performers tried to make themselves and their music sound anything but Australian. Cadd's Bootleg label released successful singles and an album by local soft rock outfit Mississippi, while Sherbet enjoyed a hit with their version of Graham Nash's 1971 song 'Chicago', about the Chicago Eight trial.

Australia's fondness for irreverent humour was evidenced in new LPs from The Captain Matchbox Whoopee Band plus The Indelible Murtceps, with their album *Warts Up Your Nose*. The 69'ers were wowing audiences with their cheeky and frequently obscene songs. Spectrum transmogrified into Ariel, and their debut album, *Strange Fantastic Dream*, proved controversial: its cover featured a hypodermic needle, and the album included song titles such as 'Chickenshit' and 'Confessions of a Psychotic Cowpoke'. There were calls to have it banned.

A number of bands were formed in Australia in 1973 that would go on to international success. One emerged in Brisbane as Kid Galahad and the Eternals but would soon adopt the name The Saints. Cold Chisel began in Adelaide covering songs by Deep Purple and Led Zeppelin. And the two younger brothers of former Easybeats guitarist George Young decided to start their own band. Their father reportedly told them, 'We give you a week.

It won't last.[46] Naive to the sexual innuendo, they dubbed themselves AC/DC after a symbol on their sister's sewing machine. (God-fearing wowsers would later claim that AC/DC stood for Anti-Christ/Devil's Children.)

Two other festivals appeared in Australia that would have long-lasting impacts. The Tamworth Country Music Festival began its very long journey, and, in a northern New South Wales town tucked away amid verdant hills, there was a gathering of the counterculture to celebrate alternative lifestyles. The Nimbin Aquarius Festival evolved out of previous festivals by the Australian Union of Students. Historically, it is important because it featured the first ever 'Welcome to Country' ceremony by Traditional Owners of the land. The music performers at Nimbin were an eclectic bunch. There was the decidedly hippie-ish Lindsay Bourke, but also brilliant South African jazz pianist Dollar Brand (later know as Abdullah Ibrahim). The festival inspired a counterculture scene in the region that is still in evidence a half-century later.

Reddy or not

On the back of her hit 'I Am Woman', Helen Reddy became the first Australian to win a Grammy Award for Best Female Vocalist. During the ceremony, Reddy caused a stir by concluding her speech with, 'I want to thank God because *she* makes everything possible.'[47] Friend Flip Wilson handed over his TV show to Helen Reddy for an eight-week summer season. The *Helen Reddy Show* aired at 8pm each Thursday on NBC-TV

This was a big year for Reddy, with her single 'Delta Dawn' also becoming a huge hit. The song had already been a country and western hit for Tanya Tucker. Bette Midler also recorded it for her debut album, intending for the tune to be the lead single, but Reddy's version came out two days before Midler's. Pop music was often a cut-throat game. 'Delta Dawn' was the first of six consecutive number one hits for the Reddy in her adopted homeland.

For Australian feminists, the Whitlam federal government was a dream come true. They supported family planning services, introduced 'no fault' divorce, legislated maternity leave for women in the public service, out-lawed discrimination on the basis of pregnancy, and even created a special adviser to the prime minister's office on women's issues – a world first.

Of course, conservative voices were consistently opposed to women's rights. Amusingly, Margaret Thatcher – at the time the British education secretary – declared, 'I don't think there will be a woman prime minister in my lifetime.' But the world was changing despite conservative desires to hold it in stasis, and Thatcher would soon be a beneficiary.

A few women were also generating chinks in the male-dominated field of hard rock. Suzi Quatro had worked with her sisters in both The Pleasure Seekers and Cradle, which were managed by her brother Michael Quatro. Although trained in various instruments, Suzi played the bass guitar in both groups. Hailing from Detroit, Cradle rocked harder than any other all-female band. In 1971, Michael invited British producer Mickie Most to see the band perform. Most judged that Suzi had real stage presence, so he invited her to come to England. This led to a family rift that would last a lifetime. In London, alone and depressed, bunking in a cheap room, she experienced what she called 'the lowest point in my life'.[48] Vindictively, Quatro's father sent his daughter a cassette tape on which he had recorded the voices of various people cruelly critiquing her.

Like many others, Mickie Most was hunting for the new Janis Joplin. Quatro's debut single was a hit in Portugal but nowhere else. Most then introduced her to the songwriting team of Nicky Chinn and Mike Chapman, who agreed to pen some songs geared towards the young woman. With a newly fashioned leather-clad look, Quatro and her new band toured as a support act for Thin Lizzy and Slade. In early 1973, her second single, the thumping boogie 'Can the Can', pushed the bass to the forefront. It reached number one in the UK, Australia and in several European countries, but only fifty-six in the US. This would be the pattern for Quatro's career, with her popularity in England and especially Australia far eclipsing that in her homeland.

If anyone can explain Chapman and Chinn's lyrics on 'Can the Can', then you're a better interpreter than I. Why is she telling women to can the can in order to make a stand for their man? And what's with all the eagle metaphors? 'Can the Can' was all thumping hook. It was rapidly followed by three more Suzi Quatro hits, '48 Crash', 'Daytona Demon' and 'Devil Gate Drive', each selling over a million copies. Quatro also released her debut LP, which was a commercial success, particularly down under, where it went to number two. Australia would continue to be a Quatro stronghold.

Blondie's Debbie Harry has suggested that Quatro was too far ahead of her time for the US market. Indeed, Harry wrote that at the time 'there weren't any girls leading rock bands'.[49] Of course, that's not quite true, but even so there can be little doubt that Quatro was a trailblazer for women rock performers. As she once put it, she played the boys at their own game. Yet in 1973 she was inclined to distance herself from the women's liberation movement, voicing concerns that movements cause people to follow like sheep rather than stand up as individuals. It may have been a naive position, but at least Quatro was walking the talk. Her influence on people like Joan Jett, Cherie Currie, KT Tunstall, Kathy Valentine and Chrissie Hynde is well documented. As Jett put it, 'She was integral to me figuring out who I was, finding my own style and, you know, becoming my own person.'[50] Talking Heads' Tina Weymouth was sufficiently impressed by Quatro to put away her folk guitar and instead pick up a bass.

There were now various women challenging male dominance in the music industry. Betty Davis – model, composer and former wife of Miles Davis – released her debut solo album of raunchy funk. Asked to describe her music, she said, 'I'd just say it was raw.'[51]

Olivia Records was established as an all-female record label, signing up Meg Christian, Linda Tillery, Mary Watkins and Sweet Honey in the Rock. The Berkeley Women's Music Collective was formed by four lesbian feminists, who began to write songs celebrating their own experiences. As member Nancy Vogl put it, '[B]y our mere existence we provided an alternative to self-medication and an alternative to self harm and there were a shit ton of women who were stuck in that dynamic.'[52] Out of Manchester, England, appeared The Northern Women's Liberation Rock Band, self-described as professional feminists living on the dole. Their sister band in London was The Stepney Sisters, performing songs about toxic masculinity and speculum exams. And American bluegrass performers Hazel Dickens and Alice Gerrard were among the first women to record in the bluegrass genre.

Acceptance of gays and lesbians also took a huge step forward when the Australian Medical Association removed homosexuality from its list of illnesses and disorders, two months before the American Psychiatric Association did the same. A National Lesbian Conference at UCLA in America was attended by 1500 people, the first such conference ever assembled.

Raw and influential

Although London is commonly viewed as the epicentre of punk, in fact the movement really started in New York (notwithstanding Detroit-based proto-punk outfits like MC5, which date back to the 1960s).

Creem magazine's readers' poll famously voted the New York Dolls as the best new group and simultaneously the worst new group. Such a confused response perfectly suited a band that refused to be pigeonholed. A decade later, vocalist David Johansen, a chameleon in the Bowie tradition, would develop a whole new alter ego as Buster Poindexter, a lounge music performer. But in 1973, the New York Dolls' first album, produced by Todd Rundgren, met with solid critical acclaim and poor sales. It would have a pivotal influence on later bands such as the Ramones, The Damned and Guns N' Roses.

The Stooges' *Raw Power* was finally released. It went for more of a heavy rock sound, thanks to the addition of guitarist James Williamson, but it's still uncooked, ear-splitting, butt-clenching, garage punk. What MC5's *Kick Out the Jams* was to the 1960s, *Raw Power* was to the '70s. Too primeval for radio airplay, the album again sold badly, but it is today recognised as one of the more influential discs in rock history. Certainly, *Raw Power* has been name-checked by many luminaries of the punk movement. Even Nirvana's Kurt Cobain claimed it was his favourite all-time album. Mötley Crüe's Nikki Sixx and Red Hot Chili Peppers' John Frusciante have also heaped praise on the LP.

The key track is the opener, 'Search and Destroy', in which Iggy Pop describes himself as a social outsider seeking revenge through destruction, with his heart full of napalm. The loner persona permeates the whole album, but the sharper focus of Pop's aggression was his own body, evidenced not only in his self-harming stage performances but also in the song 'Penetration', in which he asks to be brutally penetrated. Punk would soon pick up this thread of self-loathing and misanthropy.

Avoiding the present

France continued its atomic tests at Mururoa Atoll, and Greenpeace were now savvy to the power of media images. So when their yacht was overrun by French commandos, who proceeded to beat Captain David McTaggart, nineteen-year-old New Zealander Ann-Marie Horne was able to sneakily take photographs. Horne smuggled her exposed film off the vessel by placing it in her vagina. Retrieved and disseminated, the resulting images shocked the world. As *The Washington Post* put it, 'McTaggart's actions were among the most effective in the history of protest'.[53]

By the end of 1973, the UK government of Ted Heath had taken the extraordinary step of limiting electricity consumption across the commercial sector to three days a week – thus enforcing a three-day working week. The year was also beset with aircraft hijacks and bombings, and the Middle East was emerging as the globe's most significant flashpoint. Arabs and Jews were struggling over the existence of Israel, and America found itself wedged. The Organization of the Petroleum Exporting Countries (OPEC) represented the globe's principal oil exporters, including Saudi Arabia, Kuwait, Iran and Iraq. As the West continued to guzzle oil for vehicles, plastics, fertilisers, plus hundreds of everyday products, OPEC found itself in an increasingly powerful position. Targeting nations that supported Israel, the Arab members of OPEC turned off the oil tap to the UK, US, Canada, the Netherlands and Japan. In America, as queues at gas stations got longer, tempers began to fray, with fistfights and even gas station homicides occurring. Society itself seemed to be unravelling.

The events and turmoil of the late 1960s and early '70s had worn many people down. Americans began to look back with longing towards a more simple, less chaotic time in their history. Suddenly, nostalgia was big business.

The original production of *Grease*, a musical set in 1959, opened in New York in 1972, eventually moving to the Royale Theatre, where it ran until 1980. In 1973, *Grease* also made its London debut.

The British movie *That'll Be the Day*, a coming-of-age story set in the late 1950s and early '60s, starred rockers David Essex and Ringo Starr, with Billy Fury inveigled out of retirement, and with The Who's Keith Moon and Renaissance/Strawbs keyboardist John Hawken playing smaller parts. The soundtrack was jam-packed with songs by Fury, The Everly Brothers, Buddy Holly and Ritchie Valens, and it charted in single digits.

The nostalgia boom saw Australia's first Rock & Roll Revival concert tour, featuring Bill Haley and His Comets as well as The Coasters, The Drifters and Johnny O'Keefe. *The Rocky Horror Show*, a theatrical tribute to the schlock horror films of earlier decades, premiered in London in a production directed by Jim Sharman.

American Graffiti, a movie set in 1962's California, hit the screens. Produced on a modest budget, it became one of the most profitable films ever made, raking in millions while being nominated for a best picture Oscar. The big-selling soundtrack double album featured Bill Haley, Buddy Holly, Chuck Berry, The Beach Boys and The Platters. Hot on that movie's heels was the television series *Happy Days*, again presenting an idealised version of life in the late 1950s.

Contemporary rock music appeared to be on the ropes.

1974

Whatever Happened to the Revolution?

Here we are, a decade along from the British Invasion, which began when The Beatles, closely followed by The Dave Clark Five, The Animals, The Kinks, The Rolling Stones, The Hollies and others, conquered America. Certainly, nobody in 1964 could have anticipated that rock music would erupt into such a dazzling array of divergent styles in the space of just ten years. But where could it go next? Of the half-dozen bestselling albums in the US, four were 'best of' compilations – which might lead one to think that audiences were less interested in discovering new artists than in reheating old favourites. It was a similar story in the UK, where the top ten included greatest hits albums by Elton John, The Carpenters, Simon & Garfunkel and Elvis.

Reinforcing that rear-vision focus, Bob Dylan's first full-scale tour since 1966 began in January 1974, and broke all previous ticket sale records. Backed by The Band, the tour's success was hailed as the rebirth of 1960s optimism. Activist and folk singer Phil Ochs used the opportunity to rail against the theatrics of shock rock and glam, saying:

> So young kids think, perhaps, that making music has to go hand in hand with a stupid stage show. This is ridiculous, and that's what Dylan's concerts have proved. The social value of Dylan's tour is that here is a real man, standing up on stage with no props, and making some fine music.[1]

A live album, *Before the Flood*, resulted from the tour, but it was plainly nothing new. While touring, Dylan's album *Planet Waves* was released, again with support from The Band. For the first time in Dylan's career, the album went to number one in the US, but it didn't stay there long.

Rebounding from rock bottom

January also saw Robert Wyatt released from hospital. The world that Wyatt rejoined after recuperating from his accident was decidedly miserable, yet the former Soft Machine and Matching Mole drummer proved remarkably stoic. As his biographer Marcus O'Dair put it, 'There is, in fact, a curious sense in which Wyatt actually became *less* sorry for himself once he became a paraplegic.'[2] Now paralysed from the waist down, he continued his music career with what is, in my opinion (and, thankfully, the opinion of many others), one of the finest, most original and deeply personal rock albums of all time.

Before the accident, the former drummer had been working on new material while staying in Venice, where his girlfriend, Alfreda 'Alfie' Benge, was working on the movie *Don't Look Now*. That watery environment informed much of his new work, some of it composed on a cheap, Riviera keyboard that Alfie had bought him. During his months in hospital, he also found an upright piano in the visitor's room on which he could continue to work.

Some of the new album was recorded at the farm where Wyatt and Alfie first lobbed after his hospital stint. He could no longer play a full drum kit, but he could utilise hand percussion, including various found objects. He also perfected the use of his voice as an instrument. After he moved to Virgin's Manor and finally CBS studios, with Pink Floyd's Nick Mason in the producer's seat, the recording process went very smoothly. As Mason put it, 'Exposure to Robert's fertile stream of ideas was the most rewarding musical experience I had enjoyed outside the [Pink Floyd] band.'[3] Wyatt was able to carefully assemble the most appropriate performers for each track. Among the various combinations were Hugh Hopper, Richard Sinclair, Laurie Allan, Fred Frith, Mike Oldfield, Gary Windo and the wonderful South African trumpet player

Mongezi Feza. Both sides of the LP ended with offbeat declamations by Scottish eccentric Ivor Cutler.

Wyatt's lyrics on *Rock Bottom* frequently invoke Lewis Carroll, with an uncanny melding of childlike imagery and intellectual sophistication. Musically, the album was inspired by artists as disparate as John Coltrane and Van Morrison. Of the album's intimacy, Wyatt ruminated, 'You know, people think art transcends daily life. But it may do the opposite. It feels like it's more about re-finding the animal inside the sophisticated human being.'[4]

Wyatt admitted that *Rock Bottom* wasn't rock 'n' roll, nor was it jazz or folk. It probably didn't fit into any genre, he mused: 'It's like a sort of Galápagos Island animal, some kind of underwater duck.' The tracks 'Alifib' and 'Alifie', which comprise most of side two, are a play on his wife's name. 'Alifib' begins with some superb upper-register bass playing by Hugh Hopper, before Wyatt starts singing, blubbering nonsense, while referring to Alfie as his larder – the sustenance he plainly requires. In the rejoinder, 'Alifie', Wyatt devolves to phonetic baby talk while the music becomes increasingly sinister, with Gary Windo's urgent, untamed tenor sax performing some kind of primal scream therapy. Alfreda herself finally appears, to set the singer straight. Like an evocative parable of Jungian anima–animus struggle, 'Alifie' and 'Alifib' elicit the concept of a male seeking to devour the female in order to complete himself, with the female assertively resisting to ensure they both survive and grow.

'Sea Song' is a sublime, edgy love song, loaded with dreamlike aquatic imagery and sexual metaphors. It's a eulogy to the vicissitudes of romantic attraction. Eventually, the piece resolves into Wyatt's unique free-form, impassioned vocalising. 'Little Red Riding Hood Hit the Road' becomes a plaintive self-recrimination, over a dense bed of multi-tracked trumpets with bass guitar weaving a path through it all. The album concludes with 'Little Red Robin Hood Hit the Road', featuring Mike Oldfield's soaring guitar, until we are left with Ivor Cutler's absurd surrealism accompanied by his wheezy harmonium and Fred Frith's viola. By the time the album concludes, you know you've gone somewhere no other album has ever taken you. Even the cover bucks the trend of boldly colourful artwork, instead opting for a very subtle monochrome drawing by Alfie.

One of the most disarming qualities that pervades Wyatt's solo work is that he is neither self-indulgent nor self-important. As his biographer put it, '[F]or all his insecurities, [Wyatt] is less needy and narcissistic than many singer-songwriters.'[5] In this era of ostentatious prog, attention-seeking glam and supercilious heavy metal, Robert Wyatt was certainly swimming against the tide.

Alfreda Benge attended a meeting with Richard Branson, at which the contract for *Rock Bottom* was supposed to be negotiated. Alfie wanted a clause removed that would have assigned publishing rights to Virgin Records, but Branson reportedly said, 'I don't speak to women about these kinds of things. Get a lawyer.' That turned out to be excellent advice, because their lawyer placed a limit on the ownership, resulting in Wyatt being perhaps the only Virgin artist of the era who subsequently owned their back catalogue.[6]

Rock Bottom was met with universal praise from critics, and it even sold moderately well in the US, where the specific chart that dealt with progressive rock stations saw it peak at thirteen. Today it appears on *New Musical Express*'s 500 greatest albums of all time. *Prog Sphere* calls it a 'masterpiece ... easily one of the best rock albums ever released'.[7] *Allmusic* says it is 'deservedly acclaimed as one of the finest art rock albums'.[8]

A live version of *Rock Bottom* was performed at the Theatre Royal. In solidarity with Wyatt, the musicians all sat in wheelchairs for a cover photo for *New Musical Express*. At the same time, an offbeat single was released. It wasn't a track from the home-spun album, but rather Wyatt's version of 'I'm a Believer', the Neil Diamond song made famous by The Monkees. It includes what Nick Mason described as 'a fabulously avant-garde violin solo by Fred Frith of Henry Cow'[9]. Unexpectedly, 'I'm a Believer' became a hit, something Virgin Records was completely unprepared for. Robert and friends, including pre-Police Andy Summers, were invited to mime the song on TV's *Top of the Pops*. Unfortunately, the show's producer deemed Wyatt's wheelchair to be unsuitable for family viewing. An argument erupted that lasted most of a day. In the end, the BBC relented, although the arms of the wheelchair had to be removed to somehow make the device appear seemlier. As Wyatt noted, 'It was the first time anybody had made me feel unsightly. And it was a shock.'[10]

Still progressing

For want of a better category, *Rock Bottom* is lumped in with progressive rock. Meanwhile, classic prog was progressing, classically.

Conductor Martyn Ford put Caravan together with The New Symphonia Orchestra for a concert at the Theatre Royal in Drury Lane, which was recorded and released on the album *Caravan & The New Symphonia*. As well as Caravan standards, they also played a couple of new songs, including the amusingly titled 'Virgin on the Ridiculous'.

Yes released the double album set *Tales from Topographic Oceans*, inspired by singer Jon Anderson's acquaintance with the book *Autobiography of a Yogi*. The album is as grandiose as it sounds, with four side-long tracks. Although critical opinions ranged from ecstatic praise to cries of 'boring', the buying public were decidedly accommodating, with the album going to the top spot in the UK and single digits elsewhere, including America. Much of the material is unfocused, and, as usual, Jon Anderson's voice lacks colour and timbre, while the words are deeply buried in the mix. Touring included a massive set designed by cover artist Roger Dean and his brother Martyn. But keyboard player Rick Wakeman was less than happy performing the material live, announcing his decision to leave at the end of the tour.

While touring, Wakeman managed to find time to record *Journey to the Centre of the Earth*, based on the Jules Verne novel. He had sold some of his vehicle collection and taken on mortgages to fund two sellout concerts at London's Royal Festival Hall. The concerts featured the London Symphony Orchestra, the English Chamber Choir and actor David Hemmings as narrator. A recording of the second concert generated an album, but the A&M Records executives hated it and refused to release the disc. Yet again, the studio bigwigs proved themselves totally out of touch with public taste. A cassette was sent to A&M's US co-founder Jerry Moss, who eventually approved its release. *Journey to the Centre of the Earth* ended up being the first album on the A&M label to reach number one in the UK, and it peaked at two in Australia and three in the US, generating many millions of dollars. Despite a series of heart attacks, the twenty-five-year-old Wakeman toured the show in North America, Japan, Australia and New Zealand, supported by orchestras and choirs. As music writer Charles Snider put it, 'This may have been the stuff that gave prog rock a bad rap, but the public's appetite for these grandiose works was certainly real.'[11]

Also mixing classical music with rock was Focus' *Hamburger Concerto*, which fused chamber music with jazz-rock. The title track was a side-long work based on 'Variations on a Theme by Haydn', originally composed by Brahms, with some truly awful singing by Thijs van Leer, who should have known better. Deep Purple's keyboard player Jon Lord further indulged his classical affectations with an album recorded live in Germany titled *Windows*, performed with the rock band and the Munich Chamber Orchestra. And David Bedford released *Star's End*, which was commissioned and performed by the Royal Philharmonic Orchestra, with the additions of Mike Oldfield on guitar plus Henry Cow's versatile drummer Chris Cutler.

Electric Light Orchestra, or ELO, were unsubtle in their blending of classical and pop-rock. In concert they would marry pieces like Grieg's 'In the Hall of the Mountain King' with 'Roll Over Beethoven'. Their fourth LP, *Eldorado*, was another concept album, with a narrative about a man who escapes into fantasy worlds to avoid the reality of his humdrum life. Composer Jeff Lynne told a journalist, 'The last thing you could accuse ELO of being is pretentious.'[12] Perhaps Lynne lacked perspective? The track 'Can't Get It Out of My Head', with its Beatles-like string arrangement, became a hit single in America, where the band were far better received than in their homeland. The Beatles' influence can be found elsewhere too, especially in the melody and arrangement of 'Mister Kingdom'. During the thirteen-year lifespan of ELO, they managed to shift more than 50 million records.

Yes recruited Swiss keyboardist Patrick Moraz to take over from Wakeman, and managed to record and release another LP before the year's end. *Relayer* was another strong seller. Where *Tales from Topographic Oceans* had been sprawling, *Relayer* was far more concise and complex, with the new keyboard sounds a welcome change. They were still tackling big ideas, with the side-long 'The Gates of Delirium' inspired by Tolstoy's *War and Peace*, no less. After the obligatory tour of the US, the band split up so each member could indulge their solo album caprices.

King Crimson put out two very different discs before Fripp called it quits. *Starless and Bible Black* was an album of disparate parts, most recorded live and some in the studio. Like the previous year's *Larks' Tongues in Aspic*, the LP went from high-octane fury to gentle improvisation, often within the one track. There's a truly lovely piece describing Rembrandt's painting 'The Night Watch', an excellent vehicle for John Wetton's very distinctive voice. 'We'll Let You Know' is a twisted slice of funk, and the album concludes with 'Fracture', a meaty play on the tritone, or 'devil's interval'. Although the album saw Crimson reduced to a quartet, violin and keyboard player David Cross had already departed by the time the album appeared. That left a trio of Fripp, Wetton and Bill Bruford. They sloughed off any hints of romantic delicacy to become a powerhouse, bruising outfit for the album *Red*. If heavy metal had developed beyond simple power chords and big hair in the 1970s, it would've sounded like *Red*.

Red is a showcase of guitar magnificence, propelled by Bruford's busy, articulate drumming. As the drummer wrote:

> I was steeling myself for another round of excruciating, teeth-pullingly difficult music-making … Why did it have to be this hard? … In part, because we were not drawing on a shared heritage of music-making, and our overblown sense of importance encouraged us to believe we should be reinventing music, or at least this genre of it, with every album.[13]

Thus, *Red* displays a wonderous amalgam of cerebral complexity and visceral rock dynamism. It was the worst-selling of the early Crimson albums, but has since been reassessed for its pioneering achievement, with *The Chicago Tribune* going so far as to call it 'progressive rock's finest hour'.[14] King Crimson were always ahead of the curve. Their 1969 debut, *In the Court of the Crimson King*, had pioneered the explosion of prog rock. Now with *Red*, Fripp's Crimson was signalling the beginning of the end for prog as an expansive genre. *Red* also foresaw the hybrid of prog and heavy metal that would eventually become progressive metal.

Robert Fripp dissolved the band on the eve of *Red*'s release, and headed to a retreat with no intention of returning to music. As the self-righteous doomsayer told *Melody Maker*, 'I saw in America enough evidence of the breakdown of social and economic order to know that something's fundamentally wrong and it can't be reversed.' In response, he would become, in his words, a 'small, mobile, independent and intelligent unit',[15] i.e. just himself. But, of course, the social order didn't end, and Fripp would still be touring with King Crimson fifty years later.

Gentle Giant's sixth album, *The Power and the Glory*, took the band even further down the anomalous path they had been forging, like a machete through thick jungle. This would be the band's most difficult listening, with the tunes and arrangements even more convoluted and the time signature shifts more jagged than on previous outings. Inspired by Watergate and the Cold War, the album's overarching concept was about the corruption of power; for all that, it sold surprisingly well in America.

Genesis did a Led Zeppelin and retreated to a country estate for three months to write their album *The Lamb Lies Down on Broadway*. They were now a headlining act, but all was not well with their lead singer, Peter Gabriel, who was only present for parts of the retreat, yet insisted on controlling all the lyrics. Other band members were going through their own personal crises, so the material was created under difficult circumstances.

Based around Gabriel's narrative of a Puerto Rican youth from New York going on a journey of self-discovery, the new album was seemingly pitched to appeal to American audiences. British scribe Chris Welch delivered the verdict: 'Beautiful songs, fascinating lyrics, and sensitive, subtle playing, mixed with humour and harmonies.'[16] The double disc has remained a prog favourite. The album's US tour saw Gabriel's stage theatrics again the primary focus of the critics, which frustrated the rest of the band. As Phil Collins admitted at the time, 'I'd like to see it veer away from headdresses and costume changes, and for Peter to use his hands more in mime, just in the black suit. But we haven't talked about it.'[17] However, a more straightforward solution arose just six dates into the six-month long tour, when Gabriel told the gang that he was ditching them at the end of their engagements. It didn't make for a happy tour; as Mike Rutherford put it, 'The worst thing is when someone doesn't share your enthusiasm for what you're doing anymore: the fun just goes out of it.'[18]

Supertramp was busy, like Queen, marrying pop songs with accessible prog. Their label, A&M, had packed them off to the country for yet another rock retreat, resulting in an incredible forty-two demo songs. Eight were chosen to grace the new disc, *Crime of the Century*, which was a huge commercial breakthrough. The key single from the album, 'Dreamer', performed well, as did its B-side, 'Bloody Well Right'. Supertramp's long run of success was just beginning.

As well as appearing as a guest on many other albums, Brian Eno released two of his own: *Here Come the Warm Jets* and *Taking Tiger Mountain (By Strategy)*. But perhaps the most eagerly awaited prog album was Mike Oldfield's follow-up to his smash hit *Tubular Bells*.

Oldfield was not cut out to be a rock star. The twenty-one-year-old had been adding his skills to other people's studio sessions, and was flooded with calls to perform live, but he suffered from panic attacks and preferred to keep a low profile. Asked whether success had changed him, he told an interviewer: '[I]t hasn't changed me enough. I really wish it had changed me more than this. I'm not very happy with myself as a person. I'd like a different brain, you know, I'm tired of the one that I've got. I find life a strain.'[19] *Hergest Ridge* presented another long, shifting composition covering both sides of the LP. It went to number one in the UK, only to be usurped by Oldfield's earlier *Tubular Bells* – a rare instance of an artist displacing themselves from the top spot. Unfortunately, *Hergest Ridge* was like a less-interesting version of *Tubular Bells*. The latter would be resurrected again and again over the years, including an orchestrated version courtesy of David Bedford, remixed varieties, plus three sequel albums. It was also incorporated into the 2012 Olympic Games opening ceremony.

Arty facts

Virgin Records released avant-garde rock band Henry Cow's peerless second outing, *Unrest*. Henry Cow were also invited to join quirky trio Slapp Happy at the Manor Studio to record the truly exceptional song-based album *Desperate Straights*, featuring the extraordinary voice of Dagmar Krause. If intelligent, angular, chamber-rock with hints of Kurt Weill sounds like your thing, then give *Desperate Straights* a spin.

Henry Cow toured England and Europe with Captain Beefheart & His Magic Band. Both outfits were testing their audiences. Don Van Vliet's hoarse, gruff, barely musical vocals and freeform lyrics were draped over loose, bluesy-jazz rock. His idiosyncratic anarchy would have been far less musical were it not for the exceptional musical abilities of his band. But it was a rough ride with the mercurial Beefheart. As drummer Art Tripp explained, Van Vliet may have taken composing credit, but he was really a co-composer. As Tripp put it, 'It was better when he wasn't around. We got a lot more done.'[20]

Beefheart's first release on the Virgin label, *Unconditionally Guaranteed*, was criticised for being too commercial. Immediately after recording the disc, the band fired their eccentric leader. The next album, *Bluejeans & Moonbeams*, was made by Beefheart with a new band, but he subsequently disowned both LPs, even suggesting buyers should demand their money back. Beefheart teetered on the cusp of madness and brilliance. He only enjoyed a cult status, but his influence was far-reaching. Matt Groening, who created *The Simpsons*, apparently loved Beefheart's *Trout Mask Replica* album, and Kate Bush put *Bluejeans & Moonbeams* in her top ten.

Of particular note in 1974 was the arrival of The Residents, with their debut album *Meet the Residents*. The title was ironic, given that the band members remained anonymous when performing, wearing masks including giant eyeballs on their heads. Based in San Francisco, the group created Ralph Records to distribute their eccentric music. They also began working on their next LP, *Not Available*, with the stated intention of withholding its release until the band had forgotten about its existence! They didn't end up waiting that long, as *Not Available* was set free later in 1974.

Again, there are direct correlations with the looming punk movement, particularly in The Residents' dissembling of pop and rock conventions. *Meet the Residents* includes signature elements of rock, jazz and classical tropes, strangely processed cartoon-like vocals, and snippets of sound collage. The original cover of *Meet the Residents* used defaced artwork from the *Meet the Beatles* album. The Residents' LP opens with a deconstructed version of 'These Boots Are Made for Walking', hardly recognisable under the distortion and tape manipulations. To promote the disc, 4000 single-sided eight-inch flexi discs were provided free with Canadian art magazine *File*. Ignored at the time, the album is now rightly viewed as a landmark testimonial of anti-commercial rock music.

Not Available was less harsh and better crafted, but still alien to most ears. In moments during the album, truly beautiful snatches of melody arise like oases from the lunatic vocals and bizarre soundscapes. It's not for the faint-hearted.

Continental conquests

Much was happening in Europe also. There were prog bands by the hundreds, even in countries like Yugoslavia and Hungary. One list includes over 4000 LPs by prog and avant-rock bands released across the world in 1974, the vast majority in Europe. But 1974 was also the year when electronica became mainstream, thanks primarily to two albums.

Tangerine Dream's *Phaedra* marked the beginning of the group's international success. By dint of word of mouth, it became a must-have album for serious music listeners and drug-heads. *Phaedra* will forever be regarded as the most significant breakthrough album in the history of electronic music.

Kraftwerk's *Autobahn* was a new direction for the mercurial outfit, with the Minimoog and EMS Synthi AKS providing a better-controlled output. Instead of experimental electronica, Kraftwerk had become a synth pop band, leaning heavily on drum machines like the Farfisa Rhythm Unit 10 and Vox Percussion King. Most of the album was created in Conny Plank's studio at his home outside Cologne. 'Autobahn' takes up the entire first side of the album, a hypnotically rhythmic assemblage with repeated simple melodic motifs. A three-and-a-half-minute single version of 'Autobahn' was first aired in America by a Chicago radio station, then a New Jersey company imported large numbers of the album, prompting Capitol to secure the US release of both. The disc eventually scaled the charts to single digits in Australia, the UK, US and elsewhere.

On a more mainstream European front, this was also Swedish band ABBA's breakthrough year. Like The Beatles, Björn Ulvaeus had started out playing skiffle, before moving into the Swedish folk scene with Benny Andersson. The two started writing pop songs with English lyrics on the understanding that English was the pre-eminent language of pop music. Managed by Stig Anderson, the lads teamed up with Anni-Frid 'Frida' Lyngstad and Agnetha Fältskog, both of whom already had careers in music and had released successful records. Frida also had two children from a previous relationship, and Agnetha and Björn had a child together before they became part of ABBA.

Setting their sights yet again on the Eurovision Song Contest, they won over their native land and so performed 'Waterloo' at the international pop extravaganza. Wearing ridiculous knickerbockers and knee-high boots, lots of frills and glitter, and with the orchestra's conductor dressed as Napoleon, they scooped the pool. The song's lyrics were as absurd as the band's outfits, a clunky analogy between Napoleon's military surrender and falling in love, with the woman's submission a complete capitulation to the man. Women's movement – what women's movement? 'Waterloo' became a number one hit in nine countries, and reached single digits in many others. Their studio engineer had read a book about Phil Spector, and the layering of overdubs became an essential part of the ABBA sound. The ABBA phenomenon was off and sprinting.

Things weren't going so well for The Plastic People of the Universe in Czechoslovakia. They were still persona non grata as far as the Czech authorities were concerned. The band had been playing secret gigs in countryside barns, which attracted long-haired subversives known as *máničky*. Audience members found out about the band's performances through word of mouth, and often had to trek into the woods at short notice to catch a concert. In March, thousands of fans arrived at a rural railway station hoping for a PPU show. Instead, they were confronted by police and border guards. The young music enthusiasts were photographed and fingerprinted, and some were arrested. Many were also beaten mercilessly by club-wielding police; the incident became known as the Budějovice Massacre.

Politics and music also intertwined in Portugal, where the airing of predetermined music acted as signals to begin the so-called Carnation Revolution. At 10.55pm on 24 April, Portugal's Eurovision Song Contest entry, Paulo de Carvalho's 'E Depois do Adeus', came on the radio and alerted rebel armed forces to begin their coup. Later in the evening, a song by banned folk singer Zeca Afonso was also aired, directing the armed forces to take over strategic points of power. Within hours, the government of Marcello Caetano had conceded, and many Portuguese hit the streets to celebrate.

Books and tapes

This was the year that Robert M. Pirsig's book *Zen and the Art of Motorcycle Maintenance* was released. Subtitled *An Inquiry into Values*, the bestseller was a fictionalised autobiography of a seventeen-day road trip that the author, his son and two friends supposedly made in 1968. The meta-message was about being in the moment, balancing the rational mind and the irrational or spiritual mind. But as a parable about coming to terms with our supposed true selves, the book was an important pillar in the normalisation of narcissism, with its focus on self-gratification and thus turning inward, away from community and shared responsibility. The central character is fundamentally self-obsessed and lacking in empathy for others. *Zen and the Art of Motorcycle Maintenance* is considered the all-time bestselling book on 'philosophy', having sold in the multi-millions for decades.

In a brazen display of personal greed, not to mention lack of civic duty, both Vice President Spiro Agnew and President Richard Nixon were found to have evaded paying rightful taxes, with Nixon eventually agreeing to cough up more than $400,000. The president also released 1254 pages of edited transcripts of the subpoenaed tapes from the Oval Office, but the House Judiciary Committee insisted that the actual tapes had to be supplied. Nevertheless, the transcripts were revelatory, detailing a president who frequently discussed the Watergate affair, including the suggestion of $1 million in 'hush money' to help keep the 'plumbers' quiet.

By midyear, the unprecedented stand-off between the US president and the special prosecutor over the original tapes had made its way to the Supreme Court. Nixon's obfuscations were dismissed in a unanimous decision. Within days, the House Judiciary Committee approved three articles of impeachment against Nixon, charging him with obstruction of justice and contempt of Congress, and accusing him of repeatedly violating his oath of office. For political reasons, two articles of impeachment didn't make the final cut. One related to the tax fraud matter and the other was about concealing from both Congress and the American people the clandestine bombing of Cambodia.

When it was revealed that, six days after the Watergate break-in, Nixon had ordered the FBI to cease investigating the matter, what little remained of Nixon's political and public support vanished. Three days later, on 8 August, in a televised address, Nixon resigned before he could be impeached.

Nixon thus became the first and only American president to resign from office. Trust in American public institutions would never recover. Gerald Ford was sworn in as Nixon's replacement. In his inauguration speech Ford said, 'My fellow Americans, our long national nightmare is over,' going on to say, 'In the beginning, I asked you to pray for me. Before closing, I ask again for your prayers, for Richard Nixon and for his family. May our former President, who brought peace to millions, find it for himself.' Yet Nixon had helped bring death and suffering to millions of Cambodians, Laotians and Vietnamese. What's more, he consistently lied to Congress and the American public.

It's important to remember that the Watergate scandal was not simply about the break-in into the Democratic Party's offices. Under the president's direct supervision, CREEP was also guilty of a whole bevy of criminal activities aimed at undermining the democratic process, including bribery, extortion, wiretapping, perjury and more.

Within a month of taking office, Ford issued a proclamation awarding Nixon a full and unconditional pardon for any crimes he may have committed whilst president. As musician Graham Nash put it, 'The whole Ford pardon just stunk. It really did smell of political corruption and wheeling and dealing.'[21] *The New York Times* called the move 'unjust', saying that it destroyed the new president's credibility.

Ford also issued a conditional amnesty for the millions of Vietnam War draft dodgers who had fled the US; most of them were now in Canada. However, to avail themselves of the amnesty, they had to pledge their allegiance to the US and serve two years in the public service.

By the time the OPEC oil embargo was finally lifted in March, the price of oil had risen nearly 300 per cent. The OPEC nations had discovered their global power. To meet the new fuel costs, Western manufacturers raised product prices. Post-Watergate America experienced the highest rates of unemployment since the Great Depression. Disillusionment was rife.

Of significant media fascination across the planet was the kidnapping of Patty Hearst, the granddaughter of American publishing magnate William Randolph Hearst. Responsibility was claimed by the Symbionese Liberation Army (SLA), a far-left organisation accountable for various bank robberies, murders and bombings. Two months after Hearst was taken from her Berkeley apartment, an audiotape was released on which she announced that she had joined the SLA. The group extorted $2 million from her father to fund a food giveaway to the poor. A gun-wielding Hearst was soon captured on security footage participating in a bank robbery in San Francisco. A month later, she took part in another armed robbery. Hearst would become the poster child for 'Stockholm syndrome'.

And what of forgotten Vietnam? In January, South Vietnam's President Thieu announced that the war had resumed. Northern forces continued to build up troops and supplies in the south. America had shifted its gaze from South-East Asia to South America, with the US government and its allies lining up behind the ruthless dictator General Augusto Pinochet following his coup against the democratically elected Marxist president Salvador Allende in Chile. A self-imposed right-wing dictator was deemed better for America's interests than an elected socialist government. Phil Ochs organised a benefit concert at the Felt Forum in New York's Madison Square Garden called Friends of Chile, An Evening With Salvador Allende. Performers included Ochs, Pete Seeger, Melanie, Dave Van Ronk, Mike Love, Dennis Wilson, Dennis Hopper (reading Allende's last speech) and Arlo Guthrie. Ochs even managed to convince Bob Dylan to make an appearance. Dylan arrived well ahead of showtime, filling in the waiting hours by drinking wine. By the time he hit the stage he was in his cups, barely able to stand. He sang four songs, excruciatingly badly. Van Ronk had to assist Dylan to remain upright for the finale of 'Blowin' in the Wind'.

Lost weekends

Elton John was now consuming vast quantities of drugs, later writing that 'the next sixteen years were full of incidents that would have given any rational human being pause concerning their drug consumption'. His new mate John Lennon was deep into his 'lost weekend' with Harry Nilsson in Los Angeles. But this was much more than a single weekend. Lennon and Nilsson painted the town many times over, frequently in the company of other reprobates, such as Keith Moon, Alice Cooper or Micky Dolenz. There were news reports of Lennon and Nilsson getting thrown out of clubs, as well as hurling glasses and punching both men and women. One woman took legal action against Lennon for assault.

At this time, the ex-Beatle was aiming to record an album of old rock 'n' roll songs, with Phil Spector producing. He had lost a legal dispute over plagiarising Chuck Berry's 'You Can't Catch Me' for his own song 'Come Together'. The settlement agreement with music publisher Morris Levy insisted that Lennon record three songs controlled by Levy for his next album. But the odious Phil Spector, wife abuser and later murderer, was also drinking heavily, as well as popping amyl nitrate capsules. Spector reportedly arrived at the studio in crazy costumes, one day dressed as a doctor and the next a cowboy, replete with loaded revolver. At one stage, Spector fired his gun into the studio ceiling, deafening everyone present, including Lennon. For his part, Lennon was drinking from a large jug of vodka the whole time he was in the studio. As he later explained, 'I drank too much, and I was out of control, and nobody was looking after me.'[22] Lennon was seemingly incapable of looking after himself. He was called into court as a character witness during Spector's ugly divorce proceedings, only to hear Spector unleash a terrible tirade against his poor wife, Ronnie. When Lennon and Spector fell out, the mad producer whisked the master tapes of Lennon's album away to his fortress-like mansion.

Lennon decided he also wanted to produce an album for Nilsson, so he rented a beach house for the principal musicians. Soon Keith Moon, Ringo Starr, Klaus Voorman and Nilsson were all installed, and the decadence continued. Once recording began, Lennon eased up somewhat on the imbibing, but Nilsson didn't. At one stage, Paul and Linda McCartney and Stevie Wonder dropped by the studio and bashed out some tracks that would end up on a bootleg. McCartney and Lennon even recorded themselves singing together, the only such post-Beatles opportunity for the pair to do that. McCartney also spent an afternoon jamming with Lennon at the beach house. Hatchets were being buried.

But the late nights, booze and drugs took a toll on Nilsson's once fine voice. He never let on to Lennon that his throat was bleeding and raw. Most of the vocals had to be rerecorded at a later date, by which time Nilsson had done permanent damage to his vocal cords. The eventual album was ironically titled *Pussy Cats*. The album title was a riposte to the bad boy behaviour that was being widely reported at the time. The cover featured Lennon and Nilsson in a doll's house. There are alphabet blocks on the floor, with the letters D and S separated by a rug: yes, it's a rebus. Half the tracks are covers and the rest originals, but the album is below par in comparison to Nilsson's previous work with better producers, and it would be all downhill for Nilsson until his death in 1994.

Does humour belong in music?

Harry Nilsson wanted to call his next album *God's Greatest Hits*, but his label, RCA, wouldn't allow it. In response to criticisms of the *Pussy Cats* album, Nilsson told an interviewer, 'We thought it had a sense of humour. I don't know ... I guess I'm just bitter about it. I think that sense of humour is the single most lacking thing in popular music. It's the single most lacking quality in the people that present popular music to the public.'[23] On being asked why he never performed live, Nilsson said, 'I prefer playing dead.'[24]

Randy Newman was not one to shy away from ambiguity or controversy. His album *Good Old Boys* featured a song simply titled 'Rednecks'. Sung from the perspective of a hick, it referenced smartarse Jews and keeping niggers in their rightful place. Some listeners couldn't discern that Newman was singing with his tongue in his cheek. The artist would again court controversy with his satirical 1977 tune 'Short People', an ironic swipe at prejudice that many humourless folk mistook for the composer's actual beliefs.

Irony was a style of humour perhaps more suited to British culture. 10cc achieved their big breakthrough with the LP *Sheet Music*, which included 'The Worst Band in the World', plus hits 'The Wall Street Shuffle', lambasting the world of high finance, and 'Silly Love', which ridiculed love songs. This was a band simply bursting with musical and thematic ideas. Their comparatively complex songs took pop and rock to a high art form without resorting to the self-importance of prog. They incorporated plenty of radio-friendly hooks and incredibly clever vocal arrangements. The song

'Clockwork Creep' is about a bomb on a jet airliner. 'Hotel' ridicules wealthy musicians living in the Caribbean. 'Somewhere in Hollywood' exposes Hollywood's exploitation of vulnerable starlets, 'Baron Samedi' lampoons spiritual charlatans, and the closer, 'Oh Effendi', takes on oil tycoons.

Like 10cc, Frank Zappa insinuated humour into his more elaborate rock compositions. *Apostrophe (')*, recorded at the same time as 1973's *Over-Nite Sensation*, included one of Zappa's conglomerate narratives, this time about a dream in which Zappa became an Eskimo. The album opens with 'Don't Eat the Yellow Snow' – because that's where the huskies go – an edited-down version of which became Zappa's first *Billboard* Top 100 hit. Like 10cc, Zappa also had a crack at gurus and psychics in 'Cosmik Debris'. With the Western world in economic and political turmoil, the rush to find spiritual meaning was leading many people down rabbit holes, which irked the fiercely agnostic Zappa. *Apostrophe (')* would be Zappa's biggest album success, rising to ten on the *Billboard* chart.

For my money, the release of Zappa's double album *Roxy & Elsewhere* later in the year was far more gratifying. Assembled from three live shows, it managed to capture all the elements that made Zappa performances such a rewarding live experience, from musical virtuosity and super-tight arrangements to quirky humour and audience participation – although, it has to be said, also with a degree of chauvinism. This was the period when Zappa had two incredible drummers in his band, Ralph Humphrey and Chester Thompson. In a *Rolling Stone* interview, Thompson explained how exacting Zappa's music was:

> I had been getting into odd times, but not at the level Frank was doing it. Frank was doing time within time. We wouldn't just play a song in five. He would have subdivisions within a bar. He might have some fives and sevens instead of triplets, things like that. It was a real wake-up call.

Thompson also noted, 'If you were in Frank's band, you had to be willing to be silly. You couldn't take yourself that seriously.'[25]

Disco deliveries

In 1974, the twelve-inch single arrived. The LP-sized, 45rpm format was not only higher in fidelity and louder than a standard single, it was also twice the length. Designed for deejays, many were produced with a vocal version on the A-side and an instrumental mix on the flip side, allowing deejays to have both versions on separate turntables and thus extend the song as long as they wished. The twelve-inch 45 was the music industry's first new commercial format in almost three decades, and by 1976 it would also become available to the general public.

R&B was moving increasingly towards heavy percussion with robotic precision. Philadelphia International Records (PIR) was at the forefront of this shift. Their integrated house band, MFSB, released the album *Love Is the Message*, which included the track 'TSOP (The Sound of Philadelphia)'. This became the theme tune for the TV show *Soul Train*, while the album was a staple at block party events as well as on discotheque turntables. Kenneth Gamble and Leon Huff, along with Bunny Sigler, were responsible for what became known as the 'Philly sound', its lush, sweeping string arrangements and punchy horns melding R&B with funk and soul. Gamble and Huff wrote and produced an incredible 175 gold and platinum records.

Tom Moulton, of Fire Island's Sandpiper disco, was pushing record companies to take dance music seriously, emphasising the bass and drums on recordings. He found himself employed by various record companies to remix their existing recordings for rerelease as disco tunes. Moulton's remix of The B.T. Express tune 'Do It' did not go down well with the band, particularly the new emphasis on percussion and the loss of vocals, but it became a hit. In some ways, disco echoed the early 1960s, when record companies dictated exactly what artists could and couldn't do.

Disco music ignored musical nuance. What's more, the personalities of performers were sublimated to the beat. Gloria Gaynor's rehash of The Jackson 5's 1971 hit 'Never Can Say Goodbye' became a dance floor sensation, and arguably the first real disco hit to reach the charts.

Tom Moulton also remixed three songs from Gaynor's *Never Can Say Goodbye* album into an uninterrupted eighteen-minute dance suite.

Other danceable songs that helped propel early disco were George McCrae's 'Rock Your Baby', Hues Corporation's 'Rock the Boat' and Carl Douglas's curiosity 'Kung Fu Fighting'. Douglas was a Jamaican working in the UK. If you're wondering about the martial arts reference, this was the height of the 'chopsocky' film craze, where Hong Kong moviemakers were churning out kung fu action movies. Bruce Lee's *Enter the Dragon* had been a box-office smash in 1973 and the *Kung Fu* television series was going strong. 'Kung Fu Fighting' was supposed to be the B-side to Douglas's single release, 'I Want to Give You My Everything'. Indeed, it was tossed off in the studio, recorded in the last ten minutes of studio time in just two takes. But it began to garner popularity in the dance clubs, going on to sell eleven million copies and becoming a number one hit in seventeen countries, and, incredibly, one of the biggest-selling songs of all time.

Barry White had produced a successful girl group with the awful name Love Unlimited, a Motown-style singing trio based on The Supremes. He had also released solo material of his own. In 1973, he put together a forty-piece orchestra, originally as backing for Love Unlimited. However, White soon decided to use The Love Unlimited Orchestra for himself, recording his own composition 'Love's Theme', one of the few orchestral singles to rise to number one in the pop charts. It's an instantly recognisable tune of the era, cannily melding *Shaft*-style wah-wah rhythm guitar with strings. White also had other huge hits featuring his sexy, deep-voiced pillow talk.

The rap about hip-hop

While disco was becoming overt, rap was still under wraps. Gil Scott-Heron and keyboardist Brian Jackson released *Winter in America*, using both traditional African plus R&B music as a bed for Scott-Heron's poetry. The poet was moving closer to traditional song structures, and so this album had an influence on the nascent hip-hop and rap music scenes. A single released from the LP, 'The Bottle', critiqued the culture of alcohol abuse that was endemic in black ghettos. To avoid making money off poor black people, Scott-Heron charged just one dollar to attend his concerts.

Big Brown was an African-American beat poet and street performer who had influenced Dylan's early songwriting. In 1973, Brown recorded his album *The First Man of Poetry, Big Brown: Between Heaven and Hell*, which was a long, two-sided poem recited over music performed by Rudy Ray Moore's funky band. Meanwhile, Moore was recording his own funk with part-sung lyrics and spoken word poetry. Moore would be cited as a significant influence by later rap artists such as Snoop Dogg. In 1974, Moore spent all his savings making a low-budget blaxploitation movie, *Dolemite*, which spun into numerous sequels, as celebrated in the 2019 movie *Dolemite Is My Name*, starring Eddie Murphy as Moore.

While an estimated 300 gangs roamed New York's streets at this time, in the Bronx district deejays were developing a style of music that was inspiring some young men of colour to engage in wars of dancing rather than hostilities with knives and guns. People like Afrika Bambaataa were determined to steer impoverished youth away from gang warfare. Bambaataa introduced many young ears not only to the bands Parliament and Funkadelic, but also to The Rolling Stones and Grand Funk Railroad. Bambaataa loved to trick his dancers by tossing in repeated rhythmic sections of 'Sgt. Pepper's Lonely Hearts Club Band' or The Monkees' 'Mary Mary'. He would shock his dancers by telling them afterwards what it was they were dancing to. Other pioneering deejays included Pete 'DJ' Jones, Cordie-O, Disco Bee and his brother Theodore, plus Joseph 'Grandmaster Flash' Saddler. Sometimes the record mixing was left to the deejay while the hyped-up jive talking was performed by an MC.

There were now celebrated b-boy dancers with names like the Nigger Twins, Bumpy Faced Melvin, Sau Sau and Flippin' Mike. At the time, dance competitions were called 'up-rocking' or 'top-rocking', with new techniques like freezes and spinning being introduced. Generally, the dancers performed on sheets of cardboard to prevent grazes and bruises. It was a decidedly macho environment, reminiscent of the Brazilian capoeira, which incorporates martial arts and acrobatics into a form of stylised dance.

DJ Hollywood, born Anthony Holloway, had been spinning discs since 1972 and was now introducing 'rhythm talk' into his deejaying, making his voice flow with the records. Invited to work at Club 371 with its quality Technics turntables and sunken dance floor, he found his metier. His teenage assistant, Junebug, was from Puerto Rico, and they soon developed a routine of rhyming voice raps over music intros and outros. As Hollywood himself put it, 'I brought polish to the game.'[26] DJ Hollywood became a superstar among people of colour in New York.

By the way, it's not simple to parse hip-hop versus rap. Where hip-hop generally referred to the music, rap was initially black slang for talking. In the end, however, the terms were often interchanged.

Aussie acts

Hip-hop and rap would largely pass Australia by in the 1970s. Local Indigenous performers like Col Hardy, Jimmy Little, Lionel Rose and Vic Simms were mostly performing country and western music.

The Sunbury '74 festival has gone down in history thanks to British act Queen famously being booed off the stage. Or were they? This seems to be more urban myth than fact, with Daddy Cool's Ross Wilson insisting Queen not only finished their set but that the crowd requested an encore. Some suggest that any booing occurred only because they arrived late and the audience was frustrated. Others say it was because they were the only imported act playing before a jingoistic crowd on an Australia Day weekend. There are also suggestions that drunken yobbos didn't react well to Mercury's camp persona. Certainly, it seems true that Freddy Mercury told the audience that their next visit would see Queen touring as the biggest band in the world. There was quite a bit of boisterous booing going on throughout the festival. Even local legend Johnny O'Keefe was booed when he was announced.

Another band that copped boos at Sunbury '74 was Skyhooks, which had begun as a fully formed concept of bass guitarist Greg Macainsh. The band were a weird combination of British glam rock married with the silliness of the Bonzo Dog Doo-Dah Band. They may have had their roots in underground music, but the accessibility and topicality of their songs endeared them to a broader audience. Not everyone was impressed, of course, with Cold Chisel's Jimmy Barnes describing them as 'more like a glam band that didn't play their instruments that well ... They were one of those bands you either loved or hated. I hated them at first.'[27]

After their poorly received performance at Sunbury, Skyhooks' lead singer Steve Hill decided he was in the wrong band and quit. Graeme 'Shirley' Strachan was co-opted as his replacement and the band never looked back. Strachan had been dubbed Shirley by his surfing mates on account of his curly blond hair invoking Shirley Temple. The band were signed to Mushroom Records, managed by Michael Gudinski and produced by Daddy Cool's Ross Wilson. Zany costumes were designed by Ursula Flett, and the lads daubed themselves with silly theatrical make-up. Like a more musically literate New York Dolls, this was a band purposely designed to upset conservative sensibilities. Mature Australians were suitably shocked by the band's camp appearance, not to mention their candid songs about drugs and sex.

Skyhooks' first single, 'Living in the 70's', peaked at number twenty-eight on the charts. The song described the general unease that many were feeling about the times, referencing pollution, fast food and tranquillisers. The album of the same name took a while to take hold, but eventually *Living in the 70's* spent sixteen weeks at the top of the charts to become the bestselling Australian album to date, moving 226,000 units in a country where 20,000 units was considered a success. This was despite a radio ban being placed on more than half the tracks by the Federation of Australian Commercial Broadcasters. That ban was like the proverbial red rag to the bullish new ABC youth station, 2JJ. They chose the banned track 'You Just Like Me 'Cos I'm Good in Bed' as their first ever song when they began broadcasting in early 1975.

By the end of 1974, Mushroom Records had released a second Skyhooks single, 'Horror Movie'. It went to number one and would win the 1975 King of Pop Awards for Australian Record of the Year. The song pointedly referred to TV news broadcasting, comparing the reality of wars, riots and mayhem to the impact of horror movies. Importantly, it reinforced the youthful view that adults were screwing up the planet. This was, of course, a suppurating global phenomenon, as MC5's Wayne Kramer put it: 'There was an unspoken agreement among people of my generation that the direction that grown-ups were taking the world was a disaster in the making.'[28]

The Skyhooks album also contained 'Whatever Happened to the Revolution?', a song asking why revolutionary fervour had died. The social commentary continued with 'Smut', about attending an adult movie where the seats are sticky and the singer ejaculates into a Twisties packet. 'Balwyn Calling' was a bit of misogynist fearmongering about women who lure men into suburban mediocrity, while another tacky song compared motorcycles with women.

Another eclectic band equally out of step with the pub rock scene was former New Zealand outfit Split Enz. They had their own version of elaborate costumes, wild hairstyles and garish make-up. To get themselves heard, Split Enz began a series of radio-sponsored 'buck-a-head' shows in theatres and concert halls. Meanwhile, Sherbet was riding high with their third album, *Slipstream*, plus more hit singles, and were voted Most Popular Group in the annual King of Pop Awards for the second time. The run of Sherbet accolades would continue until 1978, while singer Daryl Braithwaite also enjoyed an equally successful parallel career as a solo artist.

Just six weeks after forming, AC/DC recorded their first single, produced, of course, by Vanda and Young: 'Can I Sit Next to You Girl'/'Rockin' in the Parlour'. By midyear, the band were garnering a positive reputation for their live performances and found themselves supporting a tour by Lou Reed. At this point they were dressing as glam rockers, however by the end of the year the glam was ditched, along with their lead singer. At the suggestion of his sister, the diminutive Angus Young took to wearing schoolboy uniforms, a trademark that would last for years, with his sister sewing various versions for him. AC/DC's new singer, Ronald Belford

Scott, was, like Malcom and Angus Young, born in Scotland before his family emigrated southwards. He was dubbed Bon at school in Australia, the word being a diminutive of 'bonnie Scotland'. Even though he was almost a decade older than Angus, the merging of Scott and the Young siblings was a match made in rock heaven.

The real dynamo in the band was Angus Young, already playing his guitar while duck-walking, rushing about or spinning on his back on the floor. This latter trick came about after he tripped over a cable at one performance and flailed around like an upturned beetle to make it seem as though the fall was intentional. The audience enjoyed it so much it became his chef d'oeuvre.

Meanwhile, Radio Birdman was formed by Deniz Tek and Rob Younger in Sydney. With nascent punk ambitions, they purposely aimed to challenge rock orthodoxy. The band's name was a 'mondegreen' – a misheard lyric – from The Stooges' song '1970', the actual lyric being 'radio burnin''. Punk had not yet been defined, let alone infiltrated the Australian music scene, so it was hard going for the fledgling (pun intended) band.

Ayers Rock released an excellent debut album, *Big Red Rock*, blending mainstream blues-rock with prog and jazz fusion. This was more sophisticated fare than most Australian offerings, offering up some truly crackerjack playing. *Big Red Rock* went through two recording attempts. The first produced a result that the band found lacking in oomph, so they tried a live-in-the-studio approach, which produced a feel more to their liking. Indeed, it's staggering to listen to the album with the understanding that it was recorded in one hit without overdubs (although spoken voices were added on 'Crazy Boys'). Cementing their fusion credentials, the album includes a cover of Weather Report's 'Boogie Woogie Waltz'. What's more, Frank Zappa's influence can be discerned on cuts like 'Crazy Boys' and 'Get Out to the Country'. The title track sees the band using textural flourishes to evoke the Uluru landscape, including guitar with wah-wah to invoke a didgeridoo. Don't be put off by the comparatively lightweight opener, 'Lady Montego', with its 'Moondance'-like riff, as the album just keeps getting better, and really takes off from track four onwards.

Signed with Mushroom Records in late 1973, Ayers Rock were pushed by Michael Gudinski in the US when he travelled there to sell Skyhooks, Daddy Cool and Madder Lake. Ayers Rock became Mushroom's first artists to sign with an international label, A&M Records. While touring the US in support of Bachman–Turner Overdrive, Status Quo and Lynyrd Skynyrd, Ayers Rock also became the first Australian act to play big stadium concerts in America. In many ways, they helped pave the way for the likes of AC/DC, Little River Band, Air Supply, Men at Work and INXS.

On 8 November, a new pop/rock television show called *Countdown* was aired on the ABC. Based on similar British pop music shows, with idiosyncratic presenter Ian 'Molly' Meldrum, it would quickly become the most popular music show on Australian television. *Countdown* gave Skyhooks plenty of coverage via its fifty-two transmitters broadcasting across the wide brown land. As Skyhooks' Red Symons put it, '[I]f you'd been seen on *Countdown* you could go to Wagga, you could go anywhere in Australia, and people would say: "you're those guys we saw on telly."'[29]

Women generating sparks

Joni Mitchell's sublime *Court and Spark* album was a decisive step towards jazz. The single 'Help Me' became a top ten hit in the US, but 'Free Man in Paris' is the real album highlight, with lyrics describing record executive David Geffen's visit to Paris. The track also heralds her move into observational songwriting, shifting away from navel gazing and towards sociological intricacy. It had been just over a year since her last LP, *For the Roses*, with the interim being used to explore new approaches to music. This time she assembled an all-star cast, the principal band being Tom Scott's L.A. Express, a jazz fusion quintet. Also roped in were members of CSNY, The Band, plus Wayne Perkins, José Feliciano and even Cheech and Chong, and the whole thing was produced by Mitchell.

For Tom Scott and his team, all of them seasoned professionals and session players, working with Joni proved challenging, primarily because she had no technical training. Reportedly, she couldn't even name the notes on a piano keyboard. But Scott said he responded to her perfectionism. The critics were almost universally enraptured with Joni's new, bigger sound. *Rolling Stone*'s Jon Landau wrote that the songs were 'sung with extraordinary beauty, from first note to last'.[30] The album would prove to be Mitchell's most successful disc, rising to number two in the US, one in her country of origin, Canada, and being voted best album of the year in *The Village Voice*'s Critics Poll.

Every track on *Court and Spark* offers a fresh perspective on life and love, focusing on the grey areas and nuances, not the typical broad brushstrokes of romantic pop. It also marks a clear turning point in Joni Mitchell's career: from here on, jazz would rub shoulders with folk rock in truly inventive ways (particularly when she teamed up with Pat Metheny and Jaco Pastorius). *Court and Spark* had a profound influence on many existing and wannabe musicians, perhaps none more so than a young Madonna, who told *Billboard* that in high school she worshipped Joni Mitchell and sang every song from the album, calling it 'my coming-of-age record'.[31]

Joni Mitchell concluded the year with her first official live album, amusingly titled *Miles of Aisles*, again backed by the L.A. Express. The double album sold well, with a live version of her signature song 'Big Yellow Taxi' also released. It now performed better in the charts than her original version of 1970. Mitchell was also featured on the cover of *Time* magazine.

Linda Ronstadt was another Asylum recording artist to achieve huge success in 1974, although contractual obligations meant that her *Heart Like a Wheel* album went out on her previous label, Capitol. It rocketed to number one in the US, and the lead single, a cover of Dee Dee Warwick's 'You're No Good', also peaked at number one. Ronstadt was symptomatic of the new country rock spinning out of Los Angeles, the city that had spawned folk rock in the mid-1960s. Poco, The Flying Burrito Brothers and Emmylou Harris were also part of the country-inflected smoothie that oozed from the LA blender.

Olivia Newton-John had been born in England before moving to Australia aged six. Using prize money from a TV talent contest, she shifted back to Britain in 1966. After various ups and downs, in 1974 she represented the United Kingdom in the Eurovision Song Contest, singing 'Long Live Love', with a thumping oompah beat not dissimilar to ABBA's winning entry 'Waterloo'. She also had an international number one hit, 'I Honestly Love You', and released albums as well as garnering Record of the Year and Best Pop Vocal at the Grammys. But when she was named female vocalist of the year by the Country Music Association, it prompted an outcry over the sanctity of country music. George Jones and Tammy Wynette led the dissent and formed an alternative organisation, the Association of Country Entertainers, convincing fifty Grand Ole Opry members to join them, aiming to 'preserve the identity of country music as a separate and distinct form of entertainment'. It was sour grapes writ large, particularly as Newton-John was not a Nashville insider. Stella Parton, Dolly's sister, recorded 'Ode to Olivia', apologising about her Nashville peers and their rigid attitudes.

But perhaps the strangest female hit parade artist in 1974 was an Australian nun. Sister Janet Mead was born in Adelaide, where she formed a band at seventeen called, simply, The Rock Band. With a desire to refresh the Catholic mass, she made recordings for use in schools and churches. Festival Records invited her to Sydney to record a version of Donovan's 'Brother Sun, Sister Moon'. It was producer Martin Erdman's idea to put a rock version of The Lord's Prayer on the B-side, and so a one-hit-wonder flashed like lightning across the globe. The single became the very first Australian recording to move more than a million copies in America, reaching number two on *Billboard*'s Adult Contemporary chart. It also hit single digits in many other countries, and number three in her homeland. While the music was credited to Traditional/Arnold Strals, it remains the only top ten hit with words attributed to Jesus Christ. Mead was nominated for a Grammy, but lost to a higher power, Elvis Presley, with his gospel song 'How Great Thou Art'. Mead's heady success led to an album, *With You I Am*, but the fame also caused her to question her faith. She gave her record proceeds to charity and released *A Rock Mass* before retreating from the limelight.

Above and below average

Steely Dan were at the top of their game when they released *Pretzel Logic*. It would be the last album to be released while the band were still performing live, and also the last with the full quintet, although a conga-line of session musos helped out. The single 'Rikki Don't Lose That Number' peaked at number four. While many people assumed that the word 'number' referred to a marijuana cigarette, the truth was more prosaic: the Rikki of the song was based on a woman on whom Donald Fagen had a crush when he was in college. The album was also notable for including an honourable version of 'East St. Louis Toodle-Oo' by Duke Ellington and James 'Bubber' Miley. Overall, *Pretzel Logic* is a classy disc fusing jazz elements with rock song formulae, almost as intricate as 10cc but without the humour.

Eric Clapton had wasted three years in a dense heroin fog. His return LP was *461 Ocean Boulevard*, on which he mixed self-penned tracks with classics. 'I Shot the Sheriff' had been a reggae hit for Bob Marley only a year previously, but Clapton went for a soft rock feel by slowing it down. Even though it lacked a guitar solo, Clapton's version hit the top of the charts in America, helping spread awareness of both reggae and Marley. It's still a tedious, repetitive song, but the hook was plainly enough to guarantee its success.

Reviewing the guitar maestro's comeback tour for *New Musical Express*, Steve Clarke found Clapton's backing band 'under rehearsed' and even 'inept'.[32] Clapton may have kicked his heroin habit, but he was busy replacing it with an alcohol habit. After one performance, Steve Clarke joined Clapton and manager Robert Stigwood at an event staged in a Danish porn club. Clapton reportedly acted like a drunken bore, yelling at the female performers, and even climbed onto the stage and urinated.[33] But Clapton's truly dark side had yet to be revealed.

The amusingly named Average White Band was formed in London from Scottish stock, which is hardly the expected source for a funk outfit. They released an album, *Show Your Hand*, which didn't blow anyone's kilt up, however Bruce McCaskill, Clapton's tour manager, agreed to manage AWB and even got them signed to Atlantic Records. So AWB headed to Los Angeles, where they recorded their second album, prosaically titled *AWB*. The instrumental single 'Pick Up the Pieces' managed to reach number one, as did the LP. It amusingly inspired The J.B.'s – James Brown's backing band – to release a single under the name AABB: Above Average Black Band.

But tragedy struck AWB later in the year following a sellout concert at the Troubadour nightclub in Hollywood. At a party in the home of Wall Street whiz-kid Kenneth Moss, a glass vial containing white powder was passed around. Many assumed it was cocaine, but it turned out to be heroin. A number of people became violently ill. AWB's bass player Alan Gorrie was taken by Cher back to her apartment, where she kept him awake, putting ice packs on his head and making him walk around until he recovered. But drummer Robbie McIntosh wasn't so fortunate. He was taken by his wife to a nearby motel, where he died the next day. Party host Kenneth Moss was indicted for murder, pled guilty to involuntary manslaughter and was sentenced to 120 days in jail.

Roxy Music's *Country Life* finally propelled the band into the US market. The cover, sporting a pair of scantily clad models in transparent lingerie, was another of Brian Ferry's provocative efforts at publicity. Ferry had met the women in Portugal and convinced them both to do the photo shoot. Early US releases came in opaque shrink-wrap, and a later version used the back cover image on the front – sans women. The cover art also caused a ruckus in Spain and the Netherlands. Meanwhile, Ferry's solo career saw the tuxedoed crooner continue to drawl out cover versions of famous songs.

Queen's second album, prosaically titled *Queen II*, was a mix of prog and heavy rock which failed to set the rock world on fire, although it did manage to reach number five on the British charts. Later in the year, *Sheer Heart Attack* was less prog and more straight-ahead rock, climbing to two in the UK. From that album flew 'Killer Queen', their first international hit, a song about a high-class callgirl. 'Killer Queen' not only established the band's radio sound, it also cemented their inimitable selling propositions: Mercury's wonderful voice harmonising with May and Taylor, theatrical flourishes, and the excellent guitar chops of Brian May.

Elton John's album *Caribou* continued his run of chart-toppers. During recording of 'Don't Let the Sun Go Down on Me', Elton had thrown a tantrum, telling everyone how much he hated it. He even told producer Gus Dudgeon that he would murder him with his bare hands if the song found its way onto the album. It went to number two in the US. Elton also used the sessions to record a slow version of The Beatles' 'Lucy in the Sky with Diamonds'. John Lennon – working under the pseudonym Dr Winston O'Boogie – helped out with harmony vocals and guitar. He even suggested that Elton try a reggae feel on the middle section. The single topped the US charts.

Lennon's *Walls and Bridges* album was recorded in New York, and everyone, Lennon included, was sober this time. Overall, the album is suffused with Lennon's romantic frustrations. 'Whatever Gets You Thru the Night' became Lennon's first US number one single as a solo performer. 'Scared' begins with a wolf howling, before becoming a thudding blues about the singer's deep-seated fears, harking back to 1970's primal scream therapy. It's a cracking tune doing what Lennon did best: rip away all façade to unveil the rawness of his feelings. Bobby Keys plays some tortured sax, and the guitar soloing, presumably by Jesse Ed Davis, wails superbly. Lennon's son Julian performs drums on the (thankfully brief) cover of Lee Dorsey's 'Ya Ya'. But *Walls and Bridges* would be Lennon's final album of original material for the rest of the decade.

Madison Square Garden hosted one of Lennon's extremely rare stage appearances, which came about as the result of a bet. Lennon had invited Elton John to play on his new album, notably on 'Whatever Gets You Thru the Night'. Elton reckoned it was going to be a number one hit, but Lennon didn't agree. In the euphoria of the moment, Elton said if he was proven right, then Lennon had to play the song on stage with him. And so it came to pass that a terrified John Lennon, having first vomited out of stage fright, walked onto the Madison Square Garden stage to be greeted with a crowd response that Elton reckoned was the biggest roar he had ever experienced from any audience. The house lights were turned on, as all 18,000 people took to their feet and thundered their approval for ten minutes. Lennon was surprised, later stating, 'I was quite astonished that the crowd was so nice to me, because I was only judging by what [the] papers said about me. And I thought I may as well not be around.'[34] When the crowd had finally settled down, the pair performed 'Whatever Gets You Thru the Night' and 'Lucy in the Sky with Diamonds'. They then tucked into Paul McCartney's 'I Saw Her Standing There'. After Lennon left the stage, Elton performed 'Candle in the Wind', and for the first time ever the audience lit cigarette lighters in the darkness.

John and Yoko were still estranged at this point. Yoko was not supposed to attend the Elton John concert as a condition of Lennon's agreement to participate. However, she did attend, so Elton made sure she was out of the sightline from the stage. After the concert, Yoko joined them both backstage and then at a hotel bar, which led to John and Yoko getting back together.

After an absence of four years, CSNY were again touring, and if you read Graham Nash's quotes in *Melody Maker*, you might think it was all love and peace in the band. 'I think before we didn't feel solid enough inside ourselves to be totally comfortable all the time,' he said. 'Now that we've grown up a little, now that we've proven that we can all move people individually, we know we want to be a band.'[35] The truth was very different. Neil Young travelled from gig to gig in his own motorhome, studiously avoiding the rest of the gang. The drug-fuelled David Crosby had two women to sleep with every night and carried a pistol in a backpack, even on stage. As Young's biographer Jimmy McDonough put it, 'CSNY was divided into four separate camps, down to the roadies.'[36] Percussionist Joe Lala noted that when someone would ask for help with an amplifier, the roadie was likely to opine, 'I work for Stephen,' and suchlike. As Mac Holbert described it, 'None of 'em are relating to each other at all – there's no band going on, no common consciousness happening.'[37] The tour crew included a fellow who was employed just to secure and provide cocaine.

Everything was excessive, from private jets and helicopters, expensive hotel suites with their logo on the pillows, right down to custom-made leather luggage tags. As Nash naively said, 'We didn't realize we were paying for all of it.'[38] Gosh knows who he thought was paying.

During the CSNY tour, Bob Dylan turned up in Minneapolis, so Stephen Stills and bass player Tim Drummond whisked him away to a hotel room, where Bob gave a private concert of tunes from his new album, *Blood on the Tracks*. Coked out of his head, Stills reportedly told Dylan that his songs weren't very good. As Drummond later said, 'I was so goddamn embarrassed ... Dylan, being the arrogant man that he was, said, "Well, Stephen, play me one of your songs." That was the end of it. Stephen couldn't even find one string from another at that point.'[39]

The Rolling Stones were also spending time apart. A concert film, *Ladies and Gentlemen, The Rolling Stones* was premiered, and Bill Wyman's first solo album, *Monkey Grip*, was released, as was Ron Wood's *I've Got My Own Album to Do*. Keith Richards was nominated 'The World's Most Elegantly Wasted Human Being' in *New Musical Express*, and came up with the line, 'I only ever get ill when I give up drugs.'[40] Jagger's marriage to Bianca was increasingly shaky, and even she admitted that he only married her because they looked similar.[41] The Rolling Stones' album *It's Only Rock 'n Roll* as usual went to single digits across the globe. This time it was produced by Richards and Jagger, billed now as The Glimmer Twins. The cover painting by Guy Peellaert had the band members as gods descending a staircase from a temple, being worshipped by Grecian women. Perhaps Peellaert was satirising the band and they were now too arrogant to notice?

The album's contents had little of relevance to youth culture, arguably marking the beginning of the band's dull, self-satisfied afterlife. The title track, like the album itself, was a muddy, ordinary slice of rock, with none of the pizzazz required for a self-congratulatory rock 'n' roll anthem. The promotional film clip for the single had the band all dressed in sailor suits and wearing eyeliner, with Jagger camping it up. It makes one wonder what they were thinking. Was this the Bowie influence?

The Glimmer Twins were lousy producers who had not mastered the finer points of mixing. Mind you, Keith Richards' substance abuse was becoming a massive headache for the band. By the end of the year, The Rolling Stones' most accomplished musician, Mick Taylor, suddenly pulled up stumps. Taylor reckoned that, with the last album, the band had begun to reek of self-parody. As he would also point out, when he first played with the band, 'Their timing was awful. They sounded like a typical bunch of guys in a garage – playing out of tune and too loudly. I thought, "How is it possible that this band can make hit records?"'[42] Asked about Taylor's replacement, Jagger crudely stated: 'No doubt we can find a brilliant 6' 3" blond guitarist who can do his own make-up.[43]

David Bowie embarked on his Diamond Dogs tour, beginning in Montreal. As critic Chris Charlesworth put it, '[T]he act that David puts over has as much to do with rock 'n' roll as Bob Dylan has with Las Vegas ... A Christmas pantomime would be an unfair parallel, but the ideas behind it were exactly the same.[44] The show was tightly rehearsed musical theatre with no room for spontaneity or embellishments. Co-designed by Chris Langhart, with influences from German expressionist films, the event incorporated a twenty-foot-high bridge that went up and down, lighting towers disguised as toppling skyscrapers, dancers, props and, as Charlesworth put it, 'some kind of phallic symbol spurting blood towards the sky'.[45] At various times Bowie would be lifted over the audience, or, like a conjuror, appear or disappear. There was no encore. For his new 'look' Bowie had dumped the androgyny, instead taking on a neat, masculine appearance with minimal make-up.

The Diamond Dogs album saw Bowie stretching beyond the glam genre, shifting more towards soul and funk in a confused amalgam of musical and thematic ideas based around an apocalyptic scenario. His head was full of half-baked projects and his overall direction was unclear. There were leftover bits of Ziggy Stardust combined with snippets from incomplete projects inspired by William Burroughs and George Orwell. Opening track 'Future Legend' sets the tone with a horror movie soundtrack, which curiously transmogrifies into the Rogers and Hart musical tune

'Bewitched, Bothered and Bewildered', from 1940's *Pal Joey*. Over that, Bowie describes a scene from a post-apocalyptic hell.

After the best tracks, 'Sweet Thing' and 'Candidate', comes a Rolling Stones–like tune, 'Rebel Rebel', which would become Bowie's most covered song. Side two opens with 'Rock 'n' Roll With Me', a tiresome, dog-eared melody and concept. Then the album sinks into Orwellian territory, with Bowie at times sounding more like Peter Gabriel. The track '1984' has echoes of Isaac Hayes, while 'Big Brother' is Mellotron-laden prog pomp. The whole thing ends with a sound collage of dubious quality titled 'Chant of the Ever Circling Skeletal Family'. As academic Dick Hebdige noted, Bowie had no interest in political or cultural messaging beyond a meta-message of 'escape – from class, from sex, from personality, from obvious commitment – into a fantasy past or a science-fiction future'.[46] *Rolling Stone*'s critic wrote of the LP:

> Aladdin Sane was frustratingly uneven, Pinups was trivial, and now comes Diamond Dogs, perhaps Bowie's worst album in six years … Bowie has tended to pander to what he thinks the public wants and to imitate those who have been more successful than he – Alice Cooper and Mick Jagger, for instance. He has deliberately cheapened himself and his music.[47]

But the disc still went to one in the UK, three in Australia and five in the US. The hideous cover art, again by Guy Peellaert, pictures a naked Bowie, part man and part hound, as a sideshow freak.

In one of the strangest events of the decade, Clifford Davis, manager of Fleetwood Mac, sent the band on a two-and-a-half month tour of America without a single member of Fleetwood Mac performing. As he told *Rolling Stone*, 'I want to get this out of the public's mind as far as the band being Mick Fleetwood's band. This band is my band. This band has always been my band.[48] The actual band had stopped touring just two weeks into a tour of America because drummer Mick Fleetwood was emotionally devastated over his pending divorce, and in any case the rest of the band needed a rest. While they were all on vacation, they received letters from Davis with an ultimatum to join his new tour. If they refused, he would put together a new band. Which is just what he did.

The whole craziness is shrouded in contradicting stories. In 2017, two of the touring band members claimed they were told that they were forming the new Fleetwood Mac. What's more, they said that Mick Fleetwood had given the project his imprimatur. Fleetwood was supposed to join them on the tour, which plainly never happened. At the first gig, in Pittsburgh, both the promoter and some of the fans realised they were being swindled and demanded refunds. The next show, in New York, was a disaster, with the lead singer claiming to have lost his voice and the band performing instrumentals. Meanwhile, the real Fleetwood Mac filed lawsuits to stop the tour, with Davis countersuing, claiming he owned the rights to the band's name, and that he held the copyright to the band's recordings.

The real Fleetwood Mac members had to move to the US as most of the legal battles were in American courts. It would take four years to settle the debacle, with the courts finally determining that the terms of the agreement with Davis were unfair and restrictive of trade, and the agreement was nullified. On a positive note, according to Mick Fleetwood, moving to the US helped the band find success there. The fake Fleetwood Mac members formed a new band, Stretch, which had a surprise UK hit with 'Why Did You Do It?'. Mick Fleetwood decided the lyrics to the song were attacking him for not joining the bogus tour.

Heavy going

Canadian trio Rush released their debut, which sounded an awful lot like Led Zeppelin, especially the rather high-pitched scream-singing. Meanwhile, Led Zeppelin presented their new label, Swan Song Records, with Maggie Bell as their debut act. The episodic launch began with a suitably decadent party at the Four Seasons hotel in New York and then at the Bel-Air hotel in LA. Now fifteen, Lori Mattix was there to take up again with Jimmy Page, but she ended up in a fistfight with another girl who had arrived with Jimmy. Richard Cole offered around a mound of cocaine on a platter. Geese (no swans were available), with weights tied to their feet so they wouldn't fly away, were chased into the traffic to meet their maker.

The British also got their chance to witness Led Zep debauchery during the UK launch of Swan Song at Chislehurst Caves, which also celebrated The Pretty Things' *Silk Torpedo* album for the label. Nuns in suspenders served drinks, while naked women wrestled in jelly and naked virgins were sacrificed on altars, and ... well, you get the picture.

Led Zep also signed up Bad Company and Dave Edmunds to Swan Songs Records. But not all of the Zep's wealth was going into the music business. They also helped finance *Monty Python and the Holy Grail*, one of the all-time great comedy movies. Zep stumped up £31,500, while Pink Floyd contributed £21,000 and Jethro Tull's Ian Anderson dug into his own pockets for £6300. Other financiers on the film included Island, Charisma and Chrysalis Records, plus Tim Rice's cricket team.

During a performance in Dallas, Gary Thain, the bass player with Uriah Heep, was shocked, literally. Heep had to cancel the rest of the tour, which was also a blow for their support act Suzi Quatro, on her first major tour of the US. Gary Thain recovered from his electrification, but his drug-taking meant he couldn't keep up with the rest of the band and so he was fired and replaced by King Crimson's John Wetton. By the end of the following year, Thain would join the 27 Club thanks to a heroin overdose. British singer-songwriter Nick Drake also died by overdosing on an antidepressant, and following two sold-out concerts at the London Palladium, 'Mama' Cass Elliot died in her sleep after suffering a heart attack.

Everything old is new again

While rock music ploughed ahead, the nostalgia bug was in plague proportions, even in Australia, where Sherbet's Daryl Braithwaite, Brian Cadd's Bootleg Family Band, plus Ernie Sigley and Denise Drysdale all had hits with revamped 1960s pop songs.

Thanks to Bill Haley's 1955 hit 'Rock Around the Clock' being used on the TV show *Happy Days*, that old chestnut crept back into the US charts, and there were plenty more hit nostalgic tunes to remind listeners of less complicated times. Bryan Ferry reprised Dylan's 'A Hard Rain's A-Gonna Fall', while Grand Funk scored with 1962's 'The Locomotion'. The Beach Boys struck a new gold seam with a double album of their hits from 1962 to 1965 titled *Endless Summer*, returning the band to the commercial success they had once enjoyed. The Drifters were also back with a sequel to their 1964 hit 'Saturday Night at the Movies', this time titled 'Kissin' in the Back Row of the Movies'. Absurdly, this found 36-year-old Roger Greenaway singing about picking up his girlfriend from school.

Carly Simon released her big-selling *Hotcakes*, a navel-gazing concept album about her privileged life with hubby James Taylor. The second hit single saw Simon duetting with Taylor on an updated version of the old Inez and Charlie Foxx song 'Mockingbird' – itself based on the lullaby 'Hush Little Baby'. With help from Dr John on piano, Robbie Robertson on guitar and a tasty sax solo courtesy of Michael Brecker, the lullaby became a rocker with the two voices interweaving.

The song charted in Australia at the same time as another version also hit the charts. Ageing Australian rock 'n' roller Johnny O'Keefe had first performed it in 1964. In 1972 he recorded a new version with vocalist Margaret McLaren. O'Keefe believed the Simon/Taylor version to be stolen from his 1972 arrangement, saying, 'I know that James Taylor and Carly Simon heard it and decided to record it.'[49] O'Keefe was incensed when Australian radio stations played the American version in preference to his own, so he visited the stations to harangue them. O'Keefe also sent telegrams to the responsible federal minister, as well as the Broadcasting Control Board. That elicited an edict that Australian stations had to play both versions or none at all. Both singles peaked at number eight. The success breathed momentary life into O'Keefe's career, and he found himself performing at venues he hadn't touched in years.

O'Keefe put together a package tour called The Good Old Days of Rock 'n' Roll, which included many of his old music friends, including

Dinah Lee, Johnny Devlin, Jade Hurley and Laurel Lee. The opening two-week season in Sydney enjoyed full houses every night. In James Brown fashion, O'Keefe dubbed himself the Granddaddy of Rock 'n' Roll. One acquaintance of O'Keefe dubbed it a 'freak show'.

Backwards and forwards

While the nostalgia craze looked back to simpler times and more un-pretentious rock 'n' roll, so too did the punks. Perhaps the real progenitors of punk music, before the coin was termed and even before The Velvet Underground, MC5 or The Stooges, were English band The Troggs. In the mid-1960s, The Troggs trotted out cheeky songs with simple riffs recorded in somewhat slapdash fashion. The Troggs pioneered garage rock, particularly on songs like 'Wild Thing' or 'I Can't Control Myself', which was later covered by punk pioneers Buzzcocks.

A musical rebellion was now underway in New York, mostly swirling around the CBGB club in the seedy Bowery district. The acronym, standing for 'country, bluegrass and blues', was something of a misnomer, as the venue became a focus for the emerging punk and new wave scene. Owner Hilly Kristal was all for giving new bands a shot in return for door takings. Once established, garage bands emerged in their hundreds to audition and perform there. Kristal added a few more letters to the club's unwieldy acronym, and it became CBGB/OMFUG, those last letters standing for 'other music for uplifting gormandizers'. In this case, gormandizer didn't mean eater of food but rather voracious consumer of music.

Television became regulars at CBGB. Their guitarist Tom Verlaine claimed he was influenced by free jazzers John Coltrane and Albert Ayler; you wouldn't find a British punk rocker who even knew who those cats were. Bass player and vocalist Richard Hell was already pre-empting punk fashion with his torn clothing and safety pins. That look had a huge impact on British fashion shop owner Malcolm McLaren when he visited New York. McLaren described Hell as 'this guy looking like he's just grown out of a drain hole ... He was this wonderful, bored, drained, scarred, dirty guy with a torn T-shirt. And this look of spiky hair, everything about it – there was no question that I'd take it back to London.'[50] The look was notably anti-glam.

Art school student, poet and rock journalist Patti Smith reviewed Television for the *SoHo Weekly News* before starting her own band, The Patti Smith Group. With funding courtesy of art collector and benefactor Sam Wagstaff, their first single was a cover of the rock classic 'Hey Joe', incorporating a spoken word dissertation about Patty Hearst. The B-side was 'Piss Factory', detailing Smith's time working on an assembly line. Like Television, Patti Smith enjoyed a residency at CBGB, and she would soon become the first of the club's acts to make it big. It has been suggested that her single 'Hey Joe'/'Piss Factory' was the first punk single, however similar claims have been made about various other recordings. Nevertheless, the single was an acidic and provocative siren call, while Smith herself injected literary leanings into the new music scene.

CBGB hosted the cream of New York's punk and new wave outfits, such as Blondie, Talking Heads, The Heartbreakers and the Ramones. Mind you, at the time, as Blondie's drummer Clem Burke explained, 'It was the same 25 or 35 people in the audience, and you would get up onstage and play, and then go offstage and hang out and watch your friends play.'[51]

Punk, like the later grunge, was a reductionist style, taking rock to its core capacity to elicit intense aggression and even frenzy. Stylistically, it harked back to the late 1950s and early '60s, specifically in terms of its simple three-chord song approach, but also in the visual look. The Ramones, for example, wore leather jackets à la rockers and greasers. Meanwhile, some new wave acts like Blondie were at this time going for a retro mods look, with Debbie Harry writing, 'Everyone in Blondie favoured the mod look, and it was easily available. And we all loved to shop.'[52]

As punk developed, it became no more or less self-important than other rock styles. Although antithetical to glam, punk was yet another avenue for performers to be noticed, particularly by adopting increasingly outrageous attire. It was also a direct repudiation of the professionalism and technical expertise that had begun to dominate rock music, most noticeably in the fields of prog rock and fusion. Punk was a conscious effort to reclaim rock by teenagers and twenty-somethings who were never going to play guitar like John McLaughlin or drums like Bill Bruford. Punks were taking rock music back to their garage and stamping ownership upon it.

The punk and new wave movements were also a product of the growing discord between what Western culture promised and what it was delivering. Americans had been told they were the chosen people in a chosen nation, marked for greatness as leaders of the free world. Such exceptionalism didn't marry with the reality of increasing unemployment and divergent living standards. Even in Australia or England, capitalism's promise of happiness through consumerism didn't align with stagflation and household struggle. These furious new rockers were youth culture's scream of frustration.

It was inevitable that neo-fascists would be attracted to punk's anti-establishment posturing, especially when punk bands began to adopt Nazi symbolism to increase their shock value. Ron Asheton of The Stooges was already appropriating swastikas, Iron Crosses and jackboots. The New York Dolls' Johnny Thunders had worn a swastika armband. For a Cleveland music event called 'Special Examination Night at the Viking Saloon', swastikas adorned the posters. Acts included The electric eels (lower case intentional), a violent band that only performed a handful of gigs. They had no drummer, but did use sledgehammers, anvils and lawnmowers. They even appropriated racist lyrics from the American Nazi Party. Dalliances with fascism would continue in the rock scene over coming years.

1975

Shadows and Light

McCartney's Wings released *Venus and Mars*, which continued the success generated by *Band on the Run*, and John Lennon finally released his *Rock 'n' Roll* album, which he had begun recording in October 1973 before his personal life had spun out of control.

As previously noted, the *Rock 'n' Roll* project was partly the product of a legal suit over plagiarism that had been brought on by Morris Levy. While attempting to get the master tapes from Phil Spector, Lennon had recorded and released *Walls and Bridges*, which clearly didn't include any tunes to which Levy held publishing rights. Lennon had to explain the circumstances about the missing tapes to Levy. When Lennon finally got the tapes, after Capitol Records had paid Spector US$90,000, only four songs were deemed useable. Levy let Lennon and his musos utilise his farm to rehearse for the rest of the *Rock 'n' Roll* set so they could complete the promised album.

But Levy's apparent generosity was a ruse. After recording the rest of the songs, Lennon gave Levy tapes containing rough mixes of the entire LP, which included the songs Levy controlled the rights to. Without consulting Lennon, Levy used the recordings to press an LP that he titled *Roots: John Lennon Sings the Great Rock & Roll Hits*, and released it on his own record label, Adam VIII. He then sued Lennon, EMI and Capitol for a cool US$42 million over their breach of contract. In response, EMI/Capitol sought an injunction, and Lennon sued Levy for releasing material without his authorisation. What a debacle!

After two trials, Levy won just US$6795 in damages and Lennon won US$144,700, as well as getting the Levy album withdrawn from sale. EMI/Capitol rushed out *Rock 'n' Roll* at a budget price. The cover was a portrait taken from The Beatles' Hamburg period. The three blurry figures walking past Lennon were George Harrison, Paul McCartney and original drummer Stu Sutcliffe. Ironically, McCartney was also set to reap some income from Lennon's *Rock 'n' Roll* album, because he now owned the publishing rights to the Buddy Holly catalogue, and thus benefitted from the inclusion of the song 'Peggy Sue'.

Rock 'n' Roll sold and charted well. Stand-out tracks are 'Do You Want to Dance', performed with a Caribbean flavour, plus an effervescent 'Be-Bop-A-Lula'. There's also a pointed rebuff to the whole plagiarism case, with Chuck Berry's 'You Can't Catch Me' performed in the same style and with the verse melody of 'Come Together'. A passionate, oddly aggressive version of 'Stand By Me' was the lead single, and charted moderately well. In Lennon's hands, the lyric comes across more like a threat than a plea. The flipside of the single was a non-album original, a rocking blues titled 'Move Over Ms L', apparently John's farewell message to Yoko. By the time it was released, however, the two had made up and were once again ensconced in the Dakota building in New York. By the end of the year, their visa issues would finally be resolved in their favour and Lennon would largely remove himself from the music business for the rest of the decade, instead concentrating on raising his new son, Sean. 'Move Over Ms L' was also recorded by Keith Moon for his *Two Sides of the Moon* solo album, which similarly harked back to an earlier era.

David Bowie was also looking backwards rather than forwards, with his *Young Americans* album indulging in blue-eyed soul. Lennon and Bowie had become friends, and the two collaborated in a recording session, working on a version of The Beatles' song 'Across the Universe'. During the sessions, guitarist Carlos Alomar improvised around a three-note riff and Lennon began to toy with the word 'fame'. That collaboration turned into the final track on Bowie's album, 'Fame'. Released as a single, it became Bowie's first number one hit in North America. 'Fame' is a funk song about the vicissitudes of celebrity, and it sounds more like Talking Heads than either Bowie or Lennon. Reviewing *Young Americans*, Michael Watts used words like 'inappropriate' and 'hollow', noting that Bowie 'patently lacks any deep emotional commitment to his material. He simply doesn't have the feel.'[1] Overall, Bowie's new direction came across as pastiche rather than an imaginative new direction.

Also looking in the rear-vision mirror was Bruce Springsteen. In his autobiography, Springsteen says he wrote the song 'Born to Run' while he was giving himself a crash course in 1950s and '60s rock 'n' roll: 'At night, I'd switch off the lights and drift away with Roy Orbison, Phil Spector or Duane Eddy lullabying me to dreamland. These records now spoke to me in a way most late-sixties and early-seventies rock music failed to. Love, work, sex and fun.'[2] Perhaps Springsteen had simply picked up on the nostalgic zeitgeist, realising that many listeners also wanted to escape the present?

With a big budget and under pressure to produce a commercially viable record, Springsteen became completely bogged down. The album took some fourteen months to record, while the song 'Born to Run' was kicked about for six months. Steve Van Zandt played a pivotal role, instructing the horn players and even suggesting a minor chord on the title track. When the *Born to Run* album was finally released, Springsteen made the covers of both *Time* and *Newsweek*. Midyear, his E Street Band played five nights at New York's The Bottom Line, which was broadcast live on radio. *Rolling Stone* magazine would later refer to those gigs as one of the fifty moments that changed rock 'n' roll. Given the lack of forward momentum in Springsteen's music, I have my doubts.

Born to Run peaked at number three on the *Billboard* 200, while the tracks 'Born to Run', 'Tenth Avenue Freeze-Out', 'Thunder Road', 'She's the One' and 'Jungleland' have all remained radio favourites. No doubt Columbia's massive US$250,000 promotional campaign (around US$1.4 million today) had a significant bearing, not to mention Jon Landau's quote, used in the marketing, that he had seen rock 'n' roll's future and its name was Bruce Springsteen. Mind you, Landau was hardly impartial, having stepped in to help Springsteen complete his disc, and then become his manager.

Springsteen was decidedly unhappy with the LP, saying, 'I hated it. I couldn't stand to listen to it. I thought it was the worst piece of garbage

I'd ever heard. I told Columbia I wouldn't release it.'[3] True or not, the question remains as to why *Born to Run* became so popular in 1975 and a classic album of the era. The opening, over-long track 'Thunder Road' throws everything at the listener: a love story, references to Roy Orbison, and self-description as a guitar player who knows how to make his instrument 'talk': cars, girls and 1950s rock 'n' roll – it's *American Graffiti* in a song with added self-aggrandisement. 'Tenth Avenue Freeze-Out' is a dull, blues-based riff with some nice horn playing, but Springsteen sings flat when he goes into top range in the bridge.

Okay, *Born to Run* is mostly good, punchy rock 'n' roll sung with a gravelly voiced, swaggering machismo, but there's nothing new happening – maybe that's exactly the point? This wasn't a new direction for rock music, just another reprise of its past glory. Even the thematic 'running' notion was a hackneyed rebel cliché: as Jimi Hendrix reportedly said, 'If I'm free, it's because I'm always running.' A description of a Springsteen concert in *New Musical Express* noted his 'knotty, out-of-tune voice', plus his efforts to 'lend the appearance of weight to a fairly inconsequential moment', and that his monologues come across as 'dumb barhouse literacy'.[4] It's nice to know it's not just me who finds the hype around The Boss a tad overwrought.

Was rock in the doldrums? Many critics certainly thought so, with Cameron Crowe asking Jimmy Page if he thought the music business was sagging. The guitarist answered, 'People always say that amidst their search for The Next Big Thing ... There's so many different styles and facets of the 360-degree musical sphere to listen to. From tribal to classical music, it's all there.'[5] The middle of the decade was certainly in a state of flux, but it wasn't moribund.

State of the union

Music journalists may have been busy decrying the state of popular music, and nostalgia was running hot, but there was actually a lot going on. Prog and heavy metal were peaking, but dance, hip-hop, new wave and punk were also starting to flex their stylistic muscles. In order to explain the development of these new music movements, it's helpful to appreciate what a mess Western culture was in, because they were a reaction to that chaos.

When President Ford greeted the new year with his State of the Union address, it wasn't the usual upbeat homily. Instead, he said, 'I must say to you that the state of the Union is not good. Millions of Americans are out of work. Recession and inflation are eroding the money of millions more.' US unemployment had reached 9.2 per cent. Even American doctors were going on strike. New York City narrowly avoided being declared bankrupt thanks to a $2.6 billion loan from the federal government.

Twenty-five Nixon administration officials, including four cabinet members, had been convicted of various crimes. Most would end up writing books and capitalising in various ways on their notoriety. The longest time spent in jail was Watergate chief operative G. Gordon Liddy, who served just four and a half years – after which his autobiography became a bestseller, he joined the lecture circuit, became an actor appearing in shows like *Miami Vice*, *Perry Mason*, and *MacGyver*, and guested on celebrity game shows. He also launched a private countersurveillance firm called G. Gordon Liddy & Associates, hosted his own syndicated talk show, and wrote a number of non-fiction books and novels. Honestly, you couldn't make this stuff up!

In Britain, inflation hit an incredible 27 per cent in 1975, while the price of petrol went up 70 per cent. Everyone and their dog seemed to be on strike. Margaret Thatcher became England's first female opposition leader, at the same time foreshadowing the lurch towards neoliberal conservatism which promised to solve all crises through unswerving faith in free-market forces and personal avarice.

Vietnam remained an embarrassment for America. As CBS anchorman Walter Cronkite told television viewers, 'In Vietnam we have reached the end of the tunnel and there is no light there.' A series of events led to the fall of Saigon. The South Vietnamese president resigned, and South Vietnam surrendered unconditionally to the north. Terrible scenes played out as thousands scrambled to escape. This is not the place to recount the tales, but Australia's actions during the withdrawal were unconscionable, not least the government's refusal to evacuate Vietnamese employees of the Australian embassy in Saigon.

On 28 April, the tune 'White Christmas' played on Radio America as a signal for all remaining CIA agents to evacuate Vietnam. In the early hours of 30 April, the last cable from CIA official Tom Polgar famously stated:

> This will be the final message from Saigon station. It has been a long fight and we have lost … Those who fail to learn from history are forced to repeat it. Let us hope that we will not have another Vietnam experience and that we have learned our lesson.[6]

For a time Vietnam remained the longest war waged by America and its allies – until the Afghanistan War claimed that dubious honour.

Not prog

Punk was a reaction to both the social malaise and the corporatisation of rock's stylistic excesses. More than anything else, punk was about defiance. Debbie Harry explained the punk/new wave crusade thus: 'I think the universal thread was that we were pointing out the inconsistencies in a hypocritical society and the foibles of human nature and what a joke it all was. A kind of big Dadaist up-yours.'[7]

Already, punk progenitors the New York Dolls were in trouble. Drug and alcohol abuse was part of the problem. For a brief time, British fashion shop owner and wannabe Svengali Malcolm McLaren became their manager, encouraging them to wear red leather outfits and to display a communist flag as their backdrop. The Dolls toured, fell apart, reformed and toured again. After they recorded just two albums, their contract with Mercury Records expired. The band would struggle on for another year.

In New York, punk developed alongside new wave. The definition of new wave is slippery. It is generally viewed as acts that appeared around the punk scene, but which were more musically adept and less hell-bent on being outrageous. They thus became acceptable to a broader audience. In Britain, new wave bands tended to be associated with the pub rock scene, while the American contingent hailed from the same New York venues as punk acts. Talking Heads and Blondie were the frontrunners of this new flavour. Interestingly, both bands incorporated women: the upfront Debbie Harry and the more discreet Tina Weymouth. Mind you, David Byrne was reportedly uneasy at first about having a woman in his band.

Blondie was named after the catcalls Harry often received from construction workers and truck drivers. It was a cartoon name for a band that was almost Warholian in its pop shtick. With Harry in little miniskirts and nipple-revealing tops, the band had immediate appeal to the lads who stood within touching distance at Max's Kansas City and CBGB in New York. Debbie Harry had once been a Playboy bunny, and now used her looks to help promote the band. She was, however, acutely aware of the contradictions she embodied: 'Since I was a front for a bunch of guys, it was like some of their perspective came through me, so I couldn't be "real cute." I was cute, but I had to be tough too. So that helped me in a way. It made me become … uh … schizophrenic.'[8] Harry also claimed to have been obsessed with Marilyn Monroe, admitting that her own 'character in Blondie was partly a visual homage to Marilyn'.[9] Blondie had yet to graduate beyond cult status, with band members struggling to make a living. As Harry wrote, her boyfriend and bandmate Chris Stein 'was on welfare, I was a bikini bartender in the financial district, and we occasionally sold some pot to make a few bucks'.[10]

Patti Smith was at some other end of the sex-kitten-androgyny spectrum, wearing decidedly non-feminine attire and eschewing glamour. Like Joni Mitchell, she had experienced teenage pregnancy and given up her child for adoption, which is a very quick ticket out of childhood. By the time Smith started her band, she had already published three books of poetry and co-authored a play with Sam Shepard. Having been signed by Clive Davis of Arista for a seven-record deal worth US$750,000 (closer to US$4 million today), Smith recorded her first album, *Horses*. It embellished punk with her poetry, bringing a rare intellectual approach to the genre.

The disc opened by explaining that Jesus didn't die for Patti Smith's sins, before devolving into Van Morrison's three-chord garage classic 'Gloria', albeit with new lyrics. 'Break It Up' was ostensibly about Jim Morrison, inspired by Smith's visit to his Paris grave, while 'Elegie' was about another dead rock star, Jimi Hendrix. The impenetrable 'Birdland' was inspired by a memoir of nutty psychoanalyst Wilhelm Reich, and 'Kimberly' was about Smith's younger sister. It's all laced with Beat poetry and lashings of Arthur Rimbaud, some of it improvised in the studio, just as Smith would improvise lyrics in concert.

When composing lyrics at home, Smith engaged a rather unusual process: 'I'd sit at the typewriter and type until I felt sexy, then I'd go and masturbate to get high, and then I'd come back in that higher place and write some more.'[11] Although she quickly became the queen of punk, Smith was more interested in rock's ability to deliver poetry than music.

Horses was produced by former Velvet Underground member John Cale, a relationship that Smith described as like a season in hell. 'All I was really looking for was a technical person,' she explained. 'Instead I got a total maniac artist.'[12] The cover for *Horses* was shot by Smith's former lover Robert Mapplethorpe, with Smith in a plain white business shirt, jacket slung over her shoulder, hair nicely dishevelled, and sporting a vaguely insolent expression. The title was a poetic symbol of Smith's desire for rock music to be rejuvenated – something about holding onto the reins. Although her label was twitchy about the androgynous look, Smith stuck to her guns. In doing so, she became a pioneering role model for women wanting to enter the rock field without having to capitalise on their sexual appeal to men. In one interview, Smith said, 'I'm a girl doing what the guys usually did, the way I look, the goals and kinds of things I want to help achieve through rock. It's more heroic stuff and heroic stuff has been traditionally male.'[13]

Today, *Horses* is ranked at number twenty-six on *Rolling Stone*'s 500 greatest LPs and twelfth on *NME*'s 500 greatest albums of all time. *NME* calls it '[s]creeching and visceral, raw with fury and full of desire ... chaotic poetry'.[14] While a handful of critics were appalled by the amateurish performances, most fell over themselves to praise the disc, and it was moderately well received by buyers, reaching forty-seven on the US charts. The Patti Smith group was booked at CBGB in early 1975 for twenty-five nights running, performing two shows per weeknight and three on weekends, which helped put the venue on the map.

Talking Heads were also hitting the CBGB stage. Unlike the punk acts who were learning on the job, this band already knew how to play their instruments. They incorporated structure and discipline into their music as well as their stage act, which diverged from punk's anarchic shambles. Within a couple of months of appearing, Talking Heads had a dedicated following and were headlining alongside the Ramones.

The Ramones were a bunch of middle-class kids from New Jersey, with their band name adopted from the pseudonym used by Paul McCartney when he checked into hotels: Paul Ramon. The Ramones would become one of the longest-lasting punk outfits, touring for the next twenty-two years. Playing only original material – 'We couldn't figure out how to play anybody else's songs,' said Johnny Cummings[15] – they went for unadorned, brief songs with basic lyrics about disaffection, all propelled by simplistic drumming.

Chris Charlesworth, writing in *New Musical Express*, visited CBGB and described it as 'a toilet … It looks as if the proprietors kick holes in the walls and piss in the corners before they let the customers in.'[16] But a few months later, the paper's Charles Shaar Murray was also at CBGB to witness the developing acts. At a Ramones gig, Murray counted an audience of just twenty-seven people, nine of whom were photographers. Of Blondie, he decided that Debbie Harry 'will never be a star simply because she ain't good enough'. Meanwhile, Richard Hell's punk supergroup The Heartbreakers were deemed to be 'dreadful', and Talking Heads played music that was 'too thin and disjointed to make it work'.[17]

Despite such misgivings, Murray was a passionate convert to the new formula. After seeing Television and Patti Smith perform at CBGB, he wrote: '[T]hat evening was one of the most exciting rock experiences I've had for a long, long time … both acts have something that rock 'n' roll desperately needs.' His conclusion: 'Something's happening.'[18]

Disco

As inevitably as night follows day, James Brown took credit for inspiring disco music, just as he claimed he had done with soul and rap. He attempted to cash in on the new disco scene by releasing an album with an image of himself on the cover overlaid with the words *Sex Machine Today* spelled out in nude human figures (he had released an album in 1970 titled simply *Sex Machine*). Subtitled *Disco Soul Dance Dance Dance*, the new LP resurrected earlier hits such as 'Get Up (I Feel Like Being a) Sex Machine' and 'I Feel Good', and added the revoltingly banal 'Deep in It', in which the singer begins by simply yelling: 'Sex!' It's truly awful stuff.

Journalist Nik Cohn was quick to document the new dance floor phenomenon. He noted that when Van McCoy's hit song 'The Hustle' was played, 'everybody would line up and do pre-ordained steps … The leader would sort of call out the claps, and that was the earliest form of disco dancing.'[19] *Melody Maker*'s Chris Charlesworth did the rounds of New York's discotheques with Billy Smith, the first record company promotion man to focus on getting discs played by deejays. Smith claimed, 'Rock is dead, I tell you. Kids want something different, and this is it.'[20]

Charlesworth noted two types of discos. There were those operating 9pm to 4am, with a $20 entrance fee, which included a couple of alcoholic drinks, and were open to all comers. The second was more 'cultist', for 'serious dancers', staying open until six or seven in the morning and restricted to members and guests. No alcohol was served in these latter establishments and the attendees were mostly gay men. The music never let up and the deejays never spoke, with around twenty to thirty records being rotated. According to Smith, 'These people buy the records and dance at home.'[21] Plainly uncomfortable, Charlesworth wrote, 'And if the sight of a dance floor occupied solely by males is mildly disconcerting at first, you've got to admit they're great dancers.'[22]

The demand was for songs with a steady 4/4 beat that had a similar tempo – around 120 beats per minute. Donna Summer grabbed the disco crown in 1975. The Boston-born Summer was married to Austrian actor

Helmuth Sommer and had been living in Europe for a number of years, where she met up with Giorgio Moroder and Pete Bellotte. Together, they transformed disco music. As Moroder put it, 'The disco songs we had before 1975 had drums. Just normal drums, like a rock group. Then in 1975 we started to put in the bass drum. We called it "four on the floor" ... We kind of exaggerated.'[23]

Moroder and Summer worked on a song called 'Love to Love You Baby'. Although she had reservations about the saucy lyrics, Summer agreed to roleplay while recording. The studio lights were dimmed, candles were lit, and Summer lay on the floor invoking Marilyn Monroe. It ended up being a sixteen-minute song containing – according to the BBC, which obsessed over such things – twenty-three simulated orgasms. The tune reached second spot in the US and fourth in Australia and the UK, despite the BBC's refusal to play it. As Summer told *Vanity Fair*:

> I originally recorded 'Love to Love You Baby' on a dare from Giorgio that I couldn't be sexy. It was a joke that worked ... When we made 'Love to Love You Baby', we knew it was somewhat innovative, but nobody knew people would jump on that bandwagon and all of a sudden, the whole world would be going disco.[24]

Patti Labelle's 'Lady Marmalade', a song about a prostitute, with its French refrain translating as 'Do you want to sleep with me?', went to number one on the sales charts. Because disco wasn't yet considered radio fare, much of the record industry failed to notice the disco snowball building in size. Disco deejays organised themselves, sharing information and songs. They could generate 100,000 sales of a single in New York alone simply by playing it on the dance floors.

In early 1975, The Bee Gees were in trouble, reduced to performing the UK club circuit. Depending on which brother one listens to, it was either Eric Clapton or Robert Stigwood who suggested they invigorate their comeback efforts by recording their next album in Miami. As keyboard player Derek 'Blue' Weaver noted, they all wanted to 'do something that was different than ever they'd done before, but we really didn't know what'.[25] They began recording in their old ballad style, but new producer Arif Mardin wasn't satisfied. He urged them to listen to contemporary R&B artists like Stevie Wonder, and that got the creative juices flowing. The resulting album, *Main Course*, introduced a new vocal sound for the group, jokingly referred to as 'the helium years'.

According to Barry Gibb, Mardin asked him, 'Can you scream in tune? … [S]ee if you can do it in a falsetto type music, scream type voice.'[26] Barry Gibb thus discovered his inner chipmunk and the sound that characterises The Bee Gees' late 1970s material. Mardin also introducing a funkier percussion sound, but it wasn't until Stigwood and Ahmet Ertegun visited the recording sessions that the band realised where Mardin was taking them. The industry heavies reportedly listened to this new blend of pop and R&B, saying, 'Wow, this is dance music!' – which apparently took the Gibbs by surprise. Mind you, the record executives weren't very happy about their decidedly white act adopting a black R&B sound.

The Bee Gees' song 'Jive Talkin'' was inspired by a noise their car made while crossing a bridge heading to and from the studio, with Barry improvising to the clickety clack. At first, the synthesised bass line was just a sample to be replaced by a real bass, but everyone liked the synthesised sound, which was later married with bass guitar. It became one of the first examples of synth bass on a pop record.

There are reports that 'Jive Talkin'' was sent out in a plain white sleeve with no indication as to who was performing. This was a trick Robert Stigwood had used for The Bee Gees' first breakthrough hit, 'New York Mining Disaster 1941', which was at the time presumed to be a new Beatles record. In 1967 the aim was to get an unknown band on the air. In 1975, the aim was also to get airplay, but with the awareness that The Bee Gees were radio poison at the time. *Rolling Stone* reported that only 20 per cent of British deejays were able to identify 'Jive Talkin'' as a Bee Gees song. The Bee Gees didn't even appear on the front cover of their *Main Course* album, which instead featured an Art Deco graphic of a young woman bathing in a giant spoon. Atlantic Records didn't want their black customers to know that the band were white boys.

The 'Jive Talkin'' single went to number one in the US, while 'Nights on Broadway' went to four and the amusingly titled 'Fanny (Be Tender with My Love)' went to nine. The Bee Gees were back! They would find themselves criticised for cherry-picking ideas from other people's songs, but Barry Gibb defended this approach, saying, 'If you are a natural songwriter and your feeling is in it, it's not a cold calculating thing at all. You listen not to steal, but to find out what little things are happening in songs and making hits.'[27]

The aforementioned song 'The Hustle', by Van McCoy and the Soul City Symphony, equalled 'Jive Talkin'' on the US charts and bettered it in many other countries. The recording utilised jazz luminaries such as Steve Gadd, Richard Tee and Eric Gale. The tune will be immediately recognisable to anyone who lived through the era.

Boozer rock

Disco fever hadn't yet hit Australia. The Australia Day weekend saw another Sunbury Pop Festival, this time with headline act Deep Purple. They pocketed a hefty AU$60,000 – a few hundred thousand dollars in today's terms – whereas local acts were paid either a pittance or nothing at all.

AC/DC were scheduled to play before Deep Purple. While their roadie Tana Douglas (one of rock music's first female roadies) was trying to set up their gear, she was told by Deep Purple's crew to 'pull it'. The visitors had received word about AC/DC's onstage presence and demanded to go on first, rather than play the closing slot they had been booked for. The matter devolved into a fistfight between AC/DC and the Deep Purple crew. Douglas reportedly managed to floor a Deep Purple roadie while trying to protect her band. Eventually, security guards quelled the brawl, and AC/DC were told they could play after Deep Purple in the early hours of the morning or not at all. They chose the latter and drove back to Melbourne.

The debacle made AC/DC even more determined to demonstrate that Australian acts could be the equal of overseas bands. When Deep Purple planned an Australian tour the following year, the Musicians' Union warned them that there was still considerable resentment over the fees they'd enjoyed at Sunbury '75. To their credit, Deep Purple placed money into a fund so that artists who had appeared at Sunbury could be paid the proper musicians' rate.

Pub rock was big in England and Australia. In the UK, bands such as Dr. Feelgood, The Stranglers, Eddie and the Hot Rods, Slaughter and the Dogs, and Buzzcocks were performing loud, aggressive rock. Among the Australian pub rockers were Cold Chisel, Farm (who would soon become Midnight Oil) and The Keystone Angels (who would soon truncate their name to The Angels). And, of course, there was AC/DC.

AC/DC continued to refine their riff-based, elemental, energetic pub rock. The first single with Bon Scott as vocalist was a revamp of the blues standard 'Baby Please Don't Go', a tune which dated back to the 1930s. It had been a solid hit for Van Morrison's old band Them in the mid '60s, but in AC/DC's hands it became an explosive monster. For a performance of the song on the television show *Countdown*, Angus wore his trademark schoolboy uniform while singer Bon Scott raided the ABC studios' wardrobe department and appeared in a schoolgirl's dress, replete with Pippi Longstocking wig, make-up and earrings. During the song's instrumental break, Scott's tattooed schoolgirl casually lit a cigarette, and soon after lay on the studio floor flashing white knickers. For many, it was one of the most shocking things to have appeared on Australian TV.

The song also opened the band's debut LP, appropriately titled *High Voltage*. The reason AC/DC appealed to many listeners, particularly in a live context, was because they stripped rock music back to its metal chassis. Indeed, much of the time, that's exactly what pub rock set out to do. This wasn't music for analytical close listening. This was raw rock to accompany drinking, smoking, dancing, yelling and carousing.

It was in 1975 that the AC/DC line-up consolidated, with the addition of bassist Mark Evans and drummer Phil Rudd. The new outfit recorded the now classic 'It's a Long Way to the Top (If You Wanna Rock 'n' Roll)', which became their first top ten single. AC/DC took off for London, where they reportedly broke attendance records at the Marquee Club and released their second album, *T.N.T.* By the end of the year, Atlantic Records had signed the band to a worldwide deal.

This was also the year that Bon Scott came close to death; he was found unconscious in his bedroom after taking unspecified drugs. Roadie Tana Douglas performed CPR until the medics arrived. The rest of the band discovered that Bon suffered from asthma, which could be a complicating factor when, as Douglas put it, he was 'mixing or overindulging in substances'.[28] His days were clearly numbered.

Barbarous blimp

Led Zeppelin's *Physical Graffiti*, the band's first double album, was released on their own Swan Song Records label. It was a massive commercial and critical success, going to the top position on both sides of the Atlantic. It was also the first album ever to go platinum on the basis of pre-orders alone. The songs covered a lot of territory, from the expected hard rock to progressive rock, plus world music influences as on 'Kashmir'. There are Gentle Giant–like jagged, syncopated rhythms on 'Trampled Under Foot', wistful soft rock on 'Down by the Seaside', and a folk guitar instrumental 'Bron-Yr-Aur'. 'Sick Again' was a nasty song about an underage groupie, with the cruel misogyny of the lyric defended by Plant, who said 'the words show I feel a bit sorry for them (groupies)'.[29] He wasn't sorry enough to treat them with any respect, however. As he would later say, 'Yeah, shoving the Plaster Casters' cast of Jimi Hendrix's penis up one of the girls' assholes at some hotel in Detroit was quite fun, actually.'[30]

Musically, my personal misgivings about *Physical Graffiti* are entirely a product of Robert Plant's tiresome voice. But there's no doubting that Led Zeppelin were one of the few heavy bands that liked to stretch their musical boundaries. One surprising example of Zep's eclectic musical influences surfaced in a *Rolling Stone* interview, with Jimmy Page saying:

I have to do a lot of hard work before I can get anywhere near those stages of consistent, total brilliance. I don't think there are too many people who are capable of it. Maybe one. Joni Mitchell. That's the music that I play at home all the time, Joni Mitchell ... She brings tears to my eyes, what more can I say?[31]

By the time of its release, the band had already embarked on their tenth American tour. They would not return to live in their homeland for another twelve months thanks to the tax problems that preoccupied successful British rock stars. Not everyone was supportive of their tax exile, with a writer to *Melody Maker* saying:

Has [Robert Plant] forgotten that some people still play music just for the fun, and that some of his fellow superstars use their privileged positions to help the less fortunate? ... Is Plant seriously trying to tell us that he could not live and work in Great Britain and earn as much after tax as the average coal worker or nurse, who works just as hard, and performs just as useful a service for the community as he does?[32]

The new tour got off to a shaky start when Page broke the tip of his ring finger after catching it in a train door. A new playing technique was required, plus some changes to the set list, along with plenty of codeine and Jack Daniels. Heroin had also now been added to their long list of intoxicants, and the tour was the usual trail of carnage and debauchery.

Riots occurred when tickets went on sale in various US cities. The worst incident was in Boston, causing the local authorities to cancel Zep's concerts there. In Greensboro, 500 ticketless fans attempted to storm the auditorium, wielding scaffolding and missiles. Three of the band's limousines were damaged before police brought matters under control. Police and audience also clashed in Pittsburgh, and a punter was seriously beaten in front of the stage in Philadelphia. Tour manager Richard Cole used his own method of keeping the crowd from reaching the band: it's been reported that he would get underneath the stage and bash their kneecaps with a hammer.

As journalist Chris Charlesworth noted, Led Zep and its staff acted 'as if they were a law unto themselves'.[33]

The band's performances were mostly lacklustre, marred by alcohol, cocaine, heroin, Quaaludes and sleep deprivation. Page's playing was increasingly sloppy. Bonham kept a bag of cocaine between his legs while he sat at his drum kit, rubbing handfuls into his face as he performed. Offstage, he was out of control. At one point, he grabbed a stewardess in a chokehold and pulled up her skirt with the aim of raping her, until she was rescued by tour manager Peter Grant. He also punched a woman in the face because he didn't like the way that she looked at him, assaulted a salesman at Tower Records, and sent *Sounds* correspondent Andy McConnell flying across a room. One evening, Bonham trashed his room before passing out on the mattress with a lit cigarette. The bed caught fire, the sprinkler system was activated, firemen arrived and Led Zeppelin were evicted.

While Zep toured and created havoc, all their previous albums simultaneously entered the Top 200. They thus became the first band to have six albums in the US charts at the same time. But their other Swan Song Records acts were being ignored.

The band made a dash back to London to perform a series of sellout shows at Earl's Court. This was Led Zep on its last legs, before various tragedies struck. Those calamities began when Plant, his wife Maureen and their three children were involved in a car accident while holidaying on the island of Rhodes. Maureen was driving, and she suffered a broken pelvis, leg and fractured skull, coming close to dying through blood loss. Their six-year-old daughter broke her wrist, their four-year-old son suffered a broken leg, while Plant broke both legs and an arm. All were whisked out of Greece before the police could investigate. The family were flown to England for treatment, but because of his tax issues, Plant was shifted to Jersey, which had offshore tax status. Led Zeppelin had been due to start another US tour in three weeks' time, but that had to be cancelled.

By the end of the year, still wheelchair-bound, Plant had relocated to Malibu to meet up with the rest of the band and start working up new material. But bass player Jones, who had previously attempted to quit the band, was not fully participating. Meanwhile, Bonham was missing his British home and taking it out on bottles of liquor while rampaging on Sunset Strip. Page's heroin habit saw him disappear into a void with his occult books. Managers Peter Grant and Richard Cole were also in the grip of drug addictions. Nothing creative was happening, and the American tax laws meant they couldn't stay in California for too long, so they again decamped to Munich, where they somehow managed to record the next LP in rapid time – fundamentally because they only had eighteen days before the Stones were booked into Giorgio Moroder's studio. The new disc, *Presence*, was rewarded with gold status in the UK and platinum in the US on the day of its release, but it wouldn't sell like their previous six albums.

Aerosmith front man Steven Tyler, like members of Led Zep and many other rock stars, was overly fond of underage girls. He described one girl thus: 'She was sixteen, she knew how to be nasty, and there wasn't a hair on it. With my bad self being twenty-six and she barely old enough to drive and sexy as hell, I just fell madly in love with her.'[34] Tyler does seem to confuse lust with love. There were real legal issues for bands that attempted to travel across US state lines with underage girls in their company. At one stage Tyler successfully convinced a girl's parents to sign papers for him 'to have custody' of her ahead of a tour, 'so I wouldn't get arrested if I took her out of the state'.[35] The girl in question became pregnant. To avoid the obvious legal ramifications, he allegedly coerced her to get an abortion. Decades later, she would take legal action against Tyler for sexual assault and battery, as well as for plying her with drugs and alcohol.

Opera plus soap

Queen's fourth album, *A Night at the Opera*, was named in honour of the Marx Brothers' movie, which the band reportedly watched during breaks from recording. It was the most expensive album ever made at the time of its release, with seven different studios being utilised over a four-month period.

Queen were a very focused, hugely ambitious and undoubtedly talented band. The LP included everything from driving hard rock to gentle romantic ballads, a touch of operetta and even Dixieland jazz. The palette was almost as sweeping as The Beatles' *Sgt. Pepper's Lonely Hearts Club Band*, and it took Queen from popularity to superstardom. Freddie Mercury's promise to the Australian audience at Sunbury '74 was coming true. *A Night at the Opera* was very much a collaborative effort, with all band members encouraged to contribute compositions, including drummer Roger Taylor, who came up with the mildly satirical 'I'm in Love with My Car'. With punk nipping at their heels, some critics were already wary of arty-farty adventurism in music, but record buyers knew what they wanted. Speaking of flatulence, Mercury told an interviewer, 'We don't believe in having any session men; we do everything ourselves. From the high falsetto to the low bassy farts, it is all us.'[36]

Despite the success of their world-wide hit 'Killer Queen', the band were skint when they set about recording *A Night at the Opera*. Of some note, therefore, was the opening track 'Death on Two Legs (Dedicated to …)', which was written by Freddie Mercury about their original manager Norman Sheffield. According to Brian May, 'I think we were a bit taken aback with how vicious Freddie wanted it to be.'[37] Although the song doesn't mention Sheffield by name, he sued both band and record label for defamation, in the process outing himself as the subject of the song. The result was an out-of-court settlement.

But it was the breathtaking sweep of 'Bohemian Rhapsody' that stole the show. Over six minutes long, the song transitions from ballad to guitar solo, and operetta to hard rock. It was actually a conglomerate of separate tunes stitched together. Recorded on twenty-four-track tape, various mixes were bounced up to eight generations, resulting in some 200 overdubs. Famously, the record executives at EMI were opposed to releasing the song as a single. In a story not dissimilar to Dylan's 'Like a Rolling Stone' in 1965, a copy of 'Bohemian Rhapsody' was leaked to UK radio disc jockey Kenny Everett, who played it fourteen times over two days. Paul Drew in the US also heard the song and began to give it airtime on his radio network. In both countries, the record labels were forced to release the song by popular demand. Although it didn't perform as well in America, 'Bohemian Rhapsody' hit number one in the UK, Australia and elsewhere, selling six million copies across the globe. It eventually became one of the best known and most loved rock songs of all time – one of the few progressive rock tunes to achieve the status of rock classic.

As it really couldn't be mimed on *Top of the Pops*, the band convinced EMI to fund a film clip – or, as it was called at the time, a pop promo. Although bands had been making such promos since the 1960s, the success of the 'Bohemian Rhapsody' video was a watershed moment, after which promotional videos became a mandatory tool in the marketing of songs. The 'Bohemian Rhapsody' clip was shot in just four hours, with the lighting and video effects achieved in the camera rather than in post-production. As Joe Smith, chairman of Elektra Records, later gushed, 'It took over three weeks to cut this one single. But the layers of guitars and the overdubs of vocals, and then when I got to see the video and you realise that Freddie Mercury was so charismatic and so unique!'[38]

Speaking of opera, the soap opera that was Fleetwood Mac continued to play out like a daytime TV serial. Mick Fleetwood was so busy managing his band that he didn't notice how neglected his wife, Jenny, was feeling. During a barbecue at their Topanga Canyon house, Jenny flipped out and began screaming hysterically while punching her husband. She was put to bed, where she started having convulsions. This was stress in extremis. The couple soon divorced, and Jenny took the kids back to England. Meanwhile, John and Christine McVie's marriage was also on the rocks, with Chris engaging in a secret affair with the band's lighting director, who was subsequently fired. Stevie Nicks and Lindsey Buckingham, who had only recently joined the group as a couple, were also in strife.

The band members somehow kept their professional lives and private lives compartmentalised. They managed to keep touring and released yet another self-titled album – the first eponymous disc had been released in 1968. To distinguish it, the 1975 LP is often referred to as their *White Album*. It spawned three charting singles, 'Over My Head', 'Rhiannon' and

'Say You Love Me', setting the group on its course towards mass popularity. As Mick Fleetwood put it, 'That album was the first time, but far from the last, that we relied on cocaine to fuel the long hours of work … Let's just say that Sound City wasn't just made of bricks and mortar, there seemed to be white powder peeling off the walls in every room.'[39] The band were also drinking heavily. An attempt to jokingly document the drinking by storing empty bottles in a corner of the recording studio quickly became an embarrassment and was discontinued.

Old guard, new songs

Reviewing a Rolling Stones concert, one critic wrote, 'A lot of the macho-sadist excess has been pruned back, and although Jagger cavorts and leaps and pouts as much as ever, he seems more like an irresistible clown than any Lucifer figure.'[40] With change in the air, many 1960s acts were beginning to worry about their relevance. Pete Townshend was concerned that The Who had already become a 'golden oldies' band, saying, 'It's just that when I'm standing up there on stage playing rock 'n' roll, I often feel like I'm too old for it.'[41]

Self-reflection was also at the heart of Bob Dylan's 1975 outing, disturbingly titled *Blood on the Tracks*. Many of the songs looked backwards, often referencing his earlier songs and those of his formative influencers. Although the album received a lukewarm response from many critics, it has retrospectively been hailed as one of Dylan's best. Certainly, it was an album born of personal pain, which is arguably why it achieved some degree of greatness.

Bob's son Jakob would eventually describe the disc as being his estranged parents talking to one another. One must wade through side one and arrive at the second track on side two to find a ballad that isn't a personalised song about forsaken love. However, there are a few beautiful songs on the disc. *Blood on the Tracks* ranks as the ninth-best album of all time in *Rolling Stone*'s top 500 list. Reviewing the album for *Melody Maker*, Michael Watts found it all rather tepid, saying, 'It's just this healthy sense of rage that I miss now in Dylan ... Blood on the Tracks is not reassuring as a reconciliation of his past with his present.[42]

Paul Simon hadn't released a new studio album since 1973's successful *There Goes Rhymin' Simon*, so his next outing was much anticipated. *Still Crazy After All These Years*, like Dylan's *Blood on the Tracks*, was written during marital estrangement. Despite its generally dour subject matter, four Top 40 hits were gleaned. 'Gone at Last' is an up-tempo gospel song about fighting depression while receiving support from unexpected quarters, with co-vocalist Phoebe Snow going for broke on the outro. The religious theme was taken a step further in the deceptively titled folk-psalm 'Some Folks' Lives Roll Easy', in which Simon recognises the role of fate while acknowledging that he needs assistance from the Lord.

He admitted to weeping while writing 'I Do It for Your Love', about a man trying his hardest to make a relationship work. Emotional chaos was also at the heart of the track 'Night Game', which uses baseball as a metaphor for personal loss and perhaps even death. Musically, however, these tunes all pale in comparison to the title track. 'Still Crazy After All These Years' is a complex song about regret and thoughts of suicide, with shifting time signatures and changes in key. There's also a somewhat discordant orchestral section that resolves into a soaring sax solo by Michael Brecker. As a piece of songwriting, it's a tour de force.

The most acerbic number on the disc is 'My Little Town', in which Simon takes a swipe at American small-town thinking, with its inherent racism and dead-end opportunities. The song was originally intended for an Art Garfunkel solo album, but when Simon played it for his old partner, they automatically began to harmonise, and so it ended up becoming a duet on this LP. On the TV show *Saturday Night Live*, the pair sang this as well as some old favourites, generating an avalanche of media interest about the old partnership reforming. As well as winning Grammys for Album of the Year and Best Male Pop Vocal, *Still Crazy After All These Years* would be Simon's only number one album on the *Billboard* charts. He would dabble in filmmaking, but not release any new studio albums for the next five years.

Joni Mitchell was taking rock music somewhere even more exciting. *The Hissing of Summer Lawns* continued her experiment combining jazz with observational songs of great lyrical substance. As Stephen Holden put it in *Rolling Stone*, Mitchell had 'moved beyond personal confession into the realm of social philosophy', with characters 'who act out socially determined rituals of power and submission in exquisitely described settings'.[43] Thus 'Edith and the Kingpin' is as fine a piece of observational poetry as one can find in songcraft, describing an underworld gangster and his women in superb detail.

A couple of songs on the LP deal with women and their social position vis-a-vis males, 'Don't Interrupt the Sorrow' and 'The Hissing of Summer Lawns', while 'The Boho Dance' is a swipe at those critics who claimed Mitchell had sold out. The album concludes with 'Shadows and Light', a dense, multitracked, metaphysical poem describing the way humans make judgements based on prescribed standards of good and evil.

Some critics used their own prescribed standards to judge the album harshly, with *Rolling Stone*'s Stephen Holden describing it as poetry with a distracting soundtrack. Those who went searching for confessional exposure à la *Blue* came up empty-handed, and thus deemed the album to lack authenticity and to be pretentious. In fact, the characters that populate these songs, especially the women, are struggling with issues far more profound than simple romantic encounters. Mitchell was now a mature, fierce and provocative documenter of American culture. *The Hissing of Summer Lawns* had an acknowledged influence on many later songwriters, notably Björk and Kate Bush.

Boundary riders

Boundaries were still being pushed by various artists. Brian Eno was much in demand as a producer, including for the amusing Portsmouth Sinfonia, an orchestra of musicians only semi-competent on their instruments (classical punk perhaps?). He also toured with Robert Fripp, performing their minimalist Frippertronic soundscapes. Eno also established the short-lived but hugely important Obscure Records label to provide broader exposure to avant-garde artists like Gavin Bryars, John Adams, David Toop, John Cage, Harold Budd and The Penguin Cafe Orchestra. This year also saw the release of Eno's third solo album, *Another Green World*, with contributions from various prog and avant-rock performers.

Synthesisers were making great strides at this time: 1975 saw Moog introduce the Polymoog, with seventy-one notes on its keyboard. Finally, more than one note could be played at the same time. It would be followed by other polyphonic synthesisers, such as the Yamaha CS-80, the Prophet-5 and the Roland Jupiter-4. The first digital synthesiser, the Synclavier, commanded a price tag north of US$75,000 (over US$400,000 dollars today). This was a major investment, yet it found homes with innovators like Stevie Wonder and Frank Zappa.

Tangerine Dream performed a concert of their atmospheric electronica at York Minster in complete darkness, while their album *Rubycon* went to number ten in the UK.

Out there on a left field of his own making was Ivor Cutler, whose classic *Velvet Donkey* on Virgin Records continued his eccentric output of peculiar ditties, this time with assistance from Henry Cow's Fred Frith on viola. Henry Cow, meanwhile, absorbed Slapp Happy into its ranks to record their masterpiece *In Praise of Learning*.

Robert Wyatt toured with Henry Cow to promote his new solo album, *Ruth Is Stranger Than Richard*. He also sang on Michael Mantler's *The Hapless Child and Other Inscrutable Stories*. This brooding material set the words of modern gothic illustrator and author Edward Gorey to Mantler's chamber-jazz. Wyatt's idiosyncratic voice was perfectly suited to the ominous mood of the material.

Other classic prog and avant-rock albums appeared by Gentle Giant, Hatfield and the North, Caravan, Goblin, Magma, Jade Warrior and many more. Greek keyboardist Vangelis had been invited to England to audition for Yes after the departure of Rick Wakeman. Instead, Yes hired Patrick Moraz. But Vangelis wanted to live where the action was, so he moved to London, set up a sixteen-track studio and negotiated a recording deal with

RCA. His first solo disc, *Heaven and Hell*, demonstrated an impressive command of contemporary keyboards enhanced by the English Chamber Choir in a somewhat *Carmina Burana*-ish opus.

Following the unbridled success of *Dark Side of the Moon*, Pink Floyd eventually came up with *Wish You Were Here*. The first track saw Floyd reverting to their old trick of long, noodling suites, this time a five-part tune titled 'Shine On You Crazy Diamond' – the diamond being former band member Syd Barrett. Barrett visited the band unannounced during the recording of the album, but his appearance had altered so dramatically that Nick Mason didn't recognise him at first. As Mason put it, 'We had all played some part in bringing Syd to his present state, either through denial, a lack of responsibility or downright selfishness.'[44]

Wish You Were Here received some brickbats on release. *Melody Maker*'s critic, Allan Jones, said it was 'unconvincing in its ponderous sincerity and displays a critical lack of imagination in all departments'. He went on to deride Gilmour's guitar playing, Waters' lyrics and every other aspect of the disc, crystallising his opinion with: 'Wish You Were Here sucks. It's as simple as that.'[45]

But the album has since been assessed far more favourably. In 1975, it went number one in the UK, US, Australia and elsewhere, and it has sold some 20 million copies. Band members Richard Wright and David Gilmour have both cited it as their favourite Floyd album, with Gilmour saying it's 'probably the best-balanced album in terms of the music having the emotional strength on its own. To me that works better than Dark Side of the Moon does.'[46]

Calamitous acts

Alice Cooper had been banned from entering Australia by Immigration Minister Clyde Cameron, who claimed the performer was a 'degenerate'. As Cooper responded, 'Isn't that crazy? People still think I kill chickens on-stage.'[47] But the ban was lifted by Cameron's successor, James McClelland, in time for Cooper's 1975 world tour. However, logistics meant that he couldn't stage his Welcome to My Nightmare show in the antipodes, because there were no venues big enough to accommodate it. Elsewhere, his sixty-five-city global tour was one of the largest stage spectacles of the decade. But the tour was not without its hiccups, with Cooper being propelled off the stage by a giant toybox, breaking ribs and requiring stitches to his head. He also collapsed on stage three days after that incident. As well as injuries, the show furnished Cooper with a wife: the eighteen-year-old ballerina who danced during 'Only Women Bleed'.

Welcome to My Nightmare was Cooper's first LP as a solo performer, without his old band. A concept album, the songs are linked by a journey through the nightmares of a child. 'Only Women Bleed' sounds like a tacky song about menstruation, and many assumed so, with some feminist groups even protesting. In fact, it's a song about domestic violence, and how women are mentally and physically subjugated by men. The song is sung from the woman's perspective, and it became the biggest hit from the album.

The Rolling Stones were still wedded to their bombastic machismo. Their 1975 tour included a twenty-foot penis that inflated on stage next to Jagger. The singer would at times sit astride the enormous phallus, although in Memphis the member didn't make an appearance following a warning by the local police about consequences. Also included in the stage extravaganza was a giant lotus-shaped stage that unfolded, plus more stage lights than any other show in history. The whole spectacle cost a reported US$1.6 million to create. As for the music, the band had no new material to unveil, relying instead on their back catalogue.

Elton John's ninth studio LP, *Captain Fantastic and the Brown Dirt Cowboy*, was a joint autobiographical account of Elton's and lyricist Bernie Taupin's collaboration during the early stages of Elton's career. The album was certified gold before being released and went straight to number one in its first week. As Elton put it, there were '[s]ongs about trying to write songs. Songs about no one wanting our songs.'[48] The single 'Someone Saved My Life Tonight' was about his failed engagement to Linda Woodrow in 1968. The 'someone' in the song was not Woodrow, but bandleader Long

John Baldry, who convinced Elton to leave his miserable relationship and focus on his music. But perhaps the thankyou was also self-directed by Bernie Taupin, who had pulled Elton's head out of an oven following the breakup. Elton John would later say that the album was his finest work because no effort was made to make any of it commercial. The launch was marred, however, when a media event in a private cinema devolved into fisticuffs. Temperamental Elton was incensed by the quality of the hi-fi system, because of which he repeatedly punched a sound engineer.

Elton John had never enjoyed a number one single in his homeland. In America, however, he was the most-listened-to artist, outselling The Beatles many times over. As demonstration of his pop status, he was even featured on a Bally pinball machine. In 1975, the mayor of LA, Tom Warson, declared 20–26 October to be Elton John Week, during which John's star was unveiled on the Hollywood Walk of Fame, outside Grauman's Chinese Theatre. Not since The Beatles in 1966 had a performer been allowed to stage concerts at Dodger Stadium. The songster flew his mother, grandmother and various friends to LA to experience the shows.

But the drugs, insecurity and stress were taking their toll, as was Elton's disintegrating relationship with manager/lover John Reid. The twenty-eight-year-old might have been the biggest pop star in the world, but he was utterly miserable. In characteristically flamboyant fashion, he announced to the many family members and friends who were staying in his Benedict Canyon mansion that he had taken a fistful of Valium and was about to die, and then dramatically threw himself into the swimming pool. Of course, with so many willing hands, he was quickly rescued, and medics soon arrived to make him vomit up the tablets. According to Elton, one thing he remembers from the episode was his grandmother pragmatically saying, 'Oh, we might as well bleedin' go home then.' As he put it, 'I couldn't stop myself laughing. That might have been exactly the response I needed. I was looking for "oh, you poor thing", but instead I got "why are you behaving like such a twat?"'[49] A day later he was onstage performing.

Elton also made time to record and release *Rock of the Westies*, the title being a spoonerism. The new disc repeated the accomplishment of going number one in its first week, but it would be the artist's last chart-topping album in the US. Musically, it was also a retreat to contrived commerciality.

While Elton John preferred playing to enthusiastic American audiences, American band The Eagles preferred to play to British audiences. As Glenn Frey put it, 'What I like about playing in England is the attentiveness of the audience. In America we tend to play to very boisterous crowds, but in England they sit and listen.'[50] The Eagles' breakthrough album, *One of These Nights*, was an international smash yielding three top-selling singles, 'One of These Nights', 'Lyin' Eyes' and 'Take It to the Limit'. As Don Henley explained: 'It was a dark time, both politically and musically, in America. There was turmoil in Washington and disco music was starting to take off … We wanted to capture the spirit of the times.'[51]

Like many successful bands, members of The Eagles were narky with one another. Guitarist Don Felder referred to the recording studio as being like a 'pressure cooker', with the arguments becoming increasingly 'explosive'.[52] Members of The Who were also largely avoiding each other. They had worked on the movie version of *Tommy* and John Entwistle was keeping himself busy performing solo gigs, but the curmudgeon Pete Townshend was experiencing a serious bout of writer's block. Not only was he depressed by turning thirty, he was also fed up with the music industry. What's more, the 'void' between him and Roger Daltrey had become a yawning chasm. Townshend's New York lawyer gave him some cogent advice, which was to hand more control to Daltrey. So Townshend wrote to his bandmate with the aim of burying hatchets and dusted off all the songs he had in the drawer, throwing the lot at Daltrey with instructions for the singer to choose which would make up the new album. Letting go of control wasn't easy, but Townshend could see the sword of Damocles hovering over his band.

For my money, all this emotional turmoil is what makes *The Who by Numbers* so exceptional. Townshend ignores the disc in his autobiography, while Daltrey in his says, 'In some ways, *The Who By Numbers* is my favourite album.'[53] *NME* called it a suicide note. The songs expose Townshend's and the band's vulnerabilities in ways that were extremely rare for swaggering macho rock stars.

The title of the album suggests the band were simply going through the motions. Far from it. 'Slip Kid', a leftover from the *Lifehouse* project, opens the disc, with Daltrey and Townshend alternating on lead vocals. The lyrics are about the burden of responsibility as one grows up. This leads into the straightforwardly titled 'However Much I Booze', supposedly penned the night Townshend gave up drinking (the sobriety didn't last long). It's loaded with self-deprecation and loneliness, the singer viewing himself as a charlatan. If ever there was a cry of pain from the pit of depression, this song is it, the subject contrasting with its up-tempo instrumentation. Daltrey found the tune far too personal and refused to sing it, leaving that task to the song's author. In similar vein is 'Dreaming from the Waist', which was originally titled 'Control Myself', with the fixation this time being sex rather than booze.

According to Roger Daltrey, when Townshend was writing 'How Many Friends', he was sitting in his loungeroom, stoned and crying, feeling detached from the band and the world. It's a towering, urgent cry about Townshend's deep-seated aloneness, his lack of trust in others and the hurt engendered by criticism. The wailing guitar and crashing drums turn this into one of rock's greatest laments. The one upbeat number, 'Blue Red and Grey', is like a cognitive behavioural therapy session, with Townshend valiantly trying to count his blessings. The song is just Townshend's voice with strummed ukulele, sparingly supported by John Entwistle on horns.

Townshend tended to turn his personal turmoil onto others, often publicly. From Daltrey's point of view, 'Pete ... could only communicate his musical struggles through the press. He never came to us when he was in trouble. He never shared his problems ... He just told journalists in order to tell us how bad we were.'[54] In one *NME* interview, Townshend also made judgemental statements about The Bay City Rollers, Jeff Beck, Pink Floyd, Yes, ELP and Gary Glitter. It was a 'pox on all your' houses position, with Townshend concluding that 'on most levels rock has become a spectator sport. It's not so important as a method of expression as it once was. Today something else could quite easily replace it.'[55] Townshend's lowest ebb is reflected in the last track on *The Who by Numbers*: 'In a Hand or a Face' finds him so drained of compassion that he can feel no empathy for a tramp seen rifling through rubbish bins. Instead the sight of the character only elicits hate.

This most exceptional of rock albums did manage to reach single digits in the UK and US. But if rock is to be considered art, and if honesty is one yardstick by which we might judge great art, then critics and historians should be falling over themselves to praise *The Who by Numbers*, just as they continue to do for Joni Mitchell's *Blue*.

The Who's UK and European tour was the first to employ laser lighting. Keith Moon was grumpy about the associated costs. He berated some hapless British Airways ground staffer, resulting not only in his arrest but also in the band being banned from commercial flights. They were thus forced to charter their own plane, which ate up even more of the tour profits. The drummer was on a rapid downhill slide, lost in booze and barbiturates while tearing hotel rooms apart. He was also spending up big on cars and all manner of material goods. At the end of the tour his personal profit was reportedly just £47.35.

Since killing his friend and bodyguard in 1970, Moon had a sort of death wish. Karen Carpenter also found a means of slowly killing herself. She had become obsessed with dieting when still in high school, and by 1975 she weighed just 41 kilograms. Fans were shocked to see how thin she had become. A tour of Britain was cancelled, blamed on stress plus 'spastic colitis' – what we today call irritable bowel syndrome. Carpenter's eating disorder and abuse of laxatives (she reportedly took eighty to ninety tablets each night) was out of control. Someone who took a faster way out was Pete Ham, the lead vocalist, guitarist and founder of Badfinger, who hanged himself in his garage, becoming yet another member of the 27 Club.

Tim Buckley had celebrated the end of a brief sellout tour with a weekend of drinking with bandmates and friends. When his friend Richard Keeling offered a bag of heroin, Buckley availed himself of a snort or two. Buckley's friends took him home, where his wife put him to bed. When she checked on him later, he was blue.

Egos down under

Australia's symphonic rock band Sebastian Hardie released their album *Four Moments*, which rose to twelve on the local charts. In true prog style, the title track took up an entire album side, with the disc referencing the likes of Emerson, Lake & Palmer, and lumbered with even more clichés. But the big hitmakers in the land of Oz were the perennial Sherbet plus Skyhooks, who provided three of the songs in the year's top ten: 'Horror Movie', 'All My Friends Are Getting Married' and 'Ego Is Not a Dirty Word'.

If there is one song that pinpoints the shift from the collectivist 1960s to the self-centred '70s, it is Skyhooks' 'Ego Is Not a Dirty Word'. Indeed, it could be viewed as an anthem for the self-esteem and New Age movements. The LP of the same name went gold twice in pre-release, then spent eleven weeks at the top of the Australian charts, selling 210,000 copies. That meant one in every sixty-five Australian men, women and children owned a copy. With cheeky irreverence, the album was peppered with double entendres and goofiness. As Red Symons put it, 'I think Shirley and I always had a sense that rock and roll potentially was a subset of vaudeville and we were inclined to go in that direction.'[56]

Michael Gudinski had entered a deal with Phonogram Records to license Skyhooks' records outside of Australia and New Zealand, and the band embarked on an American tour, where they found themselves opening for Joe Cocker, Styx and Uriah Heep. It was a trip beset with problems, beginning with bass player Greg Macainsh falling ill and having to be replaced. The band's hotel rooms were robbed while they were playing their first gig, and locals pulled guns on them on the highway.

Kiss had already commandeered the 'zany make-up' corner of the rock market, so Skyhooks simply looked imitative, while the larrikin Australian humour was lost on American audiences. As Red Symons later acknowledged, 'It was never going to be an overnight success. The way to succeed is to relocate there and work out what works for Americans and adapt to that.'[57] Instead, the Hooks returned to their homeland with a renewed sense of what it meant to be Australian, embarking on another national tour amusingly titled The Brats Are Back. Three more albums would appear in ensuing years – *Straight in a Gay Gay World*, *Guilty Until Proven Insane* and *Hot for the Orient* – before the band folded, and lead singer Strachan gravitated to television with his own children's show.

Skyhooks may have failed to make inroads in the US, but another group was pitched more squarely at that market. Little River Band were considered a supergroup by local standards, with almost every member hailing from previously well-known outfits, including Drummond, The Twilights, Axiom and Mississippi. They secured the managerial services of the irrepressible Glen Wheatley, signed with EMI locally and recorded their self-titled debut album. It managed to go gold in Australia, as did their debut single 'Curiosity (Killed the Cat)'. As guitarist Graeham Goble put it:

> The whole idea of the band was never to just play in Australia. It was always geared towards the American market. And so as soon as we had the record, and we had our record deal with EMI, Glen Wheatley went to America to talk to all the major record companies. And he literally did it with an American Express card. He had to come back with a deal ... because he had no way of paying it back.[58]

While Wheatley's expenses in the US maxed out his credit card, the band signed to Capitol Records with an eight-album deal and a million-dollar advance for each album. What LRB offered was American West Coast, harmony-driven soft rock.

John Paul Young also had a modicum of US success with his single 'Yesterday's Hero', penned by the prolific Harry Vanda and George Young. It went to the top ten in Australia and made it to forty-two in the US. What JPY didn't realise until much later was that the song 'was about what they [Vanda and Young] went through after The Easybeats'.[59]

Australian director Jim Sharman's film *The Rocky Horror Picture Show* was based on the musical stage production *The Rocky Horror Show*.

Although reception of the film was at first extremely negative, it soon turned into a cult classic. At the Waverly Theatre in New York, midnight screenings saw attendees dressing as characters from the film. In Pittsburgh, audience members began acting out roles in front of the screen. The international following elevated the movie to become the longest-running theatrical release in film history. The soundtrack album was also a hit.

Renée Geyer sang the song 'Turn on the Lights' for the Liberal Party's 1975 federal election campaign. The politicos were hoping to emulate Labor's success with 'It's Time' from 1972. Geyer would later claim that the only reason she did the gig was to make enough money to record an album in the US, where she was signed with Polydor Records. But even Geyer's assistance couldn't get the conservatives across the line. However, Labor's victory would end in tears. The conservatives who controlled the Senate successfully blocked supply, thus denying the Whitlam government the capacity to carry out government business. As a result, in a hugely contentious act, Governor-General Sir John Kerr dismissed the elected government. Whitlam's progressive but wildly erratic approach was already on the nose with much of the populace, who instead chose a conservative government under Malcolm Fraser.

The heart of the matter

Before the Labor government was ousted, the prime minister's wife, Margaret Whitlam, attended the world's first Conference on Women, in Mexico City. The United Nations had designated 1975 to be International Women's Year, and the global focus on women's issues was now unavoidable. Rock music, however, remained stubbornly male-centric, particularly in the field of heavy metal.

One exception to the 'cock rock' that defined that genre was American band Heart. They sported sisters Ann and Nancy Wilson. Heart lucked upon a gig opening for Rod Stewart in Montreal. Their debut album, *Dreamboat Annie*, sold over a million copies, generating hit songs 'Crazy on You', with its memorable riff, and 'Magic Man', with an unfortunate lyric about a girl leaving home for a man who offers to help her get high. Like Led Zeppelin, the band's music crossed over from heavy metal to ballads and folk rock, but Heart would far outlive Led Zep, becoming a mainstay for decades to come. Importantly, like Suzi Quatro, the Wilson sisters helped blast away barriers for women in hard rock. Heart also demonstrated that hard-rocking women could be both alluring and ferocious.

Meanwhile, Suzi Quatro released her new album, appropriately titled *Your Mamma Won't Like Me*. Although Quatro opened for Alice Cooper on his Welcome to My Nightmare tour and was featured on the cover of *Rolling Stone*, real success in the US market continued to elude her. Not so in Australia, where the album performed best. The opening track, and second single, 'I Bit Off More Than I Could Chew', written by her producers Mike Chapman and Nicky Chinn, is a propulsive cracker with a tight horn arrangement. Another song, provocatively titled 'Strip Me', is not an appeal to get naked, but instead a story about a wealthy man's mistress who gives away all of her material property. The album's low point is a desultory version of 'Fever', the classic raunch song made popular by Peggy Lee in 1958.

Loretta Lynn hit peak controversy this year with her country tune 'The Pill', about a woman celebrating freedom from her husband's control thanks to the contraceptive pill. As Lynn described it:

> It's just a wife arguin' with her husband. The wife is sayin', 'You've kept me barefoot and pregnant all these years while you've been slippin' around. Now you straighten out or I'll start, now that I have the pill.' It's a husband and wife, not two unmarried people, so that's not dirty.[60]

When listening to the song, look out for the chicken and incubator analogy! 'The Pill' was banned from country radio stations, which inevitably led it to rise to five on the *Billboard* Hot Country chart. The headstrong Lynn would go on to have fourteen songs banned over the course of her career.

That's prophetic

At the end of the year, flyers started to appear all over New York saying, 'Punk is coming.'. Everyone was thus asking, 'What is punk?' The flyers were forward promotion for *Punk* magazine, but they were also a prescient warning about a looming musical revolution.

1976

Blitzkrieg Bop

Record sales were now so numerous in the US that a new certification was officially established by the Recording Industry Association of America. Platinum eclipsed gold, representing 1 million copies for albums and 2 million for singles. Although previous albums had sold over a million and been informally dubbed platinum, The Eagles' compilation LP *Their Greatest Hits* became the first authorised platinum album. At the time of writing, it remains the biggest-selling album of all time in the US – bigger even than Michael Jackson's *Thriller.*

The Eagles also released their album *Hotel California*, which sits at third position on the all-time sales list. Between them, these two Eagles discs, both released in 1976, account for 64 million LPs sold into the US market. Mind you, not everyone was impressed, with Tom Waits saying that Eagles albums were 'good for keeping the dust off your turntable, and that's about all'.[1]

Peter Frampton's double live album, *Frampton Comes Alive!*, was released in the first week of 1976, remaining in the charts for almost two years while selling more than 11 million copies worldwide. *Rolling Stone*'s readers' poll voted it album of the year. By 2012, readers of *Rolling Stone* still ranked it third in a poll of all-time favourite live albums. Three hit singles were lifted from the disc, 'Baby I Love Your Way', 'Do You Feel Like We Do' and 'Show Me the Way', the latter two utilising the Heil Talk Box.

Arguably, the response to Frampton was the same sort of reaction that Bruce Springsteen engendered with *Born to Run*: many people simply wanted straight-ahead rock, with plenty of hooks and drive, embellished with high-quality, expressive guitar playing. In other words, like Springsteen,

Frampton was dealing in formula. It wasn't as aggressively threatening as most heavy metal, and Frampton wasn't trying to make deep, political statements (although he would become politically engaged later in his career). It helped that the former member of Britain's Humble Pie was easy on the eye, and that his record company was massively supportive. On learning that his album had hit the top spot in the US, Peter Frampton phoned his parents in the UK, waking them up. As he described the moment, 'I didn't cry ... but I sure came close. I'm shaking just talking about it now.'[2]

Just as Frampton's album hit the shelves, Fleetwood Mac came off the road. 'Rhiannon' was climbing the charts and they wanted to record a new album. They booked the Record Plant studio near Sausalito, California, as well as a nearby house for the entire band plus hangers-on to reside in. Sensibly, the two female band members instead opted to rent a nearby apartment. As Mick Fleetwood described the process, band members spoke to each other in 'clipped, civil tones while sitting in small airless studios listening to each other's songs about our shattered relationships ... Immediately rumors began to fly about who was seeing whom after hours.'[3] As their new, inexperienced producer Richard Dashut reported, 'All I can say is that it was trial by ordeal, and the craziest period of our lives. We went four or five weeks without sleep, doing a lot of drugs. I'm talking about cocaine in such quantities that at one point I thought I was going insane.'[4] Arguments raged, and participants regularly stormed out. Girlfriends were swapped, while Mick Fleetwood's ex-wife returned from England and took up with one of his best friends.

After two months of Sausalito madness, they went back to LA and listened to the tapes. But whichever studio they played them in, the tapes sounded wrong. Worried they might have to start all over, they eventually found a mixing suite where the recordings sounded useable. New tracks were recorded, and the process ground on. Abandoning their recording efforts, they went on tour, often supporting the soaring, bickering Eagles. Girls would turn up to concerts dressed like Stevie Nicks in black chiffon and top hats. Lindsey Buckingham was still pining for

Stevie, but she was being courted by The Eagles' Don Henley, as well as by Mick Fleetwood.

After the band completed a brief tour in the UK, American authorities threatened to deport its British members for lack of visas. While green cards were sorted out, earlier drug convictions for marijuana possession became an issue. Mick Fleetwood had to remarry his ex-wife so they and his daughters could remain in the States. They even had to live together. By the end of the year, the new album was finally completed, and given an appropriate title: *Rumours* (spelled the English way). It would have to wait until 1977 to test the market.

Bob Dylan's seventeenth LP, *Desire*, saw seven of the nine tracks penned in collaboration with theatre director Jacques Levy. Backed by his Rolling Thunder Revue band, and with backing vocals from Emmylou Harris and Ronee Blakley, it became one of Dylan's bestselling albums, going to number one in the US and Australia. *Rolling Stone* critic Dave Marsh noted that Dylan's attitude towards women had improved over the years, but the songs still evoked 'a man on the run from something he can't define'.[5] As well as his 'Hurricane' single, there was also a lionising tribute to mobster Joseph N. Gallo, which got up many people's noses.

The Rolling Stones released *Black and Blue*, an album that *Creem* magazine's critic Lester Bangs called 'meaningless'.[6] Bondage was something of an obsession for the Stones. To promote the new LP, a huge billboard on Sunset Boulevard displayed a bruised and bound woman – model Anita Russell – next to the words 'I'm "Black and Blue" from the Rolling Stones – and I love it!' Pretty soon some new words were added by spray can: 'This is a crime against women.'

David Bowie came up with *Station to Station*, which some regard as his best work. It presented yet another persona, this time dubbed the Thin White Duke, after lyrics in the disc's title track. It's a much darker LP than previous Bowie offerings, combining his interest in funk with elements of Krautrock. Like so many of his peers, Bowie was battling a cocaine addiction and was riven with paranoia. According to one biographer, at this time he was living on capsicums, milk and cocaine.

In early 1976, ABBA had four singles in the US charts, but their *ABBA* album couldn't ascend above 174 on the *Billboard* 200. In Britain they were being snubbed, with Benny Andersson admitting, 'England has been a most difficult market for us.'[7] Australia, however, was a very different story, thanks in large part to strong support from Molly Meldrum and his TV show *Countdown*. Release of ABBA's *Greatest Hits* album spawned a new single, 'Fernando', which went to number one in thirteen countries. In Australia, the song stayed at the top spot for fourteen weeks, becoming the longest-running chart topper in the nation's history for the next four decades. (It was eventually pipped by Ed Sheeran's 'Shape of You' in 2017.) In a nation of 14 million, the song sold a staggering 860,000 copies. Interviewed by Meldrum, manager Stig Anderson said in his stilted English, 'If I had come like a year ago and if I had told people that we will be bigger in Australia than anybody else before, I mean they had sent me to the hospital, I think.'[8]

Before the end of the year, ABBA's new LP, *Arrival*, delivered a further string of hit songs, the biggest of which was 'Dancing Queen'. Another was 'Money, Money, Money', which didn't raise eyebrows, even though the uber-wealthy songsters were singing about how strange it must be to live in the 'rich man's world'. Oddly, for all their focus on the singles charts, Benny Andersson complained, 'What I wish is that we could become an albums band.'[9] Clearly it was a plea for greater respect, but they continued to punch out pop singles with inane lyrics.

A new age

Canadian band Rush were in financial strife due to poor album sales and a decline in audiences, but their label granted them one last chance with a fourth album. Titled *2112*, it would sell more than 3 million copies. The twenty-minute science fiction suite that was the title track was inspired by Ayn Rand's novella *Anthem*. All members of the band had read the book, but they were stung when *New Musical Express* linked Rand with Nazism.

Over many years, Rand had been giving talks to students at colleges across the US, during which she frequently took positions that were controversial. For example, she believed that homosexuality was immoral and advocated that all laws pertaining to same-sex-attracted people should be repealed. She also argued that European colonisers had every right to take land from Indigenous Americans because the native peoples had failed to develop either their own culture or the land.

By now America's cultural shift from collectivist thinking to narcissistic selfishness was sufficiently pronounced that it inspired author Tom Wolfe to pen a cover story for *New York* magazine titled 'The "Me" Decade and the Third Great Awakening'. Wolfe outlined how and why America had abandoned communal and progressive politics, swapping it for a preoccupation with self-development that he dubbed 'atomised individualism'. Of course, this was exactly what Rand and her acolytes idealised: a neoliberal society of individuals fixated on aspirations of personal success while displaying complete indifference to the struggles or suffering of those less fortunate.

In Australia, a maths teacher named Greg Lindsay was sufficiently inspired by the writings and philosophy of Rand, as well as those of economist Friedrich Hayek, to establish the innocuous sounding Centre for Independent Studies (CIS). It was the first of many conservative think-tanks that would have a substantial influence not only on political decision-making, but also on public thinking. Almost half a century later, journalist Gareth Hutchens noted that the Reserve Bank of Australia had both a board member and a non-executive director who were members of the CIS.[10] As the CIS website states today, 'Since 1976, CIS has played an important role in changing the climate of opinion ...'[11] Many other neoliberal think-tanks, from the H.R. Nichols Society to the Institute of Public Affairs, would also aim to influence popular values. Similar pressure groups appeared in other Western nations. Most, of course, have been fierce proponents of small government and laissez-faire capitalism, while also being vehemently opposed to the science of climate change.

New Musical Express was correct in aligning Ayn Rand's views with Nazism. In her philosophy, inequality was normalised, being the inevitable and rightful by-product of superior people like herself. After decades of heavy smoking, Rand underwent surgery for lung cancer. Her obstinate sense of superiority refused to countenance any relationship between her smoking habit and her ailment.

The cult of self-indulgence which Rand and her acolytes promoted was now playing out across Western culture, with popular music an important transmitter of the new mindset. Glam may have been the most obvious example, but punk and disco, with their emphasis on unending self-indulgence, also carried the torch.

In 1976, another crusade was underway that would run parallel to the burgeoning self-esteem obsession: the New Age movement. American theosophist David Spangler developed the idea of a New Age movement when he visited the Findhorn commune in Scotland. Spangler channelled his wisdom from a couple of spiritual entities, not Celtic fairies but more prosaically named John and Bob. He/they believed the Earth was headed for a new cycle of enlightenment known in astrology as the Age of Aquarius, a time when new energies from the cosmos would become available to the human race. The collapse of the hippie movement had clearly left a vacuum aching to be filled, and Spangler helped do so with popular books, notably *Revelation: The Birth of a New Age* and *Towards a Planetary Vision*. At the same time, Paul Hawken released his bestseller, *The Magic of Findhorn*, about the cooperation between the Findhorn community and nature spirits, which allowed the commune to grow oversized vegetables on barren sand dunes.

As the New Age movement mushroomed, shops appeared that specialised in New Age books and esoterica like healing crystals. The movement, with its emphasis on personal transformation through meditation, yoga, astrology, rebirthing, past-life regression and so on, even inspired a whole musical genre. Mike Oldfield's *Tubular Bells* became something of a template, as did albums by Krautrock's Deuter. In the US, The Paul Winter Consort's explorations of world music began incorporating the sounds of whales, eagles and wolves. Windham Hill Records was also founded this year, starting with a humble US$300 investment that would become a US$26 million gross income just a decade later. Before the end of the 1970s there would be New Age albums by Kitarō, Andreas Vollenweider, Shadowfax and Mannheim Steamroller. In the 1980s the Grammy Awards would add a prize category for Best New Age Album. New Age thinking fitted perfectly with the self-esteem movement and even neoliberalism, as they all embraced an obsessive focus on the self.

Many rock stars were also avid supporters of esoteric ideologies, from the Indian mysticism promoted by George Harrison, Pete Townshend and John McLaughlin to Robert Fripp's obsession with spiritual philosopher and mystic George Gurdjieff. Even L. Ron Hubbard's zany Scientology sucked in members of The Incredible String Band, plus fusion keyboardist Chick Corea, whose band Return to Forever's album *Romantic Warrior* was dedicated to Hubbard.

Of course, many rock stars didn't need spiritual gurus to provide inspiration. Some believed they were getting their inspiration via colossal levels of drug and alcohol consumption. As The Who's Pete Townshend put it, 'Everybody credited everything innovative and exciting to drugs.'[12] Yet despite the almost religious zeal with which mind-altered states were embraced, drugs didn't really make anyone smarter, nor necessarily more creative. Nevertheless, huge swathes of music were being produced under the indulgent influence of pot, cocaine, acid, barbiturates, heroin, booze and a mind-boggling array of pharmaceutical substances.

Punk takes off

The seeming antithesis of indulgent, bourgeois hippies were punks. January of 1976 saw the first issue of the American independent magazine *Punk*, created by cartoonist John Holstrom. The first cover featured Lou Reed, followed successively by Patti Smith, Joey Ramone and Iggy Pop, with contents that mixed *Mad Magazine* cartooning and rock journalism. Not only did *Punk* help popularise what was happening at CBGB, it cemented the term 'punk' as a catchall phrase. It also heralded a range of fanzines that would appear across the globe, with *Sniffin' Glue* magazine notable in the British scene.

Punks tended to view bands like The Who and The Rolling Stones as social-climbing, money-grubbing dinosaurs. From punk's perspective, rock music – which was supposed to be rebellious – was being performed by ridiculously wealthy drug addicts for preposterously large crowds who were well-removed from the performers in giant stadiums. The Clash's Paul Simonon said just looking at a Led Zeppelin album made him feel sick. The new scene was happening in pubs and makeshift clubs, not arenas and concert halls. The physical division between audience and performer was nil. Out went all reverence for musical virtuosity, including guitar and drum solos.

The mainstream music industry initially ignored punk. So punk artists created their own underground music industry, putting out singles on bespoke labels that were often recorded and mastered in a matter of hours. In some ways, punk replicated the skiffle craze of the early 1960s with its DIY attitude.

Unlike many other punk acts, The Damned were musically accomplished. They were the first British punk band to release a single, 'New Rose', on Stiff Records. The B-side was a cover of The Beatles' 'Help!' played at break-neck speed. Stiff also signed up many of the new wave acts, including Nick Lowe, Wreckless Eric, Ian Dury, Devo and Elvis Costello. Stiff cut a deal with CBS Records for US distribution.

What had begun in New York was now being empowered in London. As a social movement, punk became more prevalent in Britain than anywhere else. It was also more aggressive, and far more fashion-oriented. The Sex Pistols are most people's first thought when punk is mentioned, even though they had many progenitors. For a band that produced little music and survived only briefly, The Sex Pistols made a huge impact. In large part that was thanks to their Machiavellian manager, Malcolm McLaren, and his sometimes wife Vivienne Westwood, both of whom knew a media opportunity when they saw one.

Before becoming The Sex Pistols, they were The Strand, and band members hung out at McLaren and Westwood's clothing shop, which was brazenly named SEX. The boutique had begun as Let It Rock, pitched at 'teddy boys', and then became a retro shop called Too Fast to Live, Too Young to Die. In 1974, they decided to change the focus of the shop to anti-fashion S&M attire. After McLaren's stint in New York, where he experienced the proto-punk scene in the form of Television and the Ramones, and even briefly managed the New York Dolls, he returned to London brimming with punk ideas and soon took charge of The Strand. The band changed its name to QT Jones & The Sex Pistols and went hunting for a front man. It was Vivienne Westwood who suggested they try an acquaintance of hers called John.

John Lydon was spotted wearing a Pink Floyd T-shirt with the words 'I hate' handwritten above the band's name and holes scratched through the eyes. He couldn't sing or keep in time, but he had attitude, so he got the job. He was dubbed Johnny Rotten due to his bad dental hygiene. It later transpired that Westwood had meant they should try John Beverley, not John Lydon. Beverley (born John Simon Ritchie) would become Sid Vicious.

With McLaren and Westwood's encouragement, the new band reduced their moniker to The Sex Pistols – a nice marketing tie-in with the SEX clothing store. The group played badly, but, as McLaren said, 'they were so good at being bad'.[13] Careering between pure rage and self-destruction, they quickly became the unbridled id of the punk scene. Despite their name, they were largely disinterested in sex, which was also a fundamental departure from the Adonis posturing of many big-name rock acts. The Pistols quickly developed a coterie of followers, known as the Bromley Contingent. They included Siouxsie Sioux (Susan Ballion), Steven Severin and Billy Idol, each of whom would form their own band.

In a brazen cross-promotion, McLaren and Westwood had The Sex Pistols wear clothing printed with slogans, and those same slogans would appear on garments in their shop. The band were advertising mannequins. As McLaren later told *The Times*, 'As long as a group has the right look today, the music doesn't matter too much.'[14] Thanks to Vivienne Westwood's designs, the ideal UK punk look became bondage pants, parachute shirts and a T-shirt with a confronting or obscene slogan from a Pistols song. Such clothing could be bought from SEX at £50 for trousers, £30 for a shirt and £8 for a T-shirt – this at a time when the average weekly wage was around £72. Chrissie Hynde was working at SEX, and her description of Westwood and McLaren is revealing: 'They saw things differently to everyone I'd ever met. They were "straight" for a start. They didn't take, and never had taken drugs. They weren't even pot smokers.'[15] The costumes designed by Sue Blane for *The Rocky Horror Show* and *The Rocky Horror Picture Show* also became templates for punk fashion. Mind you, most punk audience goers were wearing DIY outfits, with lavatory chains, dog collars and safety pins added. Their appearance was the sartorial equivalent of a 'fuck you' to civilised society. In the UK, punks were presenting themselves as symbols of social decay.

At the end of 1976, SEX changed its name yet again, this time to Seditionaries, selling clothing labelled as 'Malcolm McLaren and Vivienne Westwood Seditionaries, Personal Collection'. The anarchist symbol of an A surrounded by a circle appeared on many items, as did Nazi symbolism, including swastikas. Sid Vicious even wore a tampon – embellished by a red pen – as a fashion accessory. This rebellious, misfit, shock-value symbolism had its equivalence in heavy metal when that genre began to adopt skulls and rotting corpses for its album covers and T-shirts.

McLaren organised the 100 Club Punk Special, a festival with The Pistols headlining. Also on the bill were The Clash, Buzzcocks, The Damned, The Vibrators, French outfit Stinky Toys and a group that was put together just for the occasion, Siouxsie and the Banshees, who played a totally chaotic set improvising on 'The Lord's Prayer'. One British critic said of The Clash, 'They are the kind of garage band who should be speedily returned to their garage, preferably with the motor running.'[16]

Over in New York, the Dead Boys were building on Iggy Pop's self-destructive stage act, with singer Stiv Bators slashing his stomach until it bled and strangling himself with the mic lead until he passed out.

CBGB owner Hilly Kristal was impressed enough to become the Dead Boys' manager. Meanwhile, the Ramones were the second New York punk act to sign a record contract, following the trail blazed by Patti Smith. They released their debut album on then independent label Sire Records, which had been built on progressive rock acts.

The *Ramones* LP contained fourteen songs, the longest being just two minutes and thirty-five seconds. Amid all the mayhem was a tribute to 1960s pop, 'I Wanna Be Your Boyfriend', but the rest had titles like 'Blitzkrieg Bop', 'Now I Wanna Sniff Some Glue', 'Judy Is a Punk', 'Chain Saw' and 'Beat on the Brat', about a child being belted with a baseball bat. Again, critics fell over themselves to heap superlatives on this simplistic, stripped-back sonic fury, with many noting not only the intensity and urgency of the music, but also its assault on existing musical aesthetics. The album didn't sell very well in the US, but it became decidedly persuasive for the British punk scene.

The Ramones travelled to London, where they played a notable performance at The Roundhouse alongside The Flamin' Groovies and The Stranglers. They even handed out promotional miniature baseball bats. Some music historians argue that *Ramones* is the most influential album of the post-Beatles era, and that the band is the most important. Their leather and long hair was not pure punk, but there's no denying their essential role in the dissembling of the rock idiom. In part, their impact was due to their ability to shape and nurture their own publicity.

Although The Sex Pistols weren't impressed by the look and style of the Ramones, the release of an album by a punk act was a wake-up call. McLaren signed the Pistols with EMI for a £40,000 advance. With that money in the bank, he also charged the band 25 per cent of earnings as his management fee. What's more, McLaren legally controlled the band's name. The Sex Pistols' debut single, 'Anarchy in the UK', was released to both acclaim and opprobrium, pinning ears back with its seeming endorsement of an anarchic world of violent insurrection. The song went to thirty-eight in the UK charts and thirty-three in the US, but it would live on forever in the history of rock.

Pioneering punks The Vibrators recorded sessions for John Peel at BBC Radio 1, and Buzzcocks released their debut EP, *Spiral Scratch*, on their own New Hormones label. In that regard, they had actually been pipped by The Saints in Australia, who had already established the Fatal Records label for their debut single '(I'm) Stranded'. This milestone recording predated anything by The Damned, The Sex Pistols and other British punk acts. The Saints even resolved the matter of how to garner gigs in their hometown of Brisbane by establishing their own club in a vacant shop, which became known as Club 76.

Released initially in a run of just 500 copies, '(I'm) Stranded' was only available on import in the UK, although the band sent review copies to music magazines. *Sounds* magazine, in particular, sang its praises. By the end of the year, The Saints had signed a three-album deal with EMI in the UK. Meanwhile, Radio Birdman were Sydney's major outlaw act, drawing inspiration from MC5, The Stooges and Blue Öyster Cult. They also ran their own gigs at the Oxford Tavern, and released an EP, *Burn My Eye*, famous for utilising the sound of beer cans being smashed against heads as a percussion device.

Fascist leanings

The National Front were encouraging fascist ideologies in Britain. David Bowie didn't help matters when he performed a Nazi salute at Victoria Station after returning from Berlin, nor when he quipped to Cameron Crowe that 'I might have been a bloody good Hitler. I'd be an excellent dictator.'[17] In a long interview for *Playboy*, again with Cameron Crowe, Bowie said:

> And, yes, I believe very strongly in fascism. The only way we can speed up the sort of liberalism that's hanging foul in the air at the moment is to speed up the progress of the right-wing, totally dictatorial tyranny and get it over as fast as possible ... Adolf Hitler was one of the first rock stars.[18]

Fans often excuse Bowie's dalliance with fascism as being a product of his cocaine addiction, but cocaine doesn't generate political leanings. Bowie was naive, stupid and self-righteous, but Eric Clapton was worse. He roared his support for the National Front, as well as controversial Tory MP Enoch Powell, during a concert in Birmingham. He asked the audience if there were any foreigners present, and then told them:

> I don't want you here, in the room or in my country ... I think Enoch's right, I think we should send them all back ... The black wogs and coons and Arabs and fucking Jamaicans ... don't belong here, we don't want any black wogs and coons living here.[19]

Clapton was not only a bigot but a hypocrite. His formative influences were black artists, and much of his own music appropriated black stylings. He had recently enjoyed a number one hit with a version of Bob Marley's reggae tune 'I Shot the Sheriff'. Clapton attempted to sidestep the inevitable criticism by saying that he found his rant funny. But there were serious ramifications from such vitriol, particularly for minority groups. As Debbie Golt put it, 'The National Front were so strong in those days, literally beating people up in the streets.'[20]

Clapton's incendiary outburst provided much of the impetus for the creation of Rock Against Racism. RAR attempted to drive a wedge into the punk scene, separating out the liberals and deliberately pairing punk bands with reggae acts at concerts. This was never easy. Sham 69 were a punk band that supported RAR's objectives, but they also had skinhead fans, with the result that skinheads made havoc at some RAR concert events.

Pretty in punk

Within punk, women fared better than people of colour. Indeed, many punks were more accepting of women rock musicians than were the perpetrators of prog, metal, soft rock, fusion and other genres. In part, punk was a reaction against the status quo in rock music, and that status quo included male dominance. What's more, punk partly rejected the macho posturing and braggadocio of the likes of Rod Stewart, Mick Jagger and Robert Plant. Punk's approach to sex was far more ambivalent. Many of the women who participated in British punk – Siouxsie Sioux, Lene Lovich, Lora Logic, Poly Styrene and Gaye Advert, among others – were not trading on their femininity, unlike Blondie's Debbie Harry or members of The Runaways in the US.

The Runaways had been formed in 1975 by drummer Sandy West and guitarist Joan Jett, encouraged by producer Kim Fowley. While Fowley certainly helped pull the all-female band together and get them signed to Mercury Records, he also appears to have been a sexual predator. The Runaways' bass player, Jackie Fox, claimed that he raped her when she was sixteen years old while others watched.

The Runaways' debut self-titled album performed best in Australia, while their single, 'Cherry Bomb', inspired by vocalist Cherie Currie's looks and name, went to sixth position in their home country. There was an affected insolence in both The Runaways' music and their approach to traditional role modelling. Girls weren't supposed to scream 'you drive me wild', let alone look impudent. Runaways guitarist and vocalist Joan Jett would form her own label in 1980, Blackheart Records, pioneering another path for women in rock.

A sort of equivalent in the UK were all-female punk band The Slits. Ari Up (Ariane Forster) had witnessed a Patti Smith gig and determined she would start her own band, which she began the very next day. She was just fourteen years old at the time. The Slits appear to have been the first British all-female punk band.

Women in British rock were given a boost by the airing of the BBC's television series *Rock Follies*. The successful show followed the trials and tribulations of a fictional female rock band called The Little Ladies. The cast included Julie Covington, and the songs were written by Roxy Music's Andy Mackay. The soundtrack album to the first series, simply titled *Rock Follies*, went to number one in the UK.

Go-go disco

Punk audiences 'pogoed' up and down on the spot, a form of dance that avoided the messy business of having to secure a dancing partner. It was a far cry from the stylised flashiness of disco dance floors. Disco music was now dominating the US charts, with tracks such as The Bee Gees' 'You Should Be Dancing', KC and the Sunshine Band's 'Shake Your Booty', and Hot Chocolate's 'You Sexy Thing'.

'You Should Be Dancing' perfected The Bee Gees' disco sound, utilising Barry Gibb's newfound falsetto. It was the first single off their album *Children of the World*, and it went to number one in America. Due to label links, Arif Mardin could no longer produce for the band, so Barry took over producing while also bringing in Albhy Galuten as music adviser. But the credits on the album sleeve included another curious name. Keyboardist Blue Weaver had added the band's roadie, Tom Kennedy, to a blackboard list of album credits as an in-house joke. Little did he realise that his prank would make its way through to final printing. In the end, both the lead single label and the album sleeve stated: 'By arrangement with The Robert Stigwood Organisation and Tom Kennedy.' Even the gold record incorporated the joke.

Meanwhile, Stigwood's RSO label opened its international headquarters on 57th Street in New York, where fans could purchase souvenirs and T-shirts plastered with images of The Bee Gees. The album cover also rolled through New York streets on the backs of buses. For almost a month, the brothers Gibb gave countless interviews at the Sheraton Hotel on 7th Avenue. As Robin put it, 'People in America love this kind of thing. They like to have things put smack bang in their faces.'[21]

The struggling Motown label had its first disco hit with Diana Ross's 'Love Hangover', but the surprise hit of the year was a satire on disco music titled 'Disco Duck' by Rick Dees and His Cast of Idiots. The crass novelty tune featured a voice reminiscent of Donald Duck's, and it flew to number one in the US.

Annus horribilis

When EMI reissued a box set of all twenty-two previously released Beatles singles, plus a new version of 'Yesterday', the twenty-three singles all charted simultaneously. Meanwhile, Paul McCartney and Wings released their fifth album, *Wings at the Speed of Sound*, and although critics were less than impressed, it still went to single digits around the globe. Single 'Silly Love Songs' was McCartney's most successful US release since his Beatles days, staying at number one for seven weeks. It was also McCartney's twenty-seventh number one hit as a songwriter, setting an all-time record. Cowritten by Paul and Linda, it was McCartney's riposte to those critics who complained that his music was trivial. Stylistically, the song also paid lip service to disco.

The band embarked on their Wings over the World tour – the first time McCartney had performed live in the US since 1966. Rather than drag their young family with them, Linda and Paul rented houses in four different US cities, and after each performance flew a specially chartered plane to whichever house was the closest. At an LA show, Ringo appeared and handed his old bandmate a bunch of flowers onstage. A triple album, *Wings Over America*, was released at the end of the year and also went to number one in the US.

George Harrison's legal case over 'My Sweet Lord' finally wound up. The matter went before Federal Court judge Richard Owen, himself a classical composer and musician. In the end, the court found that Harrison was guilty of unconscious plagiarism. He was ordered to pay the American publisher of The Chiffons' song a total of US\$1,599,987. The whole affair would roll on still further, with Allen Klein ultimately purchasing the rights to 'He's So Fine' and suing his former client, Harrison. The debacle didn't end until 1998, just three years before Harrison died.

Led Zeppelin's movie *The Song Remains the Same* was released, with critics calling it dumb, embarrassing and narcissistic. The Zep had also studiously ignored the needs of their private label, and thus its roster of artists, and their business empire was crumbling around them. Band members were too busy feeding their drug addictions to take stock of the situation.

The Who's Keith Moon was also slip-sliding away. His marriage to model Kim McLagan had ended in divorce, and the pining drummer had purchased a beach house next door to screen legend Steve McQueen's in Malibu. When bandmate Roger Daltrey arrived for a visit, he found the loungeroom empty except for a couple of sofas and a Persian rug. On the rug were piles of dog excrement. Unbelievably, Moon had installed spotlights to shine on McQueen's property, supposedly in the hope of seeing a nude Ali MacGraw, McQueen's wife. In response, McQueen had craned in large trees to place along the joint boundary in the hope of deterring Moon's perving. The neighbour dispute ended up in a meeting at the district attorney's office, at which Moon chose to wear a Nazi uniform. As Daltrey put it, 'I could see he was out of control in California. He had no money and any money he could get his hands on, he was spending.'[22] Moon borrowed US$10,000 from the band's agent, and spent it in a week.

A tour by The Who saw drummer Moon, loaded with brandy and barbiturates, collapse just two songs into a show. He was rushed to hospital. The following night, released to his hotel, Moon somehow managed to sever an artery in his leg. Again, Daltrey went to the hospital, where he found his teary bandmate filled with remorse for the killing of his chauffeur and the loss of his wife. He was now at the very steep end of the slippery slope.

Keith Richards was also descending. As he put it, 'Anita [Pallenberg] and I had become two junkies living separate existences, except trying to bring up kids.'[23] New son Tara was only a month old, but Richards went on tour, taking seven-year-old Marlon with him. As they drove between gigs in Europe, the father gave his young son the task of keeping an eye on the map and warning him before they approached any national borders, so Daddy could either shoot up or else conceal his heroin. What's more, Richards was keeping a gun with him. Accordingly, when he was due on stage, security would send young Marlon to wake him up, just in case his unpredictable nature led to a shooting accident.

Driving back from the Knebworth Festival, Richards fell asleep at the wheel and ran his car into a tree. There were seven of them, including Marlon, in the bent Bentley. When the police arrived, they inevitably found drugs on Richards. Luckily for him, he was let off with a fine, but things were about to go from worse to worser. Marlon and his dad were on tour in Paris when word came through that the new baby, Tara, had died. Rather than head home, Richards opted to keep playing and touring. In his autobiography, he admits that his decision 'is something I can't forgive myself for. It's as if I deserted my post. Anita and I, to this day, have never talked about it.'[24]

The Allman Brothers Band had triumphed over all manner of tragedies to enjoy ten gold and platinum records, but an investigation into police corruption in Georgia brought about the band's demise. As part of the investigation, Gregg Allman's personal roadie, John 'Scooter' Herring, came under investigation for having been supplied drugs by a local dealer. Scooter had often been detailed to score cocaine for his boss. Allman had only just married Cher, and, as he put it, 'The whole thing became a tabloid event overnight. Because of Cher, because of the band, I was front page news every day.'[25] Allman cut a deal granting him immunity from prosecution in exchange for testimony against his roadie and former friend. Scooter copped a seventy-five-year sentence. As Allman wrote:

> The whole mess with Scooter was the last straw for the band. As if the financial mess we'd gotten ourselves into wasn't enough, most of the guys felt I'd sold Scooter out ... And none of this was helped by the fact that we'd all been doing so much coke we were in a permanent state of paranoia.[26]

With the band breaking up, Cher copped some of the blame, becoming, as Gregg Allman put it, 'the Yoko Ono of the Allman Brothers'.[27] Scooter ended up serving just eighteen months in jail.

Deep Purple also split up this year. Tommy Bolin, who had replaced Richie Blackmore on guitar, now formed his own band and was touring the US as the opening act for Peter Frampton and Jeff Beck. Backstage in Miami, he told a journalist that he was intending to be around for a long time. A few hours later he was found dead by his girlfriend, having ingested a cocktail of heroin, alcohol, cocaine and barbiturates.

This was also a bad year for Bob Marley. Two days before he was to play at a concert to celebrate peaceful unity in Kingston, seven or eight armed men arrived at Marley's residence. Marley's wife, Rita, was shot in the head. The gunmen then moved through the house, shooting randomly. Marley and his band were on a break from rehearsing, and many of them hid in a bathroom. Marley had a bullet graze his chest and another lodge in his arm, while manager Don Taylor copped five bullets in the legs and torso, and employee Louis Griffiths was also shot in the torso. Incredibly, none were killed. Marley's private security detail had mysteriously disappeared just before the attack.

The assassination attempt was part of the ugliness of Jamaican politics. The planned concert event had the endorsement of the ruling progressive People's National Party, and elections were looming. Some of the gunmen were caught, tried and executed. According to Marley's manager, one of the shooters claimed the job was done at the behest of the CIA, in return for cocaine and guns. In any case, the concert went ahead, and a bandaged Bob Marley and the Wailers performed.

Yobbos from down under

Australian rockers were now making waves on the international stage. AC/DC's album *High Voltage* was compiled from their Australian albums *High Voltage* and *T.N.T. Rolling Stone* magazine referred to the band as 'Australian gross-out champions', arguing that 'the genre has hit its all-time low'. The reviewer, Billy Altman, concluded with: 'Stupidity bothers me. Calculated stupidity offends me.'[28] *Melody Maker*'s critic was also unimpressed with the band's barebones approach to rock: '[I]t's the same old boogie, the same old sub-metal riffs you've heard a thousand times before. Too many of the songs sound the same.'[29] But the LP would go on to sell 3 million copies in the US alone.

A follow-up album, *Dirty Deeds Done Dirt Cheap*, went six times platinum in both Australia (where platinum equalled 70,000 sales) and the US (where platinum meant 1 million sales). It included an uncharacteristically slow blues, 'Ride On', which many fans deem to be a classic, even though it illuminates the vocal deficiencies of the frequently off-pitch Bon Scott. Angus's guitar solo is worth the admission fee, however. The band also set off for a tour of Britain but found themselves labelled as a punk band. Following a lacklustre performance at the Reading Festival, brothers Malcolm and Angus ended up in a punch-up, with third brother George joining in for good measure. After a show at the Lyceum, Angus also punched bass player Mark Evans in the face.

Angus Young had taken to mooning the audience. The saving grace for the young guitar whiz was that he eschewed both alcohol and drugs, unlike his lead vocalist, who was busy dabbling in the hard stuff. Back in Australia for a tour promoted as AC/DC's Giant Dose of Rock 'n' Roll, the band was asked to pose for press conference photo. When Angus dropped his daks and bared his cheeks, a female reporter stormed out. He then repeated the stupidity at a function for the band's gold and platinum awards.

In the program notes for the tour, bassist Mark Evans was reported as saying that he'd like to make enough money to fuck Britt Ekland. Rumours swirled about young girls giving themselves AC/DC tattoos, with a member of parliament suggesting authorities should police tattoo parlours to prevent underage girls from receiving such adornments. The media were abuzz about the bad boys of rock. Radio station 2SM banned their records, regional shows were cancelled, and police attended gigs, ready to pounce if Angus dropped his strides. On the back of all the bad press, some of their shows were poorly attended, and Atlantic Records in America started getting twitchy, so AC/DC headed back into the studio to record another album.

Little River Band flew to the UK and supported Queen in a show at London's Hyde Park. They toured Europe with The Hollies and opened for The Average White Band in the US, where their song 'It's a Long Way There' garnered some chart success. Sherbet also enjoyed their only international hit with the cricket-inspired song 'Howzat' going to single digits in various countries. Songwriter Garth Porter admitted the influence of 10cc, particularly the layered vocals, but also acknowledged that the song had 'dumb lyrics'.[30] Meanwhile, Graham Russell and Russell Hitchcock, both former cast members of the stage show *Jesus Christ Superstar*, formed Air Supply, who would also find international stardom.

The Australian pub rock scene was going gangbusters with a plethora of hard-driving, hard-drinking and often drug-addled bands. Rose Tattoo began its gradual ascension this year, while the New Zealand–originated Dragon signed with CBS Records. Dragon supported a tour by Status Quo and recorded a single called 'This Time'. As Jimmy Barnes noted, '[I]t shot up the charts. I use the term "shot up" carefully because that happens to be the biggest problem Dragon had in those days. Some of the members were junkies.'[31] Indeed, not long after recording 'This Time', Dragon's drummer, Neil Storey, died of an overdose.

Filmmaker and musician Chris Löfvén wrote, directed and co-produced the feature film *Oz – A Rock 'n' Roll Road Movie*, about a sixteen-year-old groupie who has an accident and wakes up in a fantasy world. Plainly paraphrasing *The Wizard of Oz*, the music was mostly by Ross Wilson, singer with Daddy Cool and Mondo Rock. Unfortunately, the movie was rush-released in Australia before the soundtrack album was out and suffered accordingly. In the US, however, it was released into New York and Los Angeles to became one of Australia's highest-grossing releases in that market. According to Löfvén, it would have performed even better had the New York opening not coincided with a devastating blizzard. Like *The Rocky Horror Picture Show*, *Oz* was destined to become a cult classic.

Potpourri of poseurs

Kiss's emphasis on showmanship didn't impress *Melody Maker*'s critic, who stated: '[W]hat Kiss hadn't got at their Hammersmith Odeon gig on Sunday night was a feeling for music. They depended on their bland pyrotechnics … but it was all so nauseatingly contrived that the showmanship meant nothing.' The reviewer went on to say that bass player Gene Simmons should 'feel the most stupid', and that rhythm guitarist Paul Stanley was 'about the worst guitarist I've ever heard'. Kiss were a cartoon version of a rock band. Mind you, lots of people enjoy cartoons.

Rod Stewart penned 'The Killing of Georgie (Part I and II)' for his album *A Night on the Town*. The song tells the story of a gay man killed in New York City. The people at Warner Bros., as Stewart put it, 'were medieval enough to fear that a pro-gay message would alienate my heterosexual following. Stuff 'em, I felt.' The song went to number two in the UK, while the album went number one across the planet.

A problem for Stewart's best mate Elton John was that he didn't pen his own lyrics, and thus couldn't match the personal revelatory style of other singer-songwriters. Tony Palmer wrote: 'Elton John bounces to the top of the charts with unnerving regularity. He has brought to popular music a refreshing, extroverted vigor. But his music, although skilfully fashioned, is empty; for some, much of it might easily – although unfairly – be mistaken for Muzak.'[32] In her *Rolling Stone* review of his double album *Blue Moves*, Ariel Swartley suggested that it was always difficult to determine whether Elton was being serious. As he didn't write the lyrics, he had never been 'an impassioned interpreter of the songs he sings', and was thus always too 'cautious'.[33] The inference that a singer of someone else's lyrics was somehow unable to invest in their meaning was patently absurd.

Blue Moves was Elton's first release on his own Rocket Records label, and went to single digits across the planet. Swartley decreed *Blue Moves* to be 'one of the most desperately pretentious albums around'.[34] The arrival of punk was making musical ostentation increasingly abhorrent. Nevertheless, prog rock wasn't ready to throw in the towel. To considerable acclaim, The Alan Parsons Project released their debut concept album, *Tales of Mystery and Imagination*, based on the works of Edgar Allan Poe. With its classical figures, and even some direct lifting from Claude Debussy, plus an all-star line-up of British talent, the album was a success.

Genesis proved there was life after Peter Gabriel, with Phil Collins taking lead vocals and managing to sound just like his predecessor. *A Trick of the Tail* is a beautifully produced LP. It opens with the muscular 'Dance on a Volcano', full of head-spinning shifts in time signature and fluctuating soundscapes. The band was still willing to take risks, but they would soon morph into a more popular – and more humdrum – hit singles band.

Jethro Tull's f-you to punk and musical fads was amusingly titled *Too Old to Rock 'n' Roll: Too Young to Die!*. Gentle Giant followed up their successful *Free Hand* disc, which had miraculously charted at forty-eight in the US, with the wonderful *Interview* album, based on their experiences with the media. It would be their last adventurous album (apart from a live double disc), before they, like Genesis, succumbed to punk's inherent criticisms and devolved to a more pedestrian sound. In the face of punk, prog was withering, although the Canterbury school of prog carried on, eking out a spartan existence, with Hatfield and the North and Gilgamesh transmogrifying into National Health, while Caravan continued travelling.

Electronica was keeping busy with albums by Klaus Schulze, Peter Baumann, Tangerine Dream and Cluster. Jean-Michel Jarre's third album, *Oxygène*, produced in his homemade Paris studio, shot to number two in the UK charts.

The Residents' *The Third Reich 'n Roll* album picked up on punk's obsession with early 1960s music, whilst lampooning its appropriation of Nazi symbolism. The LP contains side-long suites throughout which the group dismember and regurgitate Top 40 hits from the '60s. With the band's tongues placed firmly in their cheeks, the album is purportedly a commentary on how rock 'n' roll has brainwashed the youth of the world. Many of the songs are obvious, but some are so strangled as to be ambiguous. In many ways, the album points towards mashups and sampling.

Separately, The Residents released a twisted version of The Rolling Stones' '(I Can't Get No) Satisfaction' with guest star Snakefinger (Philip Charles Lithman), initially in an edition of just 200 copies. The single took on a life of its own, particularly when the British press got hold of it, requiring a further pressing of some 30,000 copies. As Snakefinger jokingly told a radio interviewer, '[T]hey forced me, tied me into the studio, and then beat me with whips while I played my guitar ... That was well before New Wave reared its ugly head. That was Some Wave. The wave before New Wave ...'[35]

1977

Go Your Own Way

Patti Smith began the year by falling off a stage in Tampa, Florida. She ended up with twenty-two stitches in her head, plus several broken vertebrae requiring months of physiotherapy. Aerosmith were performing in Philadelphia when a cherry bomb exploded on the stage. Vocalist Steven Tyler suffered an eye injury, while guitarist Joe Perry received a ruptured artery in his hand, forcing the band off the road for many months. When they returned to the scene of the crime to perform a year later, someone threw a beer bottle, which exploded on stage, sending shards of glass into Tyler's face. At the time, Tyler and Perry were known as the 'toxic twins' on account of their notorious drug consumption.

Disappearing acts

After a long absence from touring, and with Plant largely recovered from his car accident, the next Led Zeppelin tour was beset with delays, including Plant coming down with laryngitis. Eventually, they set off for the US with an entourage of personal assistants, bodyguards, physicians and flunkeys so numerous they had difficulty squeezing everyone into the chartered Boeing 707. Tour manager Richard Cole had hired John 'Biffo' Bindon to head up security, a man who had close links with the London underworld and was renowned for using his fists. Media personnel were handed printed rules, which included the warning, 'Do not make any sort of eye contact with John Bonham. This is for your own safety,' and concluded with, 'The band does not like the press, nor do they trust them.'

Hundreds of gatecrashing fans were arrested in various cities and even teargassed in Miami. In Cincinnati, a fan fell to his death. In Tampa, when Zep fled the stage due to a downpour, riot police moved in and began belting everyone within reach. In Chicago, for some reason, Jimmy Page dressed as a Nazi stormtrooper and goosestepped about. At other concerts, Page threw a trashcan at the technical crew and spat into the face of the sound man. Performances on the tour were often sloppy. Critics complained that the dinosaurs of rock were listless and boring. During one show, Bonzo fell asleep at his drum kit. Offstage, he continued to destroy hotel rooms, even managing to demolish a pool table at one establishment. And it wasn't just Bonzo going berko: all four band members trashed their hotel rooms in Cleveland.

Debauchery also persisted, with Page again hooking up with underage teenager Lori Mattix. She couldn't travel on the plane, because they were worried about the legality of trafficking a minor across state lines, so Page regularly flew to be with her. Among other shenanigans, Peter Grant handcuffed a naked woman to a bathroom sink, and the charming Bonzo bit a woman's hand until it bled. Drugs were sending tour manager Richard Cole even crazier than usual. One tantrum saw him trying to kick out a window of the aircraft mid-flight.

It all came to a head in Oakland, California. Peter Grant punched a stagehand, rendering him unconscious. Then Grant's eleven-year-old son attempted to remove a Led Zeppelin sign from one of the dressing-room trailers. A guard intervened, and so John Bonham kicked him in the groin, followed by Peter Grant and John Bindon beating the living daylights out of the poor chap while Richard Cole stood by holding a length of metal pipe. The victim, employed by promoter Bill Graham, was taken to hospital. This time, Grant, Cole, Bonham and Bindon were arrested. As Graham said, 'As far as I was concerned every one of those guys in the band was accountable for that shit, because they allowed it to go on. We weren't the only ones it happened to. We were just the last ones.'[1] All four would be found guilty and given suspended sentences. But the day after the arrests, Robert Plant received news from his wife back in England that their five-year-old son had died from a respiratory infection. Plant later claimed he gave up drugs that day. The band cancelled the rest of the tour, and Led Zeppelin would never perform in America again.

Keith Richards was keeping the tabloids busy. At Toronto airport, a small amount of hashish and a blackened spoon were found in the handbag of his girlfriend, Anita Pallenberg. Not long after, Mounties dressed as waiters raided Keith's hotel room, finding cocaine and an ounce of heroin. It took them an hour to bring the drugged guitarist back to consciousness so they could arrest him. He wasn't charged with heroin possession but with trafficking due to the amount of smack they found in his room. On that charge, Keith was facing a potential sentence between seven years and life.

Meanwhile, President Pierre Trudeau's young wife, Margaret, moved into the same hotel as the Stones and began carousing with them. Without Richards, the rest of the band and Margaret Trudeau flew to New York to escape the publicity, leaving their guitarist abandoned in Toronto. Eventually, Richards and Pallenberg were permitted to go to Philadelphia, where they were supposed to get drug treatment, while their son Marlon was farmed out to a foster family. Nineteen months after his bust, Richards would be found guilty of possession, not trafficking. The judge let him off lightly on the condition that he continue his drug treatment, and also that he play a charity concert for the blind. Richards' lawyer had successfully argued that his client didn't represent a threat to society: after all, he was sufficiently wealthy that he didn't need to steal to feed his habit. The case appeared to delineate separate rules for the rich and famous.

Further rock deaths were 1977's legacy. Three days after releasing their album *Street Survivors*, Lynyrd Skynyrd boarded a chartered Convair passenger plane. Incredibly, the plane ran out of fuel over Mississippi. An attempted crash landing resulted in the aircraft skimming treetops before hitting a large tree and splitting apart. Deaths included vocalist Ronnie Van Zant, guitarist Steve Gaines, backing vocalist Cassie Gaines and a member of the road crew, plus the pilot and co-pilot. Everyone else was injured. *Street Survivors* went gold on the first day of its release. The LP cover image had initially shown the band members surrounded by flames, but that was swiftly replaced.

Marc Bolan didn't have a driving licence, however, like so many rock stars, he owned a fleet of expensive vehicles. Heading home from a restaurant in the West End, where they had been carousing, the Mini GT driven by Bolan's romantic partner Gloria Jones left the road and hit a tree. Bolan died instantly, while Jones was trapped by her foot and suffered a broken jaw. When Bolan's funeral was held, *New Musical Express* reported that the hospitalised Gloria had yet to be informed about his passing. By the time she left hospital, fans had ransacked their home. Before she could appear in court over the incident, Jones fled the UK, taking their son, Rolan Bolan, with her.

A more consequential death was that of the King. Overweight, incoherent and stuffed full of pharmaceuticals, Elvis Presley was finding it difficult to get through his concert bookings. He did manage to release a final single, the aptly titled 'Way Down', but he was gripped by paranoia. His mental state wasn't helped by a new book called *Elvis: What Happened?*. Based on the personal accounts of three of his former bodyguards, it detailed his years of drug-taking. Elvis had made futile attempts to pay off the publishers and prevent its publication. Just a couple of weeks after the book hit the shelves, Elvis was found dead in his bathroom, having fallen off the toilet. The official cause of death was heart failure, no doubt brought about by drug abuse.

Dancing fever

Americans were living in desultory times. Their nation had just lost the longest war it had ever been involved in. Their president had been forced to resign in disgrace. Ohio, New Jersey and New York State were experiencing energy emergencies, while inflation, unemployment and interest rates were skyrocketing. The citizenry had such low expectations and limited optimism that they needed to take comfort wherever it could be found. One place was the strobe-lit, popper-fuelled dance floor.

Donna Summer's hit 'I Feel Love' was the first disco song created purely through synthesised sounds, paving the way for many more techno dance tunes. Produced and co-written by Giorgio Moroder and Pete Bellotte, it went to number one in the UK and Australia, and three in the US. Summer performed her vocal part in just one take. When Brian Eno heard 'I Feel Love', he reportedly told David Bowie that he had heard the sound of the future. Today it sounds dated and contrived, but the Moog was still making novel noises in 1977.

As James Brown noted, 'The record companies loved disco because it was a producer's music. You don't really need artists to make disco.'[2] Disco divas like Grace Jones and Amanda Lear arguably provided some proof of that. A former model and girlfriend at various times of Brian Jones, Brian Ferry and David Bowie, Lear was selected by composer Anthony Monn and label Ariola, and packaged for the disco market. Some editions of her debut album, aptly titled *I Am a Photograph*, included a poster of a topless Lear that had appeared in *Playboy*. The music was shallow, insistent, electronic dance music, with Lear's deep voice talk-singing in a come-hither manner. The track 'Alphabet' turned Bach into disco, with Lear running tunelessly through words associated with each letter of the alphabet, such as F for 'full frontal'. She claimed to be using disco 'intelligently' to improve its content!

Studio 54 opened in New York, quickly becoming the most famous nightclub in the world and the epicentre of the disco craze. The 'Disneyland for adults' was established by Steve Rubell and Ian Schrager, while their 'P.R. sorceress' was Carmen D'Alessio, who kept an invitation list of thousands of celebrity contacts, all colour coded into categories: wealthy, gay, powerful and so on. Five thousand invitees appeared on opening night. Decoration for the event included a large man in the moon snorting from an oversized cocaine spoon. Members paid an annual fee, but even being a paid-up member didn't guarantee access. Doorman Steve Rubell – the 'lord of the door' – decided from the throngs hankering at his feet which lucky few would be allowed to step past the velvet rope. It was this very exclusivity that made Studio 54 the ultimate hot spot. Being one of the chosen entrants added to one's status. This was just another facet of the new narcissistic climate, and the cult of celebrity was in full swing. Paparazzi lurked at Studio 54's door, eager to snap passing luminaries, while gossip columnists fed the media with tales of who had been seen with whom. Non-stars dolled themselves up in the hope of being viewed as sufficiently interesting to gain entry.

The Bee Gees were busy touring and recording. While they were mixing a live album, Robert Stigwood rang and said he was producing a film to be called *Tribal Rites of the New Saturday Night*, based on an article by journalist Nik Cohn that had appeared in *New York* magazine. Cohn's piece described Italian kids in Brooklyn and their disco culture. Disco was happening in select places, but it had yet to become a worldwide sensation. As Stigwood's RSO partner Freddie Gershon noted, 'Five years earlier it would have been deemed effete for men to even be on a dance floor, now men were becoming peacocks. It was Robert's instinct that a Tony Manero (the lead character in the proposed movie) existed in every community in the world.'[3]

The songs that The Bee Gees provided for the movie weren't designed to be used in that fashion. They had simply been recorded for a pending Bee Gees album. Stigwood heard the songs and convinced the band not to release the new LP. One of the songs earmarked for the film was titled 'Night Fever'. Barry Gibb thus suggested that it would make a better title for the proposed movie.

When *Saturday Night Fever* opened in cinemas at the end of the year, it had already enjoyed masses of free publicity thanks to Stigwood's mastery of cross-media marketing. The Bee Gees' single, with its suggestive title 'How Deep Is Your Love', had reached the top spot in the US charts two months before the film premiered. By the time the movie hit the screens, 'Stayin' Alive' had taken over the top spot. Every time a radio deejay spun one of these discs and mentioned that it was from *Saturday Night Fever*, the film enjoyed free publicity. Not everyone was keen on this approach to marketing, with *New Musical Express* braying:

> [W]e have now entered an era where large corporations are increasingly intent upon developing entertainment packages which appeal to the

lowest common denominator and can be readily translated from film to TV to record to book ... In this respect, Saturday Night Fever should be seen for what it is – a new mass-market innovation and a precursor of things to come: the industrialisation of popular culture.[4]

Saturday Night Fever grossed US$26 million (around US$125 million today) in its first two weeks. As well as making Stigwood and others very rich, the movie also gave licence to heterosexual white folks to become involved in the disco scene. The review in *Variety* said it was 'a more shrill, more vulgar, more trifling, more superficial and more pretentious exploitation film'.[5] But it seemed that superficiality was just what many viewers wanted.

'Stayin' Alive' would find universal appeal as a sort of anthem for marginalised groups. The drums on 'Stayin' Alive' are from a tape loop featuring just one bar of drums lifted from the song 'Night Fever'. Soon drum machines rather than tape loops would become the basis of disco drumming. With its rhythm around 103 beats per minute (as with most disco songs), 'Stayin' Alive' is still used to train medical professionals on how to perform CPR. Studies have shown that CPR is performed best when professionals are singing the song in their head. Who said disco was frivolous? Part of the appeal of 'Stayin' Alive' was the lyric, which Barry Gibb described as, 'People crying out for help. Desperate songs. Those are the ones that become giants.'[6] The same could be said of Gloria Gaynor's 'I Will Survive', released in 1978.

Guitarist Nile Rodgers and bassist Bernard Edwards had formed Chic, releasing their eponymous debut album, which spawned the disco hits 'Dance, Dance, Dance (Yowsah, Yowsah, Yowsah)' and 'Everybody Dance'. As Rodgers later said, 'Bernard and I were typical R&B and funk musicians, and we knew that if we could get people on the dance floor, we could get a record deal. It was exactly that calculated.'[7]

The Village People were even more calculated. They began as a studio project created by French producers Jacques Morali and Henri Belolo, plus singer Victor Willis. Having achieved hits in France, they moved to New York and marketed a phoney outfit they dubbed Village People. Even though the band didn't exist, their first LP became an international hit. The album cover featured a bunch of gay-looking male models in character costumes gathered around a motorcycle. With calls for live performances, Morali and Belolo hurriedly advertised for and cast a group of dancers to perform to the music. Each rookie was assigned a stereotype – soldier, construction worker, cowboy, leather-clad biker and Native American – while Willis took on the policeman role. The follow-up album, *Macho Man*, had already been recorded, but the new recruits posed for the cover.

Even Australia's John Paul Young had a worldwide disco hit, with 'Love Is in the Air' going to single digits in more than a dozen countries, including the US. Once again it was authored by Harry Vanda and George Young. As Vanda put it: 'Our biggest achievement is to write a standard, a song that hangs around for a long time. It doesn't happen to many songwriters. We've done it twice. But "Love Is in the Air" is even more accessible than "Friday on My Mind" because anyone can do it.'[8] The song was even licensed to a condom company.

Rotten to the core

On the first day of the new year, the Roxy nightclub officially opened in London's Covent Garden, with headline acts The Clash and The Heartbreakers. The venue would be the flagship for Britain's punk movement, England's answer to New York's CBGB.

The Damned scored a brief residency at The Roxy. They also released the first UK punk album, *Damned Damned Damned*. The distinguishing feature of The Damned was speed – the sheer freneticism of the music. All four members of Led Zeppelin attended one of The Damned's gigs to see what the new generation was offering. As Jimmy Page said, 'They were the best initiation one could have had. So powerful and tight. Exactly what rock 'n' roll is all about: sheer adrenaline music. I think that new wave is the most important thing that's happened since Hendrix.'[9]

The Sex Pistols were arguably no less manufactured than many disco artists, thanks to Malcolm McLaren's controlling influence. They were also aware of their own theatricality. Consider this comment made some years later by John Lydon: 'I never meant the Pistols to be a challenge to Alice Cooper. More like a compliment, thank you. You know, he had an influence on us. I think anything that Alice has ever done is good enough for me. Except golf.'[10]

When Queen pulled out of a TV interview on Bill Grundy's *Today* show in December 1976, EMI suggested The Sex Pistols as an alternative. Manager Malcolm McLaren wound the lads up before the interview, although everyone had been drinking. Siouxsie Sioux was also there, along with others from the Bromley Contingent. Grundy purposely provoked The Pistols, challenging the lads to swear on camera. When Grundy suggested that he and Siouxsie get together after the show, Jones called him a 'dirty fucker', and the whole spot was quickly brought to a close. To McLaren's satisfaction, the newspapers went ballistic and The Sex Pistols became a household name. They set out on their Anarchy Tour, supported by The Clash plus The Heartbreakers and The Damned. Due to the fierce media coverage, many gigs were cancelled, politicians expressed outrage and protests were formed. There was even more media publicity about their bad behaviour en route to gigs in the Netherlands, by which time EMI had had enough and pulled the contract, furnishing McLaren with a handsome payout.

Bassist Glen Matlock left the band, later explaining that he did so because Johnny Rotten's ego had grown too big once he had begun to appear in the media. Matlock had also started pressing McLaren to explain where the money was going. On leaving The Pistols, Matlock immediately formed a band with Midge Ure called Rich Kids.

Matlock was replaced in The Pistols by Sid Vicious, aka John Beverley/ Ritchie. Vicious had thrown a glass during the 100 Club Punk Special, blinding a girl in one eye. He ended up serving brief time in a remand centre. The real problem, however, was that Sid couldn't play guitar. As John Lydon later told it, 'Sid didn't even know how to hold the bass guitar.

Hence the original Sid stance with his legs apart ... it was the only way he could balance himself – and it became a fashion statement!'[11]

With The Heartbreakers' visit to the UK came groupie and heroin addict Nancy Spungen. Nancy's involvement with drugs had begun when she was just a toddler and doctors prescribed medication to help manage her behavioural issues. She had worked as a stripper and dominatrix to fund her drug habit. On arrival in the UK, she initially went after Johnny Rotten, but when that failed she took up with Sid Vicious. According to some reports, Sid was still a virgin and Nancy was his first love. Their emotional interdependency, not to mention their shared heroin habit, generated friction for the band. As Chrissie Hynde put it, '[T]he more his mates implored him to ditch her, the less likely it was to happen. Of course, McLaren was beside himself with frustration at her Yoko-like omnipresence, which gave Sid even more reason to refuse to budge – all he had left of his self-concept was his obstinacy.'[12]

In March, The Sex Pistols signed with A&M Records, and another £75,000 went into the account set up by McLaren. Vicious smashed a toilet bowl at A&M's offices and trailed blood through the building. After the Pistols fought with another band at a gig, A&M bailed out. It was less than a week after they'd signed the band, and the company trashed 25,000 copies of the 'God Save the Queen' single.

Next, The Sex Pistols signed with Virgin Records. According to Richard Branson, he was keen to 'remove the hippie image' hanging over the label.[13] When Virgin tried to release the 'God Save the Queen' single, workers at the pressing plant walked off the job in protest. Eventually that was resolved, and the single went out in time for the Queen's Silver Jubilee celebrations, stimulating the expected outcry. The disc became the most heavily censored record in British history, banned by radio stations and many stores. Within a week, 150,000 copies had been sold.

McLaren convinced Richard Branson to hold a party for 175 people on a riverboat on the Thames with a budget of £1500, of which Virgin would pay half. The Sex Pistols performed while slipping past the Houses of Parliament. But a scuffle broke out between a photographer and Jah

Wobble, who was a friend of Johnny Rotten. The boat operator summoned the river police, and things quickly got out of hand. Jane Mulvagh relates a story of Vivienne Westwood defiantly pulling down her pants and pissing over the side of the boat as the officers boarded.[14] As Branson put it:

> The police caused absolute chaos … It was a huge overreaction by the police, but it certainly did the reputation of The Sex Pistols and Virgin no harm at all. God Save the Queen sales went through the roof and the band's place in rock 'n' roll history was confirmed.[15]

McLaren, Westwood and others were arrested, and Branson bailed them all out the next day.

But it wasn't just the police who had it in for the Pistols and their supporters. A week after the Thames River stunt, an art director who worked with The Sex Pistols was beaten up and left unconscious. Then Johnny Rotten was stabbed in an ambush outside a pub. A Virgin Records spokesman told the media that the attackers were not teenage thugs but men in their thirties. The following day, drummer Paul Cook was hit over the head with an iron bar at a Tube station. Being seditious was dangerous work.

In the end, 'God Save the Queen' made it to second place on the UK charts, just behind Rod Stewart's 'I Don't Want to Talk About It'. According to McLaren, distributor CBS had admitted that The Sex Pistols had outsold Rod Stewart, but they stymied further outrage by preventing it from peaking on the charts. For his part, Stewart reckons that's nonsense.

A Scandinavian tour saw Johnny Rotten pose for photos while wearing a swastika and giving a Nazi salute. Back in the UK the band undertook a tour using pseudonyms to avoid having their gigs cancelled. Recording for their album took place largely without Sid Vicious on bass, with guitarist Steve Jones performing the bass parts on all but one track. *Never Mind the Bollocks, Here's the Sex Pistols* was released in October, with Paul Nelson in *Rolling Stone* hailing it as 'the most exciting rock & roll record of the Seventies'.[16] Inevitably, it was banned by some retailers and blasted by moral custodians. Police swooped on shops that dared to display the cover, even arresting a Virgin Records shop manager. The album went to number one on the UK chart.

Like a eulogy to Ayn Rand, in the song 'No Feelings' Rotten sings about how he has no emotions for others because he's too busy loving himself. On 'Pretty Vacant', Rotten places the emphasis on the last syllable, over a riff inspired by ABBA's 'SOS'. 'Anarchy in the UK' seems to sanction violent insurrection. 'Bodies' describes an abortion in grisly, graphic terms, with plenty of added profanity. The song was based on first-hand accounts by a female fan, but critics had difficulty rationalising the Pistols' apparent anti-abortion stance. Perhaps the song said more about Rotten's squeamishness regarding bodies and female reproduction? Certainly, critics like Robert Christgau viewed the song as anti-sex.

Mind you, the industrial music, art concept group Throbbing Gristle were trying even harder to offend, displaying images from pornography and Nazi concentration camps at their performances. Although fronted by a woman, their album *The Second Annual Report* included the track 'Slug Bait', which told the story of a boy who invades a couple's house, castrates the man, cuts the foetus from his seven-months-pregnant wife and then proceeds to bite and lick the foetus. Arguably, the story is only slightly more gross than that of the Manson Family murder of pregnant Sharon Tate – and perhaps that was the point?

On Christmas Day, The Sex Pistols performed at a benefit concert. They wouldn't perform live again in the UK for another eighteen years.

While punk was a reaction against the late 1960s and early '70s, it took many of its cues from the 1950s and early '60s. In so doing, it can also be viewed as yet another spoke in the wheel of nostalgia, hankering for a simpler era. Let's not forget that Malcolm McLaren and Vivienne Westwood's London boutique had begun as Let It Rock, selling old rock 'n' roll memorabilia and clothing from the '50s. The black leather, chains and short hair of the 1950s was the obverse of hippie couture.

The Stranglers were the real anomalies of British punk, becoming enormously successful with little support from the media. They released their first two albums, *Rattus Norvegicus* and *No More Heroes*, each selling a quarter of a million copies while generating charting singles. Pugnacious and crude, they found themselves banned from Dingwalls Dancehall after they smashed the equipment of their support band. What's more, their songs were deeply misogynistic and racist. Apologists argue that such criticism misses the satire in the band's early work, but I am doubtful they were ever that clever. Certainly, the opening track on their debut album, 'Sometimes', is about a man wanting to beat up his girlfriend. What's more, band member Hugh Cornwell told *New Musical Express* that the song was inspired by an actual incident when he hit his girlfriend, adding, 'I think a lot of men like to dominate women. A lot of women like to be dominated ... I think subservient women are a bit pitiful.'[17] The track 'Ugly' sees the male protagonist suggesting that he should have strangled his sex partner to death because she had acne. The hit single 'Peaches' is about perving on girls at the beach, 'London Lady' cruelly criticises a 'stupid' older woman who sleeps with a band member, and 'Princess of the Streets' is a put-down of a prostitute, who is described as 'meat'. It's all juvenile chauvinism, but there's no evident irony.

There was a significant difference between the punk trend in America and its more violent cousin in England. New York punks like Patti Smith, Richard Hell and Tom Verlaine were in their mid to late twenties, whereas the English scene was dominated by a slightly younger generation who were far less cerebral.

In New York, the Dead Boys cut their first album, *Young, Loud and Snotty*, produced by rock singer Genya Ravan for Sire Records. Ravan was a rare phenomenon, being a female producer and at the same time recording her own albums. The Dead Boys' track 'Sonic Reducer' quickly became a punk classic, later covered by bands such as Guns N' Roses and Pearl Jam. It was another anthem to individualism and a rebuttal of society, with lyrics about not needing anyone else, including parents or peers. It was also a wretched cry of anger on behalf of every social outcast and ostracised schoolkid.

Richard Hell and the Voidoids released their debut album, *Blank Generation*. The title track, written by Hell, explicitly focused on the vacant emptiness that punk devotees claimed as their own. The title itself was a play on Beat Generation, being the literary/beatnik movement of the late 1950s. The antisocial cool of Marlon Brando and the non-conforming James Dean, particularly his role in *Rebel Without a Cause*, were archetypes for the new punk movement. The melancholy detachment of Dean was pure US punk in its desultory passivity. Where British punk was actively aggressive, American punk was more about ennui. Idealism, purpose and issue-laden causes were the enemies of US punk. From this more obstinate stance would arise America's own version of aggressive punk known as hardcore.

The Clash's debut LP included the song 'I'm So Bored with the USA', which condemned the dominance of American culture and its values. In fact, The Clash weren't simply sitting around moaning. They promoted themselves as a concept as well as a band. Although such a notion seems to run counter to the anarchic nihilism of punk, The Clash were progressive in their politics, taking on issues such as police brutality in 'Police and Thieves', unemployment and soullessness in 'Career Opportunities', bureaucrats and big business in 'Remote Control', and personal identity in 'What's My Name'. The debut single, 'White Riot', is a high-speed attack on wealth inequality and racial divisions. Bass player Paul Simonon even said, '[I]f we do our job properly then we're making people aware of a situation they'd otherwise tend to ignore. We can have a vast effect!'[18] On the negative side, The Clash were hugely male-centric, with zero interest in the role of women, instead fixated on masculine, militaristic glory. But within this boy's own story, at least The Clash were focused on 'we' rather than 'me'.

Punk wasn't just a product of London and New York; it was also happening in downtown Brisbane. The Saints first album *(I'm) Stranded* was more 1950s music dressed up – or down – as punk. Like the Ramones, The Saints played fiercely fast, repetitive rock with unruly vocals and the usual buzz-saw distorted guitar. Their first single had snuck into the Australian charts, and in 1977 a second single, 'Erotic Neurotic', was noticed in England, where the band headed. In London, they opened for the Ramones and Talking Heads at the Roundhouse. EMI urged them to adopt the standard UK punk image of spiky hair and ripped clothing, but The Saints refused to be channelled. Guitarist and songwriter Ed Kuepper told a fanzine, 'I think the New Wave thing has lost a lot, it's got too involved in fashion, which is superfluous … just because we've been named as a punk band doesn't mean we're going to start dressing the part.'[19] Their UK single 'This Perfect Day' started its way up the charts but was frustrated by EMI's failure to press enough copies to meet demand.

Also from Australia, Radio Birdman released *Radios Appear* on the independent Trafalgar label, initially sold by mail order and from the backs of cars. 'Do the Pop' paid homage to The Stooges and MC5, while 'Murder City Nights' name-checked Detroit's iconic Woodward Avenue. Radio Birdman, like The Clash and others, were titillated by the macho notion of military engagement, labelling their tour a blitzkrieg and their gigs 'offensives'. Inevitably, the album was ignored by commercial radio, but it found a champion in Sydney's ABC station 2JJ. Both Radio Birdman and The Saints would etch their place in punk history.

Great expectorations

One of the unpleasant aspects of punk involved 'gobbing'. Hundreds of audience members would spit gobs of snot and saliva onto bands as they performed, often leaving the band covered in muck. The inspiration for this disgusting behaviour is clouded in mystery. Johnny Rotten, for example, spat on stage to clear his sinuses. Others have blamed The Damned's drummer, Rat Scabies. He reckons an early gig with both The Sex Pistols and The Damned saw Steve Jones gob first, with Scabies aiming back at him, and the whole thing escalating into audience participation. But Poly Styrene from X-Ray Spex argues that it was either Sid Vicious or one of the members of The Clash who started expectorating; Iggy Pop has also claimed to have started it by gobbing at his audience. While the provenance is slippery, it seems that a journalist from *The Evening Standard* wrote that punks liked to be spat on, and a week later everyone was spitting at gigs. The sax player with X-Ray Spex, Lora Logic, said, 'I'd wear a full-length plastic mac on stage because of all the spitting – the bell of my saxophone would be full of spit.'[20]

The phlegm projectiles may have had serious consequences. Joe Strummer of The Clash got hepatitis, and believed he'd contracted it from audience expectorant. Adam Ant got conjunctivitis. Siouxsie Sioux suffered from both. At a 1980 gig she even left the stage in an unsuccessful effort to get the audience to stop spitting. In Australia, Cold Chisel's Jimmy Barnes reckons he had to threaten audience members with violence to stop them gobbing at the band.

Another British trend, particularly favoured among skinheads, was slam dancing, where punters purposely slammed bodies together in an overexcited frenzy of pent-up aggression. Body piercing also became a part of the punk scene, with some adherents putting safety pins through their nose or mouth. Combined with flying mucus, the opportunities for infection of piercings must have been enormous.

Female punks were getting noticed. Following their makeshift performance at the 100 Club Punk Festival, Siouxsie Sioux and Steven Severin recruited a drummer and guitarist to make up The Banshees, although their initial guitarist was quickly fired for playing too well. Siouxsie engaged a guise that combined dominatrix with Halloween witch, pioneering what would become the Gothic look.

X-Ray Spex's front person, Poly Styrene (aka Marianne Joan Elliott-Said), was a wild woman who wore braces on her teeth and eschewed any effort at sex appeal. The band's 1976 debut single, 'Oh Bondage Up Yours!', sounds like an inverted feminist anthem, with Poly Styrene calling on the listener to make her a slave and thrash her. A close listen reveals the song is not about female subservience, but rather the subservience that arises out of consumerism. Banned by the BBC, it quickly became a must-have single among diehard punks.

Waving at punks

Ian Dury was signed to Stiff Records and managed by the former managers of Pink Floyd. His provocative debut single 'Sex & Drugs & Rock & Roll' coined a phrase that was not dissimilar to the title of Daddy Cool's 1972 LP *Sex, Dope, Rock 'n' Roll: Teenage Heaven*. The song lifts its bass riff from an Ornette Coleman tune, but Coleman or his bass player, Charlie Haden, had already borrowed it from a traditional folk tune. Although 'Sex & Drugs & Rock & Roll' became an anthem seemingly promoting self-indulgence, that wasn't Dury's intent. Dury said he was suggesting that there was, in fact, more to life.

The single led to a debut album with the title *New Boots and Panties!!*, which charted nicely in New Zealand and Australia and went platinum in the UK. *Melody Maker* reckoned it conveyed more about urban degradation than any other so-called new wave or punk outfit. Indeed, critics were universally enamoured with Dury's debut. The man himself was a prickly character who had been impacted by youthful polio, reducing his mobility. He often needed to be assisted onto the stage. His decidedly literate songs enjoyed plenty of wordplay, and his music borrowed from funk, jazz, reggae and rock 'n' roll, while the voice was unashamed cockney.

At the end of 1976, new wave band Blondie released their debut self-titled LP, which flopped. But *Countdown*'s Molly Meldrum caught their show in Detroit and asked if they had any videos he could use on his Australian TV show. They gave him tapes of 'X Offender' and 'In the Flesh'. As Debbie Harry explained, *Countdown* 'were meant to play "X Offender", but they played "In the Flesh" instead. So our success in Australia was one big mistake! By the end of 1977, "In the Flesh" had hit number two in Australia. It was Blondie's first hit anywhere in the world. Thanks Molly.'[21] This far-flung success led to an Australian tour. Blondie weren't exactly a dynamic stage act. When touring the UK with Television, one critic referred to them as 'sulky bastards, her musicians: not the type of boys Debbie should mix with at all."[22]

Part of Blondie's attraction was the gorgeous Debbie Harry. To promote the album, their record company, Private Stock, created a poster featuring an image of Debbie Harry, sans band, dressed in a see-through blouse. Harry wasn't happy, complaining to Private Stock Records about ignoring the rest of the band. But the band continued to capitalise on their vocalist's genetic luck, plus her Marilyn Monroe fixation, throughout their career. She was always front and centre on their LP jackets, and often the only one depicted on singles jackets.

In these early days, the band's lyrics were anything but feminist. 'X Offender' (originally titled 'Sex Offender') was sung from the point of view of a woman jailed for sex offences, who lusts after her police captor. It was released with the even more offensive 'Rip Her to Shreds', which seemed to encourage violence against women who sport the wrong fashion look.

In Australia, Blondie's Brisbane gig had to be cancelled at the last minute because Debbie Harry was ill. First-hand reports suggest that Harry had overindulged in too many cherries, though Harry said it was food poisoning; at least one attendee claimed it was a reaction to the local heroin. In any case, when drummer Clem Burke announced to the audience that they wouldn't be playing, all hell broke loose. Burke was pelted with objects, punters rioted, attempts were made to set the speakers on fire, and a few audience members began fisticuffs with Blondie's road crew. Four locals were eventually arrested. A follow-up show ten days later was poorly attended, and at the end of the gig Blondie smashed up their instruments.

Talking Heads' debut album was appropriately titled *Talking Heads: 77*. All the songs were written by David Byrne except for 'Psycho Killer', which was credited to Byrne, Frantz and Weymouth. Released as a single along with the album, it soon became something of a signature song for the band. The French lyrics came about because Tina Weymouth spoke French at home. *Talking Heads: 77* hints at the future direction of this decidedly funky new wave band, but it had a lacklustre and thin overall sound. That would improve when the band teamed up with Brian Eno for their next three albums.

Power trios were somewhat old hat in the late 1970s, nevertheless Sting (Gordon Sumner), Stewart Copeland and Andy Summers determined to make a go of it as The Police. The band attempted to win over punk audiences, but they were far too musically adept to suit punk tastes. Also new on the London music scene were The Boomtown Rats, created in Dublin and fronted by Bob Geldof. The band name was inspired by a gang of children described in Woody Guthrie's autobiography *Bound for Glory*. A *Melody Maker* review noted the similarity between Jagger and Geldof, ending with, 'You may have seen it somewhere before, but the precision and energy of this band make them a whole new experience.'[23] Precision was new? Wasn't that what prog and fusion had been on about for the past seven years?

The Boomtown Rats released their debut album. It included the frenetic single 'Lookin' After No. 1', which performed well on the Irish and British charts. It would be the first of ten consecutive singles by the Rats to get a guernsey in the UK Top 40. In an echo of The Who's 'My Generation', the chorus explains that the central character, a chap on the dole, doesn't want to be like everyone else. Was it an endorsement of selfishness or an ironic critique of entitlement? Asked this question, Geldof hedged his bets, explaining that it was both sincere and satirical. The song appeared to be a paean to the new avarice.

Swimming up the mainstream

On release, *Bat Out of Hell* took off like a … A collaboration between composer Jim Steinman and rock singer Meat Loaf (aka Marvin Lee Aday), the album developed out of a musical, *Neverland*, based on *Peter Pan*, that Steinman had written in 1974. *Bat Out of Hell* had a protracted gestation, being recorded throughout 1975 and 1976 at various studios, and was not released until late 1977. It has since sold some 40 million copies and been certified fourteen times platinum in the US. It remains the bestselling album of all time in Australia, where it went twenty-six times platinum.

It also spent 522 weeks on the album charts in the UK. Indeed, it's the twelfth-bestselling album of all time globally.

Overproduced, overegged and over-the-top, the saving grace of *Bat Out of Hell* is that it doesn't take itself too seriously – just listen to the spoken introduction to 'You Took the Words Right Out of My Mouth'. Here we have an LP that not only draws attention to the triteness of the clichés it ransacks, but simultaneously reveres those clichés, just as Frank Zappa spent much time parodying the doo-wop music that he truly loved. *Bat Out of Hell* works simply because those cheesy, dog-eared conventions of both metal and prog were so familiar to listeners by 1977.

While producing *Bat Out of Hell*, Todd Rundgren thought Steinman and Mr Loaf were parodying Bruce Springsteen. Recording sessions even included members of Springsteen's E Street Band. Some critics have also found similarities between the lyrics on 'Bat Out of Hell' and those of Springsteen's 'Born to Run'. If Springsteen was mining the clichéd conventions of rock, *Bat Out of Hell* was holding those same conventions up to a brighter, more garish light.

Bruce Springsteen hadn't released an album since *Born to Run* in August 1975, because he was embroiled in a legal dispute with his former manager, Mike Appel. The first half-million bucks from *Born to Run* had gone straight into Appel's accounts, with Springsteen receiving no funds or royalties of his own. At the time of the contract signing, Springsteen had been, in his words, 'too intimidated by the idea of the contracts to take them seriously'.[24] Now Appel wanted Springsteen to sign a new contract, again with dubious remunerations for the artist.

As Springsteen wrote, 'Mike's power, underwritten by the agreements, proved very effective in stopping my career in its tracks … Then came the depositions.' Eventually, after months of wrangling, huge legal bills, and a lot of lost sleep, a settlement of sorts was reached. Springsteen found himself 'signing more papers I hadn't, and would never, read … The money was gone but the music was primarily mine.' Having the rights to his own material was about more than just income, as he noted: 'I'm one of the few artists from those days who owns everything he ever created. All my records are mine. All my songs are mine. It's rare and it's a good feeling.'[25]

David Bowie released two albums, *Low* followed by *Heroes*. The first was made in tandem with Iggy Pop's debut solo LP *The Idiot*, during which both artists vainly attempted to sober up. Together they wrote 'China Girl', a song about a man who has swastikas floating around in his head and who dreams of ruling the world. The Fuhrer fetish was still with both Pop and Bowie.

Musically, Bowie was heading further down the electronic, ambient, avant-garde trajectory. The results so spooked the gormless executives at RCA that they refused to release *Low*. When they finally conceded to set it free, the album managed to hit number two in the UK and eleven in the US. Yet again the shiny-bums in the music biz were proven to be out of touch with audience desires. The *Low* album was notable for its drum sound, achieved by processing the drums through a pitch-shifting device. That sound, and indeed the album per se, would have a strong influence on synth-pop and post-punk bands like Joy Division, Magazine, Gang of Four, The Human League, Ultravox, Orchestral Manoeuvres in the Dark and Cabaret Voltaire. Produced by Bowie with Tony Visconti and Brian Eno, *Low* was defiant, a dense, muddy assault that presented some of Bowie's most original work.

Bowie, Visconti and Eno also teamed up for *Heroes*, which added King Crimson's Robert Fripp on lead guitar. Most of the tracks were composed in the studio, with the lyrics frequently improvised on the spot and sung with furious passion. This was the middle disc of what would become known as Bowie's *Berlin Trilogy*. Again, it's full of aggressive distortion and cryptic messaging. Several music papers were sufficiently impressed to nominate it as their album of the year. The title track, certainly the most accessible, was a moderately successful single.

A more clarifying commercial success was Billy Joel's fifth studio album, *The Stranger*, which generated four hit singles: 'Just the Way You Are', 'Movin' Out (Anthony's Song)', 'She's Always a Woman' and 'Only the Good Die Young'. The latter was given a marketing boost when religious groups tried to have it banned from radio because it criticised a Catholic girl for refusing to have premarital sex. It would be both Joel's and Columbia Records' bestselling album of the era, eclipsing Simon & Garfunkel's *Bridge Over Troubled Water.* Joel initially approached the fifth Beatle, George Martin, to produce, but Martin wanted to use session musicians, whereas Joel insisted that he use his own band. He ended up with Phil Ramone, who had produced *Still Crazy After All These Years* for Paul Simon. *The Stranger* enjoys a bright, clean production, and George Martin generously wrote to Joel congratulating him. On this album, Billy Joel sounds like a confident rock star: listen to the longest cut, 'Scenes From an Italian Restaurant', with its shifts in mood, sweeping gestures and superbly confident singing.

ABBA set off on their first major tour, starting in Europe before heading to the UK. Two concerts at the Royal Albert Hall not only sold out but generated 3.5 million requests for tickets. On that score, ABBA could have filled the venue 600 times over. The Australian leg of the tour generated scenes reminiscent of The Beatles' 1964 visit, with thousands of hysterical fans gathering outside concert venues and hotels. The Australian experience was also filmed by director Lasse Hallström for *ABBA: The Movie.* The film's release coincided with their fifth album, ingeniously titled *ABBA: The Album.*

Were ABBA a product of genuine talent or savvy marketing? It plainly vexed rock scribes as to why a Swedish band should be so successful in a medium traditionally dominated by American and British acts. Was there a magic formula? As manager Stig Anderson retorted, 'If it's a formula, why don't you go out and find it?'[26] Nevertheless, *Rolling Stone*'s Dave Marsh attempted to explain the prescription: 'Every song, not just a few, rides on sprightly rhythms, bounces from melodic hook to melodic hook and is overlaid with the chiming vocals of Agnetha and Anni-Frid (Frida).' Somehow during this busy year, as well as chiming, Agnetha managed to squeeze in the birth of her second child with Bjorn.

ABBA and Billy Joel may have been successful, but the biggest-selling album of the year across the globe belonged to the drugged, lovelorn shemozzle that was Fleetwood Mac. *Rumours* was so named because of all the speculation the band generated around their personal lives. It was, as one wag put it, a tabloid album, with many of the songs springing from the unfolding relationship tragedies. Yet *Rumours* turned into one of the bestselling LPs of all time, and the band finally cracked the top spot on the UK charts, as well going number one in the US, Australia and elsewhere.

Rumours has sold over 40 million copies worldwide, securing its place in the top ten all-time bestselling records. Singles from the LP include 'Don't Stop', 'Dreams', 'Go Your Own Way', and 'You Make Loving Fun'. Even if you don't recognise the titles, you'll have subliminally absorbed the tunes.

Of greater interest, however, is the final track, 'Gold Dust Woman'. It's Stevie Nicks' autobiographical tune about dealing with both fame and her failed relationship with the tyrannical Lindsey Buckingham. Oh, and of course, drugs. There is something depressingly misogynistic about the lyric, which argues that dominant women make for poor lovers, and that the queen in question would be better off giving up her power and selling her kingdom. It's a rock queen's acquiescence in the face of rock music's toxic masculinity.

Relationship woes are also at the heart of 'The Chain', its punchy chorus spat out with fury, with all members of the band contributing to that bitter catharsis. John McVie's fretless bass takes the song into the sped-up finale, with a screaming guitar solo by Buckingham which somehow invokes the fraught tension between the performers.

The band had progressed from touring in self-driven vehicles to chartered jets. Along with their fame came a crazy list of self-indulgent riders in their performance contracts. As Mick Fleetwood wrote, '[W]e had fourteen black limos at our beck and call, for a time Stevie wanted her room to be pink with a white piano (We'd often have to hire a crane to lift the piano in through a window), and the list went on.'[27] The touring company bought cocaine in bulk, and everyone involved would queue up after each show to collect their packet.

So what was it that made *Rumours* so successful? The production is bright and glossy, the songs are catchy and the whole thing is energised by the band's interpersonal turmoil. Having three good singers and three songwriters meant the tunes never became too similar. It is, if you like, simultaneously shallow pop and heartfelt, passionate rock: in other words, it has depth if you want to go digging, but can be taken as a light refreshment if you don't.

Progging the bear

In December 1977 Brian Eno released the best of his solo albums, *Before and After Science*. Side two of this timeless LP is definitely on my desert island list, with its elegant, wistful, sometimes lullaby-like tunes that pre-empt the work Eno would later create with John Cale. These songs have watery themes, and they flow serenely through the ears. The characters that inhabit side two of the disc are all listless, merging into their surroundings like camouflaged insects – and indeed insects become characters. Reviewing *Before and After Science* for *DownBeat* magazine, Russell Shaw wrote that the album 'is another typically awesome, stunning and numbing Brian Eno album – the record Pink Floyd could make if they set their collective mind to it'.[28] It made it onto the charts in Australia, New Zealand and Sweden.

Pink Floyd continued their successful run with *Animals*, a concept album loosely based on Orwell's *Animal Farm*. It seemed to be saying something about the political state of Britain. For all its long-form progginess, *Animals* eclipsed ABBA in the charts for a while. Similarly, Emerson, Lake & Palmer's *Works Volume 1* broke a three-year drought for the band, going to nine in the UK and six in Australia. It also proved to be about as ostentatious as prog could get. The double disc opened with Emerson's 'Piano Concerto No. 1', backed by the London Philharmonic Orchestra. Across the other three sides were original pieces alongside adaptations of compositions by Prokofiev, J.S. Bach and Aaron Copland. In some ways, the disc marks the pinnacle of excessive, indulgent progressive rock, with Emerson clearly desperate to be viewed as a modern classical composer of note. Although panned by the critics, it did generate ELP's highest-charting single, a version of Aaron Copland's 'Fanfare for the Common Man', which went to number two on the UK singles chart.

Former 10cc band members Kevin Godley and Lol Creme's operatic triple album *Consequences* was designed to showcase their Gizmotron invention. The Gizmo was a device that clamped onto the bridge of a guitar to produce endless sustain via continuously moving wheels on each string. It thus allowed the guitar to emulate the bowing of orchestral string instruments. Drugs and obsessiveness resulted in the recording of *Consequences* taking fourteen months. Endless hours were spent, for example, making a guitar emulate a saxophone or recording special effects. All the spoken character voices were performed by comedian Peter Cook – at least on those occasions when he was sober enough to perform. Cook moved into The Manor studios for three months to work on the project. Even jazz singer Sarah Vaughan was roped in.

The magnum opus was an incredibly expensive flop, with Lol Creme later admitting, 'I could see why it was laughed at, it does look like a pretentious pile of old stuff. We were self-indulgent pop stars, there's no question about it.'[29] The full triple set is difficult to find, but Phonogram/ Mercury did release an edited-down single LP that also found its way onto CD (in a two-CD set with Godley & Creme's exceptional album *L*). If you can find that, or even the whole grand folly of *Consequences*, have a listen to the Gershwin-influenced 'Lost Weekend' with Sarah Vaughan, 'Rosie' with Peter Cook, and the truly amazing instrumental 'Sleeping Earth', which is one of the cleverest *musique concrète* concoctions ever assembled.

Consequences was proudly unveiled to the record company executives in a seventeenth-century Amsterdam church beginning on the seventeenth minute of the seventeenth hour on the seventeenth day of September. As Kevin Godley reflected: '[E]nter The Sex Pistols. Oh-oh ... It suddenly became apparent that we were no longer creating the ultimate record: ourselves and the project had been instantly invalidated ... In fact, it was such an incredible failure that it forged a sort of bond between the people involved.'[30] *Consequences* became the *Heaven's Gate* of the record world.

331

While Godley & Creme had departed 10cc, Eric Stewart and Graham Gouldman operated as a duo – arguably just 5cc now – with help from Paul Burgess on the drums. 10cc's *Deceptive Bends* album still managed to generate plenty of quirky pop-for-adults, including the charting singles 'Good Morning Judge' and 'The Things We Do For Love'.

Peter Gabriel released his first solo album, a cracking assortment of songs each with a different flavour, accompanied by the likes of Robert Fripp on guitar (plus banjo!) and the incredible Tony Levin on bass. One of the most versatile bass players, Levin had already worked on Alice Cooper's *Welcome to My Nightmare* and Lou Reed's *Berlin* disc, and would soon join Gabriel's band, followed by Fripp's reformed King Crimson. On *Peter Gabriel I*, the London Symphony Orchestra was arranged by Michael Gibbs. If that again sounds like pretentious prog, in this case it's not. These are superbly crafted, intelligent pop songs, eschewing the poseur flourishes of Genesis or Yes. Gabriel would never better his audacious debut, with 'Solsbury Hill' and 'Here Comes the Flood' two of the most evocative songs of the decade. It was all produced by Bob Ezrin, who brought in Fripp and Levin to the project, instigating musical collaborations that would reverberate through the 1980s and beyond.

While Gabriel, 10cc, ELP and Pink Floyd clung tenaciously to their blueprint in the face of punk, a good deal of prog rock was busy shedding its embellishments for a harder, more direct sound. Queen's *News of the World* was a case in point. It opened with a simplistic rock anthem, 'We Will Rock You', followed by the equally anthemic 'We Are the Champions', both live crowd-pleasers. Gentle Giant also dumbed down their music for *The Missing Piece*, likewise PFM with *Jet Lag*.

The river of Oz

Little River Band's third studio LP, *Diamantina Cocktail*, hit second spot on the Australian album chart. Friction was running high in the band, so various members had to record their parts separately from the rest of the outfit. The songs had no Australian references, and it was all clearly pitched at the radio-friendly US market. By the start of the new year, the album had gone gold in the US, with LRB the first Australian band to achieve that level of success in America. Singles 'Help Is On the Way' and 'Happy Anniversary' also charted well. LRB toured long and hard.

Air Supply's second album, *The Whole Thing's Started*, failed to set the charts on fire, but the band supported Rod Stewart during his Australian tour, with Stewart inviting them to continue with him to the US and Canada. Third album *Love & Other Bruises* was recorded mid-tour in LA and released on Columbia Records, but the band wouldn't garner international fame until the next decade.

AC/DC felt they had outgrown both TV show *Countdown* and their country, not to mention the media's obsession with their Neanderthal behaviour. The band toured Britain and Europe with Black Sabbath, but there was friction between the two groups, not helped by AC/DC members standing in the wings and ridiculing Geezer Butler during his bass solo spot. It all came to a head in a Brussels hotel bar, when Butler reportedly pulled a knife on Malcolm Young. Ozzy Osbourne arrived just in time to prevent bloodshed.

Mind you, AC/DC were also pretty good at irritating each other. Bassist Mark Evans was dismissed, to be replaced by British player Cliff Williams. But AC/DC's brand of simple rock would endure for decades, without the formula ever changing. As Atlantic Records' Phil Carson put it, 'I guess the Youngs had a realisation that rock music should be a driving force that shouldn't be overburdened with complexity.'[31]

Acca Dacca's new LP, *Let There Be Rock*, was louder and more stripped-down than previous albums, with greater focus on the guitars. They toured the US supporting all manner of bigger-name bands. While there, Angus was introduced to the Schaffer–Vega diversity system, allowing him to connect his guitar to his amp without leads. No more would roadies have to trail behind the hyperactive Angus, trying to wrangle his guitar lead: he could climb speaker stacks and sit astride people's shoulders while ripping through his guitar solos.

New Zealand band Split Enz recorded their third album, *Dizrythmia*, produced by former Beatles engineer Geoff Emerick, which saw them moving away from Roxy Music–like art rock and towards a more Top 40 sound. The album charted well in Australia, and even better in their homeland, but they had yet to make inroads in the UK, despite touring there.

Fellow expatriate Kiwis Dragon released *Sunshine*, which went gold and sent forth a string of hit singles. Where Dragon had been a progressive rock act in their home country, shifting to Oz saw them exchange prog for a pop-rock sound. *Running Free* was the follow-up LP later in the year, going triple platinum. Their notoriety for onstage antics, combined with Marc Hunter's unpredictable stage behaviour, became such that the band needed a police escort to get to gigs. Whilst touring country towns, Hunter used a whip to pretend to flagellate young girls. At other shows, he would pick a young girl from the audience and mock rape her on stage. He was even known to call for all the women in the audience to take off their tops. As he told Glenn A. Baker, 'Anything went in the 70s. Everyone was really quite outrageous ... I don't imagine it'll ever be that crazy again ...'[32] His brother Todd Hunter concurred, saying the 1970s was 'a wild, and out of control time ... the darker and wilder it was the better.'[33]

As well as demeaning women, the band was overindulging in drugs and alcohol. When a venue took them to court for failing to perform adequately, the judge reportedly accepted the band's defence that drinking on stage was part of their act. But it wasn't just alcohol that fuelled Marc Hunter's performances. Before the decade ended, he would be fired from the band by his own brother Todd.

Well covered

One of the great joys of record consumption in the 1970s was the foot-square LP sleeves that integrated image with sound. Album covers cleverly designed by the likes of Hipgnosis, Roger Dean and Cal Schenkel were significant works of contemporary art that enhanced the music listening experience. This was before album sleeves shrank down to the eye-squinting five square inches of the CD, and then largely disappeared in the streaming era.

In the case of *Kew. Rhone.* by Peter Blegvad and John Greaves, released on Virgin, the LP cover was decidedly integral to some of the listening experience. As well as being highly original music, many of the songs related to the artwork on the front and back of the LP sleeve. Like a game of 'I Spy' blended with a cryptic crossword, it was all set to music that completely defied categorisation. The songs were full of puns, palindromes and humour, and there's even a superb track of proverbs selected from around the world. The title track offered an array of anagrams of 'Kew. Rhone.'.

There are insufficient superlatives to describe this magical blend of jazz, rock and wordplay, which Blegvad once described as 'a kind of love letter to influences like Robert [Wyatt]'.[34] Streaming it will still provide a worthwhile experience, but having both the lyric sheet and the images heightens the impact. Nevertheless, it's worth listing to in any form to enjoy the blending of Greaves' intricate compositions and Blegvad's clever lyrics, performed by stunning vocalist Lisa Herman, embellished by avant-garde jazz drummer Andrew Cyrille, as well as Carla Bley and Michael Mantler. Its release was badly timed, with Virgin turning their attention to punk, and that meant well away from such carefully crafted exercises in high art.

No explaining it

In 1977, Kiss were declared the most popular band in America by Gallup Poll.

1978

Music Must Change

Look Out for #1 had been the title of a 1976 funk album by The Brothers Johnson which went to the top of the R&B charts. The opening track and hit single belied the album's title: 'I'll Be Good to You' was about a man focused on his lover, not himself. But in 1978, a book was released titled *Looking Out for #1*, and it was certainly about the reader and not their significant other. *Looking Out for #1* was a huge bestseller, penned by Robert Ringer, who had already achieved success with his book *Winning Through Intimidation*. *Looking Out for #1* dovetailed neatly with the growing self-esteem and New Age movements. The book's title invoked Ayn Rand's *The Virtue of Selfishness*, with Ringer similarly urging readers to focus entirely on their own desires and wants.

What people desired was more music. According to the Recording Industry Association of America, music industry revenue in the US peaked in 1978 at US$4.1 billion, having achieved 100 per cent growth in just five years. Fifty-nine per cent of total revenue was from sales of LPs and EPs, vinyl singles were just 6.3 per cent, while eight-track tapes were 22.9 per cent and cassette tapes were 10.9 per cent. It seemed as though record executives could make silk purses from all manner of sows' ears. Barry Manilow, Barbra Streisand, The Captain and Tennille and Kenny Rogers were all pumping out middle-of-the-road bestsellers. Billy Joel's *52nd Street* LP went to the top spot in America and Australia, offering a somewhat jazzier feel while spawning plenty of hit singles. Meanwhile, disco was also hitting its straps.

The British outfit Dire Straits was formed by brothers Mark and David Knopfler with friends John Illsley and Pick Withers. They released their debut eponymous album, from which hailed 'Sultans of Swing', a song that swung into charts across the planet. The album ended up being the fourth-biggest seller for the year in the US. Other big sellers in America were albums by Blondie, The Steve Miller Band, Rod Stewart, Van Halen, Boston and Foreigner. Top of the list was the *Grease* soundtrack, which we'll come to in a moment.

But there was another album that appeared in the top ten across the US, UK and Australia: *Jeff Wayne's Musical Version of The War of the Worlds*. Based on the H.G. Wells novel, this was a rock opera with band and orchestra. Jeff Wayne had been musical director for David Essex, and also an advertising jingles composer, which becomes obvious on this assemblage of musical clichés. The whole double album is filled with hummable, repetitive motifs and imbecilic lyrics. Fantasy and science fiction were all the rage in the 1970s, when modernism itself was an elixir. What's more, the work enjoyed the participation of Essex, The Moody Blues' Justin Hayward, Thin Lizzy's Phil Lynott, and Julie Covington, whose musical career was peaking. Like the previous year's *Bat Out of Hell*, large-scale formulaic pomposity was still finding willing ears amid the rise of punk and disco.

The Rolling Stones, whose collective tin ear to racial matters was by now well established, released their album *Some Girls*, which immediately attracted a fierce rebuke from the Reverend Jesse Jackson. The title track featured a line which asserted that black girls wanted to be fucked all night long. That was just a slice of a much larger serve of misogyny, with the lyrics espousing a litany of all the horrid things that women do to men – including bearing children that weren't asked for! Rev. Jackson met with Atlantic's Ahmet Ertegun, but came away unmollified, declaring the song to be a racial insult that degraded both blacks and women. Atlantic Records and Mick Jagger claimed the song was a parody of stereotypical attitudes, but there was precious little humour evident in the predictable and musically woeful tune. Meanwhile, Bianca had filed for divorce from Jagger on the grounds of adultery; she later said, 'My marriage was over on my wedding day.'[1]

A now forgotten single, 'Take It All Away', was recorded by a band called Girlschool, who took their name from the B-side of the Wings' single 'Mull of Kintyre'. But this was no Beatles homage band. It was an all-female heavy metal group. 'Take It All Away' was heard by Lemmy from the metal band Motörhead, and he offered Girlschool a support role on the band's next tour. Thus began the world's longest-running all-female rock band. It's a remarkable achievement in a genre so dominated by testosterone.

Greasing the wheels

'Mull of Kintyre' was McCartney's love song to his home in Scotland. It became Wings' largest hit, the biggest-selling single in the UK for next half decade, and still ranks as the UK's fourth all-time bestseller. Wings hadn't released an album since 1976, with childbearing and line-up changes generating a hiatus, but *London Town* was another global success: lead single 'With a Little Luck' went to number one in the US.

Paul and his old Beatle chums became the unwitting inspiration for one of Robert Stigwood's rare failures. *Sgt. Pepper's Lonely Hearts Club Band* became a film loosely constructed around the story of a make-believe band, using reinterpreted Beatles songs as the operatic soundtrack. Even a cast that included Peter Frampton, The Bee Gees, Aerosmith, Alice Cooper, Billy Preston plus Earth, Wind & Fire couldn't rescue this turkey from being savaged by the critics and shunned by audiences. The double album soundtrack did chart, but it was also the first to go 'reverse platinum' – with millions of copies being returned from retailers to the distributors. However, Stigwood's other film project, *Grease*, was a very different story.

Nostalgia for the 1950s was still raging. Based on a successful stage musical, the movie version of *Grease* was a humongous hit. The slim story about a love affair between a greaser, John Travolta, hot from his *Saturday Night Fever* role, and an Australian transfer student, Olivia Newton-John, was entirely overshadowed by Stockard Channing's far more interesting character, Rizzo. That character had the best lines and the best clothes, and was ultimately vindicated in her promiscuity. This was a 1950s story made for a post-1960s generation, notably performed by adults pretending to be teenagers (which perhaps made a plot about pre-marital sex more acceptable).

Grease grossed US$9 million in its first weekend and ended its run to become the highest-grossing musical of all time, eclipsing *The Sound of Music*, with global takings of US$341 million. Hit songs from *Grease* were penned by Barry Gibb and Australia's John Farrar, as well as Jim Jacobs and Warren Casey. The transformation that Olivia Newton-John's character underwent in the movie was mirrored by a change in Newton-John's public persona. On the success of *Grease*, Newton-John released her tenth album, unsubtly titled *Totally Hot*. The cover image found her in stiletto heels and black leather.

Leather was also emblematic for the band Van Halen, featuring guitar virtuoso Eddie Van Halen, his drumming brother Alex, bassist Michael Anthony and singer David Lee Roth. Eddie and Alex had been born in the Netherlands to a Dutch musician father and Javanese mother. Due to prejudice against their mixed-race family, they relocated to California in 1962. The brothers formed a high-school band that eventually led to Van Halen. The outfit's 1978 eponymous debut LP perfected heavy metal stylings, although the critics were far from kind. The brief instrumental solo 'Eruption' set a whole new benchmark for guitar virtuosity, as well as showcasing the tapping technique, using both right and left hands on the fretboard. Although this manner of playing had been brandished by the likes of Canned Heat's Harvey Mandel, Randy Resnick of the band Pure Food and Drug Act, as well as Steve Hackett of Genesis, Eddie Van Halen popularised it in the world of heavy rock, along with unmatched playing precision. Van Halen's success would find each new album outselling the previous one.

Nothing exceeds like excess

Before a Jefferson Starship concert in Germany, Grace Slick was throwing tantrums and demanding more booze. Once on stage, she started goose-stepping and giving 'heil Hitler' salutes, at the same time abusing the audience, saying, 'Who won the fucking war?' She had performed a similar routine in 1969 at New York's Fillmore East, that time wearing an SS uniform. On this occasion, Marty Balin grabbed her by the head to put an end to the embarrassment. Paul Kantner sacked her on the spot. She became one of the first high-profile rock stars to publicly admit to attending AA. As she put it, 'Everybody knew I was a big drunk. Plus, booze and cocaine is an ugly combination. I loved it. I lived on it.'[2]

The Who's Keith Moon, no stranger to booze and drugs, was struggling to perform musically. Recording the track 'Music Must Change' – an almost hysterical, theatrical tune in 6/8 time – proved a challenge for the drummer. According to Daltrey, 'After four takes and countless apologies, he leapt up from behind his drums and shouted, "I'm the best Keith Moon-type drummer in the world!"'[3] Ironically, the song used music as a metaphor for drugs.

Cowed by the twin threats of disco and punk, most of the songs on The Who's new album *Who Are You* focused on the difficulties of remaining relevant. The opening track, 'New Song', acknowledges the pressure to provide another hit without breaking the band's formula. 'Sister Disco', with its swirling, proggish keyboards, asserts that the disco craze deserves to die a horrible death. 'Guitar and Pen' is about Townshend's determination to write songs and the terrible burden this placed on him. The album concludes with the title track: a chilling tune about Townshend's fear of anonymity, the shallowness of fame, and the purpose of life. It came about after Townshend had been at an all-day meeting with the band's former manager, Allen Klein, trying to resolve their legal stoush over royalties. Afterwards, Townshend went out drinking, where he met up with Steve Jones and Paul Cook of The Sex Pistols. Sometime in the wee hours, Townshend was found slumped in a Soho doorway by a policeman. He wrote 'Who Are You' the next day, and it became one of their biggest hits in the US.

Around midyear, Keith Moon relocated from Malibu (no doubt to neighbour Steve McQueen's relief) to a London flat owned by Harry Nilsson. Ominously, it was the same apartment in which Cass Elliot had died four years previously. As Pete Townshend wrote, 'At the time, Keith was juggling doctors to create confusion and to get the most medication he could …'[4] A doctor, unfamiliar with the drummer's lifestyle, prescribed him clomethiazole, a sedative generally used in a supervised environment to assist people with alcohol addictions. Moon was found dead in his bed, with the coroner noting that there were thirty-two clomethiazole pills in his body. One-fifth that number would have been sufficient to kill him. Moon, the king of excess, went out excessively.

The Who determined to keep working and begin a new tour, a decision Townshend later explained thus: 'The incredibly charged emotions around Keith's death made me lose all logic. I was convinced that everything would be OK if we could only play, perform and tour … my mind flipped.'[5] Roger Daltrey offered a more clinical justification: '[W]e wanted the spirit of the group to which Keith contributed so much to go on … I was determined that the band should survive because of the music. And, of course. there was self-interest as well. It was my profession and my life.'[6]

Alice Cooper was also battling alcohol addiction, descending into a hell of his own making. He entered a sanatorium for people with mental disorders. While incarcerated, Cooper hatched a new concept album, with songs inspired by characters he met in the institution. The lyrics were co-written with Bernie Taupin. As Cooper later acknowledged, 'This album was a total confession. The audience had been through my alcoholism with me, so let them be through the cure with me. I was sober – what if they don't like me like this?'[7] The inside opening of the LP cover featured a staged scene in a psychiatric institution. The album performed best in Australia, where it reached number twelve, but it was a lacklustre effort. On the LP sleeve were the words 'Inmates! In memory of Moonie', a homage to his old drinking buddy. Cooper would return to boozing, adding cocaine to the mix.

Terry Kath, guitarist and founding member of Chicago, was also deeply involved in substance abuse, as well as being fixated with guns. Following a party, he began to play with his weapons, twirling them around and holding them to his head. His last words to band technician Don Johnson were: 'What do you think I'm gonna do, blow my brains out?' He showed Johnson the empty magazine, put the semiautomatic pistol to his head and fired. There was a bullet in the chamber.

Murderous punk

Malcolm McLaren was determined to sell British punk to Americans. He booked the beginning of The Sex Pistols' US tour into conservative southern states, knowing it would provoke controversy. Sid Vicious was now taking heroin, alcohol, barbiturates and methadone, and was almost impervious to pain. Before stepping onto the stage in Dallas, Vicious carved the words 'gimme a fix' into his chest with a razor. He called the audience 'cowboy faggots', which resulted in a full can of beer bouncing off his head.

As McLaren no doubt anticipated, fights occurred during the attempted tour, with Vicious even being beaten up by security guards hired by the band's American label. Despite his moniker, Vicious was not a fighting man, but rather a sensitive, skinny kid from a dud family. His mother had been taking drugs as long as the lad could remember. By 1978, John/Sid was trying to live the life of a character that had been largely imposed upon him. As many of his friends have attested, underneath the artifice he was a nice, friendly guy.

The Pistols, however, were at each other's throats. The band's last performance occurred in the birthplace of the hippie counterculture, San Francisco. Johnny Rotten walked out after performing just one song, famously saying to the audience, 'Ever get the feeling you've been cheated?' Rotten was fed up not only with Sid's substance abuse, but also with McLaren's media manipulation.

The Sex Pistols had already become the harbingers of doom for punk. As Nicholas Rombes wrote, 'Punk worked best in secret, as a rumour, an expectation. In confirming the public's expectations, The Sex Pistols also destroyed them. They were against method. Which meant they had no choice but to destroy themselves.'[8]

A few weeks later, McLaren took drummer Paul Cook and guitarist Steve Jones to Rio de Janeiro for another publicity stunt: recording a couple of songs with the Great Train Robber, Ronnie Biggs. They taped the odious 'Belsen Was a Gas' and 'A Punk Prayer', but McLaren's manipulation of Biggs smacked of desperation, not clever marketing.

Meanwhile, Sid Vicious had flown to New York, passing into a drug-induced coma mid-flight and waking up in a New York hospital. In the big apple, he also returned to the dubious embrace of Nancy Spungen. The pair went to Paris, where Nancy cut her wrists, not for the first time. Then they both shifted to London, where they performed just once with a makeshift band dubbed Vicious White Kids. Johnny Rotten, meanwhile, had reverted to being plain old John Lydon, teaming up with Keith Levene, Jah Wobble and Jim Walker to record an album as Public Image Ltd.

Sid was without a career or friends, so he and Nancy went back to New York, where they aimed to insert him into the local punk scene, with Nancy acting as his manager. They holed up in the Chelsea Hotel, home to various drug peddlers, prostitutes and underground artists. A few lumpy performances occurred at Max's Kansas City. On 11 October 1978, Sid and Nancy threw a party in their Chelsea apartment. Sid reportedly took a fistful of Tuinal tablets, a highly addictive barbiturate sedative, which knocked him out. The following morning, Nancy was found dead on their bathroom floor, having been stabbed in the belly with Sid's hunting knife. The stab wound was not deep, but Nancy had died from gradual blood loss. Sid was arrested for murder. He gave the police confusing and conflicting statements, among them an admission of guilt.

McLaren believed Sid was innocent and bailed him out using money provided by Virgin Records. He then hired lawyer Francis Lee Bailey Jr, who had represented Patty Hearst. McLaren, never one to miss an opportunity, announced that The Sex Pistols would be reuniting to record a Christmas album, returns from which would fund Sid's legal defence. Vivienne Westwood began producing T-shirts emblazoned with 'She's Dead. I'm Alive. I'm Yours!'.

Out on bail, Sid was left in the care of his drug-addict mother, Anne Beverley. During this time, he slashed his arms with a broken lightbulb and was again taken to hospital. After being patched up, Sid began dating girls. Some weeks later, he was at a nightclub where Skafish were playing. Vicious was being obnoxious, distracting the band and flirting with a crew member. Patti Smith's brother, Todd Smith, asked Sid to back off, at which point Sid broke a beer bottle and shoved the glass into Todd's face. Skafish's road manager punched Vicious and threw him down a flight of stairs. A few days later, Sid Vicious was charged with assaulting Todd Smith.

The Sex Pistols had helped make Virgin Records the premier label for punk and its offshoots. Virgin had since signed The Motors, XTC, The Skids, Magazine, Penetration and The Members, all of which, according to Branson, were selling well. Punk concerts were breaking out of small venues. The Stranglers were the headline act at an open-air concert in Battersea Park, supported, oddly, by Peter Gabriel. The Stranglers arranged for five strippers to disrobe during their number 'Nice 'n' Sleazy'. The police interviewed the girls afterwards, but no charges were laid.

Over in the US, a more unusual concert was staged in the Napa State Mental Hospital. The Cramps and The Mutants somehow managed to get permission to perform for free at the institution. What's more, The Cramps' act was videoed, so you can witness the outcome for yourself. The band let rip with their standard, no-holds-barred performance. Various inmates try to dance, join in, imitate the band, grapple over access to the microphone and engage in all manner of audience participation. At one stage, front man Lux Interior yells, 'Somebody told me you people are crazy. But I'm not so sure about that. You seem to be alright to me.' For The Mutants, it was just more performance art. They had previously performed while inside large cardboard boxes, and had also played to a school for the deaf, where the kids held balloons so they could feel the music.

CBGB debuted Wendy O. Williams and the Plasmatics, possibly the most outrageous act of the era. Lead singer Wendy often sported a mohawk hairstyle, appeared in skimpy or see-through outfits, sometimes with electric tape on her nipples, and chainsawed guitars as part of the act.

Poly Styrene, from Britain's X-Ray Spex, eschewed sex appeal altogether. The band only released five singles and one album, but they hold a hallowed place in punk history. Their album *Germfree Adolescents* unpicks consumer capitalism and authenticity. The track 'Identity' unleashes on media manipulation of young consumers. 'I Am a Poseur' is an interesting double-edged song about exhibitionism and voyeurism, in which Poly Styrene attests to being a poseur but not caring what others think. As an honest statement of punk's fundamental drive to garner attention, it's arguably without peer. Throughout the LP, Poly's searing vocals cut through like a soldering iron into flesh. All up, it's a far more musically adept and interesting album than a lot of punk, with some nifty shifts in metre, and clever fills featuring Rudi Thomson's saxophone.

Siouxsie and the Banshees also released their debut album *The Scream*. The drums were recorded in sections, with bass drum and snare first, then cymbals and afterwards tom-toms. The result is the sort of machine-like percussive precision one might find in disco music. But Siouxsie's voice and the angst-ridden aggression are a long way from the stylings of disco. Their version of The Beatles' 'Helter Skelter' begins with slow buzz-saw guitar that accelerates into a thrashing onslaught, with Sioux so off-key it's unbearable.

The Saints, now based in the UK, released their second album, *Eternally Yours*, this time with a bigger sound that incorporated a horn section. It was well removed from the cookie-cutter punk of the day, with some critics falling over themselves to praise the effort, while others, like Robert Christgau in *Village Voice*, appalled by the inclusion of R&B stylings. In the same year, the former Brisbane lads released *Prehistoric Sounds*, this time with hints of jazz and soul. But EMI were unimpressed and dumped the band from its roster.

In any case, The Saints were falling apart. Guitarist Ed Kuepper and drummer Ivor Hay returned to Oz, while bass player Algy Ward joined The Damned. The last man standing, vocalist Chris Bailey, simply formed a new band to continue as The Saints.

The view from the swamp

With hypocritical indifference to Britain's colonial past, the UK's Conservative opposition leader Margaret Thatcher said, '[P]eople are really rather afraid that this country might be rather swamped by people of a different culture ... we must hold out the clear prospect of an end to immigration.' She also gave credibility to the National Front by saying that 'at least they are talking about some of the problems'.[9]

In the UK, the National Front were now a force to be reckoned with, and Rock Against Racism (RAR) were ready to do that reckoning. In retaliation, white power advocates and skinheads formed a counter organisation called Rock Again Communism, which began to harass RAR-affiliated bands. They even organised their own concerts of right-wing punk acts such as The Dentists, The Ventz and Screwdriver. This subgenre of racist, often antisemitic punk was dubbed Oi!.

One of RAR's more fervent supporters was Tom Robinson. The Tom Robinson Band had enjoyed a hit single with '2-4-6-8 Motorway'. Although it's ostensibly a song about driving trucks on the highway, the chorus was inspired by a Gay Liberation marching chant: 'Two, four, six, eight, gay is twice as good as straight; three, five, seven, nine, lesbians are mighty fine.' As well as being a champion for racial inclusion, Robinson was also one of the first 'out' gay performers, writing songs specifically for and about the gay community.

The Tom Robinson Band's debut album, *Power in the Darkness*, peaked at number four on the UK albums chart. It opened with 'Up Against the Wall', a song about the rise of fascism and the social divisions it was generating. There was also 'The Winter of '79', sung from the perspective of a distant future where the narrator looks back on 1979 as a time when gays were being jailed and blacks were getting crucified. 'Long Hot Summer' called on gays to amass in strength against persecution, with similar themes also appearing in 'Ain't Gonna Take It' and 'Better Decide Which Side You're On'. The LP's closer, 'Power in the Darkness', was sung from the perspective of a far-right bigot who wants freedom from niggers and pansies, Jews and liberals. As Robinson would later say, 'The times were in flux with no strong centre … There could have been a coup. We had no idea what was going to happen.'[10]

RAR's biggest event was held in London's Victoria Park and featured The Clash, Steel Pulse, Tom Robinson Band and X-Ray Spex. Organisers planned for 10,000 people, but 100,000 showed up. Unfortunately, the power generators and the sound system were woefully inadequate for such a large crowd, but more important was the show of strength for the anti-bigotry movement. The mainstream media ignored the event, so it received zero news coverage.

Fresh waves

Pere Ubu was an American group, named in honour of avant-garde play-wright Alfred Jarry. They had been kicking around since 1975, and finally got around to recording their debut LP, *The Modern Dance*. David Thomas, the quirky co-founder and lead singer, dubbed the band 'avant-garage'. On his website today he says: 'Pere Ubu is about ideas ... Personality cult, personal dress, sunglasses and haircuts, personal hopes and dreams and fears are tiresomely irrelevant.'[11]

Pere Ubu was always a sort of art project. All manner of left-field rock luminaries have passed through the band, from Henry Cow's Chris Cutler to MC5's Wayne Kramer. *The Modern Dance* didn't sell, but like The Velvet Underground's discs, it ended up being decidedly influential. Pere Ubu's original synth player, Allen Ravenstine, is today recognised as a true pioneer of the instrument, using it more for effects à la Brian Eno than for any melodic capability. *Rolling Stone* called the debut album 'harsh and wilfully ugly'.[12] David Thomas's unique voice gives the music much of its disquieting quality.

Pere Ubu released a second album in 1978, *Dub Housing*, which is also regarded as a classic. In distancing himself from punk, David Thomas called the punk movement backward-looking and dumb. The attitude further illustrates the schism between American bands who were reasonably literate and conscious of their roles as artistic provocateurs and the British bands who wouldn't know Rimbaud from Rambo.

While influenced by punk, new wave refused to embrace punk's musical amateurishness. Even the term 'new wave' was an academic reference to French new wave cinema, which set out to break cinematic rules. The detached coolness of new wave cinema was replicated by many new wave musicians in the late 1970s. Blondie, Talking Heads, Duran Duran and others weren't in the business of making emotionally resonant music. Rather, it was vibrant and clinical, with lyrics most often delivered in a dispassionate manner.

Blondie's second album, *Plastic Letters*, performed best in Holland and the UK. They had left their original label, Private Stock, to join Chrysalis Records, but the buyout of their contract left the band a million dollars in debt. The single 'Denis' performed well in Europe and Australia. Debbie Harry and Chris Stein had 'discovered' the song on a K-Tel compilation album. The original version, actually titled 'Denise', had been a 1963 hit for doowop group Randy and the Rainbows. Later in the year, Blondie released a breakthrough album, *Parallel Lines*, produced by Australian-born hit maker Mike Chapman. It yielded half a dozen successful singles. There was also a nasty stalking song, 'One Way or Another'. (Clearly, stalking wasn't considered a big deal at the time, as The Police would also enjoy their biggest hit a few years later with the very creepy 'Every Breath You Take'.)

Patti Smith had largely recovered from her neck injury and came up with her album *Easter*. It included a single with a sticky chorus, 'Because the Night', co-written with Bruce Springsteen. It charted exceptionally well, becoming her biggest hit. The album also included a track titled 'Rock N Roll Nigger', in which Smith attempted to cast herself as a nigger by redefining the word to mean any rebellious and honourable outsider – perhaps a play on Norman Mailer's essay 'The White Negro'. It also invoked Yoko Ono's song 'Woman Is the Nigger of the World', but inevitably, the crudity of the appropriation stuck in the craw of many critics, with Robert Christgau deciding Smith was 'full of shit'.[13] In *Rolling Stone*, Dave Marsh complained that Smith had no understanding of the word nigger's connotation, which was well removed from outlawry. For decades, Smith would pugnaciously continue to perform the song, ignoring the fact that the word was never hers to redefine. Many of her staunchest fans remain perplexed at this obstinacy. A lesser controversy relating to *Easter* was that the cover image revealed Smith's unshaven armpit. Even her label was concerned that the album wouldn't be displayed prominently in stores because of a tiny bit of body hair.

Ian Dury and the Blockheads' single 'Hit Me With Your Rhythm Stick' provided Stiff Records with its first number one hit. Co-written by Dury and multi-instrumentalist Chaz Jankel, it's an infectious, up-tempo dance number with a screamer of a sax solo, including a brief section in which Davey Payne plays two saxes simultaneously. Also worth noting is the super-busy bass line and the way the song gradually builds towards its crescendo ending.

Devo's debut, *Q: Are We Not Men? A: We Are Devo!*, was produced by the ubiquitous Brian Eno. The band attempted to turn fashion conformity into a thing of ridicule, with band members dressed in futuristically absurd outfits. Their minimalist techno-pop suggested that music, like society per se, would inevitably become mechanical and impassive: Devo was punk's nihilism in shiny plastic headgear. And, like punk, Devo were also averse to sex and, more particularly, the physical body. 'Uncontrollable Urge' demonstrated a revulsion towards basic libido, while 'Shrivel-Up' described the ageing process. 'Mongoloid' portrayed a person with Down syndrome, for no good purpose, while 'Gut Feeling' was yet another song about a man hating his female partner, ending with a repeated phrase about slapping one's mammy down.

Brian Eno also produced the far more satisfying Talking Heads album *More Songs About Buildings and Food*, which demonstrated the band's affinity with black American music. Tina Weymouth's bass and Chris Frantz's drumming propel each track, with a sound that is now polished and replete. There are also elements of the sort of guitar-driven repetitive intricacy that would become a hallmark of Robert Fripp's reconstituted King Crimson. Indeed, guitar maestro Adrian Belew would end up being a member of both outfits. At this time, however, Belew was working in Frank Zappa's band.

No more waving

At the beginning of the decade there were only a handful of words to describe rock genres, but by 1978 there were new genres popping up like weeds. No wave, for example, was largely centred in New York. No wave saw itself as a rebuttal of punk's emphasis on rock tropes and clichés, particularly its reliance on late '50s rock 'n' roll. No wave musicians experimented with deconstructing music using noise, dissonance and even elements of jazz and disco. The movement did, however, borrow punk's fundamentally nihilistic world view.

While Brian Eno was in New York to produce Talking Heads' second album, he caught performances by no wave bands DNA, Contortions, Mars, plus Teenage Jesus and the Jerks. He offered to produce a compilation album, which became *No New York*, released on Antilles. One can't help but wonder if people actually enjoyed listening to this stuff, or if it was simply an intellectual pursuit. Punk enthusiast Nicholas Rombes suggested that no wave 'boiled down' punk until it disappeared, resulting in 'self-conscious art that in order to like it you had to hate music, because No Wave is, at its heart, music for people who hate music'.[14]

Such a description, however, doesn't apply to John Lurie's outfit The Lounge Lizards, who toyed with jazz conventions, making witty music that incorporated stabs of electronica, free improvisation and *musique concrète*. David Cunningham's loose collective of avant-garde musicians called The Flying Lizards was perhaps London's answer to New York's no wave scene, their most memorable offerings being deadpan covers of pop standards 'Money' and 'Summertime Blues'.

But my personal favourite of the quasi-no-wave outfits is Peter Gordon's eccentric Love of Life Orchestra. They played their own version of funky rock, with solos that were often intentionally silly. Listen to the track 'Extended Niceties' for a good example of this approach. Less self-important than the bands mentioned above, Love of Life Orchestra parodied popular music while retaining all the pleasing hooks of the music it was lampooning.

The Police were also difficult to categorise: sort of reggae-funk. Their debut album, *Outlandos d'Amour* – the title of which Sting called 'a strange concoction of Esperanto and gobbledegook'[15] – was funded by Stewart Copeland's older brother, who owned the independent label Illegal Records. The album did deliver two moderately successful singles, 'Roxanne' and 'Can't Stand Losing You', landing the band a deal with A&M Records. It also included the song 'So Lonely', which Sting admits grafted his lyrics 'on to the chord changes of Bob Marley's "No Woman, No Cry"'.[16]

All the tracks on The Police's album were written by Sting, with Summers and Copeland getting co-writing credits on just one song each. Sting would thus receive the lion's share of the royalties, a disjunct that Sting admitted would 'render our somewhat fragile democracy somewhat tenuous', and ultimately brought about the death of the band.[17] On release, the tango-like single 'Roxanne' failed to chart. A promotional campaign was mounted claiming that the BBC had banned the song because it was about prostitution. In fact, this was a big porky pie, as the BBC had simply determined not to add the single to their playlist.

The BBC did, however, ban the second single from The Police, 'Can't Stand Losing You', a reggae tune that was structurally very similar to 'Roxanne'. The Beeb was offended by the single's packaging, which featured an image of a man hanging by the neck above a block of ice that had been partially melted by a radiator. The song, about teenage suicide, nevertheless went to number two on the UK chart.

Feverish

Like punk, disco was peaking. The *Saturday Night Fever* double album continued to stampede across the world. As well as three hits for The Bee Gees, the album also spawned hits for Tavares, The Trammps, KC and the Sunshine Band and Yvonne Elliman. At one point, the LP was selling at the rate of a million copies per week, and half of the top ten singles on the UK and US charts hailed from the movie.

Discos were no longer the exclusive province of gays and people of colour. The disco phenomenon was rapidly assimilated into all aspects of Western culture, from fashion to television. Cold Chisel's Jimmy Barnes reminisced on the strangeness of this period, where Chequers Nightclub in Sydney would have his band playing 'to an empty dance floor and then the DJ would put on Play That Funky Music, flick a switch and the mirror ball would start to spin. The dance floor would be packed, full of blokes with huge collars on their shirts and way too much chest hair showing.'[18]

The Bee Gees were now tied with Elton John for having the most number one US singles in the decade, and Barry Gibb became the only songwriter in history to have written four consecutive number one singles on *Billboard*'s Hot 100 chart.

Discos were everywhere. *Billboard* estimated that 36 million Americans went to one of America's 20,000 discos in 1978. Under flashing lights and pounding music, dancers could live out their private fantasies of exceptionalism, frequently bolstered by readily available drugs. Disco fever represented, in many ways, the zenith of the 'me decade'. Albert Goldman penned an article for *Esquire* suggesting, 'Outside the entrance to every discotheque should be erected a statue to the presiding deity: Narcissus.'[19] Chic's Nile Rodgers agreed, saying, 'It was really all about Me! Me! Me! Me!'[20]

This was disco's biggest year, thanks in large part to the success of *Saturday Night Fever* but also of *Thank God It's Friday*, which starred Donna Summer. Summer's song 'Last Dance' featured in the latter, becoming the biggest disco hit for the year and winning an Oscar for Best Original Song. Summer also released her two-disc, four-act concept album *Once Upon a Time*, an absurd rags-to-riches Cinderella story delivered as a disco opera. On top of all that, she became the first woman to have a number one single, 'MacArthur Park', and number one album, *Live and More*, simultaneously on the *Billboard* charts.

Gloria Gaynor's 'I Will Survive' was one of the few disco songs of the 1970s that had the legs to become a pop anthem. That's because it actually had some meat on its bones – certainly more thematic substance than hits like 'Dance, Dance, Dance' or 'Boogie Oogie Oogie'. Written by Freddie Perren and Dino Fekaris, 'I Will Survive' was inspired by the latter being fired from Motown Records. When Polydor asked Perren to produce Gaynor's next recording, he did so on the understanding that he could also produce the B-side. In the recording session, most of the studio time was spent on the A-side, a version of 'Substitute', which had originally been recorded by The Righteous Brothers. That left just half an hour to record 'I Will Survive'. Much of the instrumental backing for the song was improvised from chord charts without the players even hearing the vocals. Gaynor then quickly recorded her part, while wearing a back brace. Her battles with back surgery, combined with the recent death of her mother, added a frisson to Gaynor's performance, which was belted out with conviction. Having failed to convince her label to push the B-side, Gaynor's husband took it to the Studio 54 deejay. Soon other deejays were also playing the song. 'I Will Survive' has become an eternal symbol of female empowerment and an LGBTIQ+ anthem.

The Village People enjoyed a hit single with 'Y.M.C.A.', from their *Cruisin'* album. The song sold 12 million copies worldwide. Nobody seemed to care, or perhaps didn't understand, that the album title was a reference to hunting for gay sex. As Village person Felipe Rose explained:

> We were proud of our gay roots, but we rode both sides of the fence very, very cleverly. It wasn't the gays who bought the albums; it was straight girls and boys. Radical gay people said we were a sell-out, and we should say we're gay and we're proud, but our feeling was we were artists and entertainers first.[21]

Alicia Bridges' smash hit 'I Love the Nightlife (Disco 'Round)' was her breakthrough number, and another calculated hit, with Bridges later admitting, 'I noticed that there were several songs in the *Billboard* Top 10 that said "Disco" – "Disco Inferno", Disco this, Disco that. So we wrote "I Love the Nightlife (Disco 'Round)" kind of as a joke. It was a huge hit, but it tied me to the diva, disco title.'[22]

Released on both album and twelve-inch single, Rod Stewart's global smash hit 'Da' Ya' Think I'm Sexy?' spent four weeks at the top of the US charts. Close listening reveals it's actually a song about male insecurity. The narrative involves a young bloke trying to get a girl into bed, needing to know that she finds him attractive. His insecurity and self-doubt even extend to phoning his mother. No doubt Rod Stewart's womanising behaviour clouded people's perception of the tune, with most assuming he was narcissistically asking the question about himself. A dire video clip in which Rod seduces a pretty girl while watching himself on TV only reinforced the thematic confusion.

Duane Hitchings, who co-wrote the song with Carmine Appice and Stewart, argued that the song was a spoof on disco music and the disco culture, but audiences didn't see the joke. 'Da' Ya' Think I'm Sexy?' took its melody from the song 'Taj Mahal', by Brazilian musician Jorge Ben Jor, which resulted in legal action and an out-of-court settlement. Rod Stewart insisted it was 'unconscious plagiarism'.[23] Stewart also admitted to lifting the string arrangement for the song from Bobby Womack's '(If You Want My Love) Put Something Down On It'. All's fair in love, war and disco.

All manner of performers were now scrambling to jump on the disco gravy train: Cher with 'Take Me Home', Dolly Parton's 'Baby I'm Burnin'' and even jazz flautist Herbie Mann with 'Superman'. The Jacksons were back in the game with 'Shake Your Body (Down to the Ground)', and even The Rolling Stones joined the disco delirium with 'Miss You', which went to number one in the US. Jagger insisted that the song wasn't conceived as a disco tune, but Richards admitted it was indeed calculated to be a disco hit. 'Miss You' was the Stones' eighth and last number one single in the US.

The disco boom inevitably changed radio. When New York's WKTU shifted from soft rock to disco, their market share jumped from 0.9 per cent to 11.3 per cent, making them the highest rated radio station in the country. US television also began syndicating shows such as *Disco Magic* and *Dance Fever*. Disco had fomented a multi-billion-dollar industry, and it seemed everyone wanted a piece of the 120-beats-per-minute action. By the end of the year, Studio 54 had taken US$7 million, which did not go unnoticed by the IRS. The year concluded with a raid on the club, in which financial accounts, drugs and other contraband were seized, plus massive stashes of cash hidden in ceiling panels and garbage bags.

To the heights

Amid all this, nineteen-year-old Kate Bush appeared like a breath of fresh air. Her debut single, 'Wuthering Heights', based on the gothic novel of the same name, hit the top of the charts. It was full of supernatural imagery and obsessive love. The Sex Pistols' John Lydon loved the song and brought the single home to play for his mother, who reportedly said it sounded like 'a bag of cats'.[24] But Lydon viewed the idiosyncratic, fashion-ignoring Bush as a fellow renegade. More significantly, Kate Bush became the first British woman to garner a number one hit with a self-written song. Imagine it taking so long!

Young Kate had been writing songs at home, accompanying herself on guitar and piano. A family friend mentioned her to Pink Floyd's Dave Gilmour, who visited and liked what he heard. The kindly Gilmour funded professional recording of three demo songs, which culminated in Bush being signed by EMI. They put her on a retainer and stalled further recording while Bush continued her studies in dance and mime. She also hit the pubs with her own band to hone her skills.

When it finally materialised, her debut album, *The Kick Inside*, was like nothing else in the marketplace. It became a runaway success. Co-producers Gilmour and Andrew Powell convinced Bush to use top-notch studio musicians rather than her own KT Bush Band. As percussionist Morris Pert said:

> Within twenty minutes, half an hour, we realized that we were not working with your average pop singer … When all of us came out of that first session, we all went to the canteen or bar or whatever it was, and we thought, well, either she's going to absolutely bomb, or she's gonna start a complete revolution.[25]

Bush had presented close to 100 songs for consideration. The thirteen chosen songs for *The Kick Inside* were as brilliant as they were audacious. Full of literary, philosophical and often dark subject matter, they were sexy, inventive and alluring. Notably, the material was also enormously feminine, but without resorting to cliché. Bush's voice was breathtakingly unique, unprecedented in its range as well as in its ability to slice through radio and hi-fi speakers. She arrived as a fully formed artist. As one scribe summed up, Kate Bush was 'the high priestess of postpunk girl artiness'.[26]

EMI promoted *The Kick Inside* with a poster of Bush in a tight pink top that emphasised her breasts. She hated being sold as a body, and this early lesson encouraged her to take increasing control over both her product and its promotion. She quickly established her own publishing and management companies.

While EMI had been happy to wait for the first album, they now wanted a follow-up posthaste. Before the end of the year, *Lionheart* was recorded and released, but it didn't reach the giddy heights of her debut. It mostly relied on songs rejected for *Kick*, and the cover image of Bush in a silly lion's costume was ill-conceived. The singles 'Hammer Horror' and 'Wow' charted, with the latter being about a gay actor struggling with sycophantic attention. It even mentions the use of Vaseline, with Bush patting her bottom in the accompanying film clip to indicate what the reference was about.

Breaking in

While no Australian singles made it into the Australian top ten for the year, Samantha Sang's 'Emotion' and Dragon's 'Are You Old Enough?' did squeak into the top twenty. The latter was a song about a jailed man pining for some underage nookie. Despite promoting paedophilia, it received a *TV Week* award. Among Australian album sales, local acts were still languishing, with Little River Band's *Sleeper Catcher* coming in at number eighteen for the year, the only Australian act to make the top twenty-five.

More significantly, *Sleeper Catcher* peaked at sixteen in the US. It would be the first album recorded in Australia to go platinum in the American market. A compilation LRB album, *It's a Long Way There – Greatest Hits*, also performed well, with the band's undemanding soft rock finding its market. As pianist and songwriter Brian Cadd put it, 'Little River Band legitimised the Australian band thing ... from that point onwards the phrase "I've got this tape of this Australian band" meant a lot more to an American A&R guy than it had before then.'[27]

AC/DC were at make-or-break time in their efforts to dominate the American market. Tracks for the new album *Powerage* were presented to Atlantic, which couldn't find a single to release. The band went back into the studio and exited with 'Rock 'n' Roll Damnation', a rock anthem to rival Queen's 'We Will Rock You'. It was different to their usual fare, lacking a big solo from Angus, but it finally delivered their first US Top 40 hit.

In Oakland, Foreigner refused to go on after AC/DC, and another punch-up nearly ensued. A live album, with a cover featuring Angus impaled by his guitar, was released under the title *If You Want Blood You've Got It*. In the UK, Angus Young was now being feted in ways not dissimilar to Eric Clapton in the late '60s. For the next album, Atlantic insisted that they work with a new producer, forcing Malcolm and Angus to fire their older brother George.

Midnight Oil established the Powderworks label and released their debut eponymous album. Although it didn't catch on, this hardworking outfit were building an enthusiastic live audience, performing some 200 gigs in their first year.

Warner Music signed up Cold Chisel, but the band were unhappy with the anaemic nature of their debut self-titled album. As Jimmy Barnes put it, '[I]f you'd been around in 1977 and 1978, you'd know we sounded nothing like that album.'[28] The track 'Khe Sanh', a post-Vietnam story, was released as a single but banned from commercial radio, ostensibly for its sexually suggestive line about legs being open. As Jimmy Barnes ruefully noted, 'They [the censors] had to ban something once a week to keep the

Catholic Church happy.'[29] Despite its classification, the song was played on 2JJ, and quickly became the band's signature tune.

It wasn't easy being a member of some these volatile pub rock bands. As Barnes explained, he was living on whisky and 'cheap speed':

> I wanted everything around me to be out of control because that was when I felt comfortable. I could hide in amongst the chaos and no-one would see what a fuck-up I was. So whenever the boys tried to settle the whole thing down, I did my best to sabotage it. I needed the chaos.[30]

Around this time, John Woodruff, Ray Hearn and Rod Willis formed Dirty Pool Artists Management in Australia. Just as Led Zeppelin's Peter Grant had shifted the goalposts for international touring acts by demanding 90 per cent of the door takings, so Dirty Pool shifted the power hierarchy away from venue owners, promoters and agents and back towards the artists themselves. Dirty Pool booked and managed The Angels, Cold Chisel and Flowers, who would become Icehouse. Before Dirty Pool, as Jimmy Barnes put it, 'It wasn't unusual for a band to sell $5000 worth of tickets and fill a pub with drinkers but still only get paid $750. That fee had to cover PA/lighting costs, crew wages, travel and commissions before the musicians received their first dollar.'[31]

And so Dirty Pool introduced live performance contracts into the Australian music scene. Instead of a flat fee, bands kept 90 per cent of the door takings, and thus were paid according to how many punters showed up. What's more, Dirty Pool cut out the promoter, doing all the marketing themselves. In this radical shake-up of the system, popular bands could demand low-ish door fees and still make more than they had under the previous system. What's more, the publicans and venue owners no longer risked paying a fee to a band when nobody showed up to hear them: the financial risk was borne by the artist. This new approach was a boon to the local music scene. 'Live music exploded around Australia,' Barnes said. 'Dirty Pool helped save an industry that was coughing up blood and turned it into a very big business.'[32]

Leftovers

There were still diehard artists working in the prog rock and fusion fields, happily ignoring the music industry's obsessions with punk, new wave and disco. Godley & Creme's wonderful album *L*, full of complex, witty music and studio wizardry, was criminally overlooked. Yes managed to release a new LP, *Tormato*, which would be their fastest-selling disc, going platinum in the US within two months of release. ELP were on their last legs, but contractually obliged to produce another album, which resulted in the best forgotten *Love Beach*.

Genesis had shrunk to a trio of Tony Banks, Phil Collins and Mike Rutherford, and were now producing shorter songs with far less instrumental posturing. Relieving Collins from the drum stool on tour was Chester Thompson, previously of Zappa's band as well as Weather Report. Here was a black jazz drummer from the US who could read music, trying to fit in with a decidedly white British prog band whose members couldn't. As Thompson said, 'It was the biggest adjustment I've ever had to make, musically and culturally.'[33] Genesis also co-opted American guitarist Daryl Stuermer to help with their live act.

As well as producing for a range of artists, Brian Eno was exploring different roles for modern music. The first of his ambient music projects was 1975's *Discreet Music*, but the next, *Ambient 1: Music for Airports*, turned out to be far more pleasurable. The liner notes for the LP explained: 'Ambient Music must be able to accommodate many levels of listening attention without enforcing one in particular; it must be as ignorable as it is interesting.'

Eno had conceived of ambient music while he was recuperating in a hospital after being hit by a taxi. A friend had brought him an album of harp music to listen to, but it was left playing at a very low volume, and Eno couldn't get out of bed to adjust the volume. So he surrendered himself to a different way of hearing. For *Music for Airports* he marshalled assistance from Robert Wyatt on piano and three female vocalists. It ended up being an enormously influential project, with its floating, shimmering piano, ethereal vocals and tape loops all demonstrating a very different way of approaching music: pretty much the opposite of everything rock music had been attempting for more than two decades.

1979

Too Much Too Young

The year began with a Music for UNICEF Concert conceived by Robert Stigwood, The Bee Gees and David Frost. The televised concert was held in the General Assembly Hall of the United Nations and featured some of the top names in pop music: ABBA, The Bee Gees, Andy Gibb, Olivia Newton-John, John Denver, Earth, Wind & Fire, Rita Coolidge, Kris Kristofferson, Rod Stewart and Donna Summer, plus a sixty-six-piece orchestra. In truth, not all the performances were live, with ABBA and The Bee Gees lip-syncing to their songs. The performers donated copyright royalties from one song each to UNICEF. While the concert itself raised under a million dollars, the royalties garnered a reported US$100 million, and the event was broadcast in seventy countries.

The Rolling Stones performed two concerts in Ontario to benefit the Canadian National Institute for the Blind. Their motivation was perhaps less altruistic, being dictated by Keith Richards' drug sentence. While one portion of the tickets were free to blind patrons, the rest were sold to the public, with fans lining up for days to purchase them. They would be the band's only concerts during 1979. The trainwreck that was Keith Richards' private life took another deep dive when a seventeen-year-old boy shot himself in the head in Richards' and Anita Pallenberg's bed, with Pallenberg in the room to witness the act. Ten-year-old Marlon was downstairs, but his father was in Paris recording with the Stones.

Walls were big this year. Pink Floyd's album *The Wall* was America's biggest-selling LP in 1979. Third on the list was Michael Jackson's *Off the Wall*, his fifth studio album but the first on Epic Records instead of Motown. It was also the first produced by Quincy Jones, a collaboration that would see Jackson achieve stratospheric success in the 1980s. A pot-pourri of disco mixed with funk, R&B and soft rock, *Off the Wall* included tunes penned by Jackson as well as Paul McCartney, Stevie Wonder and Carol Bayer Sager, with five songs released as singles, including the chart-topper 'Don't Stop 'Til You Get Enough'. A breakthrough disc for Jackson, it was hailed by both *Rolling Stone* and *Melody Maker* as classy.

The US top ten albums also included works by The Bee Gees, Supertramp, AC/DC, The Eagles, Dire Straits, Led Zeppelin, Christopher Cross and Van Halen. Strangely, AC/DC didn't make the top ten in Australia. Again there were no homegrown acts on the Oz list, although Cold Chisel and The Angels made it into the top twenty.

Techno savvy

Although punk was really just a minority movement, its impact reverberated throughout the music business. Linda Ronstadt's LP *Mad Love* had precious little overdubbing, was more stripped-back and, as she described it, 'more rock 'n' roll, more raw, more basic'.[1] It also featured three songs by Elvis Costello and three by The Cretones' Mark Goldenberg. The album debuted at fifth spot on the *Billboard* chart, which was a first for any female artist. It was also Ronstadt's seventh consecutive album to sell over a million copies.

Punk also had a decisive impact on Fleetwood Mac's final outing for the decade, the double album *Tusk*. Having toured after *Rumours*, the romantically tortured band members took a hiatus from one another. When they reassembled to begin work on the new album, the headstrong Lindsey Buckingham was determined not to make it sound like another *Rumours*. Indeed, he is said to have blackmailed the rest of the band, threatening to quit if they didn't adhere to his new vision that incorporated elements of punk and new wave. Insiders have referred to this dogmatism as megalomania. Adding to the weirdness of the incredibly long recording process – a full year, working six days a week – were mountains of cocaine and other stimulants. Complete self-indulgence was now de rigueur among

Mac members, each of whom had a massive retinue of hangers-on. *Tusk* cost over US$1 million to create, eclipsing Queen's *A Night at the Opera* to become the most expensive rock album recorded up to that time. Mick Fleetwood asserts that *Tusk* 'proved to be an album way ahead of its time'.[2] Really?

In the end, the product is so layered and nuanced that it is far removed from the immediacy of punk. Nevertheless, the harder, edgier, more experimental sound came as something of a surprise to many fans. The double LP charted and sold well, but nothing like the figures that *Rumours* had achieved. As with The Beatles' *White Album*, *Tusk* is the work of disparate performers frequently working in isolation from one another. Three of the tracks ended up being recorded by Buckingham without any input from other band members. Listen to one of those, 'The Ledge', to get an idea of where Buckingham's head was at.

Stevie Nicks' tune 'Sara' was a minor hit and another song born of romantic turmoil. In this case, Nicks had begun a relationship with the band's drummer, Mick Fleetwood, only to discover that he had been cheating on her with one of her closest friends, named, of course, Sara. This really was the *Peyton Place* of rock bands.

Kate Bush went on her first tour, performing twenty-four shows in six weeks. This was remarkable for a couple of reasons: she wouldn't tour again for another thirty-five years, and she helped pioneer new technology. Her sound engineer, Martin Fisher, developed a wireless microphone so Bush could dance and sing without being encumbered by cables. It may have been fashioned from a wire coathanger, but it was the first example of a wireless microphone being used on stage.

In fact, the end of the decade saw many advances in music technology – ones that would change recording forever. Kate Bush was one of the first artists to use the new Fairlight Computer Musical Instrument, which was both a synthesiser and digital sampler. John Paul Jones, Herbie Hancock and Joni Mitchell also snaffled up Fairlight CMIs.

Home recording, now more commonplace thanks to punk, was also facilitated by the arrival of the Tascam Portastudio, the first four-track recorder using cassette tapes. Digital technology was also beginning to make its mark. Stephen Stills entered the Record Plant studio in Los Angeles and started recording material using their newfangled digital equipment. He thus became the first major-label American recording artist to record and master an LP with digital technology. However, a falling-out between artist and label meant the songs never saw the light of day. Midyear, Ry Cooder was the first popular music artist to actually release a digitally recorded major-label album, *Bop Till You Drop*, which charted best in Australia and New Zealand. The next digital album was Stevie Wonder's *Journey Through the Secret Life of Plants*, a documentary soundtrack which also sold well. It included the first examples of digital sampling, utilising the Computer Music Melodian. By the end of the year, Christopher Cross's self-titled album became the first digitally recorded LP to make it into the charts.

Joy Division recorded their seminal album *Unknown Pleasures* using pioneering AMS Stereo Digital Delay technology. This unit allowed performers to add delay to any signal passing through it, and to adjust that delay down to milliseconds, producing a ghostly sound that gave the album its unique tonal atmosphere.

The Sony Walkman, a small, portable cassette player, first hit the market in Japan. Suddenly, music listeners could have a personalised playlist piped directly to their ears. This was a gargantuan shift in the way music could be consumed. As the Walkman and its competitors penetrated Western society, the nature of popular music changed. Music became increasingly personalised. The cassette tape played through a headset connected to a Walkman meant actively excluding other people from the listening experience. The idea of music as a shared experience was being eroded, a trajectory that would reach its apogee in the era of streaming, where there is no physical medium at all.

Many consumers were now copying records onto blank cassettes. Where buying a record was making a financial commitment to an artist, copying a piece of music onto tape negated any consideration of investment in the artist's career. By the end of the decade, the British Phonographic

Industry claimed that home taping was resulting in over £200 million in lost record sales.

The cassette would also become a tool for social and political change across the planet. Easy to duplicate and move about, cassettes helped disseminate Western music throughout the third world and also behind the Iron Curtain.

As to where popular music had found itself at the end of the decade, Linda Ronstadt had this to say:

> Right now there is a whole lot of disco and it's just not the kind of music that inspires you or that gives you a personality to get involved with. The Seventies was a polished-up version of a lot of the things coming out of the Fifties and Sixties. I think we refined them past their prime: like racing horses that have been overbred – they run fast but their bones break.[3]

Certainly disco's bones would prove to be very fragile indeed.

Dying disco

According to one estimate, by the end of the decade there were more than 100,000 discotheques operating across the world.[4] At one point in early 1979, disco songs occupied eight of the top ten places on the *Billboard* Hot 100. The Bee Gees' fifteenth album, *Spirits Having Flown*, went to number one across the planet and yielded three more hit singles. Blondie's single 'Heart of Glass' from the previous year's *Parallel Lines* had a disco beat and became the band's first number one international hit. The song caused multiple controversies. Radio stations banned it because it included the phrase 'pain in the ass', but Blondie was also accused of selling out to disco, ostracising the band from many of their contemporaries in the new wave scene. Even the band's drummer, Clem Burke, refused to play the song live at first. But Blondie had been elevated from fringe act to mainstream hit makers, with their *Eat to the Beat* LP reaching the top of the UK charts.

Electric Light Orchestra's LP *Discovery* should have been pronounced 'disco … very'. Village People pumped out two charting LPs, while Donna Summer's *Bad Girls* LP was the biggest-selling album of her career, going platinum within a week of its release. She even teamed up with Barbra Streisand to record a disco hit, 'No More Tears (Enough Is Enough)'. Cher begrudgingly released an album full of disco tunes, but perhaps the weirdest disco disc was Hollywood actress Ethel Merman's effort, *The Ethel Merman Disco Album*, full of Cole Porter, Irving Berlin and George Gershwin tunes bastardised into disco pulp.

Melba Moore, who enjoyed a disco hit with 'You Stepped into My Life', admitted, 'We're in a period of the McDonald's of music, where it's mass-marketed like junk food. I don't know what good is any more.'[5] There was also a seedy undercurrent, where black female artists like Donna Summer and Grace Jones played up their sexiness, arguably reinforcing the myth that black women were more promiscuous.

Having swamped the public with imitative, mediocre product, the record companies were unprepared for the backlash that inevitably came. Some white males, particularly those fond of hard rock and metal, were affronted by the unbridled success of a music genre whose adherents included homosexuals, blacks and Latinos. But others were just offended by disco's banality. Suddenly, FM radio stations in America began running anti-disco campaigns. Midway through the year, Chicago deejay Steve Dahl staged a 'Disco Demolition Night' at a White Sox baseball game. More rock fans than baseball fans were among the reported 70,000 who converged on Comiskey Park. Many had brought disco records with them, in exchange for which they got to enter the stadium at a quarter of the standard admission price. Plenty swarmed the streets outside when they couldn't get in.

Between games, Dahl exploded a crate filled with disco records, which prompted hordes of rock fans to storm the field chanting 'disco sucks'. Destroying the baseball field was not part of the plan, though, and the White Sox were forced to forfeit their next game. Riot police attempted to quell the mob and remove troublemakers from the venue.

Debate still rages over whether the rioters were more concerned with disco as a music genre or with the homosexuals and blacks who participated in it. *Rolling Stone*'s Dave Marsh leant towards the latter belief, saying the Disco Demolition was '[y]our most paranoid fantasy about where the ethnic cleansing of the rock radio could ultimately lead. It was everything you had feared come to life.'[6] One first-hand observer, a gate usher, reported that folks weren't just bringing disco records but also non-disco albums by black artists like Marvin Gaye and Stevie Wonder. Nile Rodgers from the outfit Chic declared the event was synonymous with Nazi book burning. The anti-disco backlash didn't just affect disco music, but also black music more generally. Peter Braunstein in the *Village Voice* decided there were also gender issues at play, writing, 'Only by killing disco could rock affirm its threatened masculinity.'[7]

By now the co-owners of Studio 54 were in deep doo-doo. Indicted on federal tax charges, they had allegedly evaded more than US$2.5 million in taxes during the club's first year of operation. To avoid a trial, the men pleaded guilty to tax evasion. As well as making good on their unpaid taxes, they were each sentenced to three and a half years in prison plus US$20,000 fines. The judge declared: 'Your crime, I conclude, is one of tremendous arrogance. You assumed you achieved your success on your own and you owed nothing to fellow citizens ...'[8]

It was a fitting encapsulation of the disco movement and, indeed, the trajectory of Western culture towards increased selfishness and profiteering.

Rapping delightfully

One album in 1979 was a genuine portent of things to come. The Fatback Band released their disco LP *XII*. On it was a song lumbered with the awkward title 'King Tim III (Personality Jock)' – which referred to the band's vocalist, Tim Washington. A B-side to the single, titled 'You're My Candy Sweet', it is now recognised as the first commercially released hip-hop or rap song.

A few months later, The Sugarhill Gang enjoyed an international hit with their single 'Rapper's Delight', which is credited with introducing hip-hop and rap to a wider audience. More than anyone, we have Sylvia Robinson to thank for that. A Harlem-born woman of colour, Sylvia had worked in the music industry as a performer, songwriter and record producer since 1954. At forty-three, she became interested in the new sounds being generated at hip-hop parties, particularly after a deejay known as Lovebug Starski performed a rap at her birthday party. She was fascinated with his ability to rhyme while spinning records, so she and her son Joey went hunting for rappers to record.

She tried Grandmaster Flash but he didn't want to be recorded. Instead, she found three unknown rappers and put them in a studio. One was Big Bank Hank (Henry Jackson), a nightclub bouncer who also worked at a pizzeria. While he was auditioning for Sylvia in a car, another rapper, Guy 'Master Gee' O'Brien, jumped in and began competing. Then another nearby rapper, Michael 'Wonder Mike' Wright, offered his services as well. Sylvia signed them all up, recorded 'Rapper's Delight' and branded them The Sugarhill Gang. It was the first release on Sugar Hill Records, founded by Sylvia and her husband Joe.

'Rapper's Delight' quickly became a template for all manner of rap music. The song actually plagiarised Chic's song 'Good Times', which resulted in a legal action for copyright infringement, but hip-hop and rap was now out of the house parties and into the mainstream, just in time for the new decade. Sylvia and Joey had no idea how far-reaching their little experiment would be. For millions of ears that had never heard rapping or hip-hop, 'Rapper's Delight' was a revelation. It quickly became a global bestseller and was the first Top 40 song to become available only as a twelve-inch single in the US.

And, while we're rappin' about females and hip-hop, a New York outfit named Funky 4 + 1 was the first to feature a woman rapper, MC Sha-Rock (Sharon Green). Their debut single was 'Rappin & Rocking the House', soon followed by the more successful 'That's the Joint', on which Sha lets us know that she can't be stopped.

Disco may have been on the nose, but dance music was evolving, morphing into hip-hop, house, Latin freestyle, techno, EDM (electronic dance music) and more.

Crumbling walls

While disco and punk had commandeered the spotlight, there was still plenty happening in the art rock and prog areas. Drummer Pierre Moerlen had taken over Gong and come up with two truly splendiferous jazz-rock discs, *Time Is the Key* and *Downwind*. Godley & Creme released more of their idiosyncratic studio cleverness with *Freeze Frame*, which included the quirky Australian and European hit 'An Englishman in New York', highlighting the differences between British and American cultural norms.

The Police released their second album *Reggatta de Blanc*, the first of four consecutive albums by the band that would reach the number one position on the UK charts. The title roughly translated from the French as 'white reggae'. Police's blend of hard rock, reggae and new wave proved irresistible, especially the hit singles 'Message in a Bottle' and 'Walking on the Moon'. The title track even won the band their first Grammy Award.

Supertramp's *Breakfast in America* album went to the top of the weekly album charts in ten countries. Four hit singles were derived from the disc: more hits than from their first five albums combined. It's all beautifully crafted, keyboard-focused art rock – just the sort of thing punk hated.

Pink Floyd's Roger Waters was increasingly isolated from the rest of the band. At Montreal's Olympic Stadium during the Animals tour, he had even spat on the audience in frustration and refused to play an encore. Back home, Waters channelled his feelings into a new project. Incredible as it seems, this hugely successful band was experiencing financial difficulties and needed a new album to garner some cashflow. Their financial planners, Norton Warburg, had invested millions of dollars in high-risk venture capital. As Floyd's funds had been invested pre-tax, they now had a tax exposure of many millions. In a now familiar scenario, the band were advised to leave the UK for a year to avoid bankruptcy and allow time for their accountants to work on the wreckage. Within weeks, all four had fled, one to Switzerland, another to France and the other pair to the Greek islands.

The Floyd's new magnum opus, *The Wall*, was a somewhat auto-biographical piece about a character unsubtly called Pink, a jaded, depressed rock star based on both Syd Barrett and the curmudgeon Roger Waters. The narrative captured the narcissistic, bombastic and misogynistic excesses of the 1970s rock-star lifestyle in what would be a fitting climax to the era.

Waters ended up writing most of the music, with Gilmour and producer Bob Ezrin assisting on various tunes. But putting the double album together became a massive challenge for all involved, with Ezrin having to act as an intermediary between warring bandmates. As Hipgnosis album designer Aubrey Powell put it, the album 'marked a turning point towards the group's eventual disintegration, when individualism took over'.[9]

When Richard Wright refused to delay a holiday to record his keyboard parts, all hell broke loose. As Nick Mason explained, 'Whatever bond Rick had enjoyed with Roger in the previous fifteen or so years was terminally broken.'[10] Not helping matters was Wright's rickety marriage, plus he had to leave his kids back in England, where they were attending school, and he missed them deeply. Waters insisted that Wright had to leave Pink Floyd, otherwise he would sacrifice the whole project. Rather than perpetuate the battles, Wright quit the band. On some editions of *The Wall* his name didn't even appear. No longer a band member, Wright was employed as a session musician on their subsequent tour. The elaborate staging required around 130 crew, with a giant wall gradually constructed between band and audience and then dismantled. Ironically, Wright became the only one of the four to make money from the tour, as he was paid a fixed wage.

The Wall double album was eventually released towards the end of 1979, going to number one in Australia, the US and nine other countries, and number three in the UK. It would generate a movie and numerous album reissues and is one of the best-known concept albums in the rock canon. The single 'Another Brick in the Wall, Part 2' became the band's only combined UK and US number one hit. Sadly, many years of legal and personal spats would ensue, including High Court battles over use of the Pink Floyd name.

While *The Wall* was being polished, Nick Mason went to New York to work at the studios of jazz iconoclasts Carla Bley and Michael Mantler. Although the resulting album was titled *Nick Mason's Fictitious Sports* 'for ease of release and size of advance',[11] it's really Carla Bley's only rock album, as all the compositions and arrangements are hers. The support band is Bley's touring outfit combined with Robert Wyatt on vocals, Chris Spedding on guitar and, of course, Nick Mason on drums. It must have been a relief for Mason to be recording an album without all the interpersonal friction that dogged The Floyd. The *Fictitious Sports* LP wouldn't surface for another two years, and has been largely ignored, but it remains an idiosyncratic gem blending humour with big-band rock. (Even better was The Carla Bley Band's own release for this year, *Musique Mecanique*.)

The Wall kept the breakthrough album by Tom Petty and the Heartbreakers, *Damn the Torpedos*, from reaching the top spot on the US charts; it was instead held at number two for seven weeks, with Petty reportedly saying that he loved Pink Floyd but hated them that year.

Frank Zappa also continued down his own distinctive path, releasing no less than five albums this year: *Sleep Dirt, Sheik Yerbouti, Orchestral Favourites, Joe's Garage Act I* and *Joe's Garage Acts II & III*. His biggest rock opera, *Joe's Garage*, addressed all of his obsessions, including censorship, sexuality, the music industry, government and organised religion. According to son Dweezil Zappa, Frank's guitar solo on the very slow 'Watermelon in Easter Hay' from *Joe's Garage* is the best his dad ever recorded.

The double album *Sheik Yerbouti* (a pun on KC and the Sunshine Band's disco hit 'Shake Your Booty') took Zappa further into the realm of comedy songs, along with a period of decidedly healthy record sales and rare mainstream attention for the composer. Indeed, *Sheik Yerbouti* rose to number twenty-one on the US charts, and into single digits in various European countries. The disc saw Zappa return to his bawdy, juvenile role as prurient provocateur, but the music is performed with great precision by a crack band. Zappa also incorporated what he called xenochrony, where he used tapes from live performances and blended them with studio playing. 'I Have Been in You' lampooned Peter Frampton's 1977 hit 'I'm in You', as well as the vapidity of popular love songs more generally. 'Dancin' Fool' poked fun at the whole disco scene, earning Zappa an appearance on *Saturday Night Live*, and even achieving a Grammy nomination, while 'Jewish Princess' satirised Jewish stereotyping.

And although prog was somewhat on the nose, one of the greatest prog albums was miraculously produced: *Danger Money* by U.K. The band were at this time reduced to a trio of John Wetton on bass, Eddie Jobson on keyboards and violin, and incomparable drummer Terry Bozzio, fresh from Zappa's band. The album's themes are built around spying and espionage. But it's the compositions, superb interplay, Jobson's violin solos and Bozzio's muscular drumming that set this disc apart. *Danger Money* managed to scrape into the US charts and generated a minor hit with the track 'Nothing to Lose', but it was hard going for serious proggers in 1979. The band U.K. would call it quits come March 1980. As one rock scribe put it, *Danger Money* presented 'one of the last great keyboard performances of the decade'.[12]

British art rockers Bauhaus released their debut single 'Bela Lugosi's Dead', which many music historians point to as the first gothic rock release, though I would sneak Belgium's Univers Zero into that category, and they had been operating since 1974.

Joni Mitchell went out on a long limb to create her *Mingus* album, recorded in the months before jazz bassist Charlie Mingus's death. The disc experimented with Mingus's tunes married with Mitchell's lyrics, and the support band featured members of Weather Report as well as short-lived bass pioneer Jaco Pastorius. It was a very long way from *Blue* to *Mingus*, and many fans and critics were having trouble keeping up with the songstress, but it's a frequently maligned, misunderstood mini-masterpiece.

Another masterpiece was The Residents' *Eskimo*, a unique concept disc about fabricated Inuit tales, full of chanting voices, eerie electronica and otherworldly atmospherics. Even more extreme was the debut that oozed from the British band Nurse With Wound. Titled *Chance Meeting on a*

Dissecting Table of a Sewing Machine and an Umbrella, it is best described as industrial noise with free-form jamming. This was music designed to shock, if not repel. The original cover image of an S&M dominatrix was lifted from an old pornographic magazine.

Cold work in Oz

In the land down under, rock music was far less intellectual and a lot more primal. Men at Work was a band built around another UK immigrant, in this instance Scottish-born Colin Hay. Like most Aussie bands, they began by generating a grassroots following as pub rockers. INXS also performed for the first time under that moniker this year. For a period, they considered becoming a Christian band, but instead decided to join the throng of pub bands and soon found themselves supporting Midnight Oil. The Oils released their second album, *Head Injuries*, achieving gold status. As drummer Rob Hirst noted, 'Ian Meldrum took it as a personal affront for a while that we wouldn't appear on *Countdown*. *Countdown* at the time was young girls and flashing disco floors – it wasn't appropriate for us. We wanted to present ourselves in sweaty smoky pubs.'[13]

In those pubs, Cold Chisel had a reputation for hard drinking and wild living. They released their second LP, *Breakfast at Sweethearts*, which peaked at number four on the local charts and was the bestselling album by an Australian act for the year. But their producer had aimed for a polished product which ignored the band's in-your-face live approach, and singer Jimmy Barnes would later disown the disc. Nevertheless, it went platinum. They also had a minor hit with 'Choir Girl', a song that writer Don Walker admitted was about pregnancy termination. I have always felt decidedly uneasy about the lyric, which compares the protagonist to a refugee. It smacks of arrogance for a privileged white person like Walker to claim to appreciate the feelings of a genuine refugee, but millions of people appear to be less sensitive to such issues than me.

Australian music at this time was divided between sweaty pub bands and teenybopper pop bands. James Reyne of Australian Crawl recalled:

When we started in the late 70s, there was definitely a divide between what pop was and what rock was. We wanted to be an album band as opposed to a singles band because singles implied pop music, which was here today, gone tomorrow, and albums meant being taken seriously, long lasting.[14]

Epiphanies

While prog and disco were dissembling, 'middle of the road' music surged forward. On the strength of their first remarkably successful album, Dire Straits embarked on a whirlwind US tour, performing fifty-one concerts in just thirty-eight days.

Bob Dylan was so impressed with the band that he invited Mark Knopfler and drummer Pick Withers to play on his next album, *Slow Train Coming*, which firmly established Dylan's Christian beliefs and became a bestseller. Dylan won his first Grammy for the evangelical 'Gotta Serve Somebody', which prompted an irate John Lennon to write a parody titled 'Serve Yourself'. As Lennon pointed out, this was the same Dylan who had warned people not to follow leaders in 'Subterranean Homesick Blues'; Lennon jokingly added: 'Guess he wants to be a waiter now.'[15] Another performer who found God was Al Green: he fell off a stage and for some reason took it as a message from God that he should focus on gospel music.

Some rockers who experienced religious epiphanies found their rock lifestyle incompatible with their newfound faith. Little River Band's bass player, George McArdle, walked away from the band to pursue Christian studies at Bible college. As he put it, 'I wasn't living a good lifestyle at the time and God offered me something bigger than LRB.'[16] Meanwhile, Little River Band enjoyed *Billboard* top ten hits with 'Lady' and 'Reminiscing', followed by their fifth studio LP, *First Under the Wire*, which spawned more hits and became their highest-charting US album. Dire Straits' *Communiqué* didn't quite scale the heights of their debut album, but performed well nonetheless. Air Supply took off with the release of *Life Support*. The Eagles finished their run of chart-topping singles with 'Heartache Tonight', while Elton John's disco album, *Victim of Love*, missed the proverbial boat.

Two of the best albums emanating from the US this year featured women artists. The Roches introduced their wonderfully unique vocals on a decidedly self-effacing eponymous LP, produced, oddly enough, by King Crimson's Robert Fripp. Thus would begin three decades of sublime songwriting and peerless singing from sisters Maggie, Terre and Suzzy. Their complex harmonies and personality-infused songs took folk music to new realms. And Rickie Lee Jones burst onto the scene, her debut self-titled album providing the smash hit single 'Chuck E.'s in Love'. Jones' brand of jazzy pop music celebrated the seedy nightlife of diners and bars. She forged a path, alongside Joni Mitchell, for other women singer-songwriters to follow. Jones was also the first artist to be launched with a music video, with Warners not only stumping the bill for the production costs, but also installing video monitors in record stores to promote their new star. The era of the music video had arrived, just in time for the 1980s.

The artist grandly named Prince had his first hit with 'I Wanna Be Your Lover', from his second album, *Prince*, which featured a revoltingly vainglorious image of his face and naked chest on the cover. Irish band U2 also had their first success with the EP *Three*. Cheap Trick hit international stardom with their *Cheap Trick at Budokan* album going triple platinum.

Two-toned

Even at the end of the decade, there were remnants of 1960s activism. America's Musicians United for Safe Energy (MUSE) collective staged concerts at Madison Square Garden to campaign for a non-nuclear future. Over in England, Rock Against Racism's concerts continued to combine reggae with punk, and from that arose a whole new set of bands that blended Jamaican music and rock into a new subgenre, mostly released on the appropriately named 2 Tone Records label. Artists on the label included

The Specials, The Beat, Madness, all-female ska band The Bodysnatchers and Elvis Costello. Madness's debut album *One Step Beyond* ... peaked at number two in the UK and remained on the charts for more than a year. It included a twisted interpretation of Tchaikovsky's famous theme from *Swan Lake*.

The Specials' debut eponymous album was released at the end of the year on the back of their Top 10 hit 'Gangsters'. Leaning heavily on ska and reggae, the lyrics profiled the social degradation in the UK, especially on songs like 'Stupid Marriage', 'It's Up to You' and 'Too Much Too Young', plus the escalating street violence on 'Doesn't Make It Alright' and 'Concrete Jungle' – although 'Little Bitch' is a nasty song about a fashion-conscious teenage girl. Part of their animosity towards the world no doubt heralded from vocalist Terry Hall's experience of being abused by a paedophile ring at the age of twelve, when a teacher took him to France on the promise of helping him learn French.

Although he had provided a number of anti-fascist songs to the RAR movement, and performed at various RAR events, Elvis Costello found himself in deep racial waters while touring the US. Various acts who were passing through Columbus, Ohio, converged on a bar at the local Holiday Inn. By the time The Stephen Stills Band joined Elvis Costello and his band, Costello was already in his cups. Costello began mouthing off about America's hallowed rock stars, even referring to some black artists as niggers. Incensed, Bonnie Bramlett of Delaney & Bonnie punched Costello, which quickly devolved into your classic American bar brawl involving various patrons. But Bramlett chose to take the issue to the media, and Costello was publicly branded a racist, even receiving death threats. When he gave his version of events to journalists, it fell well short of an apology. The American version of Rock Against Racism picketed the rest of his concerts.

The incident not only marred Costello's US sales for a long time, it also haunted the artist. Finally, in 2013, he said, 'It's upsetting because I can't explain how I even got to think you could be funny about something like that. I'm sorry. You know? It's about time I said it out loud.'[17] Yep.

Vicious endings

The Sex Pistols saga was coming to an ignominious end. Enfant terrible Sid Vicious had yet to face trial on the murder of Nancy Spungen when he appeared in court over the assault on Patti Smith's brother. He served fifty-five days in the Rikers Island prison and was put on a detoxification program. When released, he attended a party at the flat of his friend Michelle Robinson. Sid's mother, Ann Beverley, was also there. Various people have asserted that the high-grade heroin provided at the party was injected into Sid by his mother. What we do know is that his mother eventually found him dead, lying next to the sleeping Robinson. Sid's mother admitted that she had been holding her son's heroin supply, and that it was pure and very strong – not what someone coming out of detox should be partaking of. She later asserted that her son had made a suicide pact with Nancy Spungen, and she even produced a handwritten note to prove it. Sid's mother would die of her own drug overdose in 1996.

Three weeks after Sid's death, The Sex Pistols' version of Eddie Cochran's 'Something Else' – credited only to Sid Vicious so as to capitalise on his newsworthiness – peaked at number three on the UK singles chart. The song was featured in Julien Temple's mockumentary *The Great Rock 'n' Roll Swindle*, as was a version of 'My Way', the song made famous by Frank Sinatra. In the film, Vicious parodies the crooner, before shooting audience members with a gun.

Throughout the short career of The Sex Pistols, Malcolm McLaren and Vivienne Westwood had incited the band members to engage in antisocial and frequently harmful behaviour for the purpose of publicising the band and their fashion shop. Virgin Records were also beneficiaries. None of them took responsibility for the carnage left in their wake. But it wasn't just The Sex Pistols who ended up being manipulated by the music machine. As record producers Raymond Horricks and Neil Slaven wrote in 1980:

> The Sex Pistols, The Clash and The Jam seemed to be caricatures of
> musicians, limited in their musicianship and objectionable in their

maniacal combination of outrageous behaviour and paranoid lyrics ...
The punks were so intent upon bringing down the establishment
that they didn't notice when they'd joined the club ... Far from
destroying the system, punk music helped the industry to reinforce
and consolidate its control of public taste.[18]

If punk was unwittingly manipulated by the music establishment, hardcore
was the antidote. Hardcore acts were determined to maintain the essence of
punkdom, notably by keeping the music industry at arms' length. Hardcore
was a decidedly American movement, taking punk to faster and more
aggressive musical extremes. In San Francisco, a hardcore band with the
provocative name of Dead Kennedys surfaced. Sometimes they altered their
name to The DKs, The Sharks, The Creamsicles and The Pink Twinkies.
The band were provocateurs, one of the few punk outfits to take politics
seriously, with their political messaging delivered through sarcasm and
absurdist pranks. The title of their debut single, 'California Über Alles',
referenced the first line of the German national anthem, while the lyrics
attacked the governor of the state.

As a stunt, the DKs' lead singer, Jello Biafra (Eric Reed Boucher), ran
for mayor of San Francisco in 1979, coming in fourth out of ten candidates.
His policies included making businessmen wear clown suits and establishing
a Board of Bribery to set standard bribe rates. It was a half-hearted effort,
as he explained: 'It never even occurred to me to print up much in the way
of campaign literature, or go door to door, or do very many public events.'[19]
In 2000, Jello Biafra more seriously ran for the presidency of the Green
Party, finishing second to Ralph Nader.

New wave bands were happy to keep plugging away in the mainstream.
Ian Dury and the Blockheads' new album *Do It Yourself* went platinum
in the UK. Dury was insistent that his albums not contain hit singles, so
the LP was followed by a separate single, 'Reasons to Be Cheerful, Part
3', which rocketed up the charts. The lyrics presented a shopping list of
things that pleased Dury, presented in a spoken, rapping style. Listen for
the lounge-jazz sax solo in the middle, apparently included so saxophonist

Davey Payne could earn a share of the composing royalties. Listen also for the witty guitar solo towards the end.

Women were now appearing in numerous punk acts, with the list including, but certainly not limited to, Mo-dettes, The Raincoats, Contortions, The Cramps, Bush Tetras, X, Penetration, Crass, Poison Girls, The Slits, The Fall, Throbbing Gristle, Au Pairs, The Alley Cats, Bags and Delta 5. Punk was providing an opportunity for women to shed the restrictive role of chanteuse, to de-pretty themselves, bang drums, twang guitars, and scream and screech rather than coo. They could also sing about any topic, no matter how off-limits. The Slits' anthem 'Typical Girls', from their debut LP *Cut*, listed the plethora of often conflicting character traits that Western culture imposed on young women. It was a superb rant against stereotyping. 'Spend, Spend, Spend', from the same LP, noted that consumerism preys on the lonely and dispirited.

Chrissie Hynde had been turned on to the power of rock music at a young age. Of crucial influence was Frank Zappa's 1966 opening salvo, *Freak Out*, as well as seeing The Velvet Underground play live, notably the band's female drummer, Moe Tucker. By the time she got to London during the height of the punk era, there had been other influences on her musical tastes, especially Iggy Pop and The Stooges, as well as David Bowie. After a series of missteps with various bands, including involvement by Malcolm McLaren and a stint as a writer for *New Musical Express*, Hynde formed The Pretenders. Their first major tour was with UB40, the reggae band named after the British unemployment benefits form. A review of a Pretenders show published in *Melody Maker* was full of phrases like 'best new singer in ages' and 'transfixes the listener'.[20] Chrissie Hynde's voice was, like her image, a disarming combination of defiance and vulnerability.

Included on their debut LP was a cover of The Kinks' 'Stop Your Sobbing', which led to a relationship between Hynde and The Kinks' Ray Davies. But 'Brass in Pocket (I'm Special)' was the obvious single, with its girl power strut and hooky chorus about how Hynde would use her sass to get exactly what she wanted. It was feminism turned on its head, with an assertive woman taking charge of her life by manipulating her sex appeal rather than denying it. Hynde originally hated the track, having said on the first studio playback, 'It goes out over my dead body.'[21] Thankfully, she was overruled by the rest of the band. 'Brass in Pocket' was the first UK number one song of the 1980s, going to two in Australia and single digits in many countries. *Pretenders* debuted at number one in the UK and also made the top ten in the US and Australia. Released on 27 December, it was a fitting end to the decade: more melodic than punk and dirtier than pop.

Punk would struggle on for a few more years, but audience tolerance for badly played music could only stretch so far. Punk's lasting influence would be the reinjection of primal force into popular music. The hardcore scene would also merge with heavy metal and grunge, eventually splintering into ever decreasing sub-sub-genres like death metal, D-beat, sludge metal, sludgecore, emo, crust punk, grindcore, thrashcore, beatdown hardcore, and on and on. Punk didn't die, it just began to smell funny.

In the slipstream of Bowie and Roxy Music arose yet another genre, dubbed new romantic. With its beginnings in London and Birmingham, new romantics were heavily focused on looks, particularly gender-bending, with frilly, foppish shirts, mullets and quiffs. Musically it borrowed from synth-pop, glam, disco and art rock. Key proponents were Visage, Duran Duran, Spandau Ballet, Adam and the Ants, and Classix Nouveaux, soon followed by Boy George and Culture Club. As Brian Canham of Australian band Pseudo Echo claimed, the new romantics was the last original trend in modern music – everything afterwards was retro.

Unhappy endings

The 1970s were coming to an end, and so were some of the era's biggest acts.

Led Zeppelin managed to scrape together another album, *In Through the Out Door*, and headlined the Knebworth Music Festival, putting in a patchy performance. Despite lukewarm reviews, the album sold well, as did their back catalogue, and the band scooped seven of *Melody Maker*'s annual readers' poll awards. But Jimmy had to miss the gala ceremony as he was appearing at an inquest into the death of a young photographer who had attended a booze-and drug-fuelled party at his home. Led Zeppelin played their last gig in Berlin on 7 July. A year later, drummer John 'Bonzo' Bonham would be dead.

ABBA's power couple, Agnetha and Björn, separated after seven years of marriage. Within days, Björn had a new girlfriend and Agnetha rushed off to therapy. Frida and Benny would split the following year. The outcome of all this turmoil would be a torch song with a disco beat titled 'The Winner Takes It All', penned by the two blokes. Björn reportedly wrote the lyrics in under an hour with the aid of a bottle of whisky. It is one of the outfit's least trite songs. The fractured quartet would battle on until 1982 before going their separate ways. In any case, they would make more money from the awful *Mamma Mia* stage and film contrivances than from all their records put together.

Karen Carpenter broke free from the cloying control of her brother to make a solo album with producer Phil Ramone. Richard was busy receiving treatment for his addictions at the time. While it's a good LP, the songs were only marginally distinguishable from the work she had done with The Carpenters, although some of the lyrics were slightly more risqué and the tunes had more disco thump. The A&M executives, her brother and the rest of the family cruelly bagged the album, destroying what remained of Karen's spirit. Despite efforts by Quincy Jones to have the album released, *Karen Carpenter* would remain in the A&M vaults until it was finally set free thirteen years after her 1983 death.

Patti Smith released her album *Wave* and then promptly left the music scene to live in Detroit with Fred 'Sonic' Smith, the former guitar player with MC5. Black Sabbath fired their cocaine- and alcohol-addicted singer Ozzy Osbourne, substituting him with Ronnie James Dio.

The Who played their first concerts with Kenney Jones at the drums. Pete Townshend was drinking on stage and becoming increasingly erratic. As he put it, 'I kept taking over the lead microphone and kicking off new songs. My adrenaline on stage was running so high most nights I couldn't control myself.'[22] A *Melody Maker* concert review averred, 'Townshend is just incapable of jamming interestingly.'[23]

Before a Who concert in Cincinnati, a crowd stampede to garner the best seats saw eleven fans trampled and killed in the crush, with many more injured. The band didn't learn about the tragedy until after the gig was over. They then had to face the press. Instead of staying in Cincinnati or halting the tour to show respect, the circus ground on, with Townshend becoming increasingly unpredictable. Daltrey reckoned the last ten shows of the tour were 'amongst the most intense of my life … Emotionally, it was a nightmare.'[24]

Paul McCartney's Wings released their seventh and final album, *Back to the Egg*, yet another concept album about a working rock band. It was largely pilloried by critics, with *Rolling Stone*'s Timothy White writing that 'McCartney's gross indulgence is matched only by his shameless indolence'. Even the all-star track 'Rockestra Theme', featuring guest musicians from The Who, Led Zeppelin, Pink Floyd and Procol Harum, was deemed to be 'a flat affair cooked up around one hackneyed riff'.[25] Regardless of the critics, the album charted in single digits, but McCartney's next effort would be another self-produced solo LP.

Former Wings guitarist Jimmy McCulloch was found dead from heart failure due to morphine and alcohol poisoning. Little Feat's Lowell George also died of a heart attack brought on by a cocaine overdose, and tortured singer-songwriter Judee Sill finally checked out, again thanks to a drug overdose.

Pattie Boyd had inspired a few famous songs, notably George Harrison's 'Something' and Eric Clapton's 'Layla', but she also inadvertently brought three of The Beatles together for a reunion bash. George Harrison, Paul McCartney and Ringo Starr were at Eric Clapton's Surrey home to celebrate his marriage to Boyd, whom he had wooed away from Harrison. At the event, George jammed with his old bandmates Paul and Ringo, with all of it, according to Denny Laine's first-hand account, sounding like 'rubbish'.[26] The three would reconvene following John Lennon's murder in 1981 to record 'All Those Years Ago'. Clapton had replaced heroin with alcohol abuse, and would later admit to both raping and beating Boyd. She finally divorced him in 1989.

George Harrison's biggest contribution to global culture at this time was to rescue the Monty Python movie *The Life of Brian* after EMI got cold feet and pulled out. Eric Idle called Harrison's funding the most anyone had ever paid for a cinema ticket. It would inspire Harrison to establish Handmade Films, which would make a further twenty-five movies by the end of the 1980s.

David Bowie and his old mate Lou Reed came to blows in a restaurant, with Reed having to be restrained and Bowie angrily trashing pot plants on his way out. The next day, Bowie's new single was released: 'Boys Keep Swinging'. The song appeared to be a statement about male good fortune, and how boys always get what they want. Yet the video saw Bowie supported by a chorus of drag queens and concluded with the star appearing in various versions of women's apparel. It appeared to be suggesting that boys even had the privilege to become female, should they wish – or was it all just more exhibitionism?

The song's parent album, *Lodger*, garnered mixed reviews. On the track 'Repetition', Bowie emulates Lou Reed's off-kilter singing with lyrics dispassionately describing a wife beater. The whole tone of the album is dark and desultory. Even the disturbing cover has Bowie as an accident victim, squashed under a pane of glass.

AC/DC attempted to record with their new producer, Eddie Kramer, but the band clashed with him and spat the bullet. Instead, they lucked upon Robert John 'Mutt' Lange, and the creative juices started flowing. The title track, 'Highway to Hell', was yet another self-congratulatory rock anthem about being in a band, and it became an instant classic. In Germany it stayed on the charts for forty-five weeks, while the album went single digits there and in the UK. AC/DC toured right up until Christmas. A few weeks later, singer Bon Scott would be found dead in a car, with the coroner concluding it was due to acute alcohol poisoning.

Broken

Being in a rock band was akin to being in a small street gang with shifting allegiances. All too often, tensions over leadership devolved into bullying. As Nick Mason put it, 'You have therapy to get over the business of being in a band.'[27] There was also a familiar trajectory, as Hipgnosis designer Aubrey Powell noted: 'People live in each other's pockets for years and then suddenly become extremely wealthy, they then tend to gravitate away from each other. They move to different parts of the country, and don't see each other so often and form more relationships outside the band. A grievance process starts.'[28]

For many rock stars, the high-risk game was the be-all and end-all of their self-concept. As Tom Robinson explained, 'For me I think I pinned all my sense of self-worth on the idea of having some sort of success in music – that it would validate me as a person if a lot of people loved me.'[29] Scratch the surface, and many rock stars had deep emotional needs, often established during problematic childhoods, particularly those with absent parents. Like many who seek the limelight, such individuals crave the love and adoration they missed out on as children; but millions of adoring strangers can't assuage damaged childhoods, and nor can the attention of sycophants.

Of course, many did survive, and even turned their struggle into art. One of the truly great albums of 1979, and perhaps the most fitting epitaph to the previous two decades, was Marianne Faithfull's return to recording with *Broken English*. As the former popstar and Jagger beau ruefully put it, 'Most people didn't know what had become of me. Or care.'[30] Becoming a heroin addict and an anorexic, and losing custody of her son, not to mention living rough, all impacted on her attitude as well as her voice. She was no longer a sweet soprano, but instead a deep and raspy singer of torch songs. The tunes were full of fury and bitterness.

The title track muses on the terrorist activism of the Baader–Meinhof group. 'Guilt' is Barry Reynolds' reflection on Catholic remorse. Faithful gives new gravitas to Lennon's 'Working Class Hero', taking the song to far darker places than Lennon had dared penetrate, while her new husband, The Vibrators' Ben Brierly, contributed the song 'Brain Drain', about being inveigled into the low life. But the two real standout tracks are 'The Ballad of Lucy Jordon', written by Shel Silverstein, and 'Why D'Ya Do It', the closing number, credited to Heathcote Williams, Faithful and three members of the backing band.

The former song had been recorded by Dr. Hook & the Medicine Show, but in Faithfull's hands the harrowing story of a bored housewife driven to suicide sounds like an impassioned elegy for a dead friend. 'Why D'Ya Do It?' is a gut-wrenching, scabrous rant about infidelity, replete with graphic sexual descriptions and tortured guitar. What starts off being told from a man's perspective quickly devolves into a spurned woman's vitriol. Heathcote Williams had intended his lyrics for Tina Turner, but Faithfull convinced him that she would be the better vessel. The song was banned in Australia, leading to the LP being released without its final track. The ABC's 2JJ and Brisbane community station 4ZZZ ignored the ban and played imported copies.

Broken English charted well in Europe and New Zealand, but only moderately elsewhere. Nevertheless, it is a masterwork, containing revelatory power and gut punches. It did garner Faithfull a Grammy nomination.

The decade ended with a genre-inclusive series of concerts between 26 and 29 December, organised by Paul McCartney and Kurt Waldheim, secretary-general of the United Nations. Titled 'Concerts for the People of Kampuchea' (now Cambodia) and held in London, the participating acts included Ian Dury and the Blockheads, The Clash, Elvis Costello & the Attractions, Queen, The Pretenders, The Specials, The Who, Matumbi, Rockpile, Paul McCartney & Wings, and concluded with the McCartney-led supergroup dubbed Rockestra, which included John Bonham, Gary Brooker, Dave Edmunds, John Paul Jones, Denny Laine, Ronnie Lane, Kenney Jones, Robert Plant, James Honeyman-Scott, Linda McCartney and Pete Townshend. It was a fitting finale to a decade of musical extravagance the likes of which we are unlikely to see again.

Final judgement

At the close of the 'me decade', Randy Newman felt the urge to pass judgement. His final album for the decade, ironically titled *Born Again*, featured a cover image of himself in a business office sporting a parody of Kiss make-up with dollar signs painted on each side of his face. The back cover had the same face but with Newman poking out his tongue à la Gene Simmons.

The opening track, 'It's Money That I Love', goes to the heart of the matter, suggesting that Americans and rock stars only care about wealth and material gratification, with greed becoming an end unto itself. Channelling Ayn Rand and her acolytes, the narrator acknowledges that he used to worry about the poor but doesn't anymore. In a clear reference to the era's rock gods, he notes that money can't buy love, but it sure as hell can buy a lot of cocaine plus a sixteen-year-old girl.

Track two, 'The Story of a Rock and Roll Band', takes a swipe at Electric Light Orchestra and their contrivances, deftly imitating the band's arrangements and idiosyncrasies, right down to the guitar solo. Then comes the unsettling 'Pretty Boy', a song about a John Travolta imitator who happens upon some genuine tough guys in the city. As well as being a song about toxic masculinity, it is a critique of the way the entertainment industry exploits gullible young men.

'Half a Man' pokes fun at the belief that homosexuality could be contagious. The final track, 'Pants', sees the rock star narrator continually threatening to drop his strides. Newman explained it thus:

> 'Pants' is about these big heavy pretentious rock 'n' roll acts like Kansas or Styx. I saw some big rock shows, in a baseball arena … and I couldn't believe what an impersonal thing it was. This kind of false sexual innuendo, you know, 'I'm gonna take off my pants!' – the whole thing was a drag, and really demeaning to the audience.[31]

The *Born Again* album drips with cynicism, but Newman's ironic humour was out of sync with his audience – so much so that it surprised him when the LP was reviewed badly and generated only lukewarm sales. As he put it, 'It was like the *Titanic*. They paid me lots of money like it was going to be big, and it was the first album I myself thought was going to be a success ...'[32]

But in 1979, very few people were ready to laugh at rock music's indulgences, let alone society's lurch towards selfishness.

CODA

The 1960s were a hard act to follow: a period of strong economic growth, virtual full employment and an overall rise in household incomes across the Western world. In this secure setting, tertiary education more than doubled, and 'elastic adolescence' saw the notion of youth extended into people's twenties. Then, rather abruptly, at the turn of the decade, the heyday began to dissolve. The boom times, which had afforded young people the luxury of 'dropping out', came to an end, and finding a job was no longer a certainty.

As the Vietnam War petered out and the global recession bit, the communion of youth culture ruptured, and the common enemy seemed more abstruse. As Robert Christgau put it, 'We all tried to forge a humane generation and ultimately fell back exhausted.'[1] The rights of women and gays progressed significantly through the 1970s, but the broader conviction of revolutionary change was left to a handful of diehard extremists.

The decade concluded with Margaret Thatcher elected as Prime Minister of England, and in a year's time, Ronald Reagan would be President of the USA. Both nations were entering a period of new politics based on old values. In 1979, *Time* magazine predicted that nobody would be inclined to look back on the 1970s as the good old days.

Music-wise, the '70s began badly, with the termination of the greatest rock band the world had ever seen. Between 1964 and 1970, The Beatles had spearheaded an incredible diversity of rock music styles, including some of its more experimental leanings. Nevertheless, rock continued to diversify through the new decade, often in unpredictable and impulsive ways.

For the consumer, central to the music culture of the 1970s was the purchasing of vinyl records. Chatting about the latest music releases was an important way by which young people related to one another. The sort of music one listened to, and the depth of one's commitment to that music, was an essential part of one's individuation. To simply loan and borrow records or, at the end of the decade, assemble compilation cassettes, was to make a statement about one's personality. Music really was the lingua franca of youth, and it's hard to imagine the artform ever becoming so intrinsic and culturally dominant again.

Compared with the 1960s, there was more music in people's lives during the '70s, because a whole lot more music was being created and performed. Rock and pop music had infiltrated the broader culture too. Most of Britain's population, for example, enjoyed watching *Top of the Pops* each week, and people of every age group held an opinion about Elton John or The Bee Gees.

One still hears the view that 1970s music, and particularly progressive rock, was self-indulgent. I don't accept that music which attempted to stretch the boundaries of rock, and which was complex and even challenging for listeners, was necessarily self-indulgent. Were Can, ELP, Gentle Giant and Henry Cow self-indulgent simply because they were excited by the possibility of trying something new? What *was* self-indulgent in the 1970s was the behaviour of many rock stars. Destroying hotels, performing while intoxicated, having sex with anything that moved, and demanding a piano filled with strawberries in every hotel room – that's the sort of thing that constitutes self-indulgence.

In part, the obnoxious behaviour of many rock stars can be explained as people achieving more fame and wealth than they had the maturity to manage. Autobiographies by the worst offenders inevitably put their excesses down to the boredom and/or the stress of being on tour. But many touring musicians did not succumb to Dionysian excess, and there were alternative ways to deal with the vicissitudes of touring that didn't involve the destruction of property and the abuse of young women.

Those who overindulged in drugs and alcohol inevitably suggest that such behaviour was normalised by the milieu. Debbie Harry, for instance, wrote, 'Getting high was just part of the music and band culture that we came up in. It didn't seem like anything extraordinary. *Everyone* at all the clubs drank or got stoned with almost no exception.'[2] Most also argue that they weren't aware of the realities of addiction. However, there was ample talk about the addictive nature of drugs and alcohol in the 1970s, so naivety is really no alibi. Furthermore, the decision to consume vast amounts of drugs or alcohol was a conscious one, and not something that can be blamed on other people inhabiting the same social scene. Artists like Frank Zappa, Angus Young and Bruce Springsteen managed to eschew drugs and excessive alcohol.

Some readers may perhaps think that I am engaging in 'presentism' – that is, judging the past by today's standards. While we may be clearer about certain moral values today, let's not pretend that it was socially or legally conventional for a twenty-five-year-old to have sex with a fourteen-year-old in the 1970s, nor that heavy drug abuse and the trashing of hotels was broadly tolerable behaviour. I am no prude when it comes to sexual matters, but we must draw the line at abusive sexual behaviour, and even more so where it involves a power imbalance.

At the beginning of the decade, it wasn't unseemly for young music consumers to be into folk rock, R&B, heavy rock and psychedelia all at once. Music genres were less defined, and often, like progressive rock, not yet named. But as rock music diversified during the decade, there arose a need for catch-all phrases to define what was happening. By the end of the 1970s, listening habits appeared to become much more segmented into subcultures. As Rod Stewart described it, '[T]here was soul and there was heavy metal and there was punk, and so on – with their followers all in separate trenches with bayonets drawn.'[3]

Indeed, the diversification of music in the 1970s could be viewed as a series of clashes: disco versus punk, bubblegum versus heavy rock, acoustic rock versus electronica, albums versus singles, music versus theatrics, and even macho versus effete. Towards the end of the decade, rock music even began to rebel against itself. What's more, musicians started to openly criticise one another. Much of the camaraderie that had existed among music performers in the 1960s had evaporated by the end of the '70s.

Big-name bands who performed to giant arenas became increasingly removed from their fan base, and the performers turned arrogant and self-indulgent. As Jimmy Barnes noted when the up-and-coming Cold Chisel were booked to support a tour by the already famous Little Feat: 'They came nowhere near us. Never said a word. In fact, they made it harder for us to play than they needed to. They wouldn't give us any room to set up.'[4] Of course, not every successful act behaved like Little Feat, but by the end of the decade there was far less of a sense that, be they music performers or music consumers, we were all in this together.

Not far into the 1970s, the Western cultural focus began to shift from 'we' to 'me', and rock music paralleled that shift. The collectivist mindset of the '60s was best exemplified by President John F. Kennedy's inaugural speech, in which he intoned: 'Ask not what your country can do for you – ask what you can do for your country.' The new self-centred mindset that had taken hold by the end of the '70s was exemplified when Margaret Thatcher said there is no such thing as society, simply, 'individual men and women'.

Harvard's Robert D. Putnam has mapped the peaks and troughs of individual selfishness across modern American history. He found that, since the 1960s, America has become demonstrably and measurably more of an 'I'-orientated society and less of a 'we'-orientated society. The more encompassing, compassionate and communitarian position peaked around 1962, but, as he put it, 'America took a more individualistic and narcissistic turn after 1970'.[5]

Analysis of song lyrics tends to reflect the shifts that broader society undergoes. One study of lyrics from the 1950s to the present found that lyrics expressing positive sentiment dropped most markedly in the 1970s, while those expressing negative sentiment went up.[6] A 1982 study looking at romantic lyrics across the most popular songs of the previous three decades found that 89.2 per cent of songs were rated as either somewhat or very emotional in the 1950s, with that figure reducing to 71.4 per cent in the 1960s, and plummeting to 42.5 per cent in the 1970s. As the researchers put it, 'By the 1970s … persons described in modern love songs often met, spent a single night together, then parted without any emotional bond or commitment.'[7]

It should come as little surprise that the political turmoil in America during the 1970s also caused their citizenry's faith in government to ebb.

Trust in government in the US dropped from a high of 77 per cent in 1964 to just 29 per cent by 1978. Watergate brought the corruption of power into living rooms around the globe. As trust in public institutions collapsed, the philosophical void was gradually filled by neoliberal thinking and the myths of the self-esteem movement (and, more recently, by conspiracy theories weaponised through social media).

At the end of the 1970s, author Robert Ringer gave self-interest another boost. Flushed with the success of *Winning Through Intimidation* and *Looking Out for #1*, Ringer expanded his self-absorption theology with a new US best-seller, *Restoring the American Dream*. Today, that title invokes Donald Trump's 'Make America Great Again' slogan, and the similarities don't stop there. On the very first page, Ringer's book states:

> The time has come. The citizens of this country either must draw the line and take America back from the politicians who control it, or they must be prepared to relinquish forever their remaining claims on liberty. The American Dream is about individualism and the opportunity to achieve success without interference from others.[8]

One could also add, 'and without empathy for those less fortunate'. As academic Lisa Duggan put it, 'The culture of greed is the hallmark of the neoliberal era, the period beginning in the 1970s ... The unifying threads are meanness and greed, and the spirit of the whole hodgepodge is Ayn Rand.'[9]

Mind you, Western culture's normalisation of self-interest wasn't going unnoticed. American history professor and social critic Christopher Lasch was sufficiently concerned to release a book in 1979 titled *The Culture of Narcissism: American Life in an Age of Diminishing Expectations*. Lasch was disturbed by the growth of 'pathological narcissism', manifested in a lack of empathy for others and an unremitting search for personal power.

President Jimmy Carter also voiced his concerns about the direction American culture was headed. In a 1979 address, known as the 'malaise speech', he spoke of a national 'crisis in confidence':

We can see this crisis in the growing doubt about the meaning of our own lives and the loss of unity of purpose for our nation ... Human identity is no longer defined by what one does, but by what one owns. But we've discovered that owning things and consuming things does not satisfy our longing for meaning ... You see every extreme position defended to the last vote, almost to the last breath by one unyielding group or another. You often see a balanced and a fair approach that demands sacrifice, a little sacrifice from everyone, abandoned like an orphan without support and without friends.

That picture, painted by Carter at the end of the 1970s, is even more evident today. The solution, from Carter's point of view, was for greater comity:

There are two paths to choose. One is the path I've warned about tonight, the path that leads to fragmentation and self-interest. Down that road lies the mistaken idea of freedom, the right to grasp for ourselves some advantage over others. That path would be one of constant conflict between narrow interests ending in chaos and immobility. It is a certain route to failure.

Carter's speech was a desperate plea to reverse the tide of selfishness. Instead, the post-Rand/Hayek neoliberal revolution consolidated under Reagan and Thatcher, with the deregulation of business and banking, the sale of public utilities, the dismantling of arts funding, the removal of protections for workers, the demonisation of welfare recipients and the lowering of taxes for the extremely wealthy. Eventually, across most Western nations, everything would be viewed through the singular prism of the economy, with seemingly no other means of measuring a society's progress. It would take decades to debunk the neoliberal myth of trickle-down economics; meanwhile, executive salaries ballooned and inequality worsened.

During the 1970s, the reductionist ideology of the self-esteem movement became something of a core belief in the West. Self-esteem was portrayed as a magic elixir that would reduce crime, teenage pregnancies, antisocial behaviour and just about every other social ill. It was a seductive hypo-thesis: after all, who doesn't want to be more confident and less fearful? But it wasn't based on anything more than a hunch. Indeed, we now know, with empirical evidence in support, that there is no causal relationship between high self-esteem and positive outcomes. Indeed, various studies show that people with high self-esteem may be bullies, do not perform better at tasks, and are more likely to be prejudiced and to cheat. What's more, high self-esteem has been shown to amplify antisocial behaviour, such as cruelty towards others. Many of the world's worst despots had or have high self-esteem.

Piggybacking on the self-esteem obsession was the New Age movement, which was also fixated on personal gratification and empowerment. Of course, not everyone was sucked into this vortex: as Chrissie Hynde of The Pretenders wrote, 'As far as self-esteem and all the New Age psychobabble stuff, I didn't worry about that. I read the Bhagavad Gita and knew all that ego and self-esteem stuff was a load of hooey anyway.'[10]

But many 1970s rock stars became exemplars of the cultural shift towards self-interest. It may have begun in the '60s, but the '70s consolidated an acceptance of selfish indulgence. The most high-profile rock artists epitomised unabashed avarice, reflected in their lavish lifestyles, colossal incomes and efforts to avoid paying tax. These were the people millions of young music consumers looked up to.

And what of music then and now? Although rock music was expanding like a supernova in the '70s, it was still possible to keep up with music's trajectory by sifting through the 'new release' section of one's local record shop, visiting an import record shop or purchasing one of the many music and culture magazines available. When I say 'local' record shop, in the 1970s any average-sized suburban shopping precinct had its own record store. Where I lived, in suburban Sydney, there were two within easy reach.

Of course, today the range of music on offer is so immense as to be mind-numbing. As Australian music manager John Watson put it, '[I]n the age of streaming where 75,000 new songs are released every single day, even big hits don't register with lots of people because they don't fit their algorithm.'[11] It is no longer possible to keep track of everything being produced in popular music. We live in an era of oversupply, and I'm not sure we are the better for it.

With the offer of ready access to millions of pieces of music, streaming services have reduced music to a disposable commodity of diminishing significance. Listening to music today is like turning on a faucet: it's taken for granted. That's not good for those who wish to make music their profession. Roger Daltrey put it well in his autobiography: 'All the internet has done for most musicians is rob them of their income … The way it is today, it's very hard for anyone starting out in the business. We thought we had a hard time back in the sixties but at least we got paid … sometimes.'[12]

Thankfully, music is remarkable. As *Rolling Stone*'s Ben Fong-Torres said, '[M]usic will always have more of a function than just entertainment.'[13] Songs have been used throughout human history to disperse and reinforce ideas. They have been used to rally citizens to action and to inspire them. Music has also been utilised to help listeners make sense of their world.

Music improves wellbeing. A recent meta-analysis of twenty-six separate scientific studies conducted across various cultures found that music can measurably boost mental health. The effects were similar whether the participants sang, played or simply listened to music. The authors concluded that the benefit of music for wellbeing was not dissimilar to that gained from physical exercise.[14]

Researchers have also shown that the music we listen to in our youth becomes a sort of lifetime reference for everything we hear through the rest of our lives. We are constantly, if unconsciously, comparing new music with that back catalogue. This historical playlist is the music that intrinsically and continually helps us to define our sense of self. Of course, we can still discover and enjoy new musical offerings later in life, but research shows that people become less open to new musical experiences as they age. More than one study into contemporary listening habits has demonstrated that most people stop listening to new music around the age of thirty; thereafter, it's the music of their teens and twenties that they continue to rely on.

It makes perfect sense for people to be nostalgic about the comparatively simplistic music of the 1950s, the decade when rock 'n' roll was born. So too with the 1960s, the period when rock music insinuated itself into broader contemporary culture. Indeed, that era of protest anthems, intense musical innovation and mass social change still stirs many a beating heart. By comparison, the 1970s are less mythologised. For many in Western society, the decade is remembered as a period of global recession, stagflation, militant unionism, Cold War thinking and mass uncertainty. But music in the '70s was just as transformative as it had been in the previous decade. More than any other era, the '70s demonstrated that pop and rock could perform a range of functions, from intellectual art to emotional catharsis, social commentary to mindless dance music. This diversity was enabled by the many technological innovations that helped expand the possibilities for recording and performing music: new electronic instruments, huge shifts in recording techniques and massive improvements in the presentation of live music.

For all its faults, the 1970s was arguably the most innovative period in the history of popular music. The '70s built on the musical foundations established in the '60s, and by 1980 every major music genre that is still in evidence today had been instigated or signposted. After 1980, it was mostly just minor tweaking to create new sub-genres. The creative blueprint had been drawn in the previous two decades.

Of those millions of songs now being uploaded to streaming services every year, all have their formative basis in the broad swathe of electronic, industrial, avant-garde, ambient, dance, rap, folk, country, world, reggae, fusion, prog, punk, new wave, metal and soft rock that was created in the 1970s. While the '60s set the ball rolling, I believe the '70s was rock's true golden era, when popular music reached its apogee of creativity. I hope this book has made such a case.

LIST OF ILLUSTRATIONS

Yoko Ono and John Lennon perform at the John Sinclair Freedom Rally in 1971.
Creator unknown
Public domain
https://upload.wikimedia.org/wikipedia/commons/7/73/Yoko_Ono_and_John_Lennon_at_John_Sinclair_Freedom_Rally.jpg

Mick Jagger, 1976.
Creator: Bert Verhoeff for Anefo
Public domain
https://upload.wikimedia.org/wikipedia/commons/2/24/Mick_Jagger_%281976%29.jpg

Linda and Paul McCartney with Bhaskar Menon on Wings Over America tour in 1976.
Creator: Capitol Records
Public domain
https://upload.wikimedia.org/wikipedia/commons/f/f4/Paul_and_Linda_McCartney_Wings_Over_America_1976.jpg

Newspaper photograph of Kent State killings, 1972.
Creator: Yankee Poster Collection
United States Library of Congress's Prints and Photographs division under digital ID yan.1a38179
https://upload.wikimedia.org/wikipedia/commons/8/83/Avenge_LCCN2015649400.jpg

Robert Plant and Jimmy Page of Led Zeppelin perform acoustic set, 1973.
Creator: Heinrich Klaffs
Creative Commons Attribution-Share Alike 2.0 Generic
https://upload.wikimedia.org/wikipedia/commons/2/24/Led_Zeppelin_acoustic_1973.jpg

Black Sabbath (Iommi, Osbourne, Ward and Butler), date unknown, 1972–6.
Creator: Warner Bros. Records
Public domain
https://upload.wikimedia.org/wikipedia/commons/1/11/Black_Sabbath_%28Iommi%2C_Osbourne%2C_Ward_and_Butler%29.JPG

Sunbury Pop Festival, 1973.
Creator: Billybobmarley
Creative Commons Attribution-Share Alike 4.0 International
https://upload.wikimedia.org/wikipedia/commons/c/c0/Sunbury_Pop_Festival_1973_.jpg

Vietnamese Refugees on US Carrier, Operation Frequent Wind, 1975.
Creator unknown
Public domain
https://upload.wikimedia.org/wikipedia/commons/d/d0/Vietnamese_refugees_on_
US_carrier%2C_Operation_Frequent_Wind.jpg

Pink Floyd play The Dark Side of the Moon at Earls Court, 1973.
Creator: Tim Duncan
Creative Commons Attribution 3.0 Unported
https://upload.wikimedia.org/wikipedia/commons/8/8f/DarkSideOfTheMoon1973.jpg

David Bowie shooting his video for 'Rebel Rebel' on AVRO's *TopPop*
(Dutch TV), 1974.
Creator: AVRO
Creative Commons Attribution-Share Alike 3.0 Netherlands
https://upload.wikimedia.org/wikipedia/commons/2/2c/David_Bowie_-_
TopPop_1974_10.png

Joni Mitchell, 1974.
Creator: Paul C. Babin
Public domain
https://upload.wikimedia.org/wikipedia/commons/0/00/Joni_mitchell_1974_cropped.jpg

Alice Cooper, 1972.
Creator: Associated Booking Corporation
Public domain
https://upload.wikimedia.org/wikipedia/commons/f/fc/Alice_Cooper_1972.jpg

The Who in Hamburg, 1972.
Creator: Heinrich Klaffs
Creative Commons Attribution-Share Alike 2.0 Generic
https://upload.wikimedia.org/wikipedia/commons/3/32/The_Who_Hamburg_1972.jpg

Karen and Richard Carpenter, 1973.
Creator: A&M Records
Public domain
https://upload.wikimedia.org/wikipedia/commons/e/e4/Karen_and_Richard_Carpenter.jpg

Elton John on the *Cher Show*, 1975.
Creator: CBS Television
Public domain
https://upload.wikimedia.org/wikipedia/commons/c/cb/Elton_john_cher_show_1975.JPG

Peter Gabriel performing with Genesis at the Massey Hall, Toronto, 1973.
Creator: Jean-Luc
Creative Commons Attribution-Share Alike 2.0 Generic
https://upload.wikimedia.org/wikipedia/commons/f/fc/Peter_Gabriel_The_Moonlight_
Knight.jpg

Brian Eno on AVRO's *TopPop* (Dutch TV), 1974.
Creator: AVRO
Creative Commons Attribution-Share Alike 3.0 Netherlands
https://upload.wikimedia.org/wikipedia/commons/c/cc/Brian_Eno_-_TopPop_1974_12.png

President Richard Nixon with singer Johnny Cash in the Oval Office, 1972.
Creator: The Nixon Library
Public domain
https://upload.wikimedia.org/wikipedia/commons/4/4c/President_Richard_Nixon_and_Johnny_Cash.jpg

Helen Reddy on *The Carol Burnett Show*, 1973.
Creator: CBS Television
Public domain
https://upload.wikimedia.org/wikipedia/commons/1/12/Helen_Reddy_1973_%28cropped%29.JPG

The Bee Gees perform on *The Midnight Special* (TV show), 1973.
Creator: NBC Television
Public domain
https://upload.wikimedia.org/wikipedia/commons/5/53/Bee_Gees_Midnight_Special_1973.jpg

Suzi Quatro in AVRO's *TopPop* (Dutch TV show), 1973. (cropped)
Creator: AVRO
Creative Commons Attribution-Share Alike 3.0 Netherlands
https://upload.wikimedia.org/wikipedia/commons/9/9d/Suzi_Quatro_-_TopPop_1973_5.png

King Crimson playing in 1973.
Creator unknown
Creative Commons Attribution-Share Alike 4.0 International
https://upload.wikimedia.org/wikipedia/commons/5/5b/King_Crimson_Playing_in_1973.jpg

Marc Bolan (T Rex) on ABC Television *In Concert*, 1973.
Creator: ABC Television
Public domain
https://upload.wikimedia.org/wikipedia/commons/0/0e/Marc_Bolan_In_Concert_1973.jpg

Slade on AVRO's *TopPop* (Dutch TV show), 1973.
Creator: AVRO
Creative Commons Attribution-Share Alike 3.0 Netherlands
https://upload.wikimedia.org/wikipedia/commons/7/77/Slade_-_TopPop_1973_05.png

New York Dolls on AVRO's *TopPop* (Dutch TV show), 1973.
Creator: AVRO
Creative Commons Attribution-Share Alike 3.0 Netherlands
https://upload.wikimedia.org/wikipedia/commons/1/16/New_York_Dolls_-_
TopPop_1973_11.png

AC/DC's Angus Young and Bon Scott, Ulster Hall, Belfast, 1976.
Creator: Lost Parables
Creative Commons Attribution 2.0 Generic
https://upload.wikimedia.org/wikipedia/commons/8/8d/ACDC-Hughes-long_ago.jpg

Gentle Giant's Gary Green, Ray Shulman and Derek Shulman, Hamburg,
1974.
Creator: Heinrich Klaffs
Creative Commons Attribution 2.0 Generic
https://upload.wikimedia.org/wikipedia/commons/f/f2/Gentle_Giant%2C_
Hamburg_1974.jpg

10cc on AVRO's *TopPop* (Dutch TV), 1974.
Creator: AVRO
Creative Commons Attribution-Share Alike 3.0 Netherlands
https://upload.wikimedia.org/wikipedia/commons/6/63/10CC_-_TopPop_1974_5.png

Johnny Rotten performing with The Sex Pistols, student union i Trondheim,
Norway, 1977.
Creator: Riksarkivet (National Archives of Norway)
Public domain
https://upload.wikimedia.org/wikipedia/commons/2/28/Sex_Pistols_i_
Norge%2C_1977_%286263353068%29.jpg

Patti Smith, 1978.
Creator: UCLA Library Special Collections
Creative Commons Attribution 2.0 Generic
https://upload.wikimedia.org/wikipedia/commons/5/55/Patti_Smith%2C_1978.jpg

Blondie: Gary Valentine, Clem Burke, Debbie Harry, Chris Stein and Jimmy
Destri, 1977.
Creator: Private Stock Records
Public domain
https://upload.wikimedia.org/wikipedia/commons/f/fc/Blondie1977.jpg

Ramones in concert at New York Theatre, 1976.
Creator: Plismo
Creative Commons Attribution-Share Alike 3.0 Unported
https://upload.wikimedia.org/wikipedia/commons/3/3a/Ramones_Toronto_1976.jpg

The Runaways: Joan Jett, Jackie Fox, Lita Ford at Brumrock, Bingley Hall, Birmingham, 1976.
Creator: David Johnson
Creative Commons Attribution-Share Alike 2.0 Generic
https://upload.wikimedia.org/wikipedia/commons/6/6b/The_Runaways_at_Brumrock_%2776_%284_of_7%29.jpg

ABBA: Benny, Anni-Frid, Agnetha and Bjorn receive a Veronica Award in Holland, 1976.
Creator: Bert Verhoeff for Anefo
Creative Commons CC0 1.0 Universal Public Domain Dedication
https://upload.wikimedia.org/wikipedia/commons/7/76/Zweedse_popgroep_ABBA_in_Nederland_v.l.n.r._Benny%2C_Anni-Frid%2C_Agnetha_en_Bjorn_%2C_Bestanddeelnr_928-8962.jpg

Stevie Wonder, 1973.
Creator: Motown Records
Public domain
https://upload.wikimedia.org/wikipedia/commons/5/54/Stevie_Wonder_1973.JPG

Carole King.
Creator: Capitol Records
Public Domain
https://en.wikipedia.org/w/index.php?title=File:Carole_King_-_Capitol.jpg&oldid=607183052

Gloria Gaynor in Amsterdam, 1976.
Creator: Rob Mieremet/Anefo
Creative Commons CC0 1.0 Universal Public Domain Dedication
https://upload.wikimedia.org/wikipedia/commons/c/cb/Gloria_Gaynor_%281976%29.jpg

Donna Summer in the recording studio, 1977.
Creator: Casablanca Records
Public domain
https://upload.wikimedia.org/wikipedia/commons/3/3a/Donna_Summer_1977.JPG

NOTES

1970: The Revolution Will Not Be Televised

1   Roger Daltrey, *Thanks a Lot Mr Kibblewhite*, Allen & Unwin, 2018.
2   Tony Palmer, *All You Need Is Love*, Futura, 1977.
3   John Lewis, *The Best of NME 1970–1974 Vol 4*.
4   Bill Bruford, *Bill Bruford: The Autobiography*, Jawbone, 2009.
5   Marianne Faithful, *Memories, Dreams and Reflections*, Fourth Estate, 2007.
6   Bill Wyman, *Stone Alone*, Penguin, 1991.
7   Keith Richards with James Fox, *Life*, Weidenfeld & Nicolson, 2010.
8   Sean Egan (ed.), *The Mammoth Book of the Rolling Stones*, Constable & Robinson, 2013.
9   Robert Greenfield, 'The Rolling Stone interview: Keith Richards', *Rolling Stone*, 20 August 1971.
10   Greil Marcus, 'Self portrait', *Rolling Stone*, 8 June 1970.
11   Molly Meldrum with Jeff Jenkins, *Ah Well, Nobody's Perfect: The Untold Stories*, Allen & Unwin, 2016.
12   Barry Miles, *Paul McCartney: Many Years from Now*, Vintage, 1997.
13   Robert Christgau, 'Living without The Beatles', *Village Voice*, September 1971.
14   ibid.
15   Philip Norman, *John Lennon: The Life*, Harper Collins, 2008.
16   Tim Grierson, 'How a weird cult therapy inspired John Lennon to make his greatest album', *Rolling Stone*, 15 April 2021.
17   Chrissie Hynde, *Reckless*, Ebury Press, 2015.
18   Dave Simpson, 'Devo: "Richard Branson almost killed us in the Jamaican mountains"', *The Guardian*, 14 April 2022.
19   Jimmy McDonough, *Shakey: Neil Young's Biography*, Vintage, 2003.
20   Hynde, *Reckless*.
21   McDonough, *Shakey*.
22   Clive Hamilton, *What Do We Want? The Story of Protest in Australia*, National Library Publishing, 2016.
23   Ed Vulliamy, '1989 and all that: Plastic People of the Universe and the Velvet Revolution', *The Guardian*, 6 September 2009.
24   Paul Rees, *Robert Plant: A Life*, Harper, 2013.
25   *Sunset Strip*, documentary, Sunset Strip The Movie LLC, 2013.
26   Nigel Williamson, *The Dead Straight Guide To Led Zeppelin*, Red Planet, 2014.
27   Bob Spitz, *Led Zeppelin: The Biography*, Penguin Press, 2021.
28   Rod Stewart, *Rod: The Autobiography*, Century, 2012.
29   Spitz, *Led Zeppelin*.
30   Germaine Greer, 2 February 2010, quoted on ledzeppelin.com.
31   Rees, *Robert Plant*.
32   Cameron Crowe, 'Loud, lusty & live: Led Zeppelin', *Rolling Stone*, 1975.
33   Ozzy Osbourne with Chris Ayers, *I Am Ozzy*, Sphere, 2009.
34   *Classic Albums Black Sabbath Paranoid*, documentary film, © Mononoise Ltd, 2010.
35   Osbourne, *I Am Ozzy*.
36   *Classic Albums Black Sabbath Paranoid*, Mononoise Ltd.
37   Richard Green, *New Musical Express*, 26 September 1970.
38   Lester Bangs, 'Album reviews: Black Sabbath', *Rolling Stone*, 17 September 1970.

39 Osbourne, *I Am Ozzy*.
40 Mike McMahon, 'Geezer crushes stereotypes about cutting', mikemcmahanlpc.com.
41 *New Musical Express*, 4 April 1970.
42 *Melody Maker*, 11 July 1970.
43 *Super Duper Alice Cooper*, documentary, Alice Doc Inc, 2014.
44 ibid.
45 Dave Marsh & John Swenson (eds), *The New Rolling Stone Record Guide*, Rolling Stone Press/Random House, 1983.
46 *The Rolling Stone/Omnibus Press Rock 'N' Roll Reader*, Rolling Stone & Omnibus Press, 1995.
47 Gillian Brockell, 'A famed folk singer won a presidential pardon after molesting a child. Did he prey on others?', *The Washington Post*, 17 May 2021.
48 James Brown with Bruce Tucker, *James Brown: The Godfather of Soul*, Aurum Press, 2009.
49 Alexis Petridis, 'The legacy of David Mancuso: "His dancefloor was a kind of egalitarian utopia"', *The Guardian*, 16 November 2016.
50 Joni Mitchell, *Melody Maker*, 19 September 1970.
51 Graham Nash, *New Musical Express*, 14 December 1968.
52 David Crosby & Carl Gottlieb, *Long Time Gone: The Autobiography of David Crosby*, Mandarin, 1988.
53 McDonough, *Shakey*.
54 ibid.
55 Elton John, *Me*, Macmillan, 2019.
56 ibid.
57 Robert Christgau, *Any Old Way You Choose It*, Penguin, 1973.
58 John, *Me*.
59 Nick Mason, *Inside Out: A Personal History of Pink Floyd*, Weidenfeld & Nicolson, 2017.
60 ibid.
61 Mike Rutherford, *The Living Years*, Constable, 2014.
62 Marcus O'Dair, *Different Every Time: The Authorised Biography of Robert Wyatt*, Serpent's Tail, 2014.
63 Claudia Schmidt, 'Sounds of the psychedelic: The tale of the Mellotron', *Happy*, 13 April 2021.
64 Richard Williams, 'On the growing trade in "pirate" records', *Melody Maker*, 14 March 1970.
65 Pete Townshend, *Who I Am*, Harper, 2013.
66 Daltrey, *Thanks a Lot Mr Kibblewhite*.
67 Alan Smith, *New Musical Express*, 7 November 1970.
68 J.A.C. Dunn, 'Ourimbah Pop Festival's gentle chaos', *The Sydney Morning Herald* & *Sun-Herald*, 25–26 January 1970.
69 Billy Thorpe, *Most People I Know (Think That I'm Crazy)*, Pan Macmillan, 1998.
70 *The Sydney Morning Herald*, 16 February 1970.
71 Graeme Skinner, *Peter Sculthorpe: The Making of an Australian Composer*, UNSW Press, 2007.
72 Hynde, *Reckless*.
73 Eric R. Danton, 'Fanny lives: Inside the return of the pioneering all-female rock band', *Rolling Stone*, 16 March 2018.
74 Accessed at socialhistoryportal.com and also John Kifner, 'A radical "declaration" warns of an attack by Weathermen', *The New York Times*, 25 May 1970.
75 Meir Rinde, 'Richard Nixon and the rise of American environmentalism', Science History Institute, 2 June 2017, accessed at science.history.org.
76 Olivia B. Waxman, 'The story behind that famous photo of Elvis Presley and Richard Nixon', *Time*, 15 August 2017.

77   Stewart, *Rod*.
78   Townshend, *Who I Am*.
79   Paul Zollo, 'Behind the song: "Fire and Rain" by James Taylor', *American Songwriter*, 2021.
80   Mick Fleetwood & Anthony Bozza, *Play On*, Hodder, 2014.

1971: Gimme Some Truth

1   *New Musical Express*, 27 February 1971.
2   Jann Wenner, 'The Rolling Stone interview: John Lennon, part one and part two, *Rolling Stone*, 21 January 1971 and 4 February 1971.
3   ibid.
4   Robert Greenfield, 'The Rolling Stone interview: Keith Richards', *Rolling Stone*, 20 August 1971.
5   Marion Meade, 'Does rock degrade women?', *The New York Times*, 14 March 1971.
6   Jean Vallely, 'Playboy interview: Linda Ronstadt', *Playboy*, April 1980.
7   Mark Bego, *Billy Joel: The Biography*, JR Books, 2008.
8   Robert Christgau, 'Carole King: Five million friends', *Newsday*, November 1972.
9   'The 500 greatest albums of all time', *Rolling Stone*, accessed at rollingstone.com.
10   James Brown with Bruce Tucker, *James Brown: The Godfather of Soul*, Aurum Press, 2009.
11   Rod Stewart, *Rod: The Autobiography*, Century, 2012.
12   ibid.
13   Alyn Shipton, *Nilsson: The Life of a Singer-Songwriter*, Oxford University Press, 2013.
14   Elton John, *Me*, McMillan, 2019.
15   ibid.
16   Richard Nixon speaking on the White House tapes, accessed at ontheissues.org.
17   Nick Logan, *Melody Maker*, 20 November 1971.
18   Alexis Petridis, 'Why Marc Bolan was "the perfect pop star"', *The Guardian*, 4 September 2020.
19   Jon Landau, 'Paul McCartney: Ram', *Rolling Stone*, 8 July 1971.
20   Peter Doggett, *There's a Riot Going On*, Canongate, 2007.
21   Christopher Andersen, *Mick*, Gallery Books, 2012.
22   Greenfield, 'The Rolling Stone Interview: Keith Richards'.
23   Pete Townshend, *Who I Am*, Harper, 2013.
24   Roger Daltrey, *Thanks a Lot Mr Kibblewhite*, Allen & Unwin, 2018.
25   Barry Miles, *Zappa*, Atlantic Books, 2004.
26   Joachim Berendt, *The Jazz Book*, Paladin, 1976.
27   Helen Reddy, *The Woman I Am*, Harper Collins, 2005.
28   ibid.
29   Jon Casimir, 'Secret life of Matilda', *The Sydney Morning Herald*, 20 April 2002.
30   Dan Condon, 'Vale Chris Winter – ground-breaking "music guru" behind Double J and Triple J', abc.net.au, 11 June 2019.
31   Chris Löfvén, interviewed by the author, 2022.
32   Toby Creswell, *Love Is in the Air*, ABC Books, 2001.
33   Barry Gibb, interview with Lyn Redgrave, *Fighting Back*, BBC, 1992.
34   ibid.
35   Maurice Gibb, interview with Lyn Redgrave, *Fighting Back*, BBC, 1992.
36   George Kimball, *Rolling Stone*, 19 August 1971.
37   Robert Christgau, 'Black Sabbath Master of Reality review', *Village Voice*, 12 December 1971.
38   Reebee Garofalo, *Rockin' Out Popular Music in the USA*, Allyn and Bacon, 1997.
39   Ozzy Osbourne, *I Am Ozzy*, Sphere, 2009.
40   Bob Spitz, *Led Zeppelin: The biography*, Penguin Press, 2021.

41 Roy Carr, *New Musical Express*, 29 April 1972.
42 Cameron Crowe, 'Loud, lusty & live: Led Zeppelin', *Rolling Stone*, 1975.
43 Spitz, *Led Zeppelin*.
44 ibid.
45 ibid.
46 Robert Christgau, *Any Old Way You Choose It*, Penguin Books, 1973.
47 Greg Lake, *Lucky Man*, Constable, 2017.
48 Richard Green, *New Musical Express*, 12 June 1971.
49 Lake, *Lucky Man*.
50 'We didn't come tooled up', *New Musical Express*, 4 September 1971.
51 David Fenton, *Ann Arbor Sun*, 7 May 1971.
52 Bryan Burrough, 'The bombings of America that we forgot', *Time*, 20 September 2016.
53 Andy Beckett, *When the Lights Went Out*, Faber & Faber, 2009.
54 Peter Cole-Adams, 'Oz trio's "brutal" sentence in obscenity trial', *The Sydney Morning Herald*, 7 August 1971.
55 Marc Myers, 'When Marvin broke pattern', *The Wall Street Journal*, 7 June 2011.
56 'The 500 Greatest Albums of All Time', *Rolling Stone*, accessed at rollingstone.com.
57 Richard Williams, *Melody Maker*, 13 February 1971.
58 John Wetton, *Prog*, no. 49, 2014.
59 Barry Miles, *Paul McCartney: Many Years from Now*, Vintage, 1998.
60 Peter Doggett, *The Art & Music of John Lennon*, Omnibus Press, 2005.
61 *LennoNYC*, documentary, Two Lefts Don't Make a Right Productions, Dakota Group, Ltd and WNET.ORG, 2010.
62 Peter Doggett, *The Art & Music of John Lennon*, Omnibus Press, 2005.

1972: All the Young Dudes

1   Stephen Holden, 'Some Time in New York City review', *Rolling Stone*, 20 July 1972.
2   Robert Christgau, 'John Lennon's realpolitik', *Newsday*, July 1972.
3   Peter Doggett, *The Art & Music of John Lennon*, Omnibus Press, 2005.
4   Roy Carr, 'Jagger slams Britain', *New Musical Express*, 18 March 1972.
5   Paul Elliott, 'Ian Anderson interview: The beginning, middle and end of Jethro Tull', *Classic Rock*, 3 April 2020.
6   Ben Gerson, 'Thick as a Brick' review, *Rolling Stone*, 22 June 1972.
7   Robert Christgau, 'Cat Stevens', *Newsday*, November 1972.
8   Robert Christgau, 'Trying to understand the Eagles', *Newsday*, June 1972.
9   Jon Landau, 'Paul Simon: The Rolling Stone interview', *Rolling Stone*, 20 July 1972.
10 ibid.
11 Paul Simon, 'Review of Stephen Sondheim's "Isn't It Rich"', *New York Times Book Review*, 31 October 2010.
12 Paul Simon, *New Musical Express*, 1 January 1972.
13 Roy Carr, *New Musical Express*, 29 April 1972.
14 Robert Christgau, 'The Rolling Stones can't get no satisfaction', *Newsday*, July 1972.
15 Mick Jagger, Keith Richards, Charlie Watts & Ronnie Wood, *According to the Rolling Stones*, Weidenfeld & Nicolson, 2003.
16 'The 500 greatest albums of all time', *Rolling Stone*, accessed at rollingstone.com.
17 Nick Dent-Robinson, 'Marianne Faithfull: Interview', *Pennyblackmusic*, March 1995.
18 Elton John, *Me*, Macmillan, 2019.
19 Grace Lichtenstein, 'Alice Cooper? David Bowie? Ugh! And ugh again!', *The New York Times*, 24 September 1972.
20 Mike Rutherford, *The Living Years*, Constable, 2014.
21 Ray Coleman, *Phil Collins: The Definitive Biography*, Simon & Schuster, 1997.
22 Michael Watts, *Melody Maker*, 22 January 1972.
23 Michael Watts, 'Don't expect Danny La Rue', *Melody Maker*, 19 February 1972.

24 Kurt Loder, 'David Bowie: Straight time', *Rolling Stone*, 12 May 1983.
25 Michael Watts, *Melody Maker*, 22 January 1972.
26 Marc Spitz, *Bowie: A biography*, Crown Publishing, 2009.
27 Roy Hollingworth, *Melody Maker*, 22 July 1972.
28 Van M. Cagle, 'Trudging through the glitter trenches', in Shelton Waldrep (ed.), *The Seventies: The Age of Glitter in Popular Culture*, Routledge, 2000.
29 Michael Watts, *Melody Maker*, 1 July 1972.
30 Charles Shaar Murray, *New Musical Express*, 22 July 1972.
31 Tony Palmer, *All You Need Is Love*, Futura, 1977.
32 Marcus O'Dair, *Different Every Time*, Serpent's Tail, 2015.
33 Greg Lake, *Lucky Man*, Constable, 2017.
34 James Johnson, *New Musical Express*, 5 February 1972.
35 Richard Green, *New Musical Express*, 13 November 1971.
36 Nick Logan, *New Musical Express*, 19 February 1972.
37 Chris Charlesworth, *Melody Maker*, 23 September 1972.
38 Ozzy Osbourne with Chris Ayres, *I Am Ozzy*, Sphere, 2010.
39 Mark Plummer, *Melody Maker*, 14 October 1972.
40 *Super Duper Alice Cooper*, Alice Doc Inc, 2014.
41 Michael Watts, *Melody Maker*, 1 April 1972.
42 John Fordham, 'Annette Peacock: I'm the One – review, *The Guardian*, 15 July 2011.
43 Landau, 'Paul Simon: The Rolling Stone Interview'.
44 Joan Baez, *And a Voice to Sing With*, Arrow, 1988.
45 ibid.
46 Vince Aletti, 'There's a Riot Going On: Review', *Rolling Stone*, 23 December 1971.
47 'Transcript of Kissinger's news conference on the status of the ceasefire talks', *The New York Times*, 27 October 1972.
48 *LennoNYC*, documentary, Two Lefts Don't Make a Right Productions, Dakota Group, Ltd and WNET.ORG, 2010.

1973: What a Bastard the World Is

1 Ray Coleman, *Melody Maker*, 25 August 1973.
2 Charles Shaar Murray, *New Musical Express*, 3 November 1973.
3 Richard Williams, *Melody Maker*, 14 April 1973.
4 US Recorded Music Revenues by format, Recorded Music Industry Association, www.riaa.com.
5 Simon Reynolds, *Shaping the '70s: Simon Draper and the Story of Virgin Records*, daily, redbullmusicacademy.com.
6 Marcus O'Dair, *Different Every Time: The Authorised Biography of Robert Wyatt*, Serpent's Tail, 2014.
7 Richard Branson, *Losing My Virginity*, Random House, 2005.
8 Tom Bower, *Branson Behind the Mask*, Faber & Faber, 2014.
9 Reynolds, *Shaping the '70s*.
10 Eric Clapton, *Eric Clapton: The autobiography*, Century, 2007.
11 ibid.
12 Nick Kent, 'The Zeppelin road test', *New Musical Express*, 24 February 1973.
13 Nigel Williamson, *The Dead Straight Guide to Led Zeppelin*, Red Planet, 2014.
14 Pamela Des Barres, *Rock Bottom*, Little, Brown and Company, 1996.
15 Charles Shaar Murray, *New Musical Express*, 21 April 1973.
16 Bob Spitz, *Led Zeppelin: The Biography*, Penguin Press, 2021.
17 Pete Townshend, 'Eyewitness!', *The Best of NME 1970–1974*.
18 Roger Daltrey, *Thanks a Lot Mr Kibblewhite*, Allen & Unwin, 2018.
19 O'Dair, *Different Every Time*.
20 Steve Lake, *Melody Maker*, 10 November 1973.

21 Michael Watts, *Melody Maker*, 24 February 1973.
22 Michael Watts, *Melody Maker*, 27 January 1973.
23 Andrew Solt & Sam Egan, *Imagine*, Virgin, 1989.
24 Barry Miles, *Paul McCartney: Many Years From Now*, Vintage, 1997.
25 Paul Gambaccini, 'Paul McCartney is not dead (and neither is the past)', *Rolling Stone*, 31 January 1974.
26 ibid.
27 Tony Tyler, 'Holy roller: Harrison', *New Musical Express*, 9 June 1973.
28 Richard Williams, *Melody Maker*, 4 November 1972.
29 Danny Thompson, 'Part 3, collaborations with John Martyn in the 1970s', *The Music Aficionado*, 8 February 2022.
30 Mike Rutherford, *The Living Years*, Constable & Robinson, 2014.
31 ibid.
32 Richard Williams, *Melody Maker*, 12 May 1973.
33 Russell Harty Plus, *Pop*, 17 January 1973.
34 Roy Hollingworth, *Melody Maker*, 12 May 1973.
35 Chris Welch, 'David Bowie: Aladdin Sane', *Melody Maker*, 21 April 1973.
36 Nick Kent, *New Musical Express*, 26 January 1974.
37 Chris Charlesworth, *Melody Maker*, 14 July 1973.
38 Roy Hollingworth, *Melody Maker*, 17 March 1973.
39 Michael Watts, *Melody Maker*, 25 August 1973.
40 Gregg Allman with Alan Light, *My Cross to Bear*, First William Morrow, 2013.
41 Roy Carr, *New Musical Express*, 28 July 1973.
42 Mark Bego, *Billy Joel: The biography*, JR Books, 2008.
43 Elton John, *Me*, Macmillan, 2019.
44 Bruce Springsteen, *Born to Run*, Simon & Schuster, 2017.
45 ibid.
46 Jeff Apter, *High Voltage: The life of Angus Young*, Nero, 2017.
47 Helen Reddy, *The Woman I Am*, Harper Collins, 2005.
48 *Suzi Q*, Acme Film Company Production, 2019.
49 Debbie Harry, *Face It*, Harper Collins, 2022.
50 *Suzi Q*, Acme Film.
51 Rebecca Bengal, 'Betty Davis projected her own liberation – and freed up generations in her wake', *The Guardian*, 10 February 2022.
52 Berkeley Women's Music Collective, accessed at revolution.berkeley.edu.
53 'Protest on the high seas', *The Washington Post*, undated, accessed at washingtonpost.com.

1974: What Happened to the Revolution?

1   Ray Coleman, *Melody Maker*, 23 February 1974.
2   Marcus O'Dair, *Different Every Time: The Authorised Biography of Robert Wyatt*, Serpent's Tail, 2014.
3   Nick Mason, *Inside Out: A Personal History of Pink Floyd*, Weidenfeld & Nicolson, 2017.
4   O'Dair, *Different Every Time*.
5   ibid.
6   ibid.
7   Nick Leonardi, 'Review special: Robert Wyatt – Rock Bottom', *Progsphere*, 18 June 2013.
8   Jim Powers, 'Rock Bottom' review, allmusic.com.
9   Mason, *Inside Out*.
10 O'Dair, *Different Every Time*.
11 Charles Snider, *The Strawberry Bricks Guide to Progressive Rock*, self-published, 2007.
12 Roy Carr, *Melody Maker*, 2 March 1974.

13 Bill Bruford, *Bill Bruford: The Autobiography*, Jawbone, 2009.

14 Greg Kot, 'Rock 'n' roll is here to stay, from Beatles to Beck, the Rude Mutt keeps on changing', *The Chicago Tribune*, 19 October 1997.

15 Robert Partridge, *Melody Maker*, 5 October 1974.

16 Chris Welch, *Melody Maker*, 26 October 1974.

17 Chris Welch, *Melody Maker*, 25 May 1974.

18 Mike Rutherford, *The Living Years*, Constable & Robinson, 2014.

19 Steve Lake, *Melody Maker*, 16 March 1974.

20 Samuel Andreyev, *Art Tripp on working with Frank Zappa, John Cage and Captain Beefheart*, accessed at youtube.com.

21 Andy Greene, 'The oral history of CSNY's infamous "Doom Tour"', *Rolling Stone*, 19 June 2014.

22 *LennoNYC*, documentary, Two Lefts Don't Make a Right Productions, Dakota Group, Ltd and WNET.ORG, 2010.

23 Chris Charlesworth, *Melody Maker*, 1 February 1975.

24 ibid.

25 Andy Greene, 'Chester Thompson interview', *Rolling Stone*, 4 February 2021.

26 Tony Fletcher, *All Hopped Up and Ready to Go*, Omnibus Press, 2009.

27 Jimmy Barnes, *Working Class Man*, HarperCollins, 2017.

28 John Robinson, 'The Best of NME 1970–1974', *New Musical Express*.

29 Toby Creswell, *Love Is in the Air*, ABC Books, 2001.

30 Jon Landau, 'Review: Joni Mitchell strikes a delicate balance on "Court and Spark"', *Rolling Stone*, 28 February 1974.

31 Brian Hinton, *Joni Mitchell: Both Sides Now – The biography*, Sanctuary Publishing, 2000.

32 Steve Clarke, *New Musical Express*, 29 June 1974.

33 ibid.

34 *LennoNYC*, 2010.

35 Chris Charlesworth, *Melody Maker*, 10 August 1974.

36 Jimmy McDonough, *Shakey: Neil Young's Biography*, Vintage, 2003.

37 ibid.

38 Andy Greene, 'The oral history of CSNY's infamous "Doom Tour"', *Rolling Stone*, 19 June 2014.

39 McDonough, *Shakey*.

40 Massimo Bonanno, *The Rolling Stones Chronicle*, Angus & Robinson, 1990.

41 ibid.

42 Sterling Whitaker, 'The day Mick Taylor quit The Rolling Stones', *Ultimate Classic Rock*, 12 December 2015.

43 Bonanno, *The Rolling Stones Chronicle*.

44 Chris Charlesworth, *Melody Maker*, 22 June 1974.

45 ibid.

46 Dick Hebdige, *Subculture: The meaning of style*, Methuen, 1979.

47 Ken Emerson, 'Diamond Dogs', *Rolling Stone*, 1 August 1974.

48 Loraine Alterman, 'Fleetwood Mac flak: Manager takes name, not members, on tour', *Rolling Stone*, 28 February 1974.

49 Damian Johnstone, *The Wild One*, Allen & Unwin, 2001.

50 Jane Mulvagh, *Vivienne Westwood: An Unfashionable Life*, HarperCollins, 1999.

51 Caryn Rose, *Why Patti Smith Matters*, Faber, 2022.

52 Debbie Harry, *Face It*, Harper Collins, 2022.

1975: Shadows and Light

1 Michael Watts, 'David Bowie: Young Americans', *Melody Maker*, 15 March 1975.

2 Bruce Springsteen, *Born to Run*, Simon & Schuster, 2017.

3   *The Rolling Stone/Omnibus Press Rock 'n' Roll Reader*, 1995.
4   Andrew Tyler, *New Musical Express*, 15 November 1975.
5   Cameron Crowe, 'The durable Led Zeppelin', *Rolling Stone*, 13 March 1975.
6   Matt Schudel, 'Thomas Polgar, CIA official during the fall of Siagon, dies', *The Washington Post*, 31 March 2014.
7   Debbie Harry, *Face It*, Harper Collins, 2022.
8   Barbara O'Dair (ed.), *Trouble Girls: The Rolling Stone book of women in rock*, Random House, 1997.
9   Harry, *Face It*.
10 ibid.
11 Caryn Rose, *Why Patti Smith Matters*, Faber, 2022.
12 ibid.
13 Dave Marsh, 'Pattie Smith: Her horses got wings, they can fly', *Rolling Stone*, 1 January 1976.
14 Emily Barker, 'The 500 greatest albums of all time: 100-1', 25 October 2013, nme.com.
15 Johnny Cummings, in Clinton Heylin, *From the Velvets to the Voidoids: A Pre-Punk history for a Post-Punk World*, Penguin, 1993.
16 Chris Charlesworth, *New Musical Express*, 7 June 1975.
17 Charles Shaar Murray, *New Musical Express*, 8 November 1975.
18 Charles Shaar Murray, *New Musical Express*, 7 June 1975.
19 M. Bilyeu, H. Cook & A. Môn Hughes, *The Bee Gees: Tales of The Brothers Gibb*, Omnibus Press, 2000.
20 Chris Charlesworth, *Melody Maker*, 5 April 1975.
21 ibid.
22 ibid.
23 John-Manuel Andriote, *Hot Stuff: A Brief History of Disco*, Harper Entertainment, 2001.
24 Lisa Robinson, 'Boogie nights', *Vanity Fair*, 6 January 2010.
25 Bilyeu, Cook & Môn Hughes, *The Bee Gees*.
26 ibid.
27 ibid.
28 Tara Douglas, *Loud*, ABC Books, 2020.
29 Crowe, 'The durable Led Zeppelin'.
30 J.D. Considine, 'Led Zeppelin interview', *Rolling Stone*, January 1991.
31 Crowe, 'The durable Led Zeppelin'.
32 Chris Durston, 'Letters', *Melody Maker*, 21 February 1976.
33 Bob Spitz, *Led Zeppelin: The Biography*, Penguin Press, 2021.
34 Steve Tyler, *Does the Noise in My Head Bother You?*, HarperCollins, 2011.
35 ibid.
36 Julie Webb, *New Musical Express*, 27 September 1975.
37 *Queen – The Making of A Night at the Opera* (classic album), documentary, Queen Productions Ltd, 2005.
38 ibid.
39 Mick Fleetwood & Anthony Bozza, *Play On*, Hodder & Stoughton, 2014.
40 Steve Lake, *Melody Maker*, 28 June 1975.
41 Roy Carr, *New Musical Express*, 24 May 1975.
42 Michael Watts, 'Bob Dylan: Blood on the Tracks', *Melody Maker*, 25 January 1975.
43 Stephen Holden, 'The hissing of summer lawns', *Rolling Stone*, 15 January 1976.
44 Nick Mason, *Inside Out: A Personal History of Pink Floyd*, Weidenfeld & Nicolson, 2017.
45 Allan Jones, 'Pink Floyd: Wish You Were Here', *Melody Maker*, 20 September 1975.
46 *Pink Floyd: Behind the Wall*, documentary, An Entertain Me Production, 2011.
47 Alice Cooper, quoted on alicecooper.com.

48   Elton John, *Me*, Macmillan, 2019.
49   ibid.
50   Chris Charlesworth, *Melody Maker*, 12 April 1975.
51   Cameron Crowe, 'Conversations with Don Henley and Glenn Frey', *The Uncool*,
      August 2003.
52   Don Felder, *Heaven and Hell: My Life in the Eagles (1974–2001)*, John Wiley & Sons, 2008.
53   Roger Daltrey, *Thanks a Lot Mr Kibblewhite*, Allen & Unwin, 2018.
54   ibid.
55   Roy Carr, *New Musical Express*, 24 May 1975.
56   Jeff Apter, *Shirl*, Hardie Grant, 2012.
57   ibid.
58   Graeham Goble in conversation with Darryl Cotton, Birtles Shorrock Goble,
      YouTube.
59   Toby Creswell, *Love Is in the Air*, ABC Books, 2001.
60   Sterling Whitaker, 'How Loretta Lynn turned a banned song into a huge career hit',
      Taste of Country, 14 April 2022.

1976: Blitzkrieg Bop

1   Fred Dellar, *New Musical Express*, 5 June 1976.
2   Cameron Crowe, 'Peter Frampton: The year of the face', *Rolling Stone*, 22 April 1976.
3   Mick Fleetwood with Stephen Davis, *Rolling Stone: The Seventies Issue*, January 1991.
4   ibid.
5   Dave Marsh, 'Desire', *Rolling Stone*, 11 March 1976.
6   Lester Bangs, 'State of the art: Bland on bland', *Creem*, July 1976.
7   Harry Doherty, 'ABBA: Digging the Swedes!', *Melody Maker*, 31 January 1976.
8   *ABBA: Super Troupe*, documentary, Entertain Me Publishing Ltd, 2019.
9   Doherty, 'ABBA: Digging the Swedes!'.
10   Gareth Hutchens, 'There's been a "30-year war" against unions in Australia, and
      think-tanks have played a role', ABC News, 2 October 2022.
11   See www.cis.org.au/about/history.
12   Roy Carr, *New Musical Express*, 24 May 1975.
13   Jane Mulvagh, *Vivienne Westwood: An Unfashionable Life*, Harper Collins, 1999.
14   ibid.
15   Chrissie Hynde, *Reckless*, Ebury Press, 2015.
16   'The Screen on the Green, London Gig Review', *New Musical Express*, 29 August 1976.
17   Cameron Crowe, 'David Bowie: Ground control to Davy Jones', *Rolling Stone*,
      12 February 1976.
18   Cameron Crowe, 'David Bowie: A candid conversation', *Playboy*, September 1976.
19   Allison Rapp, 'When Eric Clapton's bigoted 1976 rant sparked Rock Against Racism',
      Ultimate Classic Rock, 5 August 2021.
20   Tim Jonze, '"If there are death threats, don't tell me" – how Rock Against Racism
      fought fascism', *The Guardian*, 24 August 2022.
21   M. Bilyeu, H. Cook & A. Môn Hughes, *The Bee Gees: Tales of The Brothers Gibb*,
      Omnibus Press, 2000.
22   Roger Daltrey, *Thanks a Lot Mr Kibblewhite*, Allen & Unwin, 2018.
23   Keith Richards with James Fox, *Life*, Weidenfeld & Nicolson, 2010.
24   ibid.
25   Gregg Allman with Alan Light, *My Cross to Bear*, First William Morrow, 2013.
26   ibid.
27   ibid.
28   Billy Altman, 'High Voltage album review', *Rolling Stone*, 16 December 1976.
29   'AC/DC High Voltage album review', *Melody Maker*, 30 April 1976.
30   Toby Creswell, *Love Is in the Air*, ABC Books, 2001.

31   Jimmy Barnes, *Working Class Man*, Harper Collins, 2017.
32   Tony Palmer, *All You Need Is Love*, Futura, 1977.
33   Ariel Swartley, 'Blue Moves', *Rolling Stone*, 30 December 1976.
34   ibid.
35   Snakefinger, KPFA radio interview, 1980, accessed on youtube.com.

1977: Go Your Own Way

1   Nigel Williamson, *The Dead Straight Guide to Led Zeppelin*, Red Planet, 2014.
2   James Brown with Bruce Tucker, *James Brown: The Godfather of Soul*, Aurum Press, 2009.
3   M. Bilyeu, H. Cook & A. Môn Hughes, *The Bee Gees: Tales of The Brothers Gibb*, Omnibus Press, 2000.
4   'No word-of-mouth movie, *New Musical Express*, reprinted in *Uncut Presents History of Rock in the 1970s*, Carlton Book, 2017.
5   A.D. Murphy, 'Saturday Night Fever review', *Variety*, 13 December 1977.
6   Bilyeu, Cook & Môn Hughes, *The Bee Gees*.
7   Lisa Robinson, 'Boogie nights', *Vanity Fair*, 6 January 2010.
8   Toby Creswell, *Love Is in the Air*, ABC Books, 2001.
9   Williamson, *The Dead Straight Guide to Led Zeppelin*.
10   *Super Duper Alice Cooper*, documentary, Alice Doc Inc, 2014.
11   Richard Harrington, 'The core of Rotten', *The Washington Post*, 10 July 1994.
12   Chrissie Hynde, *Reckless*, Ebury Press, 2015.
13   Richard Branson, *Losing My Virginity*, Random House, 2005.
14   Jane Mulvagh, *Vivienne Westwood: An Unfashionable Life*, Harper Collins, 1999.
15   Richard Branson, 'The Sex Pistols Thames River Party', virgin.com.
16   Paul Nelson, album review, *Rolling Stone*, 23 February 1975.
17   *New Musical Express*, 18 June 1977.
18   Caroline Coon, 'The Clash: Down and out and proud', *Melody Maker*, 13 November 1976.
19   *Gun Rubber*, August 1977.
20   Stevie Chick, 'Lora Logic interview', *The Guardian*, 28 November 2022.
21   Ian 'Molly' Meldrum with Jeff Jenkins, *The Never, Um, Ever Ending Story*, Allen & Unwin, 2016.
22   'Gig review, Hammersmith Odeon', *New Musical Express*, 28 May 1977.
23   'Gig review, Rainbow Theatre', *Melody Maker*, 19 June 1977.
24   Bruce Springsteen, *Born to Run*, Simon & Schuster, 2017.
25   ibid.
26   Dave Marsh, 'Abba: The sound of business', *Rolling Stone*, 14 July 1977.
27   Mick Fleetwood & Anthony Bozza, *Play On*, Hodder, 2014.
28   Russell Shaw, *DownBeat*, 13 July 1978.
29   Lol Creme, from unedited text of interview by Kit Aiken for *Uncut* magazine, 14 December 1997.
30   Alan Robinson, liner notes to Edsel Records CD release *Music From Consequences + L.*
31   Jesse Fink, *The Youngs*, Ebury Press, 2013.
32   Glenn A. Baker, *Marc Hunter Biography*, hotshotdigital.com.
33   Creswell, *Love Is in the Air*.
34   Marcus O'Dair, *Different Every Time: The Authorised Biography of Robert Wyatt*, Serpent's Tail, 2014.

1978: Music Must Change

1   *World Today News*, 27 July 2022.
2   Max Bell, 'The epic true story of Grace Slick and Jefferson Airplane', *Classic Rock*, 31 October 2017.

3   Roger Daltrey, *Thanks a Lot Mr Kibblewhite*, Allen & Unwin, 2018.
4   Pete Townshend, *Who I Am*, Harper, 2013.
5   ibid.
6   Daltrey, *Thanks a Lot Mr Kibblewhite*.
7   *Super Duper Alice Cooper*, documentary, Alice Doc Inc, 2014.
8   Nicholas Rombes, *A Cultural Dictionary of Punk*, Continuum International, 2009.
9   Margaret Thatcher, transcript of Granada TV interview of 27 January 1978, accessed at the Margaret Thatcher Foundation, margaretthatcher.org.
10   Tim Jonze, '"If there are death threats, don't tell me" – how Rock Against Racism fought fascism', *The Guardian*, 24 August 2022.
11   *The Pere Ubu Story*, ubuprojex.com.
12   Ken Tucker, 'Pere Ubu: The modern dance', *Rolling Stone*, 1 June 1978.
13   Caryn Rose, *Why Patti Smith Matters*, Faber, 2022.
14   Rombes, *A Cultural Dictionary of Punk*.
15   Sting, *Broken Music*, Simon & Schuster, 2003.
16   ibid.
17   ibid.
18   Jimmy Barnes, *Working Class Man*, Harper Collins, 2017.
19   Albert Goldman, 'The disco style: Love thyself', *Esquire*, 20 June 1978.
20   John-Manuel Andriote, *Hot Stuff: A Brief History of Disco*, Harper Entertainment, 2001.
21   Lisa Robinson, 'Boogie nights', *Vanity Fair*, 6 January 2010.
22   ibid.
23   Rod Stewart, *Rod: The Autobiography*, Century, 2012.
24   Caroline Sullivan, 'Running Up that Hill by Tom Doyle review – Kate Bush in pieces', *The Guardian*, 2 November 2022.
25   *Kate Bush Under Review*, documentary, Chromedreams, 2005.
26   Ann Power, 'Bohemian Rhapsodies', in Barbara O'Dair (ed.), *Trouble Girls: The Rolling Stone Book of Women in Rock*, Random House, 1997.
27   Toby Creswell, *Love Is in the Air*, ABC Books, 2001.
28   Barnes, *Working Class Man*.
29   Michael Lawrence, *Showtime: The Cold Chisel Story*, self-published, 1998.
30   Barnes, *Working Class Man*.
31   ibid.
32   ibid.
33   Andy Greene, 'Chester Thompson interview', *Rolling Stone*, 4 February 2021.

1979: Too Much Too Young

1   Jean Vallely, 'Playboy interview: Linda Ronstadt', *Playboy*, April 1980.
2   Mick Fleetwood & Anthony Bozza, *Play On*, Hodder, 2014.
3   Vallely, 'Playboy interview: Linda Ronstadt'.
4   John-Manuel Andriote, *Hot Stuff: A Brief History of Disco*, Harper Entertainment, 2001.
5   Reebee Garofalo, *Rockin' Out: Popular Music in the USA*, Allyn and Bacon, 1997.
6   Corbin Reiff, 'The Chicago White Sox's attempt to commemorate Disco Demolition Night was an exceptionally misguided exercise', *Billboard*, 14 June 2019.
7   Andriote, *Hot Stuff*.
8   David Klasing, 'Notorious tax convictions: Studio 54 owners convicted of tax evasion', Klasing Associates, 21 January 2016.
9   Peter Watts, 'They weren't pop stars', *The Best of NME 1970–1974*.
10   Nick Mason, *Inside Out: A Personal History of Pink Floyd*, Weidenfeld & Nicolson, 2017.
11   ibid.
12   Charles Snider, *The Strawberry Bricks Guide to Progressive Rock*, self-published, 2007.

13 Toby Creswell, *Love Is in the Air*, ABC Books, 2001.
14 ibid.
15 *Serve Yourself*, beatlesbible.com, 24 August 2010.
16 Jason Dasey, 'George McArdle quit Little River Band at its peak', ABC News, 25 December 2022.
17 Bryan Wawzenek, 'That time Elvis Costello incited a brawl with racist remarks', *Ultimate Classic Rock*, 15 March 2015.
18 Raymond Horricks & Neil Slaven, 'The Pop Explosion', in Peter Gammond & Raymond Horricks (eds), *The Music Goes Round and Round*, Quartet Books, 1980.
19 Johnny Black, 'Clown suits and chaos: What happened when Jello Biafra ran for mayor of San Francisco', *The Guardian*, 2 September 2020.
20 'Transfixing, Pretenders Moonlight Club, February 2', *Melody Maker*, in *Uncut Presents History of Rock in the 1970s*, Carlton Books, 2017.
21 Chrissie Hynde, *Reckless*, Ebury Press, 2015.
22 Pete Townshend, *Who I Am*, Harper, 2013.
23 'Aimlessly Frenetic, The Who Brighton Centre November 10', in *Uncut Presents History of Rock in the 1970s*, Carlton Books, 2017.
24 Roger Daltrey, *Thanks a Lot Mr Kibblewhite*, Allen & Unwin, 2018.
25 Timothy White, 'Back to the Egg', *Rolling Stone*, 23 August 1979.
26 Philip Norman, *Paul McCartney: The Biography*, Weidenfeld & Nicolson, 2016.
27 *Pink Floyd: Behind the Wall*, documentary, An Entertain Me Production, 2011.
28 Peter Watts, 'They weren't pop stars', *The Best of NME 1970–1974*.
29 *27: Gone Too Soon*, SEIS Capital Limited, 2017.
30 Marianne Faithfull, *Memories, Dreams & Reflections*, Fourth Estate, 2007.
31 Jeff Giles, 'How Randy Newman confounded expectations with "Born Again"', *UCR Classic Rock & Culture*, 27 August 2015.
32 ibid.

Coda

1 Robert Christgau, 'Trying to understand The Eagles', *Newsday*, June 1972.
2 Debbie Harry, *Face It*, Harper Collins, 2022.
3 Rod Stewart, *Rod: The Autobiography*, Century, 2012.
4 Jimmy Barnes, *Working Class Man*, Harper Collins, 2017.
5 Robert D. Putnam with Shaylyn Romney Garrett, *The Upswing*, Swift Press, 2020.
6 Will Donnelly, 'Song analysis reveals how the lyrics of music have changed throughout the decades', lottie.org, 1 March 2022.
7 Fred Fedler et al., 'Analysis of popular music reveals emphasis on sex, de-emphasis of romance', files.eric.ed.gov, July 1982.
8 Robert J. Ringer, *Restoring the American Dream*, Fawcett Crest, 1979.
9 Lisa Duggan, *Mean Girl: Ayn Rand and the Culture of Greed*, University of California Press, 2019.
10 Chrissie Hynde, *Reckless*, Ebury Press, 2015.
11 Sean Sennett, 'Suitcases, tea towels and a brand new record press: The Brisbane couple taking a punt on the vinyl revival', *The Guardian*, 14 August 2022.
12 Roger Daltrey, *Thanks a Lot Mr Kibblewhite*, Allen & Unwin, 2018.
13 *Like a Rolling Stone: The Life and Times of Ben Fong-Torres*, a Studio LA production, 2022.
14 J. Matt McCrary & Clara Kretschmer, 'Association of music interventions with health-related quality of life: A systematic review and meta-analysis', *Journal of the American Medical Association Network Open*, 22 March 2022.

INDEX

INDEX

Canned Heat 53, 64, 129, 140, 147, 339
'Canon in D Major' 38
'Can't Get it Out of My Head' 211
'Can't Stand Losing You' 351
Canterbury scene 49, 305
Capaldi, Jim 167
capitalism 5, 37, 72, 88, 123, 247, 287, 322, 344, 379
Capitol Records 93-4, 152, 172, 217, 233, 248, 279
Capote, Truman 135
Captain and Tennille, The 336
Captain Beefheart 18, 149, 161, 215
Captain Fantastic and the Brown Dirt Cowboy (LP) 273-4
Captain Matchbox Whoopee Band, The 199
Caravan (band) 105-6, 210, 271, 305
Caravan & The New Symphonia (LP) 210
'Career Opportunities' 320
'Carey' 75
Caribou (LP) 237
Carlos, Michael 199
Carlos, Walter/Wendy 153
Carly Simon (LP) 75
'Carmina Burana' 272
Carnation Revolution 218
Caroline Records 165
Carpenter, Karen 1, 39, 74, 76, 277, 381
Carpenter, Richard 1, 39, 381
Carpenters (LP) 76
Carpenters, The 1, 39, 76, 195, 206, 381
Carr, Ian 92
'Carry On' 40
Carson, Phil 333
Carter, President Jimmy 35, 392
Carter, Ron 132
Casale, Gerard 14, 15
'Case of You, A' 75
Casey, Howie 178
Casey, Warren 339
Cash, Johnny 61-2, 112
Cash, June Carter 112
cassette tapes 21, 133, 178, 201, 211, 336, 339, 364-5
Catch a Fire (LP) 196
Catch Bull at Four (LP) 130
Catherine, Philip 92
Cavett, Dick 126
CBGB (club) 245-6, 254, 256, 289-90, 293, 314, 344
CBS Records 50, 82, 290, 317
Cecil, Malcolm 136
'Cecilia' 34

'Celebration of the Lizard' 32
censorship (*including* banning of records) 6, 15, 17, 24, 30-1, 35, 44, 111, 125, 148, 177, 199, 218, 229, 272, 281, 302, 316, 317, 322, 328, 351, 357-8, 365, 385
Centre for Independent Studies (CIS) 287
Chain 96
'Chain, The' 329
'Chain Saw' 293
Chamberlain, Richard 39
Chance Meeting on a Dissecting Table of a Sewing Machine and an Umbrella (LP) 372-3
Chandler, Chas 146-7, 188
'Changes' 80
Channing, Stockard 338
'Chant of the Ever Circling Skeletal Family' 241
Chapman, Mike 201, 281, 348
Charisma Records 81, 243
Charity Ball (LP) 71
Charlesworth, Chris 240, 256, 257, 264
Cheap Trick 375
Cheap Trick at Budokan (LP) 375
Cheech & Chong 174, 232
Cher 236, 300, 354, 366
'Cherry Bomb' 296
Cherry, Don 1
Chess Records 81
Chic 313, 352, 367, 368
Chic (LP) 313
'Chicago' 199
Chicago/Chicago Transit Authority 17-18, 54, 341
Chicago II (LP) 17-18
Chicago Women's Liberation Rock Band 58
'Chickenshit' 199
Chiffons, The 11, 298
'Child in Time' 29
Children of the World (LP) 297
'China Girl' 327
Chinn, Nicky 201, 281
'Choir Girl' 373
Christgau, Robert 10-11, 43, 73, 101, 105, 126-7, 131, 132, 134, 318, 345, 348, 388
Christian, Meg 202
Christie, Julie 143
Christopher Cross (LP) 364
Christopher Street Gay Liberation Day 58
Chrysalis Records 81, 243, 348
'Chuck E.'s in Love' 375
CIA (Central Intelligence Agency) 18, 162, 253, 301

INDEX

Citizen's Commission 113
civil rights issues (*including* black rights) 14,
  59, 60-1, 84, 113, 115-7, 118, 126, 157,
  194, 223, 269, 320, 337, 346, 366-7
C.J. Fish (LP) 7
Clapton, Eric 64, 92, 99, 109, 167-8, 184,
  235-6, 258, 295, 357, 382
  comeback concert at The Rainbow 167-8
  drugs, alcohol and 167-8, 235
  racist rant 295
Clarke, Steve 235
Clash, The 290, 292, 314, 315, 320, 321,
  322, 346, 377, 385
classical music 5, 15, 24, 29, 38, 45-7, 51,
  56, 85, 89, 93, 97, 105-6, 108, 144, 145,
  147, 164, 169, 210-11, 215, 216, 251, 270-1,
  298, 305, 311, 330-1
Classix Nouveaux 380
Clear Spot (LP) 149
Cleves, The 70-1
Cleves, The (LP) 71
Cliff, Jimmy 132
Clinton, George 36
'Clockwork Creep' 224
Clockwork Orange, A (film) 153
Close to the Edge (LP) 142
Close to You (LP) 39
Closer to Home (LP) 30
Club 76 294
Club 371 228
Cluster 305
Coasters, The 205
Cobham, Billy 92
cocaine 62, 90, 100-1, 135, 147-8, 170, 197,
  236, 238-9, 243, 264, 268, 284-5, 289,
  295, 300-1, 309, 311, 329, 340-1, 362,
  381-2, 386
Cochran, Eddie 377
Cocker, Joe 129, 168, 278
'Cocksucker Blues' *see* 'Schoolboy Blues'
'Coconut' 77
Coe, Tony 182
Cohen, Leonard 54, 75, 131, 161
Cohn, Nik 257, 312
COINTELPRO 59, 113
Cold Chisel 56, 97, 199, 229, 261, 322, 352,
  357-8, 362, 373, 391
'Cold Turkey' 127
Cold War 213, 396
Cole, Richard 53, 104, 168, 169-70, 243,
  263-4, 307-8
  violence and 168, 263-4, 308
Coleman, Ornette 323

Collins, Judy 40
Collins, Phil 48, 137, 183, 214, 305, 359
Colosseum 88
Coltrane, John 183, 208, 245
Columbia Records 110, 129, 250-1, 328, 333
'Come Back Again' 96-7
Come From the Shadows (LP) 118
'Come Out Singing' 152
'Come Together' 127, 222, 249
'Coming Down Again' 175
Communiqué (LP) 374
communitarianism 72, 152, 196, 219, 391
Company Caine 97
Computer Music Melodian 364
Concert for Bangla Desh 109-10, 167
Concert for Bangla Desh (LP) 68, 109-10,
  128
Concerto for Group and Orchestra (LP) 29
Concerto Grosso per i New Trolls (LP) 108
Concerts for the People of Kampuchea 385
'Concrete Jungle' 376
'Confessions of a Psychotic Cowpoke' 199
conscription (*aka* the draft) 16-17, 54, 155,
  159-60, 220
Consequences (LP) 331
consumerism 37, 123, 247, 322, 344, 379
Contortions 350, 379
contraception 57, 151, 281
Cooder, Ry 364
Cook, Paul 317, 340, 342
Cook, Peter 331
Coolidge, Rita 361
Cooper, Alice (band and individual) 27-9,
  48, 104-5, 129, 137, 148-9, 161, 189, 221,
  241, 272-3, 281, 315, 332, 338, 341
  chicken incident 28, 272
  stage act 27-8, 137, 148-9, 189, 273
Copeland, Stewart 325, 351
Copland, Aaron 144, 330-1
Corea, Chick 149-50, 289
Cornwell, Hugh 319
'Cosmik Debris' 224
Costello, Elvis 2, 290, 362, 376, 385
Countdown (TV show) 232, 261, 286, 323,
  333, 373
counterculture 4, 7, 52-3, 62, 71, 113, 200,
  342
Country and Western Hour 60
Country Joe & The Fish 7, 111, *see also*
  McDonald, Country Joe
Country Life (LP) 236
country music 38, 60, 76, 85, 134, 152, 180,
  190, 200, 228, 233-4, 245, 281, 396

421

INDEX

ACKNOWLEDGEMENTS

I would like to thank all the terrific folk at Monash University Publishing for their support, enthusiasm and professionalism. Editor Julian Welch deserves special praise for his attention to detail and surprising familiarity with the subject matter. In a league of her own is my wonderful wife, Judy Ditter, who not only read drafts and offered sage advice, but once again supported me fearlessly throughout another episode of this crazy book-writing compulsion.

ABOUT THE AUTHOR

Tony Wellington is a writer and photographer. His previous book was *Freak Out: How a Musical Revolution Rocked the World in the Sixties.* Other books by Tony include *Happy?: Exploding the Cultural Myths about Happiness* and *Noosa and Cooloola*, a history of Noosa. He also co-authored (with John Shand) *Don't Shoot the Best Boy! The Film Crew at Work*, and he has produced several photography books, the most recent of which is *Wild About Noosa*. For many years Tony worked in the film and television industry as a scriptwriter, director and editor, and he lectured in media studies and film. He has also worked as a professional artist and illustrator. Tony has run folk clubs, hosted a music radio show and written for music magazines. He holds a degree in Media and Communications from Macquarie University and is a former mayor of Noosa Shire. He has three grown children and lives in the Noosa hinterland with his wife.

Also by Tony Wellington

FREAK OUT

How a Musical Revolution Rocked the World in the Sixties

Tony Wellington

'I literally couldn't put it down. The combination of the strong memories it evoked and the new knowledge it delivered was irresistible.'
David Williamson